WOMEN'S LEGAL STRATEGIES IN CANADA

Edited by Radha Jhappan

Have Canadian women gained from their pursuit of legal remedies to social, political, economic, and cultural inequalities? Is law a fruitful avenue for such struggles? Drawing on a number of theoretical approaches, this collection of essays confronts various feminist and leftist critiques regarding the use of law in general, and the *Canadian Charter of Rights and Freedoms* in particular, as a means for seeking social justice. Several chapters examine the strategic limits and possibilities of the approaches pursued by the Women's Legal Education and Action Fund (LEAF). Other chapters focus on legal strategies mobilized by foreign domestic workers and racialized women, lesbians, women seeking reproductive freedom, women in the childcare movement, and anti-violence advocates.

Recognizing the diversity of women in terms of class, citizenship, race and ethnicity, sexual identity, culture, and (dis)ability, this collection evaluates the efficacy of the wide range of legal and political strategies women have employed, particularly since the passage of the *Charter of Rights*. Comprehensive and wide-ranging, *Women's Legal Strategies in Canada* will be of interest to scholars and activists in a number of fields.

RADHA JHAPPAN is a member of the Department of Political Science, Carleton University.

Women's Legal Strategies in Canada

EDITED BY
Radha Jhappan

UNIVERSITY OF TORONTO PRESS
Toronto Buffalo London

© University of Toronto Press Incorporated 2002
Toronto Buffalo London
Printed in Canada

ISBN 0-8020-0721-X (cloth)
ISBN 0-8020-7667-X (paper)

Printed on acid-free paper

National Library of Canada Cataloguing in Publication Data

Main entry under title:
Women's legal strategies in Canada

ISBN 0-8020-0721-X (bound). – ISBN 0-8020-7667-X (pbk.)

1. Feminist jurisprudence – Canada.   2. Women – Legal status, laws, etc. – Canada.   3. Women's rights – Canada.   4. Actions and defenses – Canada.   5. Constitutional law – Canada.   I. Jhappan, Radha

KE509.W656 2002   342.71'0878   C2001-903967-0

University of Toronto Press acknowledges the financial assistance to its publishing program of the Canada Council for the Arts and the Ontario Arts Council.

University of Toronto Press acknowledges the financial support for its publishing activities of the Government of Canada through the Book Publishing Industry Development Program (BPIDP).

Contents

Contributors   vii

Part I Introduction: Why Do Law?

1 Introduction: Feminist Adventures in Law   3
   Radha Jhappan

2 Feminist Movement in Law: Beyond Privileged and Privileging Theory   42
   Sheila McIntyre

Part II Equality Strategies

3 Women's (In)Equality before and after the *Charter*   101
   Diana Majury

4 Towards a Democratic Practice of Feminist Litigation?: LEAF's Changing Approach to *Charter* Equality   135
   Lise Gotell

5 The Equality Pit or the Rehabilitation of Justice?   175
   Radha Jhappan

Part III Race and Citizenship

6 Negotiating the Citizenship Divide: Foreign Domestic Worker Policy and Legal Jurisprudence   237
   Daiva Stasiulis and Abigail B. Bakan

7 Beyond the Confinement of Gender: Locating the Space of Legal Existence for Racialized Women   295
   Joanne St Lewis

Part IV Family and Reproduction

8 Abortion Litigation 335
 Sheilah L. Martin

9 Legal as Political Strategies in the Canadian Women's Movement: Who's Speaking? Who's Listening? 379
 Susan Phillips

Contributors

Abigail B. Bakan is Professor of Political Studies at Queen's University, where she has held a faculty position as a Queen's National Scholar since 1985. Her areas of research include the politics of development in the Caribbean, Third World immigrant women in Canada, globalization, and employment equity policy in Canada. Recent publications include *Not One of the Family: Foreign Domestic Workers in Canada* (co-edited with Daiva Stasiulis); *Employment Equity Policy in Canada: An Interprovincial Comparison* (with Audrey Kobayashi); *Critical Political Studies: Debates and Dialogues from the Left* (co-edited with Eleanor MacDonald).

Lise Gotell is an associate professor in the Women's Studies Program at the University of Alberta. She writes and teaches in the area of feminism, law, and sexuality. She has published widely on such topics as feminist litigation, constitutional equality, pornography and obscenity law, gay and lesbian rights, and sexual assault. Some of her recent articles have appeared in *Social and Legal Studies, Constitutional Forum*, and the *Canadian Journal of Law and Society*. She is a co-author of *Bad Attitude/s on Trial: Feminism, Pornography, and the Butler Decision* (1997) and the co-editor of *Open Boundaries: A Canadian Women's Studies Reader*. She is currently working on a major Social Sciences and Humanities Research Council study, 'Canadian Sexual Assault Law and the Contested Boundaries of Consent.'

Radha Jhappan is an Associate Professor of Political Science at Carleton University. She has published in the areas of indigenous politics, constitutional law, the Charter of Rights, feminist legal theory, and race and gender essentialism. She is currently writing a book on child pornography policy in Canada, as well as a series of articles and a book (with Daiva Stasiulis) on the sexualization of children in mainstream (Hollywood) cinema.

Diana Majury teaches in the Department of Law at Carleton University. Her research interests include criminal law, feminist legal theory, human rights, lesbian issues, sex equality theory, violence against women, women's health, law and literature, and family law.

Sheilah Martin is a Professor and former Dean at the Faculty of Law at the University of Calgary. She has published widely in the areas of constitutional law, equality jurisprudence, health care, and law and medicine. She co-edited *Equality and Judicial Neutrality* and has participated in judicial education seminars in Canada, Australia, New Zealand, South Africa, and China. She has written major reports and manuals on women in the legal profession and chaired the Joint Committee of the Canadian Bar, the Law Society of Alberta, and the Faculties of Law at the University of Calgary and the University of Alberta on the Status of Women in the Legal Profession in Alberta. She has acted as Counsel for LEAF in the *DFG* case involving the legal treatment of pregnant women and the *Shearing* case involving sexual assault and evidence; for the Alberta Association of Sexual Assault Centres in *R. v. Mills* in relation to the accused's access to the medical records of victims; and for the federal government in the *Firearms Reference*. In 1996 she became Queen's Counsel and received the Distinguished Service Award for Legal Scholarship from the Law Society of Alberta and the Canadian Bar Association.

Sheila McIntyre is a feminist activist who has pursued egalitarian change in law schools and universities, in legislative reform initiatives, and in the courts for the past twenty-five years. Much of her writing explores the politics of these struggles. As a member of individual case committees and of the National Legal Committee of the Women's Legal Education and Action Fund (LEAF), she participated in developing the legal arguments for over two dozen equality test cases. Since joining the Faculty of Law at Queen's University in 1985, her areas of teaching and research have included administrative, constitutional, labour, and public law, as well as feminist legal theory.

Susan D. Phillips teaches in the School of Public Administration at Carleton University. She has published books and articles in the fields of social policy, federalism and intergovernmental relations in Canada, municipal government, social movements, interest groups and the voluntary sector, and gender issues in public policy.

Daiva Stasiulis is Professor of Sociology at Carleton University. Her areas of research include citizenship studies, international migration, critical race and feminist theories, and the sociology of childhood. Her publications include *Unsettling Settler Societies: Articulations of Gender, Race, Ethnicity and Class* (co-edited with Nira Yuval-Davis), and *Not One of the Family: Foreign Domestic Workers in Canada* (co-edited with Abigail Bakan). She is currently engaged in research on children's citizenship and is writing a book with Radha Jappan on the sexualization of children in popular cinema.

Joanne St Lewis teaches law in the area of critical race theory and equality rights in the Faculty of Law at the University of Ottawa. Her primary areas of research are legal culture and the de/construction of race. She is the author of *Virtual Justice: Systemic Racism and the Canadian Legal Profession*.

PART ONE

Introduction: Why Do Law?

CHAPTER ONE

Introduction: Feminist Adventures in Law

Radha Jhappan

The gateway to a fresh millennium seems a fair vantage point from which to survey the path recently taken in women's struggle for legal equality in Canada.[1] Among many of those hitherto excluded from the full perquisites of citizenship, the hope for social justice was somewhat refreshed by the entrenchment of equality and other rights in the Canadian constitution in 1982.[2] Yet disenchantment was soon to follow, induced by years of constitutional litigation that, with some notable exceptions, has seemingly packed the winners' circle with those already privileged by their structural positions, their socioeconomic, racial, gender, heterosexual, and able-bodied statuses. These results, together with feminist and left critiques of liberal law, rights, and the legal system (each discussed below), have produced, in some quarters, overwhelmingly negative assessments of the possibility of using law in pursuit of social justice. And yet, in spite of it all, members of oppressed groups (especially women) continue to engage with law to advance their various political / social justice goals. The authors in this collection explain in different ways and from distinctive points of view some of the reasons why this is so.

This book is a response to three main questions in fact, each of which runs through the chapters implicitly if not explicitly. First, should women persevere with the legal project despite its manifest perils? Second, by what measures and from whose point of view have women's litigation strategies been successful or unsuccessful? Third, what can we learn from the strategies pursued to date and how might they be improved in future struggles? These guiding motifs of enquiry provide a backdrop to the volume as a whole, while each of the chapters raises and responds to a range of additional questions specific to its particular subject.

The term 'law' is used in differing senses by the authors in this collection, from the traditional understanding of law as a body of customary or enacted rules recognized by a community as binding (constitutional, statutory, and common or civil law), to law as an institutional system of decision-making distinct from the political sphere of legislatures, governed by its own philosophies, norms, procedures, operating principles, methodologies, and discourses, and populated by specialized practitioners to whom access is granted. In this sense, law is about the fundamental ground rules governing the settling of disputes within a polity in an institutional locus distinct from that of political bodies such as legislatures. 'Law' is also used by some of the authors in this collection in a more postmodernist vein to refer to a site of struggle wherein marginalized discourses compete with hegemonic ones to shape social relations of power.

Women's legal strategies in Canada have been many, varied, creative and, in many cases, path-breaking. They have consisted of three basic kinds of action: the lobbying of policy-makers for fresh policies and laws or amendments to existing ones; participation at various levels in the drafting of legal instruments (including specific statutory, regulatory, administrative, and human rights acts, as well as constitutional provisions); and litigation deploying federal and provincial human rights codes, statutes, and latterly the *Canadian Charter of Rights and Freedoms* (hereafter the *Charter*) to challenge the constitutionality of other legal/policy instruments. The choice of strategy will be influenced by a range of considerations, including: the source of law (e.g., whether common law or statutory provisions are involved, or whether the project is to defend protective legislation or common law rules or to challenge discriminatory ones under constitutional law); calculation of the chances for success of lobbying over litigation, for example, given the considerable resource mobilization required for each; opportunities for participation at the drafting stage; and assessment of the political climate, including the openness of the governing party to equality claims.

The chapters in this collection analyse these types of legal strategy differentially, although the majority of them focus more on litigation than on lobbying and women's roles in the crafting of legislation, and more on constitutional (i.e., *Charter*) than non-constitutional litigation. The book's focus on litigation, especially of the constitutional variety, is a result of several factors, including: the novel opportunities the *Charter* created for after-the-fact contestation of laws and policies on constitu-

Introduction: Feminist Adventures in Law 5

tional grounds; the fact that many issues raised at tribunal or human rights commission levels ultimately have been settled by the courts, some of them at the highest level (the Supreme Court of Canada); the fact that some of the laws women lobbied for or participated in drafting have been subjected to *Charter* challenges by others; and the wide-ranging significance for many women of losses and wins at that level, especially as they have affected other political strategies. Nevertheless, although many of the chapters concentrate on constitutional litigation, most incorporate discussions of lower court, tribunal, and human rights, and non-constitutional cases as appropriate to the areas of law in question, and some focus on other non-litigation legal and political strategies as well.

The choice to draw out the litigation strand of women's legal activism of the 1980s and 1990s is not an attempt to give it pride of place among the numerous other legal strategies used, let alone among the very wide range of political strategies women have exercized before and during the period. Of these, litigation is but a small (though significant) element, invariably preceded, accompanied, and succeeded by intense movement activism on many different fronts. Legal strategies are political strategies trained upon particular sites of struggle that may require more esoteric methodologies, but they are no less political for it.

My purposes in this introductory chapter are twofold. The first is to outline and respond to analyses of some of the key hazards facing women and other marginalized groups who attempt to mobilize law, particularly constitutional law, in support of social equality and justice. These hazards are illustrated practically by the records of both political and legal activism, where women have mourned important losses even as they have celebrated significant gains on each front. It is the litigation record, however, that has drawn the lion's share of attention in recent years, with constitutional litigation under the *Charter* attracting substantial media coverage, public attention, and academic analysis. Indeed, in the Canadian context, *Charter* litigation has sparked a novel theoretical debate among feminist and left scholars on the problems and possibilities of law, rights, and the legal system under liberalism. The discussion and critique of this debate presented below, therefore, address the first two questions driving this collection in a general fashion, though my arguments should by no means be taken as representative of the positions of all of the authors in the volume.

The second purpose of this introduction is to outline the scope and contents of the book, first by addressing and explaining some of the significant absences and omissions of the text, and then by describing what is present via brief synopses of the chapters.

1 The Hazards of Mobilizing Law for Equality and Justice Claims

a *The Record of Constitutional Litigation*

The *Charter of Rights* has undoubtedly been the most significant change to the Canadian legal/constitutional system since 1867. Since its passage in 1982, Canadians have generally regarded it as a salutary development.[3] Yet, the benefits expected to accrue to the various groups of women, racialized peoples, lesbians and gays, and people with disabilities who supported (and in some cases lobbied vigorously for) inclusion of equality rights, have been diffuse, unpredictable, and sometimes contradictory since section 15 came into effect in 1985. In fact, since it is the record of *constitutional* litigation that has sparked much of the contemporary scepticism or outright pessimism about the possibility of using law for progressive social change, it is important to examine that record before turning to the theoretical debates about its significance in the two sections that follow.

A statistical analysis of the first one hundred Charter decisions from the Supreme Court of Canada showed a success rate for all *Charter* claims in 1984 and 1985 at 67 per cent, but this rate declined markedly to 27 to 32 per cent between 1988 and 1992.[4] More recently, James Kelly's analysis of the first 352 Supreme Court *Charter* decisions from 1984 to 1997 shows that, in general, Charter claimants won 118 cases (or 34 per cent), lost 217 cases (or 61 per cent), while 17 cases (or 5 per cent) were inconclusive.[5] The highest success rates were for Aboriginal rights claims under section 35 of the *Charter* (46 per cent, or 6 of 13 cases), followed by language and minority language education rights claims (41 per cent, or 7 of 17 cases), legal rights (32 per cent, or 85 of 266 cases), fundamental freedoms (27 per cent, or 14 of 52 cases), equality rights (20 per cent or 7 of 35 cases), democratic rights (20 per cent or 1 of 5 cases), and mobility rights (17 per cent, or 1 of 6 cases), while claimants in each of two cases brought under the multiculturalism and gender equality sections (27 and 28) were unsuccessful.[6]

The success rate for equality claims has increased in recent years, but only slightly. For example, a statistical study published in 1992 showed that although the number of equality rights cases decided by the

Supreme Court increased sharply in 1990 (13 cases), only two were successful from the claimant's point of view, so that the overall success rate for equality claims remained at 20 per cent.[7] Moreover, up to 1991, only two sex equality cases were decided by the Supreme Court, both involving claims by men that the section of the *Criminal Code* which made it illegal for men to have intercourse with female persons under the age of fourteen years infringed their equality rights.[8] As Kelly's figures show, then, the overall success rate for equality claims from 1985 to 1997 was approximately 20 per cent, only slightly higher than the rate for the 1980s.[9]

Statistical analyses such as those cited above must be read cautiously for several reasons. First, they focus exclusively on cases definitively resolved by the Supreme Court of Canada, and do not include the decisions of lower courts, human rights boards, or administrative tribunals, or cases not appealed (for any number of reasons) which therefore stand as precedents. Second, these statistical analyses do not include decisions on applications for leave to appeal; when an application is denied, the case is effectively decided by freezing the appellate court result.[10] Nor do the statistics usually include: cases decided without reasons; cases decided together with others raising similar issues; those decided on the basis of non-entrenched rights (e.g., through the *Canadian Bill of Rights*, 1960); cases dealing with non-*Charter* constitutional rights (such as those found in the *Constitution Act, 1867*, or Aboriginal rights in the *Constitution Act, 1982*); and cases ultimately decided on non-*Charter* grounds (such as the division of powers).[11]

In fact, to my knowledge, there has been only one in-depth study of sex equality cases at various levels of court, and that is now more than a decade old. This study, by Gwen Brodsky and Shelagh Day,[12] followed Kathleen Lahey's oft-cited analysis that showed that as early as two years after section 15 came into effect, male complainants were making and winning ten times as many equality claims as women.[13] In their analysis of 591 reported and unreported decisions from all levels of court between 1985 and 1989, Brodsky and Day showed that women had been neither the chief initiators nor the predetermined beneficiaries of sex equality claims. Of forty-four sex equality cases, thirty-five (or 79 per cent) had been made by or on behalf of men, with only nine made by or on behalf of women.[14] The authors noted that these figures represented only those claims explicitly framed as sex equality issues; the picture would have looked worse for women if many other cases framed in different ways but still having serious impacts on sex equality had been included (e.g., men's challenges to sexual assault laws and to women's reproductive freedom via 'fetal rights' claims).

According to Brodsky and Day's study, up to 1989, the section 15 cases had been 'baffling and disappointing,' as they were not about systemic inequality but 'about drunk driving, marketing boards, the regulation of airline landing fees, and the manufacture of pop cans.'[15] The case record showed that the equality section had not been used as anticipated by its framers and those who supported it (mostly traditionally subordinated social groups), but had been commandeered by a range of unexpected claimants including, for example, criminals claiming a right to trial by judge instead of jury; drunk drivers claiming discrimination because of variations in provincial laws; drivers protesting mandatory seat-belt laws; male academics seeking the suspension of mandatory retirement; men trying to get access to the few benefits available to women (such as welfare benefits for single mothers, or maternity benefits for adoptive parents) or contesting affiliation and child support orders against men only; and assorted dangerous offenders, sex offenders, rapists, and other accused criminals challenging criminal procedures (including rape shield laws), sentencing, prison, and release.[16] Unfortunately, no follow-up study comparable to that by Brodsky and Day has been conducted, so we do not know what the data for the decade since 1989 might show. More recent data focus on ultimate resolutions of cases at the Supreme Court level, thus accounting for only a small proportion of the cases decided in the lower courts. Our sense of the fate of equality issues before the courts is therefore partial, particularly if we take into account that many cases argued on grounds other than equality may nevertheless have significant effects on women's equality rights.

Given the limitations of the data available, it is perhaps not surprising that most commentaries on equality rights claims tend to focus on cases settled by the Supreme Court of Canada, and particularly those argued in terms of constitutional rights. Because the highest Court's decisions are both definitive and (usually) open to influence by a host of competing intervenors (not to mention being easily accessible as texts in libraries and online databases), they receive most of the academic and public attention. This does not mean, however, that they are the most significant for the everyday lives of women and other marginalized groups. Nor does it mean that they are not subject to further action by legislatures, which may open up fresh opportunities for political struggle. Nevertheless, Supreme Court cases have been important focal points for feminist litigators and activists because they can set the parameters of public policy-making by fleshing out the content of otherwise indeterminate constitutional rights and articulating, on a case-by-case basis, the fundamental principles with which statutory law must be consistent. As such, constitutional litigation at the highest level is attractive to feminist activists and litigators, who have made use of the opportunity to participate as litigants or intervenors where other political strategies have not produced desired results, or where gains made through those means are under attack from others.

Many of the essays in this volume discuss constitutional cases decided by the Supreme Court, particularly those that featured interventions by equality-seeking groups. In fact, much discussion in this volume is devoted to the interventions of the Women's Legal Education and Action Fund (LEAF) in constitutional equality litigation. Founded in 1985 following feminist successes in lobbying for the inclusion of equality rights in the 1982 *Constitution Act* (in sections 15 and 28), LEAF was originally (and more or less remains) an organization of feminist lawyers 'dedicated to litigation of *Charter* issues before Canada's highest courts' to 'ensure that the promise of section 15 [is] converted into tangible gains.'[17] Although some of its activities are geared towards educating the public (and the judiciary) about women's equality issues, the bulk of its work has focused on the litigation efforts of LEAF's legal committee, whose mandate is to 'select and manage LEAF's litigation ... working toward the development of a comprehensive theory of substantive equality for all women [and] developing fundamental principles of legal analysis.'[18] A non-profit organization run by a national board of directors and relying mostly on volunteers, LEAF has branches across Canada, and has been working in recent years to form coalitions with other women's organizations and to increase representation of non-lawyers in the work of the legal committee. As the lead feminist equality rights intervenor, participating in more equality-related cases than any other social movement organization, LEAF has played a critical role in coaxing the Supreme Court away from its previously formalist understanding of equality to a more nuanced, contextualized, and substantive vision. Although the courts' adherence to the latter approach is often unreliable,[19] LEAF has nevertheless played a very significant role in the evolution of constitutional equality jurisprudence in the *Charter* era.

Since 1985, LEAF has participated in what are regarded as important cases in different areas of law. In fact, of the twenty-three *Charter* cases in which LEAF intervened at the Supreme Court level between 1985 and 1996, the organization was on the winning side in seventeen of them (by my estimation, four were losses and one was an inconclusive result). This is an impressive record for an organization whose approach has challenged so many of the legal system's habitually sexist (and racist) constructions of rights.

LEAF's 'wins' (or cases that were 'successful' according to the claimant involved and to LEAF litigators) include the first major equality rights decision, *Andrews*,[20] in which the Supreme Court of Canada adopted LEAF's innovative view that equality should be understood as a substantive, rather than merely a procedural right. In the area of reproductive freedom, although LEAF had not intervened in the 1988 *Morgentaler*[21] decision that decriminalized abortion (creating a negative liberty though not a positive right to abortion), it did so in *Daigle v. Tremblay*,[22] a defensive civil law action brought under the *Quebec Charter of Human Rights and Freedoms*, which ultimately resulted in the Supreme Court of Canada's definitive rejection of fetal and paternal rights claims. This finding was confirmed more recently in *Winnipeg Child and Family Services*,[23] which upheld the liberty rights of a pregnant woman who had been apprehended to 'protect' her fetus against the effects of her glue-sniffing.

LEAF has intervened in two recent cases that were ultimately successful at the Supreme Court: *Vriend*,[24] in which it was found that Alberta's *Individual Rights Protection Act*, which excludes sexual orientation from the prohibited grounds of discrimination, violates section 15 of the *Charter*; and *M. v. H.*,[25] which found that Ontario's *Family Law Act*, in defining 'spouse' as heterosexual, is discriminatory. In addition, LEAF has been involved in a range of cases that dealt with sex/gender discrimination specifically, including: *Brooks*,[26] which found the exclusion of pregnant women from the employee group health insurance plan to be sex discrimination, thus overturning the *Bliss*[27] decision; *Janzen*,[28] which recognized sexual harassment as sex discrimination; *Canadian Newspapers*,[29] which upheld a publication ban on the identity of sexual assault complainants; *Butler*,[30] in which the Supreme Court of Canada upheld the obscenity provisions of the Criminal Code on the grounds that degrading and dehumanizing pornography offends women's equality rights; *Shewchuck*,[31] which upheld allegedly discriminatory child support and paternity determinations as they served to place the financial burden of care for children on fathers rather than on the state; and *Conway*,[32] in which privacy rights of male prisoners were found not to be violated by the employment of female prison guards. LEAF was also on the winning side when it intervened in: *Keegstra*,[33] which upheld the Criminal Code's provision against the 'willful promotion of hatred'; *Eldridge*,[34] in which a provincial health scheme was found to discriminate against hearing-impaired individuals in that it did not provide for sign language translation services; and *R. v. S. (R.D.)*,[35] which rejected an accusation of bias against an African-Canadian judge who had noted the existence of systemic racism in the context of a criminal trial.

While LEAF's consitutional litigation record is formidable, it must be seen in context. First, it represents a tiny fraction of the cases decided in lower courts on equality and various other grounds that nevertheless have substantial effects on women's equality. Second, not all of the cases have been decided on s. 15 / equality grounds (*Morgentaler* and *Daigle*, e.g.), and even in those that have, the Court has not necessarily accepted LEAF's version of equality as opposed to those of the many other groups intervening or, indeed, the Court's own deference to the formalist tradition. Moreover, while it is arguable that at least some Supreme Court (and lower court) decisions have delivered significant gains to women in general or at least to some classes of women, few of LEAF's interventions have enjoyed unanimous support from women's organizations. Indeed, some of LEAF's positions have been extremely contentious among feminists, with its radical feminist pro-censorship approach to pornography in *Butler*, for example, precipitating a particularly fractious politic within Canadian women's move- ments.[36] In fact, the contestations of many of its positions played a significant role in LEAF's decision in the early 1990s to build coalitions and to intervene in cases in conjunction with other organizations to integrate more complex and intersectional analyses into its model of equality.[37]

In addition, LEAF's 'wins' at the level of high constitutional law are offset by the losses, among them: the now infamous *Seaboyer*[38] decision that struck down the rape shield law that had prevented accused rapists from using their alleged victims' past sexual history to imply consent; the *Canadian Council of Churches*[39] decision that upheld changes to the *Immigration Act* that made it more difficult to make refugee claims; *Schacter*,[40] which complicated the maternity benefits scheme under the *Unemployment Insurance Act*; the *Thibaudeau*[41] decision that upheld the *Income Tax Act*'s provision that allowed non-custodial parents (98 per cent of whom are men) to deduct child support payments from their taxable income, while custodial parents were taxed both on their own portion of child support *and* that of the non-custodial parent; and the *O'Connor*[42] decision that allowed a Roman Catholic bishop accused of raping a number of young First Nations students in a residential school in the 1960s access to their therapeutic and school records. As well as these cases, there were others in which neither LEAF nor other feminist organizations intervened and in which equality was nowhere raised as an issue, but which damaged gender equality anyway; the *Daviault*[43] decision in which the Supreme Court accepted extreme intoxication as a defence for rape is a case in point. It should be noted that some of these 'losses' were subsequently addressed by corrective legislation on the part of legislatures,[44] but such corrections cannot be assumed.

The inconsistency of the courts' responses to equality, together with the discordant responses to the nature of constitutional interventions among feminists, signal the need to interrogate the very meaning of 'success' and 'failure.' While the discussion above referred to cases as 'wins' or 'losses' from the point of view of the litigants and/or of LEAF counsel, it was not intended to suggest that cases are so handily categorized. Virtually every 'win' is contestable *within* as well as outside of the terms of feminist theory and practice, especially as feminist politics have become increasingly complex with the development of such antiliberal analyses as critical race theory, postmodernism, and poststructuralism. The chapters in this volume engage, in different ways, the question, 'what constitutes a win and in whose view?' As noted above, LEAF is not the only constitutional litigator, and its approach to equality is by no means hegemonic within the community of so-called equality-seekers.

b Feminist Critiques of Law

The overall results of constitutional litigation have been explained by some progressive social activists, and in various bodies of literature, as the inevitable proceeds of a liberal legal system that conceals both social injustices and its elite-serving design behind a veil of neutrality. For example, in recent years, significant intellectual challenges to the positivism of traditional academic disciplines have been mounted by feminists, antiracists, postmodernists, and deconstructionists. In particular, for several decades feminist legal scholars have been developing feminist theories of law, approaches that explicitly reject the 'malestream' approach of patriarchal legal positivism as well as positivist law itself. Such scholarship challenges the liberal, individualistic, non-contextual approach to law, and rejects the canonization of orthodox notions such as formal equality, equality of opportunity, and the public/private dichotomy. Rather than viewing law as the impartial application of standard principles over genderless legal subjects, feminist theorists regard law as an integral, formalized carrier of patriarchal relations.

At the same time, mainstream feminism has been rigorously critiqued on the grounds that the 'essential woman' assumed by much feminist discourse turns out to be a white, middle-class, heterosexual, able-bodied (and, in the Canadian/American context, English-speaking) woman. Women of colour, Aboriginal women, women with disabilities, lesbians, and non-anglophone women have expanded feminist legal theory to recognize that the law is not only a carrier of patriarchal relations, but also of racial hierarchy, heterosexism, ablism, and Anglo-dominance, among other things.

In view of these analyses, not surprisingly, many feminists have questioned the utility of law as an instrument for addressing women's inequality, and some have become increasingly sceptical about what Carol Smart terms 'the siren call of law.'[45] Such scholars note, for example, that Canadian women's organizations (among others) fought hard for the constitutional entrenchment of substantive equality rights beyond the formal rights that had produced such unsatisfactory results under the *Canadian Bill of Rights*. Since 1985, however, experience shows that *Charter* provisions in general, and equality rights provisions in particular, have been used disproportionately by the advantaged and by men. Hence, women's legal strategies have tended to be reactive rather than proactive. A number of activists and scholars have even suggested that women's engagement with law has been counterproductive: it has largely pursued the interests of white, middle-class, heterosexual, able-bodied, English-speaking women at the expense of marginalized women; it has overinvested intellectual and other resources in the legal project to the detriment of struggles on other fronts; it is not clear that the gains have outweighed the costs; it has bought into the individualization of women's rights; and it has 'legalized' the political struggle and legitimized the 'malestream' judicial system.

However, these alarms notwithstanding, the collection of original essays in *Women's Legal Strategies in Canada* is guided by the assumption that despite its pitfalls for different women, law is an important (though often 'malevolent') site for feminist struggle. To the extent that the law itself creates, reinforces, or at the very least, fails to intervene in the inequality and subjugation of women, it exerts its power in concrete consequences for women's daily life experiences. Moreover, law is not a monolith that exists independently of human volition, but instead is fashioned and refashioned by human beings with varying agendas and for specific purposes. Since privileged interests have used the law and (latterly the *Charter*) to roll back gains women have made on both political and legal fronts, feminists will spurn engagement in the development of jurisprudence at their peril. Non-legal political strategies per se are insufficient: the law exists, it participates in the subjugation of oppressed groups, and, therefore, it must be tackled as one important element of a multipronged approach to an inclusive feminist vision.

c *Left Critiques of Law, Rights, the* Charter, *and the Courts*

Well before the *Charter* was entrenched into the constitution in 1982, debates about the nature of law and rights had been ongoing, though not especially prominent, features of feminist and left politics and scholarship in Canada. They were to take on a salience and distinctive tenor among feminists in the process leading to the entrenchment of the *Charter*, however, as the novel potential for challenging the constitutionality of laws by means of an equality rights clause presented new strategic possibilities for women to attack a wide range of discriminatory laws and policies their political struggles had not managed to shift. While the organized left (in the form of political parties and the labour movement) paid scant attention to the coming of the *Charter*, however, as noted above, the legal left and adherents of the critical legal studies (CLS) school have been vehement critics of it, and have scorned, in particular, women's resort to law, and especially to *Charter* rights. Their critiques, relying in part on a series of important losses in the courts of claims made by traditionally socially marginalized groups,[46] raise the question of whether there is really any point in those groups resorting to law at all. It is a crucial question to which I shall respond after outlining the CLS/left position.

The Canadian legal left has been strongly influenced by the critical legal studies school that is primarily American in origin, and that has become particularly visible since the 1970s. Drawing upon several intellectual traditions, the CLS school's understanding of law weaves elements of Marxism with strands of Weber's social theory, poststructuralism and postmodernist discourse analysis. These latter threads notwithstanding, CLS nevertheless offers a compelling, largely neo-Marxist/socialist, class analysis of power. It asks whose world views and whose material and ideological interests are represented in law, the legal system, processes, and discourse, and it concludes that wealthy, class privileged, and corporate interests are the beneficiaries of a system designed to serve them and legitimate their power. In fact, the legitimation thesis is the crux of the CLS analysis of law; rights claims are seen as playing into the liberal/capitalist mythology of freedom, fairness, due process, impartiality and opportunity.

Although there are some differences between adherents of the CLS school and the traditional Marxist or socialist left, the similarities between their overall analyses of law and rights are overwhelming, so I will not separate the strands here. It is not the purpose of this brief discussion to detail the fine nuances of particular authors within either school; rather, my purpose is to lay down the broad strokes of their common approach, a task that necessitates a certain amount of generalization, even caricature. The following discussion is cognizant of the debate among socialist legal theorists in Canada on the question of whether liberal 'rights,' so scorned by Marx and many of his followers, are anything more than vehicles of legitimation for liberalism/capitalism. Amy Bartholomew and Alan Hunt, for example, drawing upon criticisms of CLS by women of colour, have offered a vigorous critique of the CLS antirights position, arguing that abstract liberal rights can be very useful resources for social movements.[47] Similarly, like a number of socialist feminists,[48] Joel Bakan has recently taken the position that there may be some justification for resorting to litigation in limited (and reactive rather than proactive) circumstances, conceding that 'rights ... can be an effective strategy in progressive social struggle' and that 'the *Charter* can provide immediate relief from direct state coercion or discrimination.'[49] However, for the purposes of this discussion, I am more interested in responding to the antirights/anti-*Charter*/antilitigation writers (such as Mandel, Petter, Hutchinson, and Glasbeek) whose work has targeted the legal strategies of women and other equality-seeking communities.

The CLS/left analysis of legal culture, at least in the Anglo-American democracies using the common law system, finds that: it is rule- and precedent-bound, therefore, inherently conservative and backward-looking; it is adversarial, and thus geared towards zero-sum absolute winning/losing, rather than problem-solving, mediation, or negotiation; it is abstract in methodology, and thus wipes events and actors clean of the socioeconomic and political contexts and relationships in which they operate in the real world; it is positivist and reifies only the written provisions of black letter law and hence has no room for natural justice or natural rights; and it feigns neutrality and objectivity but is in reality built upon specific class power relations.[50] From the general character of legal liberalism to the specificities of its Canadian application, the Canadian legal left has generally bewailed the passage of the *Charter of Rights* as a capitulation to the legalization of politics and the further disempowerment of labour and oppressed groups. Left critiques of the *Charter* per se are many and varied, but their basic premises can be distilled into a few key clusters of arguments. First, it is argued that the *Charter* is a fundamentally liberal document that sees government as the enemy from which citizens have to be protected. Yet social inequality thrives, not so much in the public sphere, but in the so-called private sphere that is based on the unequal distribution of property and power, and this sphere is not touched by the *Charter* (the behaviour of private individuals and corporations is not subject to it). In fact, *Charter* rights can only be claimed when government legislation or executive acts are seen as perpetuating systemic discrimination that actually originates in the private sphere.[51] The form and character of the *Charter* thus perpetuate the myth that the state, not capitalism and the private/corporate sector, is the enemy of the people. In such a legal system, victims of capitalism (including the poor, the unemployed, the old, the injured, women, immigrants, and indigenous peoples) are treated as victims of law as they are forced to argue that it is the law that fails to provide a protection it could afford, or that the courts or administrative agencies apply and administer state schemes improperly.[52]

Second, the Canadian legal left generally objects to constitutional rights discourse on a variety of grounds. For example, the *Charter* mostly enshrines negative liberties[53] (i.e., freedom from interference by the state) rather than positive entitlements to social benefits (such as jobs, health care, social insurance, income support, collective bargaining rights), and it does not oblige government to spend money to ensure the economic well-being of citizens. The negative liberties enshrined in the *Charter* assume a robust citizenry, so that as long as they are left alone free of government interference, all will be well. Substantive inequality, however, often needs to be addressed through the redistribution of resources, and the courts are more likely to strike down legislation extending positive benefits than they are to demand that government spend in order to remedy economic inequality.[54] In fact, the question of whether governments have positive obligations under section 15 is an ongoing focus for a number of equality-seeking groups,[55] though legal left theorists usually reject the whole idea of social 'rights.'[56]

A related problem regarding rights is that *Charter* rights and freedoms are not only abstract, but also universal. They are not the exclusive instruments of dispossessed groups, but can be claimed by property owners also.[57] Because of the imbalance of resources, the wealthy actually have greater access to rights as they are able to buy the best lawyers, researchers, experts, and legal arguments, as well as call upon their networks of personal connections with policy-makers and judges.[58] In addition, the vast majority of *Charter* rights accrue to individuals rather than groups, thus pitting them against collectivities (the general populace or specific social groups). The *Charter*, therefore, reinforces the liberal illusion of disconnection, self-interest, and lack of responsibility towards others, and encourages individuals to strike out against any putative infringement of their liberty, regardless of its social purpose or effect.

The third major objection of the Canadian legal left to the *Charter of Rights* concerns the net transfer of power from legislatures to unelected, unaccountable, class-interested judges. Various studies profiling the judiciary have shown that Canadian judges are overwhelmingly male, middle to upper class, of English- or French-Canadian descent, Protestant or Catholic, over fifty years old, and active in political parties.[59] The legal left's argument is not so much that judges are wilfully and self-consciously hostile to the claims of oppressed groups (though undoubtedly some are), but that they cannot help but be biased by their social identities, their own life experiences, their indoctrination into the tradition-bound, conservative legal culture, and their mainstream ideologies that hold individuals responsible for their situations rather than social and economic structures. In view of these facts, the left lawyers would think it easier for judges to repeal the laws of nature than to overturn the hegemony of the class and economic interests of which they are both members and agents. Moreover, there is a mountain of case evidence to show how advantaged interests win, and disadvantaged groups lose quite consistently in *Charter* claims.[60]

Legal scholars of the left quite consistently conclude that pursuing social transformation through law (and particularly through bourgeois legal rights) is very nearly pointless, since the law's ultimate purpose is precisely to *prevent* radical change. Law is the codification of the status quo, courts and lawyers its collaborators, litigation its legitimation, and reform its reinforcement. As far as the legal left is concerned, the portal to the Supreme Court, like the gates to hell in Dante's *Inferno*, might as well have engraved: 'Abandon every hope, all who enter here.'[61] The left's main prescription is, therefore, that the oppressed practise politics not law, through all the traditional avenues of political struggle, including mass mobilization, community-level organizing, unionization, demonstrations and protests, boycotts, strikes, lobbying of policy-makers, electoral politics, and so on. The mobilization of collective power in the open fora of political struggle is the path to social transformation, not the abdication of authority to narrowly trained lawyers who disguise crucial social and economic issues with technical, decontextualized legalese. *Charter* politics, they argue, has not done much for disadvantaged claimants, but has encouraged them to devote their time, energy, and scarce resources to hopeless litigation.

The legal left and the CLS school are the iconoclasts of twentieth-century liberal legalism, out to destroy its images of impartiality, fairness, equality and justice, together with the idolatry of the populace that sustains them. As such, they have done an excellent job of deconstructing law and exposing its 'deep structures' to the light of critical inquiry.

While I find the legal left/CLS analysis of law and rights well grounded and substantially correct, I am less persuaded by its political prescriptions.[62] For a start, left scholars (much like postmodernists, whom they would revile) seem to think that their work is done once they have deconstructed law. Cornel West notes that in the United States CLS offers very little in the way of 'strategies and tactics for effective social change in the larger culture and society,' but instead 'tends to limit its political praxis to pedagogical reform in elite law schools.'[63] This may be less true of the Canadian legal left, though it is difficult to see what it has offered in the way of strategies and tactics for effective social change beyond the traditional politics of class struggle outlined above. In my view, legal left scholars have posited an ultimately unsustainable dichotomy between law and politics, and they make a number of curious assumptions based on it. First, they seem to assume that social activists have a choice of *either* one *or* the other, whereas social movements have been engaging in all kinds of different struggles at various levels in multiple arenas for many years, with law being only one site, and for many groups a minor one at that. Contrary to the legal left's presumption, it is not as if women or members of other oppressed groups have given up politics in the wider political sphere to pursue legal rights. On the contrary, they have continued their material and discursive struggles in non–state-focused sites like the workplace, the family, community organizations, and so on. Indeed, it could even be argued that with the ascendancy of provincial and federal governments determined to deal with debts and deficits by shutting down the welfare state and withdrawing funding from women's and other social movement organizations, litigation may be one of the few routes left open to social movements. The left is, of course, right in pointing out that litigation can be very costly, both in time (as appeals take years) and in money (as legal fees can run to many hundreds of thousands of dollars, depending on the case). On the other hand, regular politics costs time and money, too, often a lot of both, and often with little pay-off.

Second, although their own analysis is about uncovering the politics behind law's neutral façade, left scholars appear (oddly) to assume that to participate in law is not already a deeply political act of which the participants (social movement organizations intervening in constitutional test cases) are keenly aware. The 'law is politics' revelation is not new to those who have been oppressed by it. Third, the legal left seems to assume that the strategy of mobilizing and lobbying policy-makers for legislative change is somehow *not* engaging with law;[64] yet it is an attempt to set new legal rules by establishing policies to be codified through legislation. It is just not *litigation*, which is apparently their primary preoccupation. Yet for groups whose voices and interests are normally excluded from the policy-making process no matter how much they lobby, litigation is merely the after-the-fact endeavour to modify or to have invalidated legislation or executive acts; as such it is a bid for retroactive input into the policy process. Why this is not as legitimate a pursuit for the left as before-the-fact lobbying is not clear. Of course, it is more open to charges of illegitimacy by privileged interests, but then, so is every gain the marginalized make by any means.

In fact, the 'political struggle' the legal left advocates may end up producing less-lasting results than litigation, to the extent that governments can easily repeal laws passed by their predecessors. One of the benefits of constitutional litigation that left scholars seem to forget concerns the power of the new type of judicial review authorized by the 1982 *Constitution Act*; if the courts strike down an act as unconstitutional, neither level of government can enact it.[65] To the extent that the courts can establish frameworks within which public policy must be designed (though this is a double-edged sword), litigation may well ultimately save a lot of politics, time, and resources. The legal left also seems to overlook the fact that public policy-making has been rendered *less* flexible by the *Charter*, which corporate and privileged interests have used and will continue to use to thwart interventionist public policies. They will occupy, not just the equality field, but the whole *Charter*. Therefore, the strategy the legal left generally advocates would mean vacating the constitutional field in favour of those who would undo what the dispossessed have struggled for via 'politics.'

Women and other oppressed groups are not naïfs who delude themselves that a few decisions from the courts will magically fix conditions of social and economic domination; there is much evidence to the contrary, in fact. Accounts of the various conferences and meetings of the women's groups that organized to secure equality guarantees through sections 15 and 28 show that many women had serious reservations about the *Charter* and about the possible fate of the equality sections in light of their perversion under the *Canadian Bill of Rights*.[66] Even in the mid-1980s, before any major equality cases had reached the Supreme Court, feminist legal scholars and others were worried about the lower courts' construal of section 15, and they showed little faith in what the high court would do with it.[67] It should not be surprising then that today one rarely hears in social movement politics or reads in critical or (non-liberal) feminist studies anything but cautious and sometimes wholly pessimistic attitudes towards the legal project.[68]

Furthermore, although 'disadvantaged' groups have won few cases in comparison with advantaged groups, there have been more wins than left scholars admit, though many of them are in relatively discrete areas of law that do not command much public attention, but nevertheless affect *women's* lives, if not men's.[69] Although there is a range of circumstances, the most typical cases involve either an individual charged with an offence whose lawyers then pursue a constitutional attack on the criminal law, or an individual litigant who challenges a law or policy that has affected her or him directly. Social movement organizations then participate as intervenors in cases initiated by others, rarely initiating litigation themselves. This is not to deny that some cases would never go forward without the support (financial and otherwise) of social movement organizations. Nor is it to deny that such organizations look out for appropriate cases to forward their own agendas. The point is that usually cases will proceed whether they intervene or not.

In fact, one of the chief complaints and problems facing feminist organizations has been that there has been little opportunity for proactive legal actions as they have been pressed into reactive responses to cases initiated by others, often before they were ready and without the benefit of movement consultations.[70] Nevertheless, while the adversarial legal system dictates that intervenors must argue for or against a particular outcome, they are not obliged to endorse all the claims of the litigant on whose side they have ostensibly intervened. Indeed, they usually offer analyses of how the issue affects groups rather than the individual, even where these might diverge from the particular litigant's claims. Hence, given that most cases are initiated by others and will go forward regardless, constitutional cases are opportune occasions for interventions where other political strategies have failed or are simply not possible.

As for the purpose of constitutional litigation, it seems to me that the legal left has fashioned a critique from what is its own misconstruction. Certainly, if one defines its purpose as being to win legal cases, then, much like other political strategies, the litigation project has not been an unmitigated success. If the purpose is understood as being to publicize and mobilize support for particular demands, however, then it has been quite successful.[71] Sigurdson, for example, notes that various equality claimants who lost their legal cases nevertheless considered their actions successful because the publicity they generated gave them the opportunity to communicate their politics and/or to mobilize others.[72] Bad decisions (or unsuccessful actions) may have quite useful effects: many people were not aware that they did not have certain rights until the Supreme Court announced they did not have them, and such decisions may well have a politicizing effect that formal victories on narrow legal grounds would not produce. In addition, as noted above, a number of cases that have been lost at trial have nevertheless produced a policy change that at least approximated what was being claimed in the legal case. In this way, cases can be used as pressure points to induce policy shifts where efforts on other fronts have gone unrewarded, and losing a case can be a stroke of luck.

In my view, those legal left scholars who spurn constitutional litigation for oppressed groups have taken a position that is politically and practically indefensible. To criticize law as oppressive, and tell women and others not to engage with it is to ignore the fact that law as legislation has real practical impacts in the daily lives of real people. Such a position offers cold comfort to indigenous peoples, women, people of colour, lesbians and gays, people with disabilities, and others who variously need Aboriginal rights to culture, community, and self-determination, child support, reproductive choice, physical security, jobs, labour rights, harassment-free workplaces, homes, and public spaces, promotions, social benefits, and many other things. As Razack puts it, we should 'erase the line we sometimes draw between legal and political activity and recognize that when we go to court we are fighting for our lives. We are not up against a neutral arbiter, but a powerful system of symbols, rules, and practices that combine to oppress women and other groups.'[73]

The legal left has yet to show that legal strategies, and especially litigation, are less effective than the endless political struggles that have failed to overturn a wide range of discriminatory and oppressive laws. Law may indeed be treacherous, but many left scholars seem to be suggesting that we surrender this terrain, as if challenging the power of this mighty institution that holds in place relations of domination is too dangerous for us, as if we would somehow be *more* crushed by a litigation strategy that delivers fewer victories than defeats than by living with the consequences of oppressive laws every day. The sometimes patronizing tone of their admonitions to rely on politics conveniently ignores the fact, obvious to those subjugated by the law, that it is politicians who have passed discriminatory or otherwise disadvantageous laws that are being challenged through courts, and that the political process has not been that much kinder, more accessible, or more democratic than the courts.[74] When Michael Mandel glibly asks, 'Who needs a *Charter* when you hold up 52% of the sky?'[75] he should remember that women do not hold up 52 per cent of Parliament or the provincial legislatures, just as Aboriginal peoples, racial/ethnocultural minorities, people with disabilities, and working-class Canadians continue to be severely underrepresented in Canada's political institutions relative to their proportions of the population.

It is largely because there are so many uncontrollable mega-elements to the political process (such as an ideologically receptive government, bureaucratic entry points, public support or antipathy, government's financial wherewithal, sympathetic ministers, positions of opposition parties) that marginalized groups may turn to the relatively more circumspect legal process. Here there are certainly significant impediments (availability of relevant legal instruments / constitutional provisions, favourable precedents, conservative legal culture, ideological leaning of judges, personnel and financial resources to pursue litigation, good test case material), but they are more manipulable than the mega-political variables, depending on neither timing and the political climate nor the whims of the party in power.

The socialist left naturally, and with evidence aplenty, worries that the incremental improvements in everyday conditions of life wrought by liberal reform serve only to postpone if not utterly thwart the coming of the socialist revolution. Yet, it has nevertheless supported the struggles of labour over a wide range of political *and* legal fronts (including struggles for labour laws, regulatory systems, tribunals, and the use of the courts to uphold or to challenge such regimes, though not via *Charter* challenges), even as it seeks to discourage non–economically based social movements from legal reform, especially through litigation. But given that the socialist revolution seems to be off for the moment, the left position raises the question of what subjugated groups are supposed to do while waiting for it (assuming that they should be). The question is not, as is usually posed by the left, whether law can produce social (i.e., socialist) transformation, but rather, what will happen if such groups *do not* participate in legal reform? Left scholars generally conclude that because law / the legal system is tainted, biased, fundamentally conservative, and oppressive, in other words, not a neutral or perfect instrument, it therefore ought not to be used. Yet it seems to me that that is the whole *point* – if it *were* perfect, there would be no need to use it to effect change! Their assumption is that that which we want to change is independent of the legal system, and that the legal system is somehow only regarded as a tool to be used in attempts to change 'it.' But the legal system itself is a huge part of 'it,' not independent of it, but constitutive of 'it.' How are we supposed to transform 'it' by boycotting it? Ironically, its imperfections create opportunities to alter it. If this is all the revolution we are going to get for the foreseeable future, it seems to me that subjugated groups would be ill-advised to boycott law.

2 Scope and Contents of the Book

a What Is Absent from the Text

Throughout my own process of learning I have found that what is absent from a text often says as much about the assumptions, values, positionality and world view of its creator(s) as what is present; that is, omissions generally serve as fairly good clues as to what is considered significant, and hence worthy of attention, and what is not. The same is probably true of this text, though perhaps to a lesser degree as its original conception was much more inclusive and ambitious than its final configuration might suggest. Among the unintended omissions, for example, are chapters about and/or by Aboriginal women, women with disabilities, lesbians, and women in Quebec (discussed below). Among the missing areas of law are family, tax, criminal, civil, torts, corporate, and pay and employment equity law, while among the absent levels of law are the provincial human rights scene and administrative law. This is not to say that these constituencies of women, areas, and levels of law are not referred to or even featured in various chapters – it is simply that there are no chapters explicitly dedicated to them. These absences are not the results of oversights or low prioritizing. Indeed, contributions were solicited from a number of potential authors for each of these fields, but for varied reasons, in the end many were unable to contribute manuscripts. A chapter on lesbian litigation strategies was withdrawn by the authors for personal reasons late in the production process. The final collection reflects the generally overextended working lives of feminist activists and scholars rather than any editorial undervaluing of the importance of their identities, fields, expertise, approaches, positions, and their importance to the feminist legal project.

Readers will also find significant omissions in the areas of ideology, theory, and the very diverse approaches to feminism and legal projects one finds within today's feminist movements. For each chapter, numerous counterpoints could have been included as each arises from an approach and takes a position that is contested within, between, and outside feminist movements. That, however, would have been a very different and considerably longer book, for which there is also room in the Canadian literature. Nevertheless, the collection does *not* assume homogeneity among women. The chapters reflect a wide range of views and approaches to the issues raised. They do not pretend to be definitive representations of 'the feminist position' and they do not assume an 'essential woman.' On the contrary, they recognize the diversity of interests and positions among women, particularly those arising from differential socioeconomic, citizenship, racial/ethnocultural, and class situations, as well as the fact, as several chapters note, that in some instances, certain women have made legal and other gains at the expense of others.

As it has turned out, this book is about the legal strategies of women

Introduction: Feminist Adventures in Law 25

from the English-speaking provinces of Canada, not those of women of Quebec. Again, the absence of chapters on women's legal strategies in Quebec is not the result of an oversight or exclusion, but more of the overstretched working lives of the feminist scholars, lawyers, and activists who were asked to participate in this project. In view of this gap, however, a brief outline of some of the differences between the legal strategies of the women's movements in Quebec and the rest of Canada is in order.[76]

The political/legal agendas of the Quebec women's movements and those in the rest of Canada have differed quite markedly in important areas, and for good reasons. In the first place, the majoritarian (white, anglophone) Canadian and (white, francophone) Quebec women's movements have had unique histories, and their relationship has varied with the political and cultural relations between the rest of Canada and Quebec. Since the Quiet Revolution of the 1960s, the (white, francophone) Quebec women's movement has increasingly aligned itself with the nationalist movement; it has been 'stimulated and nurtured' by nationalism (increasingly of the sovereignist variety), and this has produced a distinctive feminism vis-à-vis the rest of the country.[77] Feminism and nationalism are regarded as symbiotic rather than contradictory, and the majority of both federalist and sovereignist feminists of the umbrella organization Fédération des femmes du Québec (FFQ) favour at a minimum the further devolution of powers to the Quebec government, the better to institutionalize feminism within both the state and society.[78] So, given that feminist and cultural/nationalist analyses are explicitly woven together in the mainstream Quebec women's movement, the latter has been less willing to treat gender as a separate issue from ethnicity, language, culture, and francophone self-determination.[79]

In the second place, the political/legal agendas of the majoritarian Canadian and Quebec women's movements have been quite divergent because of the very different legal systems and social policy nets facing them in their respective provinces. Over the past thirty years, the Quebec provincial state has assumed a range of what previously were federal jurisdictions, and, prodded by Quebec women's movements, has used its complement of pre-existing and new powers to pioneer progressive social policies in a number of areas (access to abortion, inexpensive day care, family law other than divorce, and labour/employment legislation, to name a few). Hence, there is a sense among Quebec feminists that women's fundamental rights are protected by the overhauled *Civil Code*, family law, social policy, the Quebec *Charter of Human Rights and Freedoms, 1976*,[80] and by a body of modern judicial precedents. There is also a sense that the Quebec legislature and administration are more receptive to the women's lobby than are their federal counterparts, or indeed, other provincial states. Women's organizations in Quebec, therefore, have felt somewhat less need to challenge social legislation and thus more loyalty to their provincial state than have women in other provinces who have looked more to the federal level of government to design national norms and standards across provincial boundaries.

The trajectories of the legal strategies of the majority women's movements of Canada and Quebec must also be explained in terms of the markedly divergent constitutional agendas of each. These stemmed in the first instance from the constitutional entrenchment without Quebec's consent of the *Constitution Act, 1982*, and the imposition of the *Charter of Rights*. Women's groups in Quebec lobbied for and supported equality rights legislation and constitutional amendments. The *Charter*, however, was viewed by nationalists, not only as inferior to Quebec's own *Charter*, but as a threat to the collective rights of francophones and a unilateral reduction in the powers of the Quebec National Assembly in favour of the federal and provincial governments as well as Canadian courts.

Subsequent attempts by the Conservative federal government of Brian Mulroney to satisfy Quebec's constitutional demands in the forms of the Meech Lake (1987) and Charlottetown (1992) accords saw serious ruptures in the relationship between the two majoritarian elements of the women's movements. The predominantly anglophone National Action Committee on the Status of Women (NAC) joined the Native Women's Association of Canada (NWAC) in rejecting the 'distinct society' language of the proposed Meech Lake Accord and were at least partially responsible for its defeat.[81] And although the schism was somewhat narrowed when NAC accepted the concept during the Charlottetown negotiations (albeit in a 'three nations' framework), in the end most Canadian women's organizations rejected the accord for a number of other reasons and it was likewise defeated. But despite the fact that Canadian feminist opposition to accords that might have satisfied Quebec's constitutional demands pivoted, for many, on the questions of the rights of indigenous and racial/ethnic and cultural minority women, such issues have not detained the white francophone Quebec women's movement.[82]

Given the lack of legitimacy initially accorded the *Charter* by Quebec's political elites (subsequently exacerbated by the Supreme Court of Canada's invalidation of parts of Quebec's language legislation), it is perhaps not surprising that Quebec feminists have had a rather different take on the *Charter* and equality rights than have feminists in other provinces.[83] This is not to suggest that gender equality is a fait accompli in Quebec, but rather to explain why, unlike those of the other provinces, Quebec women's organizations have neither undertaken a systematic legal assault on provincial laws and policies nor regarded the *Charter* as the instrument of choice with which to do so.

Feminist organizations in Quebec have participated in several legal challenges, perhaps the most high profile and successful of these being the initiative of Action travail des femmes (ATF), a group specializing in the placement of women in non-traditional jobs.[84] In the landmark case of *C.N. v. Canada*,[85] the Supreme Court of Canada endorsed ATF's claim that the Canadian National Railway's hiring and promotion policies discriminated on the basis of sex contrary to s. 10 of the *Canadian Human Rights Act*. The case was significant in that ATF successfully insisted upon the creation of an affirmative action program to combat systemic discrimination for future applicants and employees, instead of limited individual remedies (monetary compensation) for past victims. In a number of subsequent cases, employers responded to impending claims by adopting voluntary programs.[86]

Relations between Quebec groups such as the ATF and anglophone organizations from the other provinces (such as LEAF) have not been particularly close. The language/cultural divide has been a significant impediment to the development of joint strategies between LEAF and Quebec women's groups, and Quebec women's groups regard as illegitimate any attempts by anglo-feminist organizations to intervene in what they see as Quebec sovereignty matters.[87] Although LEAF established a branch in Montreal, its members decided that LEAF would not be recognized as the exclusive leader in litigation, but that instead the commitment would be to secure intervenor status for women's groups specializing in the issues raised by each case.

Although Quebec women's groups have participated in a number of important cases (mentioned above), such participation has been sporadic. This is partly because Quebec judges, like those of most other provinces (except British Columbia and Ontario), tend to grant permission for third parties to intervene quite infrequently,[88] and partly because there are very few interventions by feminist organizations at the provincial trial or appeal court levels anyway. Nevertheless, Quebec women's organizations have been conspicuously absent from several high-profile cases, some of which have had a significant impact on Quebec as well as the rest of Canada. In each of these cases, it was LEAF, not Quebec feminist organizations, that intervened to argue for gender equality: *Daigle*,[89] *Thibaudeau v. Canada* and *Caron v. R.*,[90] a challenge to Quebec welfare legislation's 'man in the house' rule at the Quebec Court of Appeal. Granted, *Thibaudeau* was not about provincial law or human rights instruments as were the other two, but it is significant that it was LEAF that made the interventions rather than Quebec organizations.

b What Is Present in the Text

As noted above, this collection of essays offers reflections on the questions of whether women should persevere with legal projects despite their dangers, whether women's litigation strategies have been successful or unsuccessful and from whose point of view, and whether and how the strategies pursued to date might be improved, the better to represent the complexity of different women's situations and interests. Each of the chapters responds in its own way to these questions. Readers will find a number of themes threaded through the essays, among them the politically disempowering critiques of liberal law and rights paradigms from the ideological left, the problems of legal equality strategies, gender essentialism, accountability of feminist litigators to broader women's movements, and the difficulties of pursuing justice through the courts.

Part One of this book is devoted to theoretical reflections from various angles about the major questions posed above. Sheila McIntyre's chapter centres on the question of whether women's participation in legal reform is ultimately worthwhile once the many negative aspects have been accounted for. McIntyre squarely addresses the phalanx of male legal scholars and political scientists of the ideological left, right, and centre, whose mission has been to denounce as antidemocratic the pursuit of *Charter* rights by those who traditionally have been marginalized. McIntyre critiques the left's legitimation theory and sets about dismantling the key elements of its case against legal activism. Her overriding purpose is to highlight some of the ways in which race, gender, and class oppression operate through 'the oppressors within,' the 'intellectual and/or professional vanguards.' McIntyre sees various instances of community activism, such as that around the struggle to end violence against women, as movement-building moments. For her, coalition work offers a sustainable model for politically empowered and accountable legal activism.

The three chapters that follow in Part Two guide our attention to the litigation strategies typically employed by Canadian feminist organizations such as LEAF. They focus in different ways on the fallibility of the equality approach that has typically isolated gender from other relations of power at the cost of capturing the complexity of diverse women's lived experiences and structural locations vis-à-vis each other as well as in relation to men.

Diana Majury takes up the themes of gender essentialism and of the problems and possibilities of legal equality strategies, noting the unidimensionality of (Euro-American) feminist equality analyses and strategies that largely hold gender as the primary root of women's inequality. Her analysis of various cases shows how the 'equality as sameness' model has persisted, even though the Supreme Court of Canada explicitly rejected the formal equality/similarly situated test in the *Andrews* case. Majury argues that the model has created new problems in the reinforcing of stereotypes of group disadvantage, as evidenced in the *Egan, McKinney, Rodriguez, Lister,* and *Thibaudeau* decisions. This is no argument for abandoning law reform and equality, however. For Majury, we should see equality, not as a destination, but as a strategy, so that the challenge is how to think strategically and critically about how it is and could be deployed.

Gender essentialism is the predominant concern in Lise Gotell's analysis of the evolution of LEAF's 'contextualized approach to sexual equality,' or CASE. Her postmodernist approach is profoundly sceptical of the concept of 'woman' as a natural subject, understanding it instead as a constructed category. Gotell points out that although essentialism characterized LEAF's litigation strategy from 1985 to 1992, the organization has since attempted to develop a less essentialist, more inclusive, and fully contextualized intersectional analysis of in/equality. Nevertheless, she remains critical of LEAF's revised approach, taking issue with the assumptions characteristic of LEAF's feminist standpoint epistemology and problematizing positivistic claims to epistemic 'truths.' Even so, Gotell's purpose is not to eschew the legal project altogether; on the contrary, she endorses LEAF's continuing efforts to forward substantive equality jurisprudence, with the benefit of the kind of constructive criticism of legal strategies that has produced recent shifts towards intersectional analyses.

Constructive criticism of feminist litigation strategies pursued to date is the principal aspiration of my own essay, which outlines a number of major problems with 'equality,' including its essentialist and assimilationist tendencies. My primary purpose in the essay is to suggest an alternative goal and strategy for feminist litigation efforts that avoids these traps and is flexible enough to encompass more complex intersectional analyses – that is, justice. Such an approach would be contextualized, substantive, and outcome- rather than process-oriented. The chapter offers some suggestions as to how such approaches could be applied in *Charter of Rights* challenges using sections 7 and 1.

The third and fourth parts of this book move from general/theoretical to more specific/applied modes of analysis. They are devoted to practical assessments of whether feminist legal enterprises have been worthwhile in discrete issue areas. Part Three focuses on racialized women and their various struggles for the rights of citizenship.

Daiva Stasiulis and Abigail Bakan provide a layered analysis of citizenship issues tied to a strand of immigration policy that is designed to secure a supply of cheap, in-home, domestic labour for middle- and upper-income Canadians, in the form (almost always) of poor women from developing countries. This analysis of necessity reaches far beyond gender issues to encompass the complex class, race, ethnic, neocolonial, and international relations that are reflected in what the authors call 'the citizenship divide' between populations of the North and South. Wealthy states' increasingly stringent enforcement of border control, state security and sovereignty, they argue, reflects a system of 'global apartheid' in which those states band together to ensure that migrant workers from poorer countries, especially women, have minimal access to citizenship rights in the highly industrialized countries. Stasiulis and Bakan show that Canadian policy on foreign domestic workers abrogates the basic human and worker rights of female migrant live-in caregivers, and this further skews the power relations intrinsic to their situation in favour of employers. Their analysis of litigation efforts by domestic workers and their associations shows that courts have deferred to the border control and sovereignty assertions of the Canadian state rather than to *Charter* principles, thus allowing both state policies and the private power of employers to trump the human and labour rights of female migrant workers.

Introduction: Feminist Adventures in Law 31

The need for intersectional analyses is the dominant theme of Joanne St Lewis's essay. Her concern is to explain why feminist legal theorists must draw upon the expertise of racialized women in their litigation efforts, from the formulation of concepts to methodologies and strategies. She argues that, contrary to its projected image of race-neutrality, Canadian law 'has always borne the "race" and culture of its progenitors,' whose world views and interests it was designed to serve. The sham of race-neutrality is amply illustrated by the recent charge of judicial bias against an African-Canadian woman judge in *R. v. R.D.S.* St Lewis tracks the ways in which feminist litigation strategies have moved through phases of 'race-denial' (pre-1970s), to gender essentialism (1970s and early 1980s) and finally, to race consciousness. Urging feminists to give voice to racialized women to express their own needs, interests, and political agendas, St Lewis argues that critical race theory offers an exciting, rather than divisive, opportunity for the refinement of feminist legal theory and practice.

Part Four of the book features two chapters that centre to varying degrees on law, family, and reproduction.

Sheilah Martin's essay, 'Abortion Litigation,' focuses on an issue that perhaps has been less contentious within western women's movements (though challenged by women of colour and women in or from poorer countries),[91] that of women's control of their reproductive potential, especially through access to abortion. Nevertheless, Martin notes that in Canada, as in the United States, litigated cases have been extremely important in the determination of access to abortion, not to mention the mode and temper of public debate. She analyses the various impacts of the *Morgentaler*, *Borowski*, and *Daigle* cases on the lives of women, noting throughout the many limitations of the legal system, the judiciary, and the confusing and contradictory nature of the decisions. Although it is difficult to define success and failure, and to assess what effects litigation and other legal strategies have (given the myriad other social and political forces in play), Martin's view of law, in the end, is relatively optimistic. Like others, Martin warns against the tendency to legalize complex social problems into 'rights talk' abstractions that can eclipse real and immediate needs and practical policy, but in her view, legal strategies and litigation *can* yield some positive results in conjunction with other strategies on other fronts.

Finally, returning to the 'law or politics' question, Susan Phillips reminds us that legal strategies are political strategies and that the pursuit of political goals via litigation accounts for a relatively small proportion of the political activities of the women's movement. She looks at the impact of certain legal cases on broader movement politics in two major areas of feminist activism – the pursuit of a national day-care program and the struggle against violence against women. Phillips suggests that although *Seaboyer* was an excellent example of how a legal case can instantly undo long struggled-for gains, it nevertheless brought together local and national as well as privileged and minority women, and it contributed to the democratization of feminist legal strategy. Phillips also outlines some of the difficult politics surrounding the federal government's Panel on Violence Against Women, especially those of representation and voice. The chapter traces movement attempts to secure a national child-care program, explaining the failure of this lobby in terms of the shift in the political opportunity structure attending the ascendancy of neoconservative ideology, social policy, and fiscal restraint that produced a resistant state. After examining the role played by the *Symes* case in shifting the discourse on child care, Phillips sees legal cases as important opportunities for political mobilization and alliance-building that cannot be understood independently from the intense, multifaceted, and complex movement politics preceding and succeeding them. Indeed, the same is true of all the cases and litigation strategies discussed in this volume.

Although all of the authors contributing to this book are at least uneasy about feminist litigation strategies (and several show that, in discrete areas of law, litigation has yielded relatively small returns on relatively costly efforts), interestingly, none advocates jettisoning them entirely. Instead, most seem to lean towards the view that we can take as much instruction from past problems, errors, and losses as from our breakthroughs and triumphs. Feminist adventures in law in the twenty-first century will no doubt remain contentious, complex and risky – but such is politics in the real world.

Notes

1 I am grateful to the anonymous reviewers of the first draft of this chapter for their excellent comments and suggestions, and hope I have done justice to them here.
2 *Canadian Charter of Rights and Freedoms*, Part I of the *Constitution Act, 1982*, being Schedule B of the *Canada Act, 1982* (U.K.) (1982) c. 11.
3 For example, a 1989 national study of Canadians' attitudes towards the

Charter found that 90 per cent of women and 88 per cent of men felt that it was a good thing for the country; 95 per cent of respondents felt the equality guarantee was important; and only 2 per cent of women and 3 per cent of men did not agree with the view that every person in Canada is entitled to the same rights and protections. The *Attitudes toward Civil Liberties and the Canadian Charter of Rights Project* data are referred to in Sandra Burt, 'What's Fair? Changing Feminist Perceptions of Justice in English Canada' (1992) 12 *Windsor Yearbook of Access to Justice (WYAJ)* 349. National surveys of 1987 and 1999 found that 82 per cent of Canadians regarded the *Charter* as 'a good thing.' See Joseph Fletcher and Paul Howe, 'Canadian Attitudes toward the Charter,' paper presented at the Annual Meeting of the Canadian Political Science Association, Université de Sherbrooke, 8 June 1999, at 4, 9.

4 Frederick L. Morton, Peter H. Russell, and Michael J. Withey, 'The Supreme Court's First One Hundred Charter of Rights Decisions: A Statistical Analysis' (1992) 30, 1 *Osgoode Hall Law Journal (OHLJ)* 9.

5 James B. Kelly, 'The Charter of Rights and Freedoms and the Rebalancing of Liberal Constitutionalism in Canada, 1982–1997' (1999) 37 *OHLJ* 641.

6 Ibid., Table 5 at 648.

7 Peter Russell, 'The Supreme Court in the 1980s: A Commentary on the S.C.R. Statistics' (1992) 30, 4 *OHLJ* 788.

8 *R. v. Nguyen* and *R. v. Hess*, [1990] 2 S.C.R. 906. The claims, which were heard together, ultimately succeeded on s. 7 grounds. Of the remaining equality cases, six were age-discrimination claims, two involved mental or physical disability, one concerned religious rights, while others concerned province of residence and various other grounds analogous to those found in s. 15.

9 The success rate for equality claims between 1985 and 1992 was 19 per cent. See Kelly, 'The Charter,' 631.

10 See Morton et al., 'Supreme Court,' 49.

11 Ibid., 50, 51, 52.

12 Gwen Brodsky and Shelagh Day, *Canadian Charter Equality Rights for Women: One Step Forward or Two Steps Back?* (Ottawa: Canadian Advisory Council on the Status of Women, 1989).

13 Kathleen Lahey, 'Feminist Theories of (In)Equality,' in Sheilah L. Martin and Kathleen Mahoney, eds., *Equality and Judicial Neutrality* (Toronto: Carswell, 1987) 82.

14 Brodsky and Day, *Canadian Charter*, 49. Similarly, in 'Legitimizing Sexual Inequality: Three Early Charter Cases' (1989) 34 *McGill Law Journal (MLJ)* 360–2, Andrew Petter notes that of the first thirty-five sex discrimination

cases, twenty-five (70 per cent) were brought by men, and of eleven successful cases, seven (65 per cent) involved male litigants.
15 Brodsky and Day, *Canadian Charter*, 103.
16 Ibid., 49–67.
17 Women's Legal Education and Action Fund (LEAF), *Equality and the Charter: Ten Years of Feminist Advocacy before the Supreme Court of Canada* (Toronto: Emond Montgomery, 1996) xv, xvi. For an analysis of LEAF's interventions and equality discourse, see also Sherene Razack, *Canadian Feminism and the Law* (Toronto: Second Story Press, 1991).
18 LEAF, *Equality and the Charter*, xvii.
19 See Margot Young, 'Change at the Margins: *Eldridge v. British Columbia (A.G.)* and *Vriend v. Alberta*' (1998) 10, 1 *Canadian Journal of Women and the Law (CJWL)* 244.
20 *Andrews v. the Law Society of British Columbia*, [1989] 1 S.C.R. 143. The Court found that the B.C. Law Society's exclusion of non-citizens from the bar violated the equality rights of otherwise qualified non-citizens, in this case, a landed immigrant from Britain who had passed his bar exams in the province. As many have observed, it is ironic that the first significant s. 15 case should have upheld the equality rights of a healthy, wealthy male of British origin, rather than a member of a group that has been historically oppressed. It is also ironic that the decision has not been applied by the courts to other non-citizens (such as foreign domestic workers) who suffer serious disadvantage in the sense that they are excluded from labour code provisions governing health and safety, hours of work, minimum wages, unionization rights, and the like.
21 *R. v. Morgentaler*, [1988] 1 S.C.R. 30.
22 *Daigle v. Tremblay*, [1989] 2 S.C.R. 530.
23 *Winnipeg Child and Family Services v. G. (D.F.)*, [1997] 3 S.C.R. 925.
24 *Vriend v. Alberta (A.G.)*, [1998] 1 S.C.R. 493.
25 *M. v. H.*, [1999] 2 S.C.R. 3. The successful claims in *Vriend* and *M. v. H.* follow losses in *Canada (A.G.) v. Mossop*, [1993] 1 S.C.R. 554 and *Egan v. Canada*, [1995] 2 S.C.R. 513.
26 *Brooks v. Canada Safeway Ltd.*, [1987] 1 S.C.R. 1219.
27 *Bliss v. A.G. Canada*, [1979] 1 S.C.R. 183.
28 *Janzen v. Platy Enterprises*, [1989] 1 S.C.R. 1252.
29 *Canadian Newspapers v. Canada (A.G.)*, [1988] 43 C.C.C. (3d) 24 (Supreme Court of Canada).
30 *R. v. Butler* (1992), 70 C.C.C. (3d) 129.
31 *Re Shewchuck v. Ricard* (1986) 28 D.L.R. (4th) 429.
32 Also known as *Weatherall v. Canada (A.G.)*, [1993] 2 S.C.R. 872.

Introduction: Feminist Adventures in Law 35

33 *R. v. Keegstra*, [1990] 3 S.C.R. 697.
34 *Eldridge v. British Columbia (A.G.)*, [1997] 3 S.C.R. 624.
35 *R. v. S. (R.D.)*, [1997] 3 S.C.R. 484.
36 For critiques of LEAF's approach in *Butler* and anticensorship positions, see e.g., Brenda Cossman, Shannon Bell, Lise Gotell, and Becki Ross, *Bad Attitude/s on Trial* (Toronto: University of Toronto Press, 1997).
37 Frequent partners in Supreme Court interventions have thus included the National Action Committee on the Status of Women (NAC), the Aboriginal Women's Council, the Native Women's Association of Canada, the Canadian Association of Sexual Assault Centres, the Disabled Women's Network of Canada, and the Canadian Disability Rights Council, to name but a few.
38 *R. v. Seaboyer*, [1991] 2 S.C.R. 577.
39 *Canadian Council of Churches v. Canada* (1992), 88 D.L.R. (4th) 193.
40 *Schacter v. Canada*, [1992] 93 D.L.R. (4th) 1. See Michael Mandel, *The Charter of Rights and the Legalization of Politics in Canada* (Toronto: Wall and Thompson, 1994) 391–6.
41 *Thibaudeau v. Canada*, [1995] 2 S.C.R. 627.
42 *O'Connor v. the Queen*, [1995] 4 S.C.R. 411.
43 *R. v. Daviault*, [1994] 3 S.C.R. 63.
44 After *Seaboyer* a new rape shield law was developed with in-put from women's organizations (see McIntyre's chapter in this volume); after *Thibaudeau*, the Liberal government amended the *Income Tax Act* to stop taxing custodial parents (usually mothers) for the child support they receive from non-custodial parents (usually fathers) who had previously enjoyed a tax credit for such payments; and after *Daviault*, the federal government passed Bill S-6, *An Act to amend the Criminal Code (dangerous intoxication)*, S.C. 1995, c. 32.
45 Carol Smart, 'Feminism and Law: Some Problems of Analysis and Strategy' (1986) 4 *International Journal of the Sociology of Law (IJSL)* 111.
46 The 'Labour Trilogy' of cases in which the Supreme Court repelled the idea of a constitutional right to strike and other hard-won union rights fuelled much of the criticism from the left. See Mandel, *Charter of Rights*, chap. 5.
47 Amy Bartholomew and Alan Hunt, 'What's Wrong with Rights?' (1990) 9 *Law and Inequality (LI)* 1.
48 See, e.g., Shelley Gavigan, 'Law, Gender and Ideology,' in Anne Bayefsky, ed., *Legal Theory Meets Legal Practice* (Edmonton: Academic Publishing, 1988); and Susan Boyd, 'Child Custody, Ideologies and Employment' (1989) 3 *CJWL* 111.

49 Joel Bakan, *Just Words: Constitutional Rights and Social Wrongs* (Toronto: University of Toronto Press, 1997) 56. Yet despite this concession, Bakan argues throughout his book that 'the *Charter* does not further democratic and egalitarian values, except in narrow and exceptional circumstances ... and even then, not substantially' (at 7), that 'it is unlikely that any meaningful movement towards *social* equality will result from the [Supreme] Court's apparently progressive approach [to equality]' (at 47), and that 'the *Charter* has done little to advance social justice in Canada, despite its just words' (at 144). While this is not the occasion for a lengthy critique, Bakan's position, like that of the left approach, in general, seems economically deterministic. Though he claims to have avoided class reductionism (at 148) by recognizing that other social relations such as gender, race, and colonialism intersect with class, his analysis throughout is overwhelmingly fixed on class and economic relations (passim, but see also his summary of the focus of each chapter at 146), and as a result Bakan under-estimates the importance to a variety of social movements of their non-economic claims in the pursuit of social not just economic justice.

50 These analyses are found in various forms in the works of Canada's leading left legal scholars and proponents of the CLS school, including the following: Judy Fudge, 'What Do We Mean by Law and Social Transformation?' (1990) 5 *Canadian Journal of Law and Society* (*CJLS*) 47–69; Judy Fudge, 'The Effect of Entrenching a Bill of Rights upon Political Discourse: Feminist Demands and Sexual Violence in Canada' (1989) 17 *IJSL* 445–63; Harry Glasbeek, 'Some Strategies for an Unlikely Task: The Progressive Use of Law' (1989) 21, 2 *Ottawa Law Review* (*OLR*) 387–418; Michael Mandel, *Charter of Rights*; Joel Bakan, 'Constitutional Interpretation and Social Change: You Can't Always Get What You Want (Nor What You Need),' in R. Devlin, ed., *Canadian Perspectives on Legal Theory* (Toronto: Emond Montgomery, 1991) 445–66; and three articles by Andrew Petter and Alan Hutchinson, 'Daydream Believing: Visionary Formalism and the Constitution' (1990) 22 *OLR* 365; 'Rights in Conflict: The Dilemma of Charter Legitimacy' (1989) 23 U.B.C. Law Review (*UBCLR*) 531; and 'Private Rights / Public Wrongs: The Liberal Lie of the Charter' (1988) 38 *University of Toronto Law Journal* (*UTLJ*) 278.

51 Fudge, 'What Do We Mean,' 60.

52 Glasbeek, 'Some Strategies,' 388.

53 Bakan, *Just Words*, 49–50.

54 Fudge, 'What Do We Mean,' 57.

55 See, e.g., Martha Jackman, 'Women and the Canada Health and Social Transfer: Ensuring Gender Equality in Federal Welfare Reform' (1995) 8

CJWL 371. Indeed, *Eldridge* would be a good example of a successful attempt at forcing extension of a government benefit plan; *Egan* and most other lesbian and gay rights claims for benefits would be examples of unsuccessful ones.

56 See Bakan's argument against a social charter in *Just Words*, 134–41.
57 See, e.g., Judy Fudge, 'The Effect of Entrenching,' 449; and Elizabeth Kingdom, 'The Legal Recognition of Women's Right to Choose,' in J. Brophy and C. Smart., eds., *Women and Law* (London: Routledge and Kegan Paul, 1985).
58 Glasbeek, 'Some Strategies,' 388 and 401.
59 Peter McCormick and Ian Greene, *Judges and Judging: Inside the Canadian Judicial System* (Toronto: Lorimer, 1990) 79.
60 The most thorough analysis of the case law in various areas from a left perspective is found throughout Michael Mandel's book, *The Charter of Rights and the Legalization of Politics in Canada*. For a more detailed exploration of the left position, critiques of the *Charter* from the ideological right, and a response to both, see Richard Sigurdson, 'Left- and Right-Wing Charterphobia in Canada: A Critique of the Critics' (1993) 7–8 *International Journal of Canadian Studies (IJCS)* 95–116.
61 Dante Alighieri, *The Divine Comedy of Dante Alighieri: Inferno* (New York: Bantam Books, 1980, trans. Allen Mandelbaum), Canto III, 21, line 9.
62 Sheila McIntyre's chapter in this volume provides the finest response to the left/CLS position I have seen. Also, Richard Sigurdson has offered an excellent set of critiques of their political prescriptions in 'The Left-Legal Critique of the *Charter*: A Critical Assessment' (1993) 13 *WYAJ* 117. I will not repeat their analyses here, but will add some of my own.
63 Cornel West, *Keeping Faith: Philosophy and Race in America* (New York: Routledge, 1993) 203, 224. Similarly, Donna Greschner criticizes CLS for its tendency to study doctrine, esp. historical doctrine, and to focus 'too much on abstract ideas and not enough on people and the conditions of their lives,' whereas feminist jurisprudence starts with the experiences of women and develops theory from there. See Donna Greschner, 'Judicial Approaches to Equality and Critical Legal Studies,' in Martin and Mahoney eds., *Equality and Judicial Neutrality* 67.
64 Judy Fudge acknowledges this point, but she still regards lobbying as preferable, partly because legislatures have different 'institutional dynamics, roles, and principles of legitimation' from those of courts. See 'The Public–Private Distinction: The Possibilities and the Limits to the Use of the Charter to Further Feminist Struggles' (1987) 17 *IJSL* 546.
65 Governments can re-enact legislation that has been found to violate ss. 2 or

7–15 of the *Charter* by invoking s. 33, the notwithstanding clause on a five-year renewable basis. However, s. 33 has been used only three times since 1982, and in only one case as a response to a legal decision – Quebec's blanket invocation of s. 33 following the Supreme Court's invalidation of a section of Quebec's language law in 1988 (see Mandel, *Charter of Rights* 159–65). Governments apparently prefer to avoid the political costs of re-enacting laws the courts have declared to be infringements of Canadians' constitutional rights.

66 See Penney Kome, *The Taking of Twenty-Eight: Women Challenge the Constitution* (Toronto: Women's Educational Press, 1983).
67 See, e.g., Mary Eberts, 'Risks of Equality Litigation,' in Martin and Mahoney, eds., *Equality and Judicial Neutrality* 89–105.
68 See, e.g., Margot Young's analysis of two *successful* cases in which she suggests that 'one ought to remain less than sanguine about the future of equality law and its potential for social change,' in 'Change at the Margins: *Eldridge v. B.C. (A.G.)* and *Vriend v. Alberta*,' (1998) 10, 1 *CJWL* 245.
69 For an overview of the sex equality cases prior to 1989 in the areas of family law, personal injury, employment, human rights, prisons, and reproductive autonomy, see Brodsky and Day, *Canadian Charter Equality* 49–56. For more recent cases/wins, see various chapters in this volume.
70 See the chapters by Martin and McIntyre in this volume, as well as Brodsky and Day, *Canadian Charter Equality*, 134–7. The latter text notes (at 103) that the largest body of equality cases up to 1989 concerned criminal law, and about half of LEAF's interventions have been in cases involving violence against women.
71 Judy Fudge, a socialist feminist who shares many of the legal left's critiques of law and the *Charter*, nevertheless recognizes that even the demand for simple formal equality is important for women because the assertion of constitutional and legal rights acts as a catalyst to mobilize political action, as in the *Morgentaler* case. See Fudge, 'What Do We Mean,' 54–6.
72 Richard Sigurdson, 'The Left-Legal Critique of the *Charter*: A Critical Assessment' (1993) 13 *WYAJ* 116–55, at 128–9. This is also an important part of Didi Herman's argument in *Rights of Passage: Struggles for Lesbian and Gay Legal Equality* (Toronto: University of Toronto Press, 1994).
73 Sherene Razack, 'Using Law for Social Change: Historical Perspectives' (1992) 17 *Queen's Law Journal (QLJ)* 49.
74 Sigurdson, 'The Left-Legal Critique,' 130.
75 Mandel, *Charter of Rights*, 386.
76 I use the term 'Canadian' in this context while noting the ever more

Introduction: Feminist Adventures in Law 39

common usage among Quebec francophones of the term 'Quebec and Canada' as signifying their understanding of two already separate entities, rather than one as a subset of the other. I use it, however, as terms such as 'Rest of Canada,' seem unsatisfactory for other reasons, as does 'English Canada,' *for example*, which in truth is less and less English as it is more and more multicultural.

77 Micheline Dumont, 'The Origins of the Women's Movement in Quebec,' in Constance Backhouse and D.H. Flaherty, eds., *Challenging Times: The Women's Movement in Canada and the United States* (Montreal and Kingston: McGill-Queen's University Press, 1992) 89.

78 See Clio Collective, *Quebec Women: A History*, trans. by Roger Gannon and Rosalind Gill (Toronto: Women's Press, 1987).

79 See Marie-Claire Belleau, 'L'Intersectionalité: Feminisms in a Divided World,' in Dorothy E. Chunn and Dany Lacombe, eds., *Law as a Gendering Practice* (Toronto: Oxford University Press, 2000) 19–39.

80 *La Charte des droits et libertés de la personne, 1975*. R.S.Q. c. C-21.

81 The issues were much more complex than my synopsis can describe in short form. It is probably fair to say that for Aboriginal women, the issue was the negation of their nationhood and the possible effects of the 'distinct society' clause on Aboriginal rights in Quebec, whereas for non-Aboriginal women, the issues were much more bound up with changes to the federal spending power and the effects of the clause on women's equality rights. For an excellent discussion of the constitutional positions of the Aboriginal, Quebec, Anglo-Canadian, and racialized minority, disabled, and lesbian elements of the women's movements through the 1982, 1987, and 1992 constitutional rounds, see Jill Vickers, 'The Canadian Women's Movement and a Changing Constitutional Order' (1993) 7–8 *IJCS* 261–84. For accounts of Aboriginal women's various positions and a critique of 'three nations,' see R. Jhappan, 'Inherency, Three Nations and Collective Rights: The Evolution of Aboriginal Constitutional Discourse from 1982 to the Charlottetown Accord' (1993) 7–8 *IJCS* 225–60.

82 In contrast to the mainstream Canadian women's movement that in recent years has been forced to grapple with questions of difference, diversity, racism, heterosexism, and 'ableism,' the white, francophone women's movement of Quebec has kept these issues at the margins, despite the affiliation to the FFQ of several organizations of minority women. This may be in part because of the incompatibility of the FFQ's sovereignist stance with the competing claims to 'nation' and cultural community of indigenous peoples and other ethnocultural minorities. For a provocative discussion of these and related issues, see Daiva Stasiulis, 'Nationalisms,

Feminisms, Racisms,' in Caren Kaplan, Norma Alarcon, and Minoo Moalem, eds., *Between Women and Nation* (Durham and London: Duke University Press, 1999).

83 Andrew Heard's statistical analysis of the success of *Charter* claims in Quebec courts between 1982 and 1989 showed that while, in overall terms, Québécois made roughly as many *Charter* claims that were accepted roughly as often by Quebec courts as elsewhere in Canada, Québécois made fewer *Charter* equality claims and Quebec courts accepted significantly fewer of those that were made than did other Canadian courts. However, his data were not disaggregated to distinguish gender from other types of equality claims. Nevertheless, one surprising observation was that while in other provinces there were more claims against federal than provincial laws, in Quebec the reverse was true. Heard also noted the tendency for Quebec claimants to invoke the *Quebec Charter of Human Rights and Freedoms* either instead of or concurrently with the Canadian *Charter*. See 'Quebec Courts and the Canadian Charter of Rights' (1993) 7–8 *IJCS* 153–66.

84 I am grateful to Suzanne Boivin for the remainder of this account of Quebec women's legal strategies since the 1980s.

85 *C.N. v. Canada (Canadian Human Rights Commission)*, [1987] 1 S.C.R. 1114; *Action Travail des Femmes v. C.N.R.*, [1987] S.C.J. no. 42.

86 According to Suzanne Boivin (in a personal communication with the author), based on the credibility ATF attained in previous cases, it was granted intervenor status in a 1996 Quebec Court of Appeal case dealing with the interpretation of the Quebec *Charter* and the powers of the commission.

87 LEAF has never, in fact, been as widely accepted or promoted in Quebec as it has been in Ontario and elsewhere in Canada, though some francophone legal feminists have been members of LEAF's national legal committee and board of directors, or have served as counsel in cases in which LEAF has intervened. Although LEAF has attempted to include some French services at conferences and in its newsletter, *LEAFLines*, communications (meetings and conference calls) are for the most part conducted in English, and this restricts participation to anglophone or bilingual women.

88 Heard, 'Quebec Courts,' 157, notes that, becuase of very restrictive rules, individuals or groups were granted permission to intervene in only 3 per cent of Quebec *Charter* cases.

89 In fact, some well-known *Quebec* legal feminists appeared as counsel for LEAF, including Suzanne Boivin, Lucie Lamarche, and Michelle Boivin.

90 *Caron v. Sa Majesté La Reine*, [1991] Q.C.A.; *R. v. Caron*, [1988] 20 Q.A.C. 45.

91 For example, Navsharan Singh points out that while western (white) feminists have characterized reproductive issues as 'rights' issues, specifically the 'right' to abortion, many women in poorer countries have had to struggle against *forced* abortion in the context of coercive patriarchal practices and population control policies. Singh also outlines some of the other reproductive issues facing women in poorer countries that are not represented in the abortion-dominated discourse of western feminist movements. See 'Of Victim Women and Surplus Populations: Reproductive Technologies and the Representation of Third World Women' (1997) 52 *Studies in Political Economy* 155–73.

CHAPTER TWO

Feminist Movement in Law: Beyond Privileged and Privileging Theory

Sheila McIntyre

The authority to enunciate rules ... so easily asserted by [white political theorists] ... percolates into their personal environments from the larger topography of empire, past and present. That empire ... continue[s] to assure that both exploitation and its critique ... remain, by and large, attached to white persons, white theories, and white languages. It is thus 'natural' for the white [progressive] to assume ... she has the right (indeed the mission civilisatrice *and 'manifest destiny') to set me, a perfect stranger, straight on this subject; and to do so in a manner that marks me as either child or miscreant, but certainly not political co-worker, let alone sister.[1]*

Long before any women in Anglo-American legal systems acquired legal personhood, were permitted to enrol in law schools or, having graduated, permitted to practise law, were allowed to serve on juries or hold public office, or acquired the right to vote, the written and unwritten constitutional norms that distinguish Anglo-American legal systems had been elaborated and endlessly debated by privileged, white, male constitution drafters and theorists.[2] Central among the matters elite men debated was the appropriate division of constitutional powers between the (white, male, rights-holding, and propertied) voters and legislators entrusted with enacting laws in the public interest and the (white, male, rights-holding, and propertied) judges entrusted with monitoring the conduct of government actors to ensure they do not exceed their constitutionally assigned powers. In liberal democracies, political controversy has always attended the resulting divisions of power because they authorize an unelected, unrepresentative, and politically unaccountable judiciary to invalidate as 'unconstitutional' public laws that, at least in theory, codify the will of the majority of the electorate. Defenders of such judicial review of legislation seek to demonstrate how it does or could protect and give continuing life to the core values underlying liberal democratic orders; detractors underline the anti-democratic and/or anti-egalitarian nature or outcomes of judicial review.[3]

Although these debates have never been quiescent, with the entrenchment of the *Charter of Rights and Freedoms* in the Canadian Constitution,[4] debates have proliferated and intensified about both the principle and the potential or actual results of enhancing Canadian judges' powers to strike down legislation they deem an infringement of citizens' rights. A corollary debate about the social and political merits of pursuing rights litigation or, indeed, any form of "rights" activism, to advance social justice claims has also flourished. For the past twenty years, the back-and-forthing among constitutional theorists in the disciplines of law and political science has remained overwhelmingly white, male terrain.[5] Save for a handful of liberal idealists who defend judicial review in theory, if not in present practice,[6] white male academics on the political left,[7] the centre,[8] and the right[9] are approaching consensus in opposing the changes to historic political and legal divisions of power crystallized and accelerated by the advent of the *Charter*.[10] They isolate the same concerns – the 'legalization' or 'judicialization' of 'politics," the 'abstract' and 'indeterminate' language of rights, and the bypassing of electoral processes and/or popular political action – as threats to the 'democracy' each ideological camp champions. Male elites' arguments against rights litigation also betray a similarity of posture towards rights-seeking groups: a pervasive intellectual and political condescension, a presumption of ownership over the premises of 'law' and 'politics,' and a tendency towards pulling rank and crude stereotyping when describing those who do not share their personal and political world view.[11] This posturing combines the privilege of ignorance – the right not to know the Other described but to pronounce and prescribe the Other's best interests nonetheless – and ignorance of that privilege.

Even were this offensive posturing less pronounced, the apparent closing of ranks by otherwise ideologically divided male academics against rights litigation and rights activists in favour of 'old-style' political struggle (the left version) or 'traditional' or 'legitimate' political lobbying (the right version) should cause equality-seeking groups pause. Their common front has emerged at precisely the moment in history when law's historic outsiders – white women, people of colour, Aboriginal women and men, out lesbians and gays, and disabled people of all races – are the primary agents of substantive egalitarian change in and through Canadian educational and legal institutions. The division of political labour is striking. On the one hand, white male scholars are verbally denouncing the 'anti-democratic' features of rights activism and litigation in books, academic journals, conferences, and the classroom. On the other hand, those populations that law and legal education have most consistently excommunicated from full citizenship – that is, those with most reason to be sceptical of law's and democracy's formal promises – are achieving substantive egalitarian change in and through the universities, political lobbying, law reform initiatives, and the courts. They are doing so animated, among other things, by the logic and discourse of rights, though not necessarily by the formalist logic or abstract discourse ascribed to them or deployed against them so often by white male professionals in law and the universities.

This is not to say that substantive equality activists have proceeded in the absence of critical theory tracking the legitimating dynamics of liberal legalism. But the theory in question is less bloodless and less disembodied than the critiques of rights litigation currently emanating from the (white, male) left, primarily because it has been forged in and from ongoing political struggles, not from analyses abstracted at a distance from the (often romanticized) past. Its strength and weakness are its immediacy because its authors fashion theory from their lives as outsiders working inside oppressive and hostile systems for egalitarian change and as insiders institutionally, if not socially, remote from the broader constituencies they seek to serve. The jurisprudential as well as political inquiry at the heart of such insider/outsider praxis has not been *whether* liberal democracy's historic and continuing 'Others' should persevere with using any dimension of law – legal discourse, existing legal doctrines, legislative lobbying, or litigation – in pursuit of egalitarian change, but *how*. More specifically, as with most feminist activists, the focus of my own engagement with law is not whether, in theory, to use 'law' in general or rights litigation in particular, as an instrument of social change, but how to do so accountably to the constituencies of women I seek to serve, mindful of how power and privilege operate through *all* legal actors, including me and my feminist peers, and with an eye towards building political movement.

This chapter begins with a general critique of the left/progressive case against the *Charter*. I argue that the left critique goes both too far and not far enough in calculating the political and material risks, costs, and successes of rights activism, including rights litigation. Both failings, in my view, derive from generalizations ungrounded in the particularities of the actual political and/or legal strategies and processes adopted by distinctive equality-seeking constituencies in different equality pursuits at different times and over time, in different contexts in different legal and/or non-legal fora. Its (selective) scorecard of litigation wins and losses, and its predictions about the politically demobilizing and antidemocratic dimensions of rights litigation, in short, attend too little to *how* particular rights activists have advanced equality claims: by what processes, in what formations, with what relation to political action in other fora, with what arguments, and with what goals. I hope to expose the politics and operation of privilege in the patterns of overstatement, omission, reductionism, and stereotyping that permeate this scholarship and in the selective measures adopted to pronounce rights activism misguided, antidemocratic, and demobilizing. This feminist critique of the left's case against *Charter* activism is followed by a brief legal history of one systemic feminist struggle – the struggle to end male violence against women. This history will illustrate, on the one hand, how hegemony operates in and through all liberal political and legal instruments with or without rights discourse and, on the other, how feminist legal activists have sought to resist hegemony's operation, including in their own practices. The weak link in *Charter* activism is not, I argue, the left's caricature – a duped citizenry and their naive or despair-ridden legal advocates squandering hopes and resources on the false promise of rights in elite arenas that are ideologically and structurally stacked against the systemically disempowered. Much more dangerous are intellectual and/or professional progressives unmindful of how race, gender, and class oppression operate through 'us' when we theorize and/or practise resistance to a liberal legal order. The risk that rights activism will yield antidemocratic, co-opted, depoliticizing, and inequality-entrenching outcomes is real enough. But it is privilege operating through rights activists as much as the system-legitimating tendencies of rights discourse as interpreted by a politically unaccountable and unrepresentative judiciary that produces such outcomes. The chapter concludes with a description and endorsement of the collective structures and coalition formations adopted by the feminist antiviolence movement when pursuing legislated or litigated egalitarian change as mechanisms that not only inject political representativeness and accountability into legal advocacy but that democratize the law reform process.

The history of the feminist antiviolence movement confirms that deep ambivalence about the possibilities and risks of working within and through dominant institutions like law – in any of its forms – to secure systemic egalitarian change is an obvious prerequisite of responsible political activism. But it also discloses an obvious corollary of registering that relations – plural – of domination are systemic: declaring any dominant institution, including rights discourse and rights litigation, unambiguously off-limits is indefensible in theory as in practice. Likewise, this history underlines why measuring whether, how much, and with what judge-delivered results a movement resorts to rights litigation will reveal very little about that movement's political health and efficacy, democratic or antidemocratic tendencies, and contribution in advancing the substantive equality of its own constituents and of other equality-seeking groups. For over twenty-five years, the movement to end male violence against women has engaged, often brilliantly, in systemic political struggle. Such struggle has been waged by grass-roots activists and by feminist professionals, against and within dominant institutions other than law, as well as in the see-saw between legislatures and courts, propelled to and by theory and political consciousness built from the realities of violence against women: violence facilitated and normalized by systems, violence practised by individual men emboldened and excused by such systems, and sometimes violence perpetuated and obscured by the theories and practices of privileged professionals, male and female. Its record indicates that each site of struggle is inextricably interrelated; each can be and has been compromised by progressive as well as reactionary moves emanating from one of the other sites. Yet, this movement has generated, corrected, and reconstructed theories and practices that have yielded systemic changes unthought of twenty-five years ago (and disregarded by the male left today). Its history, if contradictory, offers a more politically engaging prescription for democratic and egalitarian change than the contradictory theoretical utopianism and impossibilism emanating from the left.

The Left Critique of Rights Litigation

Reduced to its essentials, the argument of the left is that it is naive and futile (hence a wasteful diversion of limited human and financial resources) as well as antidemocratic (hence antithetical to progressive principles and struggle) to rely on the *Charter* to bring about social, by which is usually meant socialist, transformation. *Charter* litigation will unavoidably prove an unequal resource in an unequal society, serving ultimately to augment existing social, political, and economic inequalities. The left case against the *Charter* relies upon a number of constant subthemes.[12]

First, the rights and freedoms enumerated in the *Charter*, as well as the 'reasonable limits' clause, which allows judges to uphold state action that 'justifiably' infringes citizens' democratic rights,[13] are so abstract and open-ended that their actual meanings are indeterminate. Accordingly, they can be enlisted by any ideological camp and any interest group in support of claims on all sides of any political divide. Although they *can* be deployed to advance creative progressive claims, they *will* disproportionately be used as instruments to shore up existing inequalities of wealth, power, and social status. Litigation is an expensive enterprise, therefore relative access to the courts that will give meaning to *Charter* guarantees, will be skewed in favour of privileged interests. Moreover, the open-ended language of most guarantees falls to be interpreted by judges. If they look (backward) to precedent for interpretive guidance, they will entrench an inegalitarian status quo. If they draw on their own values and world view, they will constitutionalize the perspectives of privilege. Legal history supplies ample evidence that, either way, judges will prove hostile to legislative incursions on private property and contract rights, or on white or male privilege; and they will be predisposed towards individualistic rather than collective rights claims and towards formal rather than substantive interpretations of *Charter* guarantees.[14] By constitutionalizing judicial review, then, the *Charter* not only enhances the power and status of a politically unaccountable judicial elite, it allows courts to mask the power relations codified in their judgments behind the abstract, but legitimating, rhetoric of liberal rights and freedoms.

Second, because progressive lawyers recognize the limits of courts and of liberal law, and/or because they are socialized in legal culture, they will feel forced or will be inclined to mould their arguments, language, selections of precedent and choice of remedies conservatively – that is, in terms least jarring or most palatable to judicial understandings. In this process, political claims will be submerged in the abstract discourse of rights; substantive claims will be refashioned to formalist conventions; and judges may be encouraged to do the right thing for the wrong reasons.[15]

Third, they caution that litigants cannot use the *Charter* without reinforcing the public/private distinction defining liberal legal orders as regimes in which the best state is the one that least intrudes on the private sphere and on private freedoms. Liberal constitutions protect private corporations, private contracts, and free enterprise, no less than individual citizens, from illiberal state interference. Their structure fosters and codifies the illusion that citizens have more to fear from the welfare state than from abuses of private concentrations of power which have been checked by the regulatory state. They make redistributive state benefits vulnerable to well-resourced *Charter* challenges by the privileged, while leaving private sector exploitation and discrimination beyond constitutional review. As a result, the new legal order marketed as a transfer of 'power to the people'[16] is likely to prove a potent asset for rolling back the welfare state by authoritarian judicial decree.

In aggregate, this legalization of politics will legitimate antidemocratic rule by judges, increasingly channelling political conflicts into courtroom debates by elite players deploying apolitical discourses to engage in elite accommodations. It may empower and enrich lawyers and will enhance the authority of judges, but it will effectively disenfranchise citizens, weaken the effectiveness of the one-person–one-vote model of participatory democracy and promote this regressive trend as an advance in Canadian citizens' fundamental rights and freedoms.

The left concedes that rights litigation does yield periodic wins for disempowered groups. But these are not net gains: they could, or would, and, hence, should have been won through grass-roots 'political' lobbying,[17] or they simply do not dent, far less eliminate, the oppressive conditions under which new rights must be exercised.[18] Periodic progressive gains will be outweighed by cumulative losses: gains secured by litigation will trigger a backlash because they are secured from judges, not the democratic process; each isolated win will encourage further overreliance on elite practices and liberal norms as the primary vehicle of social change; reliance on the few good cases or selective progressive judicial dicta will legitimate their antidemocratic source while foreclosing protest when powerholders exploit the far larger cache of antiprogressive rulings;[19] and even the most progressive rights arguments or gains will be reabsorbed into and limited by the liberal discourse and ideology of the dominant.[20] Nor are cases yielding progressive interpretations of rights guarantees or material wins self-enforcing. Many will have to be litigated again and again to force powerholders to comply with judicial mandates. To the extent left scholars venture alternatives to rights activism, they offer rhetorical prescriptions (abandon liberal individualism, democratize our electoral system, challenge authoritarianism, prioritize class analysis and struggle) or wax romantic about genuine 'political struggle' without any blueprint addressing how such ends might practically be pursued.[21]

There is a right-wing narrative on each of these subthemes. It, too, decries the open-ended, indeterminate, and malleable language of *Charter* guarantees as a vehicle that allows judges to constitutionalize the ideology of dominant elites. However, in this account, an organized coalition of 'materialists, feminists, and post-materialists'[22] dominates the law schools. Working with or on behalf of 'special interest groups' mobilized around particular *Charter* guarantees, they have generated a wave of constitutional outcomes consistent with their illiberal political agenda. The power of this 'Court Party' is 'unimaginable.'[23] Its politically driven scholarship, conferences, speeches, teaching, popular writing, and lobbying influenced the wording of the *Charter*, defeated the Meech Lake Accord, and, in between, served to influence judicial appointments, legal and professional training, the mass media, legislators, and judges to endorse redistributive legal reforms it could never have achieved through electoral politics. As a result, this unrepresentative elite has successfully promoted judicial, over parliamentary, supremacy; a proactive, expansionist state over the traditionally liberal non-interventionist ideal; (special interest) group claims over individual rights; and 'life-cycle' or 'life-style' rights claims over the 'natural' rights guaranteed under principles of formal equality.[24] It has also subverted the public/private distinction. That state funding supports many of these interest groups and the scholars who champion their claims and equality-based *Charter* litigation underlines the extent of their influence.[25] In the result, conservative groups who have launched or intervened in *Charter* cases have consistently lost. Worse, the entire point of constitutions – the codification of neutral and predictive rules for resolution of legal disputes and the entrenchment of time-tested, permanent civic commitments insulated from easy amendments pandering to fleeting political whims – has been subverted. Immutable, universal rights have collapsed into relativist values; judicial impartiality has given way to results-oriented partisanship and social engineering; law has become policy-making by undemocratic means.

While left theorists tend to emphasize those *Charter* decisions amounting to losses for organized labour and wins for corporations, and to devalue gains by feminist legal activists, the right cites decisions failing to strike down social welfare or existing labour legislation, and inflates wins by feminist litigators as proxy for gains to all disadvantaged groups.[26] While the left concedes the inegalitarian dynamics of our current electoral system, the Right concedes no such thing. For the right, one-person–one-vote equals equality; systemic inequality is either an unsubstantiated thesis of malcontented interest groups pressing their political claims[27] or a product of natural endowments or lifestyle choices properly beyond redress by the liberal state.

A Feminist Critique of the Left Critique

Suppressing the knowledge produced by any oppressed group makes it easier for dominant groups to rule because the seeming absence of an independent consciousness in the oppressed can be taken to mean that subordinate groups willingly collaborate in their own victimization. Maintaining the invisibility of [subordinated groups] and our ideas is critical in structuring patterned relations of race, gender, and class inequality.[28]

As a feminist who has been active in test case equality litigation for over a decade,[29] I find the left critique wholly convincing on its own terms and, ultimately, politically paralysing because its basic critical insights could, and in my view should, be applied to all the other forms of activism I have pursued in and outside of law.[30] The logic of this extension of the left critique is that all resistance within and against institutions of domination is inherently suspect: more often than not elite-driven and/or antidemocratic in process, depoliticized and depoliticizing in its direct outcomes and, in the result, reinforcing and legitimating of the systemic inequalities normalized by liberal law and ideology. The logic of this analysis may be pure; but as a political stance it is a luxury of privilege. Pending some non-utopian blueprint for procedurally and substantively democratic political struggle towards systemic egalitarian change that is immune from system legitimation, and pending identification of a political discourse invulnerable to liberal appropriation within a liberal regime, it is not obvious that imperfect activism is more system legitimating or more demobilizing than theoretical critiques dictating inaction within and against dominant institutions like law. Dissociation from rights activism is not just a luxury of white, male, class privilege, it is the political flaw in the left case against the *Charter*, a flaw that correlates perfectly with privilege. The white male left offers false universals generalized from its partial world view, from what it is positioned to see and not see. Left *Charter* critics see what is most accessible to them: the pre-*Charter* legal record of judicial conservatism, the texts of reported *Charter* cases viewed through the framework supplied by left legitimation theory, and the critique of rights articulated by the critical legal studies (CLS) movement.

Divorced from the movements and from the political results of progressive struggle in and through institutions other than courts, the left case against the *Charter* is very persuasive. But to theorize the politics of the *Charter* from what judges write is to abstract a lot, to generalize too much from too little. Differences among rights theorists and claimants, the political and legal strategies they deploy, and the results they achieve are erased; differences among the kinds of claims and claimants electoral majorities support or revile are unaddressed; the relationship of litigation to the grass-roots and institutional activism that precedes and succeeds individual cases is overlooked.[31]

Many, but not all, of the left's low expectations of the *Charter* have been vindicated in cases decided to date, and the left's aggregated scorecard of twenty years of case law is far more credible than the right's. With the exception of *Charter* litigation launched by defence lawyers to keep accused individuals – mostly men – out of jail,[32] the first wave of *Charter* cases was dominated by privileged players attempting to roll back social welfare, consumer protection or egalitarian reforms, to evade legal sanctions or obligations under laws less than 100 per cent universal in their application, or to extend the range of their inequitably accrued powers and freedoms.[33] Courts dismissed union challenges to legislation that curbed free collective bargaining and its functional prerequisites, but upheld a number of corporate rights claims.[34] The Supreme Court refused to grant public interest groups legal standing equivalent to that of private, individual rights-holders to launch constitutional challenges.[35] And the private sector was largely insulated from *Charter* review.

Nonetheless, the case law reveals that the left's undifferentiated pessimism about the *Charter* is overstated, particularly in respect of equality litigation. On the basis of decidedly non-liberal feminist argumentation, the Supreme Court of Canada's first decision applying the *Charter*'s equality guarantees endorsed a substantive approach to section 15.[36] *Andrews* not only explicitly rejected the dominant formalist approach which is designed to change nothing, but diminished the standing of privileged individuals or groups to demand that if they cannot have access to those state benefits available to less advantaged individuals, no one should have them. Some challenges grounded in the individualistic and formalist abstraction that animates the civil libertarian tradition were defeated on the basis of the substantive equality interests of groups.[37] Neither should have happened by the logic of the left critique. Working women, if not the (male-centred) labour movement, directly benefited from judicial endorsement of feminist litigators' interventions.[38] Where legislation discriminates through under-inclusive coverage, some courts have extended the formal recognition of rights to stigmatized or, merely, overlooked minorities whom legislators persistently abandon to appease bigoted majorities or comparatively advantaged Canadians pressing for tax cuts.[39] The language and articulated values in a number of decisions has often been anything but abstractly liberal or opaque,[40] and even regressive decisions legitimated by abstraction did not dupe the public about the politics in play.[41]

Splits among and within courts are not predictable from case to case. Although this may vindicate claims about the 'indeterminacy' of rights guarantees, it also underlines that 'the courts' are not monolithic. More, it vindicates those critical scholars whose research provided not only the analytic underpinnings but the 'authorities' progressive litigants could cite when advancing claims without liberal legal precedent. Unlike the left, the right recognizes that such scholars' departure from the conventions of so-called disinterested scholarship is part of a larger political project of challenging the conventions of liberal formalism.[42] Even though much progressive litigation was reactive to challenges launched by the privileged against social benefits or other remedial legislation, it was not the wasteful diversion of resources suggested by the left. The Women's Legal Education and Action Fund (LEAF), for instance, would have adopted a far more incremental litigation strategy had challenges initiated by male liberals and conservatives not spurred it to intervene to advance substantive arguments.[43] And had the LEAF arguments which prevailed in *Andrews* been tabled for even five years, a differently composed Supreme Court of Canada might well have entrenched deference to dominant and/or majoritarian prejudice as the Canadian approach to constitutional equality rights.[44]

This scorecard of litigation results and of the divergent critiques they have spawned on the left and the right suggests that the political significance of the *Charter* over twenty years is as open to partisan interpretation as is the 'indeterminate' language of the *Charter*. What I wish to underline is that even the few progressive gains I have noted were sufficient to trigger a concentrated counter-offensive from the right, often abetted by the mainstream media. As predicted by the left, the right denounces as 'illegitimate' those substantive equality gains secured from courts rather than through ordinary electoral politics. Some voices on the right have called for the rescission of the *Charter*,[45] others merely for rescission of those provisions protecting group rights or open to substantive equality claims.[46] The left has rationalized this 'backlash' rather than acknowledge it as evidence of a politicization of law inconsistent with the left thesis that the *Charter* can yield only the legalization of politics with antidemocratic results. This evasion is obscured by the left's failure to remark on what activists have had little choice but to notice: substantive egalitarian reforms secured through the electoral process[47] and by majoritarian decision-making within the universities that employ *Charter* sceptics on the left have also been excoriated by the right as 'illegitimate' and 'undemocratic.'[48]

At bottom, the right attack on the *Charter* turns on the substance, direction, and sources of political change, not on the legal process by which social change is being secured. However exaggerated the takeover claims of the right, its counter-offensives against substantive egalitarian change do signal that something deserving of the name 'political struggle' has not only survived, but has intensified in the post-*Charter* era. The centuries-old purchase of formal equality has weakened in the past twenty years. What was an interpretive monopoly is now publicly contested terrain. Far from containing power struggles to abstract legal arguments framed by lawyers for courtroom consumption, *Charter* and other rights litigation in concert with coincident political struggles in and through other dominant institutions have made competing models of equality the topic of widespread public debate.

The male left's inattention to the political significance of this shift is paradigmatic of the insular world view of privilege. Decades of antiracist, feminist, and queer intellectual, political, and personal struggle produced this result. What began as a pursuit of formal equality, led to a compelling critique of liberal formalism, and yielded a precarious foothold for substantive arguments and wins in law, the universities, and other public institutions implicated in the reproduction of systemic inequality. The measure of the political significance of this delegitimation of formalism is the measure of concerted resistance to it in the form of intellectual, political, and personal counter-attacks, including in the academic institutions which supply salaries, research resources, and influential platforms to the male scholars who pronounce rights activism futile, antidemocratic, and depoliticized/depoliticizing. Insofar as the most highly publicized eruptions over feminist and antiracist activism in Canadian universities have been in faculties of law and departments of political studies,[49] it is difficult for me to find a benign explanation for the male left's characterization of rights activism as depoliticized or depoliticizing. The (mostly) conservative 'backlash' to substantive egalitarian change in the universities, like the 'backlash' to substantive equality gains secured through litigation (and legislation), relies rhetorically and ideologically on the classically liberal equation of formal equality with democracy. As the left critique of abstract individual rights underlines, that rhetoric and that ideology sustain and legitimate institutions of domination. From a formalist perspective – that is, from the dominant perspective/the perspective of domination embraced primarily, but not only, by the right – pursuit of group rights through equality of results is, by definition, illegitimate in 'Our' liberal legal order. It is 'illiberal' whether secured through majoritarian electoral processes, 'special interest' group social activism, or the courts. Politically speaking, what is illegitimate is equality in substance, instead of equality of mere form. Socially speaking, illegitimacy inheres in those liberalism constructs as 'Them' and in 'Their' disregard for the premises of the rule systems that keep 'Them' outsiders. Substantively speaking, backlash is the forceful (re)assertion of race, gender, class, and heterosexual privilege legitimated by the abstract language of rights.

The backlash's bottom line is that 'Our' liberal system is not meant to enfranchise 'Them,' those deprived of full personhood, voice, self-possession, and self-determination in western liberal culture. If 'They' bypass the processes and majorities that have proved systemically resistant to 'Their' subaltern claims in order to secure rights from courts, of course, those possessed of systemically exclusionary political entitlements will construe such gains as 'illegitimate' because 'undemocratically' secured. This is simply to define legitimacy and democracy in dominant and dominating terms – on precisely the terms that delegitimate the substantive claims and the full legal and political personhood sought to be advanced by such claims. When left scholars denigrate rights activism as a system-legitimating diversion distinctive from and demobilizing to 'real' political struggle, I hear privilege talking. Either they are oblivious to the racist, heterosexist, and classist stereotypes, denigration, threats, sanctions, and outright violence directed at white feminists, students, and faculty of colour and lesbian and gay equality activists of all races, in their own workplaces, or their definition of 'political struggle' excludes feminist, antiracist, and antiheterosexist equality activism in professional settings and the violent resistance that it elicits. More importantly, when left men rationalize hostility to court-won egalitarian change as a predictable 'backlash' to the bypass of majoritarian 'democratic' processes, they legitimate such backlash as well as the political processes that have proved only formally, not substantively, accessible and accountable to the systemically dispossessed. They theorize as if the (re)assertion of white, male, class, and heterosexual privilege and supremacy were not the common thread linking what kind of activism and whose counts as 'illegitimate' in all dominant institutions.

Arguing against litigated egalitarian change on the basis of its perceived illegitimacy to those served by majoritarian processes is like arguing against affirmative action on the basis that its actual or deemed beneficiaries will be stigmatized as unqualified and undeserving by those shored up by the biases embedded in systemically exclusionary 'merit' systems. There is a material difference between being unemployed because one is deemed unqualified by virtue of one's race or gender or national origin, and employed but still deemed unqualified on the same bases. But the stigma of deemed non-entitlement is constant. The perceived illegitimacy and undeservingness of those constructed as outsiders by liberal democracy is the dominant order. It precedes and rationalizes 'backlash.' The only way of preventing backlash is cooperating in one's own systemic exclusion. Rights activism is an impossible struggle against the odds of illegitimacy and legitimation. The left grasps only half of the legitimation equation. The false promise of abstract rights is system legitimation; the real promise of rights is self-assertion, meaning: asserting the long-denied entitlements of a rights-bearing individual. System legitimation through rights recognition is what the dispossessed desire, notwithstanding their awareness that this same system delivers their dispossession.

Many scholars of colour, mostly American, have compellingly accounted for this contradiction and have exposed the race privilege in the de-raced critique of rights produced by left-leaning white men in the CLS movement.[50] Although the left critique of rights in Canada draws heavily on or strikes common themes with CLS writing and thinking, I have found only three passing references in the literature to minority critiques of CLS theory.[51] The left's failure to engage this extensive literature does worse than de-voice those whom liberalism has also de-voiced; it sustains a privileged narrative that positions white, male, progressives as more politically advanced and intellectually sophisticated than minority activists. By default, feminist and minority rights activism appears to be false consciousness rather than articulated critical consciousness divergent from the left's prescriptions. This political positioning naturalizes paternalist presumption: authority to issue political correction; authority to dictate the politically correct path to inclusive democracy; the privilege of prescribing self-suppression pending a discourse and model of political activism endorsed, if not defined, by elite white and/or male theorists.

This left presumption turns on an oddly benign portrait of the alternatives to litigation, where it addresses concrete alternatives at all. Close scrutiny of progressive struggles via majoritarian political processes, for instance, would confirm that: legislatures are not significantly more demographically representative than courts or more ideologically disposed than courts to counter-hegemonic claims; their accountability to the public – particularly on feminist, antiracist, antiheterosexist, and antipoverty issues – is more formal than substantive; the financial costs of campaigning for legislated reform through the mass media, public and institutional lobbying, consultation processes, brief-writing, and legislative committee appearances, many of which processes require the assistance of progressive (usually elite) lawyers, can be and often are significantly higher than appellate interventions; reforms secured through legislation ranging from our highly juridified and pro-capital regime of labour law to pay and employment equity legislation to gay and lesbian human rights protection, have been easily as compromised, system-legitimating, and depoliticizing as any landmark litigation gains; the open-ended language of any and every statutory reform in the areas of, say, labour or employment standards, human rights, pay equity, sexual assault, welfare or family law reform has proved as amenable to erosion, outright inversion, and manipulation by privileged litigants backed by superior resources and hegemonic credibility and as enriching of inventive lawyers as *Charter* litigation; reforms closing down one avenue of economic, sexual, or racist abuse typically restrain powerholders only temporarily until they identify loopholes or invent new practices to bypass the intent of such regulatory restraints; and no democratically secured statutory grant or restraint is self-enforcing, with the result that most must be substantively sustained by defensive and proactive litigation as well as lobbying. In sum, the liberal political order, not just liberal courts interpreting liberal rights instruments, restrains and contains movements for radical social transformation (and radicals) all the while legitimating the systemic inequalities endemic to liberal legalism.

Although substantial left male and socialist feminist scholarship exists to illustrate most of these realities,[52] the left critique of rights litigation makes only passing and generic references to the limits of majoritarian politics and almost none to their legitimating dynamics. It makes little effort to particularize which constituencies and what kinds of claims will never secure majority support within a liberal order. Accordingly, it offers no blueprint for interim relief until that time when the state withers away or when a genuinely democratic process of political struggle yields majority support for redistributive justice. It simply extrapolates from the purity of theory that securing progressive precedents from courts under the rubric of rights will almost certainly prove worse in terms of legitimating an elitist, antidemocratic, and authoritarian mechanism of social ordering than securing nothing from majoritarian legislative processes. The left's preference for legislated over litigated change also ignores the significant role of state bureaucracies in tempering, containing, or flatly resisting substantive and democratic change.[53]

Litigating rights or any social reforms is financially costly and politically risky, and it is often pursued in abstract and depoliticized language. Genuine successes can be inverted and deployed directly against the most disempowered or invoked to legitimate a systemically unequal order. It is simply insulting to imagine all or most equality activists are unaware of such Politics 101 basics, more so to portray equality activists for public consumption as naive romantics ignorant of the anti-egalitarian history of judicial review and inclined to look exclusively or primarily to the courts for egalitarian change. This demeaning portrait of *Charter* activists is constructed in no small measure by the nearly total absence in left *Charter* theorizing of any reference to thirty years of feminist legal scholarship, fifteen years of critical race theory, and a burgeoning reservoir of queer legal theory, or the political struggles that produced them, launched from them, or emerged in reaction to them. This scholarship tracks oppression and its legitimation through legal discourse, legal education, legal doctrine and process, professional gatekeeping and streaming, law enforcement, and judicial bias. Whether its large erasure from left male theory stems from the theorists' intellectual ignorance, privileged self-referentiality, or conscious or unconscious bias, the effect of such privileged exclusion is not only the public projection of intellectual illiteracy and, hence, political immaturity on non-liberal legal activists, but a public misconstruction and trivialization of their political project.

Those who trouble to read what has thus been rendered invisible would fairly conclude that few feminist or critical race (or, more recently, queer) scholars and legal activists operate from the 'naive, almost silly' belief that all they have to do 'is cook up imaginative legal arguments and go to court for the realization of an egalitarian and just society' or require reminding that 'progressive change follows from mobilization and organization by oppressed and disempowered people, not the 'benevolence' of those who have power.'[54] Few deserve admonishment that a transformative approach to law 'entails much more than pouring new legal wine into old institutional bottles' or requires 'critical understanding of the political nature of legal structures' mindful of 'historical and political contingency' and 'framed by concrete realities.'[55] Few need to be cautioned that political action should not begin and end in rights litigation. There does seem to be an old-fashioned double standard operating here. For instance, how is applying old legitimation theory to new political formations and contingencies without regard for such movements' actual histories or aspirations consistent with these admonitions? How will public delegitimation of rights-inspired legal activists and activism by progressive white men combined with the left's persistent refusal to venture concrete blueprints for exiting the impasse of legitimation theory convert into political mobilization? How does public trivialization of feminist, antiracist, and/or queer activists not resonate with, reinforce, and even legitimate the systemically entrenched devaluation of such outsider groups? How does public denunciation of rights litigation not deliver to conservative governments and the right a discourse on rights that can and will be used to discredit equality activists and rights litigation? What solidarity among new political movements and the (old) left is imaginable in face of such white, male condescension?

My version of Politics 101 would begin with this concrete reality: the legal scholarship authored by (non-liberal) feminist and critical race scholars is necessarily innovative, not 'cooked up.' In a precedent-based legal system in which legislative and constitutional deal-making, drafting, and interpretation have been until very recently a monopoly of elite white men, all women, like minority men, have had to construct authority from and despite social and legal erasure. From this perspective, the 'indeterminacy' of *Charter* guarantees has supplied a small, because unprecedented, opening to challenge the dominant ideologies embedded in the liberal laws securing and legitimating white, male, and class privilege. But for the enterprise of feminist, critical race, queer, and disabled scholars who have produced citable, interpretive authorities for substantive and systemic arguments while elite male theorists produce critiques of judicial review, the substantive jurisprudence on which activists continue to build as litigants and as lobbyists for legislated reforms would not exist.

My version of Politics 101 would question any elite theory that relies on false universals premised on the erasure of situated and politically significant differences among rights litigants. The left scorecard on *Charter* results fails utterly to differentiate among distinct constituencies pursuing rights claims, their distinctive strategies and political processes, and their legal and political impacts. For instance, not all litigants have framed their claims in abstract, individualistic, and formalistic terms. Most powerholders did, and did so calculatedly. Only by abstract equation, for instance, could regulation of corporate advertising be argued to be as illiberal as censorship of individual political dissent. But the false symmetries of liberal formalism have always served the powerful: 'free trade,' 'academic freedom,' 'freedom of contract,' sexual 'consent' come to mind. The *Charter* supplies the most resourced with a new legitimating vehicle for bypassing the rare checks on the abuse of power secured by majority will. Quite apart from the *Charter*, abstraction and liberal ideology along with the concrete threat of corporate relocation are working fine to dismantle the regulatory state while demobilizing political resistance. Corporate *Charter* victories are but a spit in the bucket of restructuring and deregulation, little more than symbolic victories against the governments that corporations have so largely enlisted in their service.

Many arguably progressive litigants also have framed their claims in abstract, individualistic, and formalist terms, but for different reasons. Some did so as a matter of professional mindset as well as practical exigency. Criminal defence lawyers do not function as an organized political lobby pursuing systemic change, and they do not coordinate to anticipate and avoid the long-term negative consequences of the isolated, individualized, and largely abstract *Charter* arguments that they advance to keep accused individuals out of jail. Abstraction is instrumentally useful to take the focus off bad facts and actors and onto the winning hypotheticals of which criminal law is woven. In an unsuccessful attempt to appease longstanding judicial anti-unionism, some union lawyers also have offered liberal abstractions ('freedom of expression' and 'freedom of association') to secure constitutional recognition of collective labour actions instead of good facts[56] or documentation of the material and systemic inequalities defining particular labour–management relations and disputes. By contrast, gay (and more rarely, lesbian) litigants have offered the courts highly sympathetic facts in order to displace homophobic and heterosexist stereotypes enough to argue for no more than formally equal treatment in law. These 'sameness' arguments have generated considered criticisms from proponents of substantive equality.[57] However, only those ignorant of the material and social injuries and physical endangerment associated with legally sanctioned non-personhood could reduce litigated achievement of formal legal recognition to a negligible, depoliticizing gain or a net loss to the fabric of participatory democracy. Because most disability rights claims have challenged purportedly neutral laws or policies that disproportionately exclude or fail to advert to and accommodate the specific needs of people living with particular disabilities, by definition they not only advance a substantive rather than formal conception of equality, but also contest abstract conceptions of the public interest or public good generalized from 'ablist' norms.[58] Finally, it should be noted that some rights activists who would view themselves as progressives have advanced quintessentially liberal claims because they are, quintessentially, liberal and, not coincidentally, privileged individuals. This is simply to say that they were not compelled by the abstraction of rights discourse or of rights guarantees to advance formalistic, individualistic claims: their arguments perfectly captured their personal – if socially constructed and reinforced – preferences. That they functioned like rugged individualists in pursuing public law claims purporting to represent broad constituencies with whom they did not consult, to whom they chose not to be accountable, and to whom their individualist arguments would collectively apply, is a problem of privilege, not rights activism or rights discourse as such.

Almost the only litigators who consistently have advanced non-formalist arguments are feminist and other constituency-based, public interest organizations governed by collective and/or consultative processes with some measure of accountability to the constituencies their arguments purport to represent and serve. Although such legal advocacy groups have adopted challenges initiated by individuals, their analyses and legal arguments have been theorized to extend beyond the specific facts and distinctive interests of any individual challenger.

To be sure, this theorizing from individual to collective interests risked reinforcing essentialist understandings of the groups whose unequal sociolegal status or equality interests were being argued, particularly where those doing the theorizing were not fully representative of the constituency they claimed to represent. On the other hand, the strategic effort to theorize group-based inequalities from individual circumstances by developing and testing equality arguments through collective processes does mitigate two other risks of test case public law litigation. It ensures no precedent affecting an entire class of equality-seekers will be the product of a single legal advocate's analysis, of a single litigant's political agenda, or of an atypically sympathetic fact situation. As well, to the extent that underrepresentative or underinclusive theorizing has flawed an advocacy group's work, collective case development processes with built-in accountability structures are more likely and more quickly to yield corrections than in the case of individual litigants operating autonomously without organizational or community ties.

Were left theorists to have read the facta with which I am most familiar, those authored by teams of feminist scholars, practitioners, and non-legal activists coordinated by LEAF, they would not find abstract, apolitical arguments that fail to confront squarely the systemic sexual inequalities that liberal legalism legitimates.[59] (They will, however, find some undifferentiated generalizations about 'women,' particularly in LEAF's earlier arguments.) The facta anatomize the legal and social dynamics and material specificities of male domination and of women's inequalities, not abstractions like 'equality' or 'discrimination' or 'freedom' or 'privacy' or the 'rule of law.' In cases concerning women's reproductive autonomy, for instance, the facta specifically name and contest the obfuscating abstractions and false symmetries of the liberal discourse and ideologies of fetal and father's 'rights' claims.[60] In *Moge v. Moge*, LEAF challenged the gender-neutral and formal-equality principles determining women's entitlement to financial support following marriage breakdown,[61] and in *Gordon v. Goetz*, the false symmetries of and substantive inequalities embedded in 'joint custody' ideology.[62] The many intervenor facta filed by LEAF in cases launched by men facing civil or criminal sanction for sexual offences incorporate radical, not liberal, feminist scholarship and advocacy; they do not soft-pedal the misogyny of judge-made precedent or the ideologies it reflects and legitimates; they contest the liberal construction of rape as an atypical practice of deviant individual men and articulate a systemic analysis of how liberal laws and structured relations of inequality, particularly those defined by gender, race, and disability, interact to normalize male sexual violence.[63] Nor has LEAF conceded the public/private distinction. It has sought and been granted standing to make *Charter* equality arguments in private law litigation and in non-constitutional cases concerning interpretation of family law statutes, statutory limitation periods in tort suits, and the human rights legislation prohibiting discrimination in the private sphere.[64] It also challenged, albeit unsuccessfully, the public/private distinction underlying current rules of standing.[65]

Unlike male *Charter* sceptics on the left, LEAF does not concede the unaccountability of judges; its litigation strategies begin from the premise that judges can and should be held accountable for their past biases and present political choices in the 'balances' they strike. All LEAF facta, like much of the critical legal scholarship on which the facta depend, are calculated to educate judges (and those who follow their decisions) about the disjunction between purportedly neutral legal principles, discourse, and reasoning, and their gendered (and, where relevant, raced, ablist, and/or heterosexist) genesis and sociolegal effects. Judges have not proved impervious to such feminist argumentation. In twenty-seven of its thirty-five Supreme Court of Canada interventions,[66] the position LEAF supported prevailed. Although several of those cases were decided on grounds other than those argued by LEAF, the majority reasoning in nearly two-thirds of those wins bears LEAF's imprint.[67] Two of LEAF's major losses, *R. v. Seaboyer* and *R. v. O'Connor* were succeeded by corrective legislation better than the laws which preceded the defeat.[68] In each case the legislated amendments were superior because they built on analyses developed by broad-based coalitions of LEAF and other feminist lawyers and grass-roots activists who first coalesced to theorize the arguments articulated in the facta and who, following Supreme Court losses, built on those political ties as well as on the factum arguments when pursuing statutory amendments. LEAF's overall success rate, of course, represents only a tiny fraction of *Charter* decisions issued by the courts. On the other hand, LEAF's record should not be dismissed as a statistical fluke when its processes and approach to litigation and achievements in and out of courts so contradict the male left's predictions. LEAF's record is inexplicable unless located in the broader context of thirty years of feminist political and legal activism in Canada.

Feminist Legal Activism Prior to the *Charter*

Roots in the Universities

The first significant product of postwar feminist legal activism in Canada, the *Report of the Royal Commission on the Status of Women*,[69] was decidedly liberal and formalist in its philosophy and recommendations.[70] It was produced before there were any Women's Studies programs in Canada, before most Canadian law schools had hired any women, far less, feminist faculty, before a new critical mass of (mostly white) women students and a handful of (mostly white) women faculty fought for courses in 'Women and the Law' and began to build the now-voluminous literature that documents and analyses the legal construction of women's inequality.[71] Initially, this pioneering work generated the impetus for primarily liberal reforms oriented towards eliminating overtly unequal treatment of the sexes in legal doctrines most central to 'women's' status and welfare such as those concerning employment, family, reproduction, taxation, and male violence against women. These early works also documented gender bias in legal education, the legal profession, and in the courts.[72] The cumulative yield of this issue-specific research launched a second wave of scholarship: feminist legal theory. Among other things, these first systemic analyses of how male domination is embedded in and sustained through law anatomized the relationships among the public/private distinction, women's domestic and economic subordination, and male violence against women, and exposed the limits of formal equality principles and the ideological and legitimating functions of law's claims to objectivity. The content of this new scholarship politicized many women students and faculty. So did the male student and professorial hostility triggered by producing it, studying it, seeking its incorporation into the 'core' curriculum or engaging in women-centred institutional reform initiatives catalyzed by its insights.

Few left critiques of the *Charter* make much reference to this transformative body of work or its magnitude and impact over twenty-five years or its relevance to theorizing about the possibilities and not just the risks of working from within legal institutions for egalitarian change. None acknowledges that the generation of feminist jurisprudence itself triggered a continuing political struggle within universities, much less a struggle waged by elite professional men and male students against women faculty and students through personal and professional denigration, harassment, reprisals, and sometimes violence.[73] And none tracks how legitimation has operated in university settings. In the 1970s, even the mildest liberal feminism was mocked and institutionally discredited. By the 1990s, liberal feminism was endorsed by most faculty and administrators, liberal feminists were relatively easily tenured and routinely recruited to liberalize administrative committees, and both have been used to discredit or suppress more radical feminists pressing for more than cosmetic inclusion of women and of gender awareness within their disciplines and institutions. Cumulatively, over the past three decades, inroads gained by feminists in universities were used by other excluded constituencies to legitimate their claims, and by powerholders to legitimate deferring those claims.

Gender-based reforms to admission, curriculum, language, and hiring initiatives, new sexual harassment policies, and the funding of women's conferences and journals, for instance, all created the momentum for new caucuses and the precedent for more comparable initiatives to remedy race-, sexuality-, and disability-based institutional exclusions, harassment, and disciplinary biases. In law schools, the logic of formal equality provoked and gradually secured these changes, often at a much faster pace than in other disciplines. However, even while white women's gains were showcased to market universities as open to all women and systemically disempowered men, the ruptures in male dominance produced by the inroads made by white women became an unspoken justification for delaying real institutional equity for other historically excluded groups. To the extent that equity principles have been factored into hiring at all, white women, preferably heterosexual and free of disabilities, just happened to be preferred by all-white hiring committees over candidates of colour; to the extent white male faculty have been challenged for offensive remarks or postures or underinclusive teaching materials, correction for racism proved more explosive than for sexism;[74] to the extent that a faculty complement of about 20 per cent women struck white men as a 'takeover' and as evidence that white men stood no chance of being hired, the resulting 'backlash' ensured that women and men of colour, Aboriginal scholars, out lesbian and gay scholars, and scholars known to be living with disabilities never would be hired, or if hired, would be the target of enhanced hostility.

White feminists, however beleaguered, nonetheless benefited from the results. Feminist legal scholarship and legal activism did not. Most white feminist legal scholars grew up in segregated neighbourhoods, schools, and social settings acculturated to the habits of privilege anatomized earlier in this chapter. The faculties that hired women like me were and, in too many cases, remain racially segregated and class privileging, ablist, and heterosexist in their institutional norms. Feminist scholars like me analysed our gender oppression in relation to the white, privileged men we knew socially and professionally and to the male-authored, elite white scholarship and judgments we read. Constructing 'women's' inequality disproportionately through the lens of gender alone (or, in the case of Marxist-feminists, of class alone) was habitual because all other variables determining 'women's' oppression were, by virtue of systemic inequalities, conceptually as well as physically absent from our view.[75] Overwhelmed by pioneering new pedagogies, new jurisprudence, and new institutional policies while meeting our more conventional institutional obligations and carrying the extra committee loads of token women and extra student counselling demands of token feminists, we rationalized our large ignorance about the history of racism and imperialism, ablism, and heterosexism in Canada's social formation, and defended our illiteracy in the writings which would have tempered such ignorance on the basis of being too overburdened to take on 'additional' political issues. Most white, middle-class feminists of my generation, de-raced and de-classed 'women' conceptually because we had the privilege and, hence, habit of our race and class normativity. We also evaded engagement with the role of heterosexism and ablism in the oppression of 'women,' unless we were not heterosexual and/or were living with physical and/or mental disabilities, and, even then, we sometimes evaded such engagements. With few exceptions, we fashioned theory from our insularity, erasing exactly what and how left *Charter* theory erases; and we occupied the feminist legal field often remote from the feminist grass roots and exceptionally remote from and unaccountable to the 'women' we presumed ourselves to be representing. There is now an enormous literature anatomizing the political and theoretical costs of (white) feminist essentialism.[76] Within this literature, essentialist feminist accounts of male violence against 'women' are also being corrected.[77] Few thinking feminists reject the substance of these critiques, and most thinking feminists endorse both the principles and the political necessities mandating far more inclusive feminist praxis. Yet feminist movement from substantive political principle to substantively egalitarian practice has been sporadic at best. Hegemony authorizes this inconsistency; privilege explains it.

Roots in Community

Academic feminism was never the only or even the primary site of women's political movement or of women's legal activism in Canada. Community-based feminist activism coexisted with, indeed, often galvanized feminist consciousness and activism in the universities. Some students and faculty founded local women's services or volunteered in existing feminist community services or transported grass-roots issues or skills into the universities, and on leaving university, into their workplaces and/or professional lives.[78] Some grass-roots feminist priorities have been more natural sites for such town–gown alliances and for the resulting interfusion of theory and practice than others. Self-interest may well explain why students and first-generation feminist scholars and professionals maintained direct linkages with broader-based movements , for instance, to secure abortion rights or universal day care, or equal pay and equal employment opportunities, or to curb male violence against women, and why similar interlinkages were comparatively less pronounced with antipoverty or union or antiracist activism. I also think, however, that the immediacy of such issues to the vast majority of women's lives, and the alliances they kept alive even as academic and professional feminism became more institutionalized, accelerated the democratization of feminist legal activism. Where academic and professional feminists have focused on political priorities unrelated to organizing in grass-roots feminist organizations (for instance, wages for housework or tax and pension reform) or have proceeded with and from theories untested by and unaccountable to extant grass-roots movements organized around similar political issues, they have remained more insulated from or resistant to more inclusionary and less essentialist praxis.

Over my own thirty years of feminist activism, I have been directly involved in a wide range of struggles for egalitarian change, local and national, centred in the universities, in legal institutions, and in the community.[79] None has been immune to the dynamics of system legitimation. Some have nonetheless been democratizing and movement-building. Others have morphed into new enclaves of privilege, presided over by professionalized 'feminists' who are overly possessive of and invested in fields or initiatives or networks or feminist resources that they helped build. Privileged women have been pivotal players in both scenarios. What distinguishes them is their actual rather than imagined ties to the women their work purports to serve. Even absent the proximity to power that goes with academic or professional position, privileged feminists are acclimatized to the 'larger topography of empire' naturalizing their authority to enunciate rules, strategies, and priorities.[80] Professional training compounded by constant proximity to power deforms feminists, however politically well-meaning. Ties to non-elite women can offset the gravity tug and seductions of (relative) power by reminding elite feminists to whom they are accountable as *co-workers*, not as missionaries and not as imperialists.

The balance of this chapter tracks the history of a thirty-year struggle for social and legal change which confirms that legitimation processes operate in all arenas of egalitarian struggle and that isolating any arena as particularly vulnerable to co-optation misses the agency of the relevant political actors. On the one hand, this lets a lot of people – mostly privileged people – off the hook for their political choices, and on the other, it erases the achievements of those who work against being used. The struggle by feminist activists to expose and end male violence against women has been a radical struggle against individuals, groups, and systems empowered, not just by racist, classist, and misogynist ideology, but by actual violence. Feminist litigation against laws and legal practices implicated in legitimating male sexual violence did not channel scarce resources into depoliticized discourses and depoliticizing fora; it was the occasion for building from and within and across a movement. Court defeats have neither legitimated the ideologies normalizing men's and law's violence against women, nor have they demobilized activists. Legislated or other institutionalized reforms, if compromised, have not tamed the movement; they have made the coercive dimensions of law as a vehicle of the oppression of women more transparent and more frequently resorted to than in pre-movement times when legitimation processes were largely adequate to the task. 'Backlash' is a pallid term for an escalating war on women that has nothing to do with male resentment of feminists' resort to courts in lieu of electoral politics. The left critique of the *Charter* not only misses the degree to which feminist activism to delegitimize male violence against women contradicts its critique of rights on virtually every point, it also ducks who and what is legitimized by the left's partial narrative.

68   Sheila McIntyre

The Counter-Narrative: The Movement to End
Male Violence against Women

The Royal Commission did not even address male violence against women in its 1970 Report. By 1973, the first women-run, women-centred rape crisis and battered women's shelters in Canada had been established as sites of resistance to the legal and medical systems' sexist responses to rape victims and to the social mechanisms and ideologies that serve to privatize male violence and isolate and/or pathologize individual men's individual victims. Over their first decade, these grassroots front-line organizations, working with other women's organizations, achieved two things: consciousness raising that de-privatized male violence and created the foundations for a political analysis to end it; and significant institutional reforms. Increased public awareness of the pervasiveness of male sexual violence and its relationship to equally pervasive sexism throughout the private and public sectors translated into literally countless local initiatives for change, ranging from isolated actions defacing sexist billboards, picketing pornographic films or challenging the use of pornographic images or rape jokes in university classrooms, to more organized lobbying for new broadcasting standards curbing media sexism or new procedures to address and redress sexual harassment in universities and the workplace, to scholarly writing and professional advocacy designed to eliminate sex inequality in criminal and civil sexual offence laws.

Whether by intent or in the result, the earliest of these reforms in Canada and the United States were basically liberal. This activism secured stable operating funds, rather than impermanent, project-based grants, for rape crisis centres and battered women's shelters run by feminist activists rather than health or social service staff whose professional training was sexist, if not outright misogynist. It achieved the (formal) revision of police training manuals and policing practices to reduce overt discrimination in police and Crown lawyers' (non) processing of reported rapes and wife assaults. It generated the codification of qualified protections against sexual harassment in human rights legislation,[81] and, in 1983, the first major overhaul of Canadian rape law in almost a hundred years.[82] The 1983 reforms primarily sought to eliminate formal sexual inequality in the enforcement and prosecution of rape law by eliminating the most overtly discriminatory evidence rules unique to the processing of rape complaints (the corroboration rule, the recent complaint rule, the admissibility of evidence of 'general sexual reputation,' and the unrestricted admissibility of evidence of sexual activity with individuals other than the accused), the marital rape exemption, and the male-centred definition of the crime focusing on proof of penile penetration.[83] In the hope of encouraging the gender-neutral enforcement of rape laws, the – now much-regretted – renaming of the crime in gender-neutral terms from 'rape' to 'sexual assault' was achieved.[84]

Not one of these feminist-inspired reforms has escaped co-optation, deradicalization, or organized containment and backlash. With state funding came abstract and depoliticizing discourses describing state initiatives to combat male violence or to support men's victims in gender-neutral terms such as 'family violence,' 'domestic' or 'spouse' abuse, and the 'friendly parent' rule in custody disputes. Institutionalized public funding also brought relentless pressure on crisis workers to 'professionalize' women's services: to substitute for the politics of empowering women collectively, a therapeutic model of rape relief that has reprivatized a systemic expression and vehicle of oppression into a problem of individual victimization and 'healing'; to replace collective decision-making with top-down organizational structures managed by women with professional accreditation, not feminist politics and expertise; to embrace accountability measures and reporting structures undermining of centres' autonomy and priorities; to entrust survivors facing court appearances not to seasoned front-line advocates, but to state employees providing 'Victim Witness' assistance. A slew of new professionals – some feminist, many not – emerged to make a living from the casualties of male and institutional violence. Where front-line activists seek to politicize and mobilize survivors, many of the new professionals seek to scientize them for legal, psychiatric, or scholarly consumption, systematizing survivors' coping strategies or healing options, rather than analysing the oppressive systems that facilitate, normalize, and excuse pervasive male violence. In a well-meaning effort to persuade judges out of blaming the victims of male violence, professionals analogized from the psychological traumas experienced by men as soldiers and hostages to 'rape trauma syndrome,' 'battered women's syndrome,' and 'incest syndrome.' As a result, these initiatives have functionally reinstated what the 1983 reforms formally eliminated: a new corroboration requirement to the effect that the testimony of complainants cannot be credited or comprehended unless mediated by expert interpreters. This has led to new objectifying psychosexual stereotypes of women, and new points of entry for defence counsel to intimidate and/or discredit complainants by demanding access to any and all records about their lives on which to hang the old story of her or her 'type's' unworthiness of law's protection.[85] They have also yielded the ultimate evil twin, so-called false memory syndrome, which is now deployed not only to discredit adult survivors of child sexual abuse, but to demonize feminist therapists for maliciously planting false memories in the vulnerable.[86] While antiviolence activists fight all these co-optive and deradicalizing dynamics, supporting more survivors who are daring to report and charge more and more previously immune – because privileged – men, with fewer public and private funds than a decade ago, the liberal state seeks to promote the little it is doing in support of ending male violence against women under its cynical 'law and order' agenda.

Notwithstanding all the mechanisms designed to contain the political power of the movement to end male violence against women and children, the combined labour of front-line activists and feminist legal theorists has inalterably transformed political analysis of this practice of domination.[87] By asking novel questions about the social contexts in which sexual violence occurred, about the relationship between sexually abusive men and those they abuse, and about how men stage and manage and rationalize their predations, the front lines have produced original, counter-hegemonic data not only proving that women and children have more to fear from men they know and/or love than from the aberrant, deviant, stranger of rape mythology, but exposing the relationships between institutionalized power and disempowerment and sexual violence. Over time, the aggregated accounts of individual women or children sexually abused by individual husbands, (step-)fathers, dates, employers, priests, physicians, institutional caregivers, probation officers, teachers, and pimps have revealed three transformative truths. First, vulnerability to male sexual violence and to discriminatory treatment within the justice system is directly related to victims' social, economic, and political inequality. Second, individual men's sexual exploitation of their actual or deemed unequals and their relative immunity from legal sanction for such crimes are directly related to their social, economic, and political elevation. These insights provided the grounding and validation for theoretical analyses by feminist legal and social science scholars of the relationships among systemic male domination, male violence, and domestic and international law. Third, in domestic relationships, in workplaces, and in public spaces, whenever women individually or collectively move towards greater self-assertion and self-possession, male violence escalates.

From these truths have followed analyses of rape as a direct or indirect adjunct to white supremacy, imperialism, cultural genocide, and eugenics. The rape of slave women that enriched white, male, slave owners bred more than new human property. It bred racist inversions of reality in the form of stereotypes of black women as sexually promiscuous and indiscriminate that rationalized and legalized white male sexual supremacy by deeming black women beneath the protection of (white) law; stereotypes of white women as naturally chaste and, if chaste, deserving of male and legal protection; and stereotypes of black men as oversexed, rapacious, and dangerously drawn to pure white womanhood. Lynching, segregation, antimiscegenation laws, and racist eugenics policies based on dirty science are among the offshoots of such racist rape myths.[88] In Canada, white supremacist colonialism justified culturally genocidal practices against First Nations communities that both facilitated and rationalized widespread sexual and physical abuse of Aboriginal children by white staff in the residential schools.[89] The legacy of this forcible cultural dissociation, coupled with reprogramming by sexual and physical violence, has been exceptionally high incidences of sexual violence against First Nations women within their own communities, even while sexual predation by white men rationalized by the sexual and racial devaluation of Aboriginal women continues. Both forms of violation are compounded by unjust legal treatment where survivors report their violation to a white legal system.[90] The conjunction of racism, imperialism, and male sexual violence has also been vividly exposed in Bosnia, where rape was an overt instrument of ethnic genocide.[91]

The vulnerabilities, social isolation, and sexualized stereotypes associated with disability have also now been linked to the extremely high incidence of male sexual aggression against disabled women and against disabled children of both sexes.[92] Perversely, such vulnerability to sexual exploitation or coercion spawned laws permitting forced sterilization of developmentally delayed women and of mentally healthy women deemed defective by reason of their unchastity.[93]

Nationally and internationally women have sought to expose and combat these linkages between women's systemic sexual, racial, and economic inequality, and their vulnerability to male sexual violence by a number of political and legal means. Such means include invoking 'equality rights' and 'human rights' discourses and laws, not only to eliminate systemic bias in domestic and international instruments for prosecuting male sexual crimes against women and children, but to advance women's economic, political, and social equality in order to reduce their vulnerability to abuses of institutionalized power by men. Reducing this (in)equality-driven approach to just another instance of rights talk would be to trivialize and misconstrue a profound paradigm shift in conceptualizing individual men's sex crimes and individual women's sexual victimization in *political* terms.

Feminist work unpacking sexualized violence as an abuse of institutionalized power exposed the legitimating function of equating sexual danger with the stranger, the man none of 'us' knows. Gradually the men 'we' know were exposed and, sometimes, charged. This has yielded a monstrous counter-offensive. In the context of privilege, the presumption of innocence operates at its highest pitch. Powerful men do not plea-bargain, they fund liberal civilian and military defence lawyers to invent end-runs around those few law reforms that have constrained the ability of powered men to purchase acquittals from the logic of inequality. They command three days of international media coverage of U.S. Senate hearings to out-myth each other in appointing a sexual harasser to the U.S. Supreme Court. They graft new misogynist myths (feminist therapists who induce women to lay false charges against innocent men) onto old (women's propensity to lie about rape) to justify 'whacking the complainant hard' pre-trial by invading her privacy and stripping her of her support systems. Then, if successful in inducing her to withdraw from her legalized revictimization, they pounce on her forced retreat from attempting to access the justice system as proof positive women lie about rape.[94] They use feminist statistics on the high incidence of rape to argue for the disqualification of the majority of women from jury service on the basis of rape-based bias against accused men.[95] They subpoena feminist organizations known for their activism against male sexual violence to advance such disqualification arguments.[96] To be sure, some of these newer variants on old discriminatory dodges are rationalized by defence lawyers and criminal law scholars and blessed by the Supreme Court of Canada in the abstract language of rights. But to imagine that in women's eyes this continuing war against women has been depoliticized by the *Charter* or that the *Charter* and rights discourse are responsible for its escalation or its legal normalization is to confuse form with substance. Substantively and politically, the sexual presumptions embedded in *Charter*-backed discourses about and court-defined elements of 'fair trial' rights do not differ meaningfully from other long-standing discourses of male right – property rights, conjugal rights, breadwinner rights, the right to an acquittal for an 'honest' mistake, the right to the spoils of war, for example.

From a feminist perspective, there is little to choose between elite theorists who blame the *Charter* for empowering judges to elevate the misogynist and antifeminist tactics of defence lawyers to constitutional rights and the defence lawyers who exploit and then rationalize such tactics as *Charter* imperatives over which they have no personal or professional choice. Between the voice of the left (the *Charter* made them do it) and the voice of defence lawyers (the *Charter* made me do it) coupled with the voice of approving criminal scholars (the *Charter* requires them to do it) and the voice of judges (the *Charter* requires me to do it), male agency conveniently disappears in *Charter* abstraction. Concerted and escalating male resistance to feminist change within, through, and despite law also disappears from view. A fierce, high stakes political struggle disappears from view. Not coincidentally, the pervasive nature, systemic causes, and political effects of male violence – intellectual, institutional, ideological, as well as individual – also disappear from view. This is legitimation writ large.

Feminist Legal Activism as Coalition Politics

It has become trite to urge discrete political movements to mobilize in coalitions against the awesome forces exacerbating every existing structural inequality in Canadian society and around the globe. The irresistible logic is the power of numbers; the complacent assumption is that members of disempowered groups can and should unite despite real political differences in face of a common enemy. But this logic, the logic of the dream of a common language and of universal sisterhood remains the logic of privilege. 'We' women are not similarly disempowered, and 'Ours' is not, in all contexts and all the variants of our violation, a common enemy. The fact of female gender does not neutralize race, class, heterosexual, western, or ablist privilege. Even the fact of a common site of female oppression such as, say, lack of reproductive freedom, has been manifested very differently in differently situated women's lives as a result of aggregates of legal, social, and historical domination that are not universal to all women. The forced sterilization of women of colour or women living with disabilities without their knowledge is not the same as criminal abortion regulations that forced all women to secure the approval of three doctors as the legal precondition to safe, publicly funded abortion. Nor was the experience of all women in attempting to secure three doctors' approval the same. Nor has feminist political and fund-raising support to combat the wide variety of coercive mechanisms curbing the reproductivity of mothers long deemed 'undesirable' by reason of their race, poverty, sexuality, and/or disability[97] ever approached that mobilized and sustained for access to abortion.

Political coalitions of equality-seeking women are hard, consuming, and necessarily conflictual work because the focus on relations of domination that unites 'women' in theory is what divides actual women in practice.[98] Coalition work disrupts the flow of privilege and slows it down. Coalitions amount to democratizing structures of accountability which expose and check the habits of privilege and displace ignorant presumption and privileged insularity. It is harder for the privileged progressive to rule when the knowledge and political consciousness of 'Others' are not structurally suppressed.[99] The very real risks of top-down theorizing and legal strategizing constitute the real case against the *Charter*. Because interfused relations of domination permeate all social institutions and are hegemonically enforced, there is no exit in theory or in practice from the reality of the superior resources the dominant bring to containing social transformation or from the inevitability of dominant interventions to that end. The question that remains, therefore, is not *whether* to use law for social change, but *how* to do so accountably, while keeping mindful of how power and privilege operate through us all, and with an eye towards building political movement.

There is at present a working model of coalition engaging law reform that has wedded feminist front-line activists, litigators, and legal scholars in antiviolence activism at the national level. Its genesis was a *Charter* challenge by Stephen Seaboyer against statutory amendments codified in the 1983 rape law reforms. Those amendments placed formal restrictions on the admissibility of 'evidence' of a sexual assault complainant's sexual history with men other than the accused; they placed no formal limits on the past sexual history of the complainant with the accused. Insofar as all front-line workers and many feminist lawyers insist sexual history of either type is never relevant to whether a particular woman consented to sex with a particular man (or woman) on a particular occasion, the evidence rules challenged by Seaboyer were instances of the compromised quality of legislated reformism.

When LEAF intervened in the case at the Ontario Court of Appeal, it adopted a conventionally liberal line. LEAF conceded not only that some sexual history is relevant but that in rare cases evidence of the type even Parliament had declared inadmissible is relevant, and its exclusion would deny an accused a fair trial. LEAF urged that the so-called rape shield provisions not be struck down, but that trial judges exercise discretion to declare the provisions inoperative in those rare cases where sexual history evidence relevant to a full and fair defence would be statutorily excluded.

Rebuked by feminist activists and legal scholars for advancing so compromising a position in 'women's' name, LEAF embarked on a new process to rework its argument from the ground up. Prior to intervening in the case again before the Supreme Court of Canada, LEAF initiated consultations with women's groups and rape crisis workers across the country and, in coalition with six other women's organizations, fundamentally reframed its arguments on the basis of the (in)equality analysis attributable to front-line work (which I have described above).[100] Canadian history was made when two Supreme Court judges not only grasped and applied that analysis, but held that because judges were accountable for the discriminatory rules Parliament had intervened to correct, judges could not be trusted with discretion to make evidentiary rulings on a case-by-case basis if the 1983 reforms were struck down. A seven-judge majority, however, plainly rejected the coalition's analysis, adopting one of the more breathtaking instances of privileged and privileging erasure to do so: they deemed the equality guarantees of the *Charter* irrelevant to the case.[101]

The majority decision triggered enormous public outrage. Justice Minister Kim Campbell and her advisers were of the view that the Supreme Court opinion foreclosed any substantively corrective response that could survive constitutional challenge, but she wanted to be seen to be responding to the intense public outrage. She held a quick consultation with representatives of LEAF, the National Association of Women and the Law (NAWL), the National Action Committee on the Status of Women (NAC), and the Canadian Bar Association – all elite organizations – for suggestions on how to respond to *Seaboyer*. Shortly thereafter she indicated that she would introduce some minor amendments to fill procedural gaps left by the decision. LEAF, NAWL, and NAC used their political leverage to persuade the Justice Minister to slow down and to expand the consultation process. By the second, far more broadly based consultation, nine national women's groups had agreed to demand an equality-driven substantive overhaul of the *Criminal Code*'s sexual assault provisions and a delay in the enactment of that overhaul until any new amendments had been evaluated and, if necessary, improved through national consultations with front-line workers and women's groups across the country. I have told that story elsewhere.[102]

What I wish to underline here is that the 1983 reforms which the Court struck down in *Seaboyer* were significantly inferior to the 1992 amendments which replaced them. The former codified formal equality principles; the latter redefined the offence and corollary evidentiary rules around substantive equality principles linking sexual violence to sexual inequality and the abuse of male power. That substantive shift would not have been constitutionally available without the equality jurisprudence already secured by LEAF in earlier test cases. Further, the coalition, which successfully pressed for substantive rather than procedural reforms, could not have been so quickly and effectively mobilized without the pre-existing alliances developed in working on *Seaboyer*. The actual substance of the amendments could not have been so quickly conceptualized or so persuasively proposed without the equality analysis articulated in the *Seaboyer* factum. Finally, the process of fighting for, and then proposing the outlines of the substantive amendments that finessed the *Seaboyer* decision would not have been movement-building had the prominent national women's organizations not also demanded as the price of their cooperation in the law reform project a state-funded consultation with a constituent assembly of sixty front-line rape crisis and shelter staff, feminist equality activists, and feminist criminal and constitutional practitioners and scholars.

The coalition formed to circumvent *Seaboyer* remained intact and expanded in the succeeding five years. It publicly boycotted the $10,000,000 federal Panel on Violence Against Women because the panel's leadership refused to be directly accountable to the movement it served. It met as a national formation in each year from 1994 through 1997 to supply the federal Department of Justice with the equality analysis necessary to change several federal laws and policies facilitating or exacerbating violence against women. It played an influential role in the substance of the legislated reforms that followed the Supreme Court's recognition of extreme intoxication as an exit from criminal liability for sexual assault.[103] Members of the coalition also intervened in two subsequent Supreme Court cases.[104] Their factum in *O'Connor* and the oral argument delivered by Sharon McIvor may be the most uncompromising, politically honest, and hence radical demands ever heard before the Supreme Court of Canada.[105] That factum emboldened three attorneys-general to advance arguments before the Supreme Court that were more radical than they had previously dared.

The left's *Charter* scorecard would count *Seaboyer* on the debit side of *Charter* politics. But this would divorce a single decision from a twenty-five year struggle fought in multiple arenas. Similarly, to single out the work of the coalition responsible for the post-*Seaboyer* reforms as a more accurate measure of the efficacy or democratizing potential of rights activism would idealize and abstract too much. As a model of feminist process and substance, the 1992 amendments constitute an extraordinary departure from the efforts of a decade earlier. But that success has spawned a reactionary counter-move more threatening to complainants' security of the person and to fair trials than defence lawyers had dreamed of ten years before. Then the price of access to justice for sexually abused women was law's access to their sexual histories. Now the price is law's access to their medical, educational, contraceptive, social welfare, institutional, therapeutic, employment, *and* sexual histories. With *R. v. O'Connor* and *R. v. Carosella*,[106] the Supreme Court constitutionally approved such legally extraordinary access and the overtly discriminatory logic underpinning it.[107] As was the case in *Seaboyer*, the majority opinions in *O'Connor* and *Carosella* define the substance of a constitutionally fair trial without reference to the equality guarantees of the *Charter*. And as was the case after *Seaboyer*, feminists mobilized to secure a justice minister's support for equality-driven legislation to override the *O'Connor* majority's disregard for section 15 of the *Charter*.[108]

My experience with this coalition suggests a practicable blueprint for politicized and politically empowering legal activism. I want to underline that the genesis of this blueprint was an instance of lawyering – LEAF's initial intervention in the *Seaboyer* decision – which manifested most of the failings the left ascribes generally to rights litigation. *Seaboyer* and its sequelae taught the dozens of women involved in coalition politics since then that no test case *Charter* litigation should be launched by individuals or argued by lawyers who are not directly accountable to the constituency or constituencies they purport to represent. The most obvious vehicles for such accountability are public interest organizations, preferably national, composed of members of that constituency and founded to advance their equality. Those organizations, in turn, must be mini-coalitions, demographically representative of the full diversity of their constituency. Where a particular test case may establish precedent affecting the equality claims of several disempowered groups, it should only be pursued in coalition with organizational representatives of all such groups, each functioning as a full partner in all decision-making, and each fully accountable to the others for ensuring its organization honours those decisions. Less than full partnership generates a very high risk that the interests and perspectives of the most marginalized groups and the organizations that represent them will remain in the background or be reduced to rhetorical presences in the conception, drafting, and oral delivery of the rights claim. Public law litigation, in short, should not bypass existing movement organizations and the knowledge and experience they consolidate, but should engage and empower them and give them visibility in the legal process. Collective processes defined by multiple lines of accountability are both time-consuming and costly to finance. However, rights litigation pursued without accountability and without equal input from the leadership of all communities likely to be affected by the challenge, win or lose, and without checks on the insular world views of lawyers, carries an almost certain risk of vindicating every argument against rights litigation advanced by the left.

Where governments choose to consult with individual feminist lawyers on policies related to women's inequality, those lawyers should refuse to participate in such consultation unless the input they have to offer has already been tested in coalition processes, or unless, before they attend, they can consult with and take instructions from organizations representing the most directly affected constituencies of women. When governments initiate consultations with representatives of public interest or equality-seeking organizations, those representatives should also refuse to participate unless two conditions are met: that all organizations who ought to be present have been invited and that the invitees can meet alone to define their own agenda before meeting with government officials. Because power likes dealing with power, governments are most likely to invite the most high-profile organizations to their round-tables. A high profile often can be correlated with mainstream politics, privileged credentials, and/or privileged perspectives and self-conduct. Accordingly, any consultations restricted by profile will generate exclusionary proposals irrelevant or positively harmful to those excluded. Because such invitations signal that a government believes it stands to gain something by being seen to consult with such select representatives, those with high profiles likely have the political leverage to demand a more inclusive round-table as the price of their participation. As a matter of principled, accountable, democratizing politics, if the government refuses the demand, the meeting is not worth attending.

The national Department of Justice consultations on violence against women held annually from 1994 through 1997[113] replicated the consultations that followed the *Seaboyer* decision. In my view, they offered the optimal model of principled, accountable, democratizing feminist legal activism. Sixty women attended each year and met for three days.[109] Travel, food, and hotel costs, funding for simultaneous translation, and staff support for co-ordinating the assembly were supplied by government. The cost of replacing participants for three days was born by their organizations. The government did not control either the invitation list or the agenda. Lee Lakeman, a thirty-year veteran of rape crisis work representing the Canadian Association of Sexual Assault Centres, composed the invitation list in consultation with other front-line organizations. Typically, the consultation assembly included: (1) representatives from every national feminist organization in the country and, where no national, women-only organization existed, as in the case of sex trade workers, lesbians, Métis women, and union women, representatives of regional organizations or women's caucuses; (2) representatives from approximately thirty rape crisis or battered women's centres from across the country or, where such services did not exist or had been closed down by government cuts, from regional women's centres; and (3) about four feminist scholars specializing in equality law.[110] In selecting the representatives from each subgrouping, care was taken to ensure that Aboriginal, francophone, disabled, lesbian, and racialized women were well represented.

For the first two days the assembly would meet without government officials, starting with a plenary designed to identify what each delegate viewed as the most pressing issues related to male violence against women in her own work, and to reach agreement on eight to ten strategic priorities that the assembly wished the government to address in the next year. Historically, such priorities have included reforming regulations concerning foreign domestic workers and the sponsorship of immigrants, restoring funding to federal–provincial transfer payments, instituting changes to child custody policies in the federal divorce act to respond appropriately to situations of physical or sexual abuse, and taking action to offset the effect of provincial cuts to civil and criminal legal aid as well as amending criminal laws that violate women's constitutional rights to equality. The assembly then would break into eight to ten small working groups to brainstorm around one of the identified priorities, pooling knowledge about the nature of the problem across the country, and identifying measures to address or redress it within the jurisdiction of the federal government. The results of these sessions were reported in plenary session on the afternoon of the second day. Each group offered its action plan and concrete proposals to be endorsed by the full assembly, modified with their input or dropped where consensus was lacking. On the third day, the (in)equality analysis mandating government action on all the proposals endorsed in plenary was presented to the relevant ministers (Justice, Citizenship and Multiculturalism, Solicitor General, Status of Women, Employment, and Immigration) and some forty of their staff. In between working on this primary agenda, caucuses of lesbians, Aboriginal women, and women of colour often met to identify their own priorities and/or to craft constituency-specific proposals for one or more of the priority issues identified in the first plenary.

The most significant benefit of these consultations was the opportunity for activists across the country to meet regularly, exchange information, convert isolated experiences into political analysis, strategize coordinated political action, and gain strength, resources, and political wit from each other. The extraordinary productivity of each three-day gathering exceeded that of any political project in which I have participated in twenty-five years. Some misguided state policies were abandoned on the basis of our articulated opposition. Only a few of our proposals were embraced. The inspired analysis recorded in the transcripts of each consultation is plainly having an effect on how politicians and bureaucrats think about equality, and may finally persuade some departments to direct research funding to the front lines rather than to private consultants or to professional academics. The workshops and plenaries empowered participants with equality arguments and analyses transportable to local battles. No feminist lawyer who participated failed to learn the necessity of coalition work to sound legal analysis. Sadly, Justice Minister McLellan discontinued the consultations in 1998. In my view there is little hope that the consultations will be reinstated while Ms McLellan remains Justice Minister.

Public interest organizations, like LEAF, whose mandate is to pursue test case litigation and related law reform initiatives, must not only be demographically representative in their composition and operate by collective, representative decision-making, but they should theorize no cases and make no governmental submissions without the benefit of non-lawyers expert in how the particular laws in specific test cases work in the world, not just in the jurisprudence. The work of lawyer-dominated organizations most benefits from organizational coalitions when addressing laws that affect different constituencies within their mandate differently; but such elite organizations also most threaten coalition principles and processes.

Legal training, professional status and the social habits of privilege compounded by both incline public interest litigators to treat organizations with whom they work in coalition as junior partners, not co-equals. Breaking coalition ranks in professional settings, pulling professional rank when disagreements about legal strategy occur, and closing ranks when called on such exercises of privilege are the typical dangers. The good news is that effective coalition work is a learnable skill. The bad news is that, because one privilege of privilege is the privilege of ignorance – ignorance of the knowledge and expertise and realities of Others, ignorance of the costs of such illiteracy, ignorance of one's own oppressive habits and exercises of privilege – lawyers are the least likely members of any coalition to presume that they have a lot to learn and the most likely to presume that they are so overstretched that they need not invest in the rudiments of participating as an equal in the hard work of coalition politics. Success in coalition work despite habituation to privilege requires grasping the meaning of expropriations such as extracting self-regard, self-centredness, self-confidence, self-expression from the disregard of Others, presuming the right to put the work, expertise, political analyses, and even lived experience of Others to one's personal use and benefit, and privileging privileged interests. Equal political partnerships, to say nothing of reparations, require a new division of labour. Let Others speak; read what they have long said; credit their knowledge and authority particularly when it threatens yours. Assume disentitlement to the authority to prescribe; presume your untrustworthiness; erase your self when power wants to deal with power; assume responsibility when power must be faced down.

The case against the *Charter* is, ultimately, a case against privileged theory and theorizing, a case against privileged erasures by unaccountable and unrepresentative progressive scholars and activists no less than by unaccountable and unrepresentative courts. There is an alternative that is percolating through women's movements and that is the animating principle in feminist legal activism to end male violence against women. It promises to reduce those system-legitimating dynamics that progressives can control for while respecting the real promise of rights to those most systematically denied the legitimating embrace of liberal legalism.

Notes

1 Maivan Lâm, 'Feeling Foreign in Feminism' (1994) 19 *Signs* 872–3. Lâm's text refers specifically to white women and white feminists.
2 Formal legal bars and informal norms excluded many men from full citizenship and, thus, participation in law-making as voters, jury members, lawyers, holders of public office, and judges. Chinese- and Japanese-Canadians of both sexes were denied the federal vote until 1948 (S.C. 1948, c. 46, s. 6); status 'Indians' of both sexes acquired the federal vote only in 1960 (S.C. 1960, c. 7).
3 For a brief overview of basic U.S. and Canadian schools of thought for and against judicial review, see Janet Hiebert, *Limiting Rights: The Dilemma of Judicial Review* (Montreal and Kingston: McGill-Queen's Press, 1996) chap. 5. For an elegant summary and refutation of the basic arguments in favour of judicial review, see Joel Bakan, *Just Words: Constitutional Rights and Social Wrongs* (Toronto: University of Toronto Press, 1997) chap. 2. For an overview of no less than twenty-one prescriptive theories about how judges should approach judicial review under the *Charter*, see Richard Devlin, 'The *Charter* and Anglophone Legal Theory' (1997) 4 *Review of Constitutional Studies* (*RCS*) at 44–5.
4 Part I of the *Constitution Act, 1982*, being Schedule B of the *Canada Act 1982* (U.K.) 1982 c. 11. Hereafter, the *Charter*.
5 Women wrote just two of the twenty-one articles cited by Devlin proposing interpretive approaches to *Charter* guarantees that would help legitimate judicial review. See Devlin, '*Charter*,' 44–5. Many feminist scholars have written about particular *Charter* cases or guarantees. Few have engaged in the larger debates about the politics of judicial review. Those few who have been most critical of *Charter* rights litigation include Judy Fudge, 'The Public/Private Distinction: The Possibilities of and the Limits to the Use of the Charter to Further Feminist Struggles' (1987), 17 *International Journal of Society and Law* (*IJSL*) 445; 'Labour, the New Constitution and Old Style Liberalism' (1988) 15 *Queen's Law Journal* (*QLJ*) 1; and 'What Do We Mean by Law and Social Transformation?' (1990) 5 *Canadian Journal of Law and Society* (*CJLS*) 47; Elizabeth Sheehy, 'Feminist Argumentation in the Supreme Court of Canada in *R. v. Seaboyer*; *R. v. Gayme*: The Sound of One Hand Clapping' (1991), 18 *Melbourne Law*

Review (*MLR*) 450; and 'Women and Equality Rights in Canada: Sobering Reflections, Impossible Choices,' in Susan Bazilli, ed., *Putting Women on the Agenda* (Johannesberg: Ravan Press, 1991); and Hester Lessard, 'Creation Stories: Social Rights and Canada's Social Contract,' in J. Bakan and D. Schneiderman, eds., *Social Justice and the Constitution* (Ottawa: Carleton University Press, 1992) 101.

6 Notably David Beatty, *Putting the Charter to Work: Designing a Constitutional Labour Code* (Montreal and Kingston: McGill-Queen's University Press, 1987); and *Talking Heads and the Supremes: The Canadian Production of Con-stitutional Review* (Toronto: Carswell, 1990); Patrick Monahan, *Politics and the Constitution: The Charter, Federalism and the Supreme Court of Canada* (Toronto: Carswell, 1987); and John Whyte, 'Legality and Legitimacy: The Problem of Judicial Review of Legislation' (1987), 12 *QLJ* 1.

7 See Michael Mandel, *The Charter of Rights and the Legalization of Politics in Canada*, rev. ed. (Toronto: Thompson, 1994); Harry Glasbeek, 'From Constitutional Rights to "Real Rights" – "R-i-i-g-hts Fo-or-wa-ard Ho"!?' (1990) 10 *Windsor Yearbook of Access to Justice* (*WYAJ*) 468; H. Glasbeek and M. Mandel, 'The Legalization of Politics in Advanced Capitalism: The Canadian Charter of Rights' (1984) 2 *Social Studies* (*SS*) 85; and J. Fudge and H. Glasbeek, 'The Politics of Rights: A Politics with Little Class' (1992) 1 *Social and Legal Studies* (*SLS*) 45; Allan Hutchinson and Andrew Petter, 'Private Rights / Public Wrongs: The Liberal Lie of the Charter' (1988) 38 *University of Toronto Law Journal* (*UTLJ*) 278; 'Daydream Believing: Visionary Formalism and the Constitution' (1990), 22 *Ottawa Law Review* (*OLR*) 365; A. Petter and A. Hutchinson, 'Rights in Conflict: The Dilemma of Charter Legitimacy' (1989), 23 *University of British Columbia Law Review* (*UBC*) 531; A. Hutchinson, *Waiting for Coraf: A Critique of Law and Rights* (Toronto: University of Toronto Press, 1995); Joel Bakan, 'Constitutional Arguments: Interpretation and Legitimacy in Canadian Constitutional Thought' (1989), 27 *Osgoode Hall Law Journal* (*OHLJ*) 123; J. Bakan, 'Strange Expectations: A Review of Two Theories of Judicial Review' (1990) 35 *McGill Law Journal* (*MLJ*) 439; J. Bakan 'Constitutional Interpretation and Social Change: You Can't Always Get What You Want (Nor What You Need)' (1991) 70 *Canadian Bar Review* (*CBR*) 307; and J. Bakan, *Just Words*. For differences among these *Charter* sceptics, see Bakan, *Just Words*, 6–9, and Hutchinson, *Waiting for Coraf*, 174–8. Notwithstanding their differences, all are critics of liberal capitalism and the *Charter*'s likelihood of entrenching and legitimating it while eroding the possibilities of democratic mobilization to curb, if not end, the structural inequalities inherent to liberal capitalist legal orders.

8 See, e.g., W.A. Bogart, *Courts and Country: The Limits of Litigation and the Social and Political Life of Canada* (Toronto: Oxford University Press, 1996).

9 See, e.g., F.L. Morton, 'The Charter Revolution and the Court Party' (1992) 30 *OHLJ* 627; F.L. Morton and Rainer Knopff, *The Charter Revolution and the Court Party* (Peterborough: Broadview Press, 2000) and most of the contributions in Anthony Peacock, ed., *Rethinking the Constitution: Perspectives on Constitutional Reform, Interpretation, and Theory* (Toronto: Oxford University Press, 1996).

10 It should be noted that the labels 'left' and 'right' break down when male scholars express antifeminism. On my reading, self-styled lefties like Robert Martin, a law professor at the University of Western Ontario, or University of Victoria political scientist Warren Magnussen vent their hostility to feminists in terms and via rationales indistinguishable from those typical of the religious, academic, and economic right. Martin showcases his antifeminism in *The Lawyers Weekly*. See Professor Magnussen's outraged response to what I read as a fairly commonplace campus chilly climate report entitled: 'Feminism, McCarthyism and Sexist Fundamentalism' (copy on file with author).

11 In its more overtly offensive and exaggerated stereotyping and postured political neutrality, the *Charter* literature from the right is indistinguishable ideologically and strategically from the scaremongering analysed in my article, 'Backlash against Equality: The "Tyranny" of the "Politically Correct"' (1993), 38 *MLJ* 1. Whereas the right effectively pulls social rank by trading on denigrating social stereotypes of equality-seeking groups, the left pulls political and intellectual rank. Consider the assertion by Judy Fudge and Harry Glasbeek that the 'onus' is on rights proponents to justify (presumably to the left?) the use of *Charter* litigation, in 'The Politics of Rights,' 56. See, also the patronizing punchline of Bakan's 'Constitutional Interpretation,' 328: 'it seems naive, even silly, to think that with the Charter in place all we have to do is cook up imaginative legal arguments and go to court for the realization of an egalitarian and just society' when '[h]istory would suggest that those with power do not give up so easily,' or his argument that it is 'delusions' symptomatic of 'depression' which lead progressives who are in 'despair' over the pervasiveness of social injustice to seek 'an easy way out through litigation' ('Strange Expectations,' 442). *Just Words*, Bakan's most recent and book-length treatment of the politics of rights betrays none of the condescension I find offensive in his earlier articles. For condescension mixed with antifeminism, see Mandel, *Charter of Rights*, esp. 443–54.

12 Each of these subthemes can be found, more or less prominently, in the works cited at n7 supra. Richard Devlin's comprehensive review of anglophone *Charter* jurisprudence offers an exhaustive list of scholarship sound-

ing these subthemes, 'The *Charter,*' 35–40. Devlin does not classify *Charter* rights theorists by political affiliation as I do, but simply distinguishes 'those who believe in the utility of a rights discourse' from 'those who do not, and those who resist dichotomous analyses' (ibid., 35).

13 Section 1 states that the *Charter* 'guarantees the rights and freedoms set out in it subject only to such reasonable limits prescribed by law as can be demonstrably justified in a free and democratic society.'
14 For detailed expositions on these political ramifications of the indeterminacy of rights guarantees, see, e.g., Bakan, *Just Words*, chaps. 3–6, and Hutchinson, *Waiting for Coraf*, 12–27, 88–122.
15 On this last point, see Sheehy, 'Feminist Argumentation.'
16 Mandel, *Charter of Rights*, 3.
17 This is a constant theme in Mandel's book, ibid. See also Fudge, 'What Do We Mean.'
18 See Bakan, *Just Words*, 55–62.
19 See Fudge and Glasbeek, 'Politics of Rights,' 56.
20 See Joel Bakan and Michael Smith, 'Rights, Nationalism and Social Movements in Canadian Constitutional Politics' (1995) 4 *SLS* 367.
21 Hutchinson and Petter end each of their *Charter* critiques with lofty, if empty, rhetorical prescriptions: see articles cited at n7 supra. In *Waiting for Coraf* Hutchinson proposes 'strategic scepticism' towards rights activism and the promotion of a 'dialogic democracy' as an alternative to reliance on rights discourse and activism. For a thoughtful critique of contradictions, underdeveloped ideas, and substantive gaps in Hutchinson's proposals, see Richard Devlin, 'Some Recent Developments in Canadian Constitutional Theory with Particular Reference to Beatty and Hutchinson' (1996) 22 *QLJ* 126–33. Fudge and Glasbeek prioritize development of a totalizing, normative theory to advance a coherent approach to challenging global capitalism, 'The Politics of Rights,' 61. Mandel's 461-page argument against the legalization of politics devotes a single paragraph to alternative praxis: 'bring democratic politics to the courtroom and ... the constitutional table' to 'challenge the authority of the court and thereby to challenge authoritarianism generally.' *Charter of Rights*, 461.
22 Peacock, *Rethinking the Constitution*, ix. See, too, Morton, 'Charter Revolution,' 627.
23 Morton, 'Charter Revolution,' 630.
24 Peacock, 'Strange Brew: Tocqueville, Rights, and the Technology of Equality,' in Peacock, *Rethinking the Constitution*, 127.
25 See Morton, 'Charter Revolution,' 636.
26 For Morton, the Women's Legal Education and Action Fund (LEAF) is the

'prototype' of *Charter* imperialism; ibid., 631. See also, the views of REAL Women on the power of 'radical feminists' and LEAF and for the conflation of feminist activism with gay and lesbian activism, in Didi Herman, *Rights of Passage: Struggles for Lesbian and Gay Legal Equality* (Toronto: University of Toronto Press, 1994) 94–6, 105–6.

27 See Morton, 'Charter Revolution,' 642.

28 Patricia Hill Collins, *Black Feminist Thought: Knowledge, Consciousness, and the Politics of Empowerment* (New York: Routledge, 1990) 5.

29 From 1984 to 1988, I was a member of the litigation team that unsuccessfully fought a ten-year battle to defend the existence of an all-woman teachers' union against the claim that woman-only organizations discriminate against those women who prefer mixed-sex organizations. See *Tomen and Logan-Smith v. Ontario Teachers' Federation and Ontario Public School Teachers' Federation* (1994), 20 C.H.R.R. D/257, appeal dismissed; *O.T.F. et al. v. Ontario (Human Rights Commission)* (1995), 126 D.L.R. (4th) 409 (Ont. Div. Ct.), aff'd. (1997), 153 D.L.R. (4th) 285 (Ont. C.A.). From 1987 to 1998 I worked on a variety of equality test cases argued by LEAF, including fifteen appellate interventions, eleven of which were in the Supreme Court of Canada. My contributions ranged from conceptual and/or editorial input into the collective development of arguments ultimately drafted by others, to joint authorship of individual facta according to the instructions of LEAF working committees and/or of broader coalitions of feminist organizations with which LEAF worked in partnership.

30 As a student in the early 1970s and again in the early 1980s, and beginning in 1985 as a law professor, I have been consistently active, but inconsistently effective, pressing for egalitarian change within faculties of law, in other schools and programs with which I have been formally involved, and more broadly, in university governance and university policies. Since 1991, I have played fairly significant roles within national coalitions of feminist legal activists who have mobilized to secure legislated reforms to combat federal and provincial laws that facilitate male violence against women and/or that institutionalize and legitimate substantive inequality in sexual offence law and law enforcement.

31 Very few progressive scholars in Canada have chosen to reply to left critiques of rights litigation. Those who do are similarly critical of the reductionism and overstated generalizations found in left *Charter* scholarship. See, e.g., Didi Herman, 'Beyond the Rights Debate' (1993) 2 *SLS* 25; and 'The Good the Bad, and the Smugly: Perspectives on the Canadian Charter of Rights and Freedoms' (1994) 14 *Oxford Journal of Legal Studies* (OJLS) at 589; Richard Sigurdson, 'The Left-Legal Critique of the *Charter*:

A Critical Assessment' (1993) 13 *WYAJ* 117; Byron Sheldrick, 'Law, Representation, and Political Activism: Community-Based Practice and the Mobilization of Legal Resources' (1995) 10 *CJLS* 155; and Miriam Smith, 'Social Movements and Equality Seeking: The Case of Gay Liberation in Canada' (1998) 31 *Canadian Journal of Political Science (CJPS)* 285.

32 Seventy-four of the first hundred *Charter* decisions issued by the Supreme Court of Canada dealt with substantive, procedural, or evidentiary rules of crim-inal law. See Frederick L. Morton, Peter H. Russell, and Michael J. Withey, 'The Supreme Court's First One Hundred Charter of Rights Decisions: A Statistical Analysis' (1992) 30 *OHLJ*, 20–1. Glasbeek is withering on the political emptiness of those decisions enhancing accuseds' rights. See 'Forward Ho,' 472–3.

33 See Gwen Brodsky and Shelagh Day, *Canadian Charter Equality Rights for Women: One Step Forward or Two Steps Back* (Ottawa: Canadian Advisory Council on the Status of Women, 1989).

34 It should be noted that courts also dismissed challenges to the Canadian collective bargaining regime mounted by antiunion individuals and by management. See, e.g., *Lavigne v. Ontario Public Service Employees Union*, [1991] 2 S.C.R. 211. George Adams describes the challenges brought by both sides of the labour–management divide as 'spectacularly unsuccessful'. See *Canadian Labour Law*, 2nd ed. (Toronto: Canada Law Books, 1999) 3–67. Adams's review of the case law (at 3–67 to 3–98) amply substantiates this conclusion. For an overview of the mixed success of business interests and economic rights claims, see Richard Bauman, 'Business, Economic Rights, and the Charter,' in David Schneiderman and Kate Sutherland, eds., *Charting the Consequences: The Impact of Charter Rights on Canadian Law and Politics* (Toronto: University of Toronto Press, 1997) 58.

35 See *Canadian Council of Churches v. The Queen*, [1992] 1 S.C.R. 236.

36 See *Andrews v. Law Society of B.C.*, [1989] 1 S.C.R. 143; and factum of LEAF in *Equality and the Charter*, 3.

37 See *R. v. Keegstra*, [1990] 3 S.C.R. 697; *R. v. Butler*, [1991] 1 S.C.R. 452; and *Moge v. Moge*, [1992] 3 S.C.R. 813.

38 I emphatically reject Harry Arthur's claim that when disadvantaged groups win *Charter* claims concerning employment discrimination, they benefit as disadvantaged groups, not 'workers.' See 'The Right to Golf,' in *Labour Law under the Charter* (1988) *QLJ* 23. Mandel's assertion that sex equality litigation produces 'gifts' of 'unambiguous benefit only to women who are not workers' (*Charter of Rights*, 444) is equally myopic and, judging from the surrounding text, tainted with antifeminism. Working-class, working women supported by feminist organizations and intervenors

initiated the legal actions which led to Supreme Court of Canada approval of imposed hiring quotas to remedy systemic employment discrimination (*Action travail des femmes v. C.N.R.*, [1987] 1 S.C.R. 1114); the extension of sexual harassment protection and employer liability under human rights law (*Janzen v. Platy Enterprises*, [1989] 1 S.C.R. 1219 and *Robichaud v. Treasury Board*, [1987] 2 S.C.R. 84); and the legal recognition of pregnancy discrimination as sex discrimination (*Brooks v. Canada Safeway*, [1989] 1 S.C.R. 1252). Perhaps what leads male scholars to consider these landmark decisions of no benefit to women as workers is that male workers do not need such benefits and male-dominated unions have been so slow to bargain for such protections.

39 *Schachter v. Canada*, [1992] 2 S.C.R. 679 defines courts' powers in this regard. *Vriend v. A.G. Alberta*, [1998] 1 S.C.R. 493 represents the most dramatic instance of the judicial vindication of minority rights. Faced with the Alberta government's persistent and overtly discriminatory refusal to extend the protections of statutory human rights protection to lesbians and gay men, the Court read such protection into the province's human rights act. In *Eldridge v. A.G. B.C.*, [1997] 3 S.C.R. 624, the Court ordered the province to pay for sign interpreters for deaf patients seeking medical services covered by the provincial health insurance plan.

40 Contrast, e.g., the non-abstract reasoning of Dickson in *Keegstra*, L'Heureux-Dubé in *R. v. Seaboyer*, [1991] 2 S.C.R. 577; and LaForest and McLachlin in *Norberg v. Wynrib*, [1992] 2 S.C.R. 226, with the liberal abstractions of McLachlin in *Keegstra* and *Seaboyer* and of Sopinka in *Norberg v. Wynrib*.

41 For instance, in the case of *Seaboyer* and *R. v. Daviault*, [1994] 3 S.C.R. 63.

42 Contrast Morton's denunciation of the politicization of scholarship in service of progressive advocacy in 'Charter Revolution,' 641–3 with the trivialization of such scholarship as 'naive,' 'silly,' or 'delusional,' in e.g., Hutchinson and Petter, 'Daydream Believing'; and Bakan, 'Constitutional Interpretation.'

43 See Sherene Razack, *Canadian Feminism and the Law: The Women's Legal Education and Action Fund and the Pursuit of Equality* (Toronto: Second Story Press, 1991) 51–8.

44 See the opinions of LaForest (Lamer, Gonthier, and Major concurring) and of Sopinka in *Egan v. Canada* [1995] 2 S.C.R. 513.

45 See Herman, *Rights of Passage*, 105–6.

46 See, e.g., Karen Selick, 'Rights and Wrongs in the Canadian Charter,' in Peacock, *Rethinking the Constitution*, 103; and Ross Howard, 'Reform's Grassroots Dig in On Tough Ground," *Globe and Mail*, 8 June 1996, A4.

47 See, e.g., Brief by REAL Women to the Legislative Committee on Bill C-49, Minutes of Proceedings and Evidence, May 1992, 2A: 64–81.

48 See McIntyre, 'Backlash against Equality.' On the continuity between the backlash against civil rights in the 1960s and against the modest yield of civil rights by the 1980s, see Patricia Williams, *The Rooster's Egg* (Cambridge: Harvard University Press, 1995) 16–56.

49 For an analysis of the major law school battles, see Bruce Feldthusen, 'The Gender Wars: "Where the Boys Are"' (1990) 4 *Canadian Journal of Women and the Law* 66 and sources cited therein. For feminist analyses of resistance to institutional equity in Political Science departments, see Dorothy Smith, 'Textual Repressions: Hazards for Feminists in the Academy' (1997) 9 *CJWL* 269 (University of Victoria); Haideh Moghissi, 'Racism and Sexism in Academic Practice: A Case Study,' in Haleh Afshar and Mary Maynard, eds., *The Dynamics of Race and Gender* (London: Taylor and Francis, 1994) 222 (Queen's University); and Sheila McIntyre, 'Studied Ignorance and Privileged Innocence: Keeping Equity Academic,' (1999) 12 *CJWL* 147.

50 See, e.g., Mari Matsuda, 'Looking to the Bottom: Critical Legal Studies and Reparations"' (1987) 22 *Harv. C.R.–C.L. L. Rev.* (*HCR-CLLR*) 335; Harlon Dalton, 'The Clouded Prism: Minority Critique of the Critical Studies Movement' (1987) 22 *HCR–CLLR* 435; and Patricia Williams, 'The Pain of Word Bondage' in *The Alchemy of Race and Rights* (Cambridge: Harvard University Press, 1991) 146. There are now three compendious U.S. anthologies of critical race theory in print. See Kimberlé Crenshaw et al., eds., *Critical Race Theory: The Key Writings That Formed the Movement* (New York: New York Press, 1995); Richard Delgado, ed., *Critical Race Theory: The Cutting Edge* (Philadelphia: Temple University Press, 1995); and Adrien Wong, ed., *Critical Race Feminism* (New York: New York University Press, 1997). The first Canadian book advocating rights litigation in support of racial justice is Carol Aylward's *Canadian Critical Race Theory: Racism and the Law* (Halifax: Fernwood Press, 1999).

51 The passage in Hutchinson's *Waiting for Coraf* (at 180 and note 61) is so brief and cryptic that I could not determine whether he cites two critical race scholars in support of his general opposition to rights litigation, or in support of his concession that occasionally rights litigation is strategically defensible. Bakan's book quotes one critical race response to the left critique of rights in support of his acknowledgment that litigating equality rights in particular and discrete contexts may have some positive (as well as negative) effects, particularly for dispossessed groups, and thus may play 'some role, though relatively minor' in struggles to transform the structures and institutions responsible for systemic inequality; *Just Words*, 56, 62. The third reference I found is patronizingly dismissive: see Fudge and Glasbeek, 'Politics of Rights,' 51.

52 The exception is analysis of the comparative economic costs of test case litigation and legislative lobbying. Generalizations are impossible.
53 For instances of containment, see, e.g., Sue Findlay, 'Facing the State: The Politics of the Women's Movement Reconsidered,' in Heather Jon Maroney and Meg Luxton, eds., *Feminism and Political Economy* (Toronto: Methuen, 1987) 31; and Linda Carty and Dionne Brand, '"Visible Minority" Women – A Creation of the Canadian State' (1988) 17, (3) *Resources for Feminist Research* 39. For the most dramatic recent example of bypassing government feminists, recall the efforts of the Trudeau liberals to prevent the Canadian Advisory Council on the Status of Women (CACSW) from holding a scheduled national conference on women and the constitution during the process that culminated in entrenchment of the *Charter*. See Penney Kome, *The Taking of Twenty-Eight* (Toronto: Women's Press, 1983).
54 See Bakan, 'Constitutional Interpretation,' 328.
55 Hutchinson and Petter, 'Daydream Believing,' 385. It should be noted that what provokes Bakan, and Hutchinson and Petter, to such cautions is the liberalism and/or idealism of the male theorists who have made the most extended efforts to articulate principled defences of constitutional judicial review. I object to their extrapolating a denigrating composite portrait of all *Charter* or rights activists from the political blinders of select white, male scholars – as if men remain the measure of all things.
56 Easily the most ill-conceived of these challenges was *R.W.D.S.U. v. Dolphin Delivery*, [1986] 2 S.C.R. 573 which sought to overturn twenty years of common law and statutory doctrine on secondary picketing, and to secure judicial extension of the *Charter* to purely private, commercial conduct without any factual record at all. This allowed the Supreme Court to wax abstract about 'powerful' unions and 'public interest' and, on an obiter dicta basis, to deem constitutional any legislative restrictions on secondary picketing no matter what the facts are. It also allowed judicial antiunionism to play a role in defining the scope of the *Charter*'s application, with adverse consequences to all progressive litigants.
57 See, e.g., Didi Herman, 'Are We Family? Lesbian Rights and Women's Liberation' (1990) 28 *OHLJ* 789; Jody Freeman, 'Defining Family in *Mossop v. D.S.S.*: The Challenge of Anti-Essentialism and Interactive Discrimination for Human Rights Litigation' (1994) 44 *UTLJ* 41; Shelley Gavigan, 'Paradise Lost, Paradox Revisited: The Implications of Familial Ideology for Feminist, Lesbian and Gay Engagement to Law' (1993) 31 *OHLJ* 589.
58 See *Eldridge v. A.G.B.C.* for the Supreme Court's recognition that the

achievement of equality for people with disabilities calls for a conception of discrimination quite different from the focus on wrongful group stereotyping that is central to formalist liberal approaches to discrimination.

59 Twenty-three of LEAF's Supreme Court of Canada facta have been published in *Equality and the Charter: Ten Years of Feminist Advocacy before the Supreme Court of Canada* (Toronto: Emond Montgomery, 1996).

60 Ibid., 49 and 101 for the facta in *Borowski v. The Queen*, [1981] 2 S.C.R. 575 and *Daigle v. Tremblay*, [1989] 2 S.C.R. 530. Also see factum in *Winnipeg Child and Family Services v. G.(D.F.)*, [1997] 3 S.C.R. 925 (copy on file with author).

61 Ibid., 321 for the factum. Decision reported at [1992] 3 S.C.R. 813.

62 Ibid., 469 for the factum. Decision reported at [1996] 2 S.C.R. 27.

63 See ibid. for the facta in *Janzen, Seaboyer, M.(K.) v. M.(H.)*, [1992] 3 S.C.R. 6, *R. v. M.(M.L.)*, [1994] 2 S.C.R. 3, and *R. v. O'Connor*, [1995] 4 S.C.R. 411.

64 *Moge, Norberg v. Wynrib, M.(K.) v. M.(H.)*, and *Janzen*. See also the analysis of this phenomenon by Kate Sutherland: 'The New Equality Paradigm: The Impact of Charter Equality Principles on Private Law Decisions,' in Schneiderman and Sutherland, *Charting the Consequences*, 245.

65 For a striking example of the contrast between substantive and formalist legal reasoning, compare LEAF's factum in *Canadian Council of Churches* (in *Equality and the Charter*, 245) and the reasoning of the unanimous judgment of the Supreme Court.

66 The impact of LEAF's arguments in its first twenty-three Supreme Court appearances can be tracked in *Equality and the Charter*, ibid., which follows the text of each LEAF factum with a summary of the Court's decision including those dicta which endorse or show the influence of LEAF's analysis. By December 2000, twelve additional cases in which LEAF intervened had been decided by the Court. Decisions consistent with the equality claim LEAF's argument supported have been rendered in ten of the twelve decisions. See *R. v. S. (R.D.)*, [1997] 3 S.C.R. 484, *Eldridge v. A.G.B.C.; Winnipeg Child and Family Services; Vriend v. A.G. Alberta; R. v. Ewanchuk*, [1999] 1 S.C.R. 330; *M. v. H.*, [1999] 2 S.C.R. 3; *B.C. v. B.C.G.S.E.U.*, [1999] 3 S.C.R. 3; *N.B. (Minister of Health and Community Services) v. J.G.*, [1999] 3 S.C.R. 46; *R. v. Mills*, [1999] 3 S.C.R. 668; *Blencoe v. B.C. (Human Rights Commission)*, [2000] 2 S.C.R. 307; *R. v. Darroch*, [2000] 2 S.C.R. 443; and *Little Sisters Book and Art Emporium v. Canada (Minister of Justice)*, [2000] 2 S.C.R. 1120.

67 LEAF's imprint is particularly pronounced in *Andrews v. Law Society; Canadian Newspapers v. A.G. Canada*, [1988] 2 S.C.R. 122; *Brooks; Janzen; Butler v. The Queen; Norberg v. Wynrib; Schachter; Moge v. Moge; Conway v. The Queen*, [1993] 2 S.C.R. 872; *M.(K.) v. M.(H.); Eldridge; Vriend; B.C.G.S.E.U.;*

Mills; and *Darroch*. Portions of LEAF's analysis also influenced *R. v. Keegstra* and *Winnipeg Child and Family Services*.

68 The amendments that followed *Seaboyer*, [1991] 2 S.C.R. 577 can be found in sections 273.1, 273.2, 276(1)–(3), and 276.1–276.5 of the Criminal Code; those that followed *O'Connor*, [1995] 4 S.C.R. 411 in section 278.1–278.9 of the Code. Both packages of amendments were challenged by criminal defence counsel as violations of the constitutional fair trial rights of men accused of sexual assault. The Supreme Court dismissed both challenges and upheld the constitutionality of the amendments. See *R. v. Mills* and *R. v. Darroch*. Parliament also amended the *Income Tax Act* after Suzanne Thibaudeau lost her challenge to provisions that tax child support payments as income of a custodial parent while serving as a tax deduction for the payor spouse. In coalition with three other groups, LEAF unsuccessfully intervened in support of Thibaudeau's claim that the old regime discriminated on the basis of sex. Neither LEAF nor its coalition partners played a direct role in the process that led to the new federal amendments after the Supreme Court decision.

69 Ottawa: Information Canada, 1970.

70 For criticisms of the Eurocentrism and the underinclusive and essentialist analysis used in the Report, see Mary Ellen Turpel, 'Patriarchy and Paternalism: The Legacy of the State for First Nations Women' (1993) 6 *CJWL* 174, and Toni Williams, 'Re-Forming "Women's" Truth: A Critique of the *Report of the Royal Commission on the Status of Women in Canada*' (1990) 22 OLR 725.

71 See Susan Boyd and Elizabeth Sheehy, *Canadian Feminist Perspectives on Law: An Annotated Bibliography of Interdisciplinary Writings*, Special Issue of *Resources for Feminist Research*, December 1989 (English-language writing up to 1988); and Josée Bouchard, Susan Boyd, and Elizabeth Sheehy, *Canadian Feminist Literature on Law: An Annotated Bibliography* (Toronto: University of Toronto Press, 1999) (French-language writing 1986–98, English-language writing 1988–98).

72 See analysis and listings, ibid. Later in this subsection, I address the exclusionary construct of 'women' that operated in much feminist legal scholarship authored by privileged white women unmindful of the degree to which race and class privilege flawed their/our analyses.

73 See Christine Boyle, 'Teaching Law as if Women Really Mattered, or, What about the Washrooms?' (1986) 2 *CJWL* 96; Teresa Scassa, 'Violence against Women in Law Schools' (1992) 30 *Alberta Law Review* (*ALR*) 809; and The Chilly Climate Collective, eds., *Breaking Anonymity: The Chilly Climate for*

Women Faculty (Waterloo: Wilfrid Laurier University Press, 1995), seven of whose articles address male backlash against equality activists in Canadian law schools.

74 See, e.g., the differential responses to student complaints of pervasive sexism and of pervasive racism documented in Joan McEwen's *Report in Respect of the Political Science Department at the University of British Columbia*, Vancouver, 15 June 1995; and in Patricia Marchak's partisan account of the controversy: *Racism, Sexism, and the University: The Political Science Affair at the University of British Columbia* (Montreal and Kingston: McGill-Queen's University Press, 1996).

75 See, e.g., the de-raced, classless 'woman' and 'gender' analysis in my own article 'Gender Bias within the Law School: "The Memo" and Its Impact' (1987–8) 2 *CJWL* 362.

76 Most readers of this book will be familiar with the most frequently cited works on this topic, such as those written by Americans Patricia Hill Collins, Kimberlé Crenshaw, Angela Harris, bell hooks, Audre Lorde, Mari Matsuda, Trinh Minh-ha, Chandra Mohanty, Elizabeth Spelman, and Patricia Williams, and by Canadians Marlee Kline, Roxanna Ng, Sherene Razack, and Mary Ellen Turpel. The Canadian contributions that have in every sense of the term moved me the most are Himani Bannerji, *Thinking Through: Essays on Feminism, Marxism and Anti-Racism* (Toronto: Women's Press, 1995); Patricia Monture-Angus, *Thunder in My Soul: A Mohawk Woman Speaks* (Halifax: Fernwood Press, 1995); Toni Williams, 'Re-Forming "Women's" Truth'; and volumes 20 (no. 3/4) and 22 (no. 3/4) of *Resources for Feminist Research*. I would also strongly recommend the article by Maivan Lâm quoted at the start of this article and Toni Morrison's *Race-ing Justice: En-gendering Power* (New York: Pantheon, 1992).

77 See Note, 'Rape, Racism and the Law' (1983) 6 *Harvard Women's Law Journal (HWLJ)* 103; Angela Harris, 'Race and Essentialism in Feminist Legal Theory' (1990) 42 *Stanford Law Review (SLR)* 581; Patricia Monture-Okanee, 'The Violence We Women Do: A First Nations View,' in Constance Backhouse and David Flaherty, eds., *Challenging Times: The Women's Movement in Canada and the United States* (Montreal and Kingston: McGill-Queen's University Press, 1992) 193; and Mary Eaton, 'Abuse by Any Other Name: Feminism, Difference, and Intralesbian Violence,' in Martha Fineman and Roxanne Mykitiuk, eds., *The Public Nature of Private Violence: The Discovery of Domestic Abuse* (New York: Routledge, 1994) 57.

78 For an insightful account of this cross-fertilization and its decline as feminist knowledge production became institutionalized within universities,

see Dorothy Smith, 'Contradictions for Feminist Social Scientists,' in *Writing the Social: Critique, Theory, and Investigations* (Toronto: University of Toronto Press, 1999) 15.

79 See n29 and n30 supra. For written accounts of some of my university activism and of legislative lobbying in which I have participated, see McIntyre, 'Gender Bias within the Law School'; and McIntyre, 'Redefining Reformism: The Consultations that Shaped Bill C-49,' in Julian V. Roberts and Renate M. Mohr, eds., *Confronting Sexual Assault: A Decade of Legal and Social Change* (Toronto: University of Toronto Press, 1994) 293.

80 See quotation by Maivan Lâm prefacing this chap., supra n1.

81 By 'qualified' I mean provisions which condition redress on a finding that harassment occurred on more than a single occasion and/or which imagine some harassment is 'welcome,' and/or which relax employers' liability for harassing misconduct by their employees. Each of these erosions of protection is present in Ontario's *Human Rights Code*, R.S.O. 1990, c. H-19 as amended, ss. 10 and 41(2).

82 *Criminal Law Amendment Act*, S.C. 1980–81–82, c. 25. For a thorough analysis of the ideologies underlying the pre-1983 law, the political trade-offs embedded in the 1983 package and their political risks, see Maria Løs, 'The Struggle to Redefine Rape in the 1980s,' in Roberts and Mohr, eds., *Confronting Sexual Assault*, 20.

83 See Christine Boyle, *Sexual Assault* (Toronto: Carswell, 1984).

84 See Catharine MacKinnon, 'Feminist Approaches to Sexual Assault in Canada and the United States: A Brief Retrospective,' in Backhouse and Flaherty, eds., *Challenging Times*, 186.

85 See Marilyn MacCrimmon, 'Trial by Ordeal' (1996) 1 *Criminal Law Review* (*CLR*) 31.

86 See Carolyn Enns, Cheryl McNeilly, Julie Corkery, and Mary Gilbert, 'The Debate about Delayed Memories of Child Sexual Abuse: A Feminist Perspective' (1995) 23 *The Counselling Psychologist* 185; Katherine Kelly, '"You Must Be Crazy if You Think You Were Raped": Reflections on the Use of Complainants' Personal and Therapy Records in Sexual Assault Trials' (1997) 9 *CJWL* 187; and Margo Rivera, ed., *Fragment by Fragment: Feminist Perspectives on Memory and Child Sexual Abuse* (Charlottetown: Gynergy Books, 1999).

87 For the best accounts of the radicalism of the movement to end male violence against women and of the mechanisms used to contain it, see Lee Lakeman, *99 Federal Steps: Toward an End to Violence against Women* (Toronto: NAC, 1993); Gillian Walker, *Family, Violence and the Women's Movement: The Conceptual Politics of Struggle* (Toronto: University of

Toronto Press, 1990); Nancy Matthews, *Confronting Rape: The Feminist Anti-Rape Movement and the State* (New York: Routledge, 1994); and Louise Armstrong, *Rocking the Cradle of Sexual Politics* (Don Mills: Addison-Wesley, 1994).

88 See, e.g., Harris, 'Race and Essentialism,' text and notes at 596–601; Dorothy Roberts, 'Crime, Race, and Reproduction,' (1993) 67 *Tulane Law Review* 107; Nell Irwin Painter, 'Hill, Thomas, and the Use of Racial Stereotype,' in Morrison, ed., *Race-ing Justice*, 200; Debra Lewis, 'Coercive Sterilization: Its Eugenical Underpinnings and Current Manifestations,' MA thesis, Carleton University, 1996; and Hudson Blaine, 'Scientific Racism: The Politics of Tests, Race and Genetics' (1995) 25 *The Black Scholar* 3.

89 See Assembly of First Nations, *Breaking the Silence: An Interpretive Study of Residential School Impact and Healing as Illustrated by the Stories of First Nations Individuals* (1994); Hamilton and Sinclair, Report of the Aboriginal Justice Inquiry of Manitoba, vol. 1, *The Justice System and Aboriginal People* (1991) 478–82.

90 One of the factors leading to the Manitoba Justice Inquiry, ibid., was the non-prosecution for nearly two decades of four white men known within the community of Le Pas, Manitoba, to have raped and murdered Helen Betty Osborne, a First Nations woman. For analyses of discriminatory treatment experienced by Aboriginal women who report their sexual assaults to police, see Margo Nightengale, 'Judicial Attitudes and Differential Treatment: Native Women in Sexual Assault Cases' (1993) 23 *OLR* 71; and Teressa Nahanee, 'Sexual Assault of Inuit Females: A Comment on "Cultural Bias,"' in Roberts and Mohr, eds., *Confronting Sexual Assault*, 192.

91 See Catharine MacKinnon, 'Rape, Genocide, and Women's Human Rights' (1994) 17 *HWLJ* 5.

92 See Dick Sobsey, 'Patterns of Sexual Abuse and Assault' (1991) 9 *Sexuality and Disability* 243; and Shirley Masuda with Jillian Riddington, *Meeting Our Needs: An Access Manual for Transition Houses* (Toronto: DisAbled Women's Network, 1992).

93 See, e.g., Lewis, *Coercive Sterilization*; Angus McLaren, *Our Own Master Race: Eugenics in Canada, 1885–1945* (Toronto: McClelland and Stewart, 1990); *Muir v. Alberta* (1996), 132 DLR (4th) 695 (Q.B.); and *Re Eve*, [1986] 2 S.C.R. 388.

94 See Karen Busby, 'The Rape Crisis Backlash: Raising the Spectre of False Rape Allegations' (unpublished ms. on file with author) on Clayton Ruby's misuse of police unfounding rates and suspect 'recantation' scholarship in his oral and written argument in the Supreme Court of Canada appeal of *A. (L.L.) v. B.(A.)*, [1995] 4 S.C.R. 536; and see Cristin Schmitz,

'"Whack" sexual assault complainant at preliminary hearing' *The Lawyers Weekly*, 27 May 1988, 22 for Michael Edelson's infamous promotion of pursuit of court-ordered disclosure of complainants' personal records as prelude to the 'whack' which might persuade her to withdraw charges.
94 David Paccioco, 'Challenges for Cause in Jury Selection after *R. v. Parks*: Practicalities and Limitations," paper presented at conference on Recent Issues and Developments in Criminal Law, sponsored by the Canadian Bar Association, 11 February 1995.
96 To this end, Keith Wright, a criminal lawyer defending an accused rapist, subpoenaed Metro Toronto Action Committee on Public Violence against Women and Children (METRAC), the Barbara Schlifer Commemorative Clinic, the Women's College Hospital Sexual Assault Care Centre, St Joseph's Hospital Women's Health Care Centre, Education Wife Assault, Toronto Rape Crisis Centre, and LEAF in February 1995.
97 Although manifested differently, state-authorized, and ideologically rationalized interferences with the family formation of women who are not white, not heterosexual, not middle class, and not physically and mentally 'normal' have been constant vehicles and indicia of distinguishing privileged from non-privileged women since at least the nineteenth century. Eugenic science and laws have tended to target and conflate actual or ascribed physical imperfection, mental defectiveness, promiscuity, and criminality for detection and eradication, thereby linking racist, classist, heterosexist, and ablist ideology in a single genocidal tool. Aside from overtly eugenic interventions, curbs on the reproductive generation of 'Otherness' have been tailored to the situated vulnerabilities of those constructed as less than fully human.

The continuity of Aboriginal community has been forcibly disrupted by means of, e.g., the residential school system, the legal and cultural exile of Aboriginal women who married non-Aboriginal men, the displacement of Aboriginal children from their families and communities into white adoptive families, and the relegation of Aboriginal communities to reservations lacking adequate sewage service, housing, and natural resources to sustain subsistence and protection from environmental toxins; and over-jailing of Aboriginal women and men during their peak reproductive years.

Constraints on black reproductivity and generational continuity have ranged from slave rape, sale of slave-born children, and prohibitions on slave marriage to antimiscegenation laws to involuntary sterilization and drug testing of black women to conditioning welfare entitlement on forced Norplant 'treatment' to prenatal drug testing followed by coerced choice between abortion or imprisonment for drug use and/or child neglect, to overincarceration of black males during peak reproductive years to police shootings of black people. Human genome research continues to search for a 'crime' gene that may legitimate race-based state surveillance, preventive medical 'treatment' or eugenic intervention. Racist science rationalizes racist eugenics and systemic educational and economic deprivation of the means by which to sustain healthy and intact black families.

Impediments to gay and lesbian family formation include: legal bars on marriage, adoption, foster parenting, and retention of child custody, denial to lesbians of alternative insemination, and to gays and lesbians of 'spousal' or 'family' employee benefits, denial of the full protection of human rights laws which might make existing as self-respecting lesbian and gay couples or families less socially and economically costly, and less physically, even fatally, dangerous. The continuing search for the 'gay' (and 'crime') gene may well be a precursor to prenatal genetic screening and counselling to promote the abortion of homosexually inclined fetuses.

Actual or deemed physical and mental 'defectives' have been prevented from marrying, forcibly sterilized, segregated in chronic care institutions, denied sex education, and, in the case of deaf children, denied access to the most effective means of communicating and socializing with one another as well as with hearing people. Prenatal genetic screening overtly facilitates and legitimates the abortion of imperfect fetuses. As more markers of actual or potential congenital infirmity are identified, eugenic cleansing will escalate.

98 Bernice Johnson Reagon, 'Coalition Politics: Turning the Century,' in Barbara Smith, ed., *Home Girls: A Black Feminist Anthology* (New York: Kitchen Table Press, 1983) 356.
99 See quotation by Patricia Hill Collins, *Black Feminist Thought* at note 28 above.
100 See *Seaboyer* factum in LEAF, *Equality and the Charter*, 173.
101 Early in the majority judgment is the subheading, 'Relevant Legislation' under which appears the text of the two *Criminal Code* provisions Seaboyer challenged as well as ss. 7, 11(d), and 52 of the *Charter*. Section 15 is not on the list of relevant provisions. Section 15 is mentioned in exactly two sentences of the lengthy majority judgment. In one passage, it is acknowledged as an 'interest' subsumed within s. 7; in the other it is a passing reference in the s. 1 analysis.
102 McIntyre, 'Redefining Reformism,' 293.
103 See *R. v. Daviault*. The subsequent amendments, *An Act to Amend the*

98 Sheila McIntyre

     Criminal Code (dangerous intoxication) S.C. 1995 c. 32, may now be found in s. 33.1 of the *Criminal Code*.
104 *R. v. O'Connor* and *A. (L.L.) v. B. (A.)*.
105 See *O'Connor* factum in LEAF, *Equality and the Charter*, 427. Text of Sharon McIvor's argument on file with author.
106 [1997] 1 S.C.R. 80.
107 See MacCrimmon, 'Trial by Ordeal,' and Karen Busby, 'Discriminatory Uses of Personal Records in Sexual Violence Cases' (1997) 9 *CJWL* 148.
108 For approximately a year prior to the release of the *O'Connor* decision, the federal Justice Department had been preparing legislation to curtail defence lawyers' access to complainants' personal records. The process included several consultations with a variety of groupings of criminal and constitutional law scholars, defence and Crown lawyers, feminist lawyers who represent sexual assault survivors, and feminists involved in the post-*Seaboyer* coalition. Initially, in the wake of the *O'Connor* decision, the department's lawyers watered down the draft legislation. A coalition of feminist legal activists helped conceive the equality-driven legislation that overrode *O'Connor*. The result is Bill C-46, *An Act to amend the Criminal Code* (production of records in sexual offence proceedings) S.C. 1997, c. 30, s. 1. Bill C-46 survived constitutional challenge. See *R. v. Mills*.
109 Historically, the consultations have been held immediately before the annual meeting of the National Action Committee on the Status of Women, which spares some organizations the cost of flying delegates to NAC.
110 Along with lawyers representing LEAF, the National Association of Women and the Law or other national or front-line organizations, there were usually no more than ten lawyers. I consider this six-to-one ratio of non-lawyers to lawyers ideal.

PART TWO
Equality Strategies

CHAPTER THREE

Women's (In)Equality before and after the *Charter*[1]

Diana Majury

Equality is an amorphous concept – slippery, uncertain, flexible, dynamic, by definition comparative, by implication restrained. These attributes are at the same time the potential and the limitations of equality, and the reason equality is controversial, both as a goal and as strategy for women.

Equality has been, and continues to be, a cornerstone and watchword of feminist struggles, particularly in the context of the law. But, all the while, there has been ongoing disagreement among feminists about the appropriateness and effectiveness of the focus on equality. Even among feminists who have adopted equality, as either a means or an end (or both), there is disagreement on what equality means and how we might attain it.

As women, we live with and have internalized inequality on many levels and in many different forms, and we experience these inequalities differently. Many, perhaps most, women experience inequalities that are rooted in multiple sites of oppression – sex, race, class, sexual identity, disability, and/or age among them – and that are mediated by multiple sites of domination. While the inequalities are interactive and complex, feminist legal equality strategies have been, and often still are, simplistic and one-dimensional, focusing on gender at the expense of other categories, as if gender is the only, or at least an isolatable, discrete, source of inequality for women.[2] This restrictive focus is in part a function of how our law and legal system work and in part a function of equality as a concept. The tension between the complexity of gender inequality as experienced by women and the oversimplification involved in legal approaches to equality raises fundamental questions about our continuing commitment to working in and with law and to working with equality as a primary principle.

Systemic inequality is so entrenched in our institutions, and in our ways of thinking, so deeply rooted and so complex, that it is difficult to imagine our way out of inequality. The difficulty is compounded when one considers trying to employ the very institutions in which systemic inequalities are so firmly entrenched – law in the context of this discussion – to assist us in pursuing our imaginings of equality. Nonetheless, despite the manifest dangers that inhere in the resort to law, feminists continue to struggle in law, and with law, to try to reduce women's inequalities and promote equality. The dangers are not unique to law; fighting for social change in any arena of power is necessarily dangerous and risky. But the analysis of arenas of power has shifted so that most of us no longer see them as so formidable or so powerful. Using law against itself, seeing law simultaneously as tool, as foe, and as focus for change, demystifying law as institution, and recognizing law as presenting multiple sites of struggle rather than a solid one-dimensional monolith may by now be postmodern truisms, but these understandings provide grounding for contemporary feminist legal equality struggles, as in the past the grounding may have been provided by the liberal promise of equal opportunity.

While I think we need to approach both law and equality with a great deal of scepticism, I also think that we need to engage fully and actively with both of them. It would be foolish to ignore or boycott law or concede the legal terrain; law simply provides a powerful forum for struggle.

For this chapter, I was asked to provide a brief background to section 15 of the *Canadian Charter of Rights and Freedoms*[3] and a brief discussion of some of the issues that have arisen in the courts' applications of section 15. The focus on section 15 is because this provision has become a primary symbol of, and vehicle for, feminist legal equality struggles. I am not in this chapter providing a comprehensive analysis of equality under the *Charter*, nor even a cursory review of section 15 decisions. I am more interested in raising questions and concerns about the meaning(s) of equality under the *Charter* so that we can think strategically and critically about our engagement with law in this context.

A huge number of vastly important equality issues are being addressed under section 15 of the *Charter*; a huge number of issues cannot be addressed under the *Charter* because they do not fit within its narrow confines; and a huge number of equality issues have yet to be raised under section 15 of the *Charter*. In what follows, I refer to only a few of this multitude and variety of issues, because of time and space limitations, as well as the limitations of my own perspective. I write this piece as a white, non-disabled, Christian-raised, middle-class, anglophone lesbian. There is no doubt that all of these pieces of myself inform what issues and inequalities I even recognize as such and which of those I choose to discuss. One of the problems of equality is that, despite its mythic promise of universal application, our individual and collective understandings of equality are only ever partial and circumscribed. The critiques of universality as invoking false and oppressive generalizations that perpetuate dominance apply to equality in very similar ways. However, to me the promise of equality lies not in its universality, but rather in its potential for particularity and in its uncertainty, openness, and fluidity. It is a promise that can be furthered when these qualities are directed to the elimination of dominance and subordination, and when they are informed by an understanding of underlying, intersecting inequalities and the power dynamics that maintain those inequalities. This to me is the possibility of equality.

(In)Equality before the *Charter*: The Historical Backdrop

Equality has been, and remains, a key component of liberal political theory. Individual equality, defined in terms of equality of access, equal opportunity, and the right to equal treatment, is a cornerstone of the liberal concept of democracy. The unstated norm underlying this notion of equality is that of the prototypical person, the person who is from the dominant groups in all aspects of himself, that is the oft-referred to white, heterosexual, non-disabled, Christian, middle-class, male (hereinafter referred to as the prototype). It is he who represents the goal (members of non-dominant groups are assumed, or expected, to aspire to be him) and the standard by which the right to equality is measured (to qualify for equality, members of non-dominant groups have been required to prove they are just like him). Under this liberal model, equality action is directed towards the removal of overt barriers and the elimination of differential treatment; the rest is left up to the individual – to prove herself equal.

The image of the 'level playing field' has dominated liberal equality discourse, with its implicit assumption that we are all into 'sport' – that we all should and do want to play a game under the rules created by the prototype in his own image to showcase his particular skills and reflecting his particular understanding of the world. In this context, members of oppressed groups (women, racialized people, people with disabilities, Aboriginal peoples, poor and working-class people, lesbians and gays, transgendered people) have been expected to direct their equality-seeking activities towards proving that they are the same as members of the dominant group. To qualify for equal treatment, one had to demonstrate that there were no substantive differences between oneself and the prototype, and thereby one had the right to be treated the same. This model of equality is clearly and unapologetically one of assimilation.

Oppressed groups have participated, to varying degrees, in this assimilationist model. White women have a long history of trying to fit within the liberal equality paradigm, of trying to prove ourselves just like, that is equal to, the prototype. There have always been some members of each oppressed group who have resisted the assimilationist model and demanded equality on their own terms and in their own image; some groups have been more sceptical than others about the potential for liberation under the rubric of equality; and some have rejected the language and concept of equality altogether.[4] For those who are members of more than one oppressed group, it has been harder and more complex to try to prove they are equal. The less one is like the prototype, and the more ways in which one's 'differences' are apparent, the more difficult it is to prove that those differences do not matter, and probably, as well, the less one is likely to be willing to deny or disown one's 'differences.' It may be for this reason that those who are oppressed on compounded grounds have often had the most clear and radical insights into the limitations of the liberal model of equality.

Historically, women have been regarded by western culture as inherently different from men, in terms of biology, psychology, and culture. Women were clearly not seen as like the prototype; that is, women were clearly not the same as men, and hence there was no obligation to treat them as equals. Traditional liberal notions of equality generally did not include women. The barriers and restrictions placed on women in all aspects of their lives were seen as consistent with liberal philosophy. In nineteenth- and early twentieth-century Canada, women's legal status was very much one of inferiority.[5] Women were almost totally excluded from participation in the public sphere; women were unable to vote, hold public office, sit on juries, or practise most trades and professions. Women were ghettoized and underpaid in terms of paid labour; women's work in the home was devalued to the point of rendering that work invisible. Married women were by law clearly and in every way subservient to their husbands; they were unable to own or dispose of property in their own right, or to enter into contracts, or to retain their nationality or domicile. While women generally had the work and responsibility of child care, fathers had legal authority over their children and exclusive right to custody of their children on separation of the parents.

Women were regarded as intellectually and physically inferior to men and in need of protection in their essential roles as child-bearers and child-rearers. This prevailing view ignored the realities of working-class women and women of colour, most of whom worked at poorly paid menial jobs under extremely poor working conditions, in addition to caring for their own children and domestic work in their own homes. Cloaked in the rhetoric of protection and deference, women were kept in a state of inequality in which their domestic and reproductive labour (and their paid labour for those who had it), their sexuality, and their economic and physical security were largely under male control.

Over the past century, the impediments and double standards imposed by law on women, in both the so-called public and private spheres, have largely been eliminated.[6] Up to, and even shortly after, the advent of the *Charter*, white women's fight for legal equality in Canada focused primarily on the attainment of full legal 'personhood,' that is, on obtaining the rights and privileges accorded to men under law. In law reform efforts and litigation, women's fight for equality was, for a long time, largely a fight for inclusion. It was premised on the notion that if women were just allowed in, we could prove that we are just as good as men. This model of equality, now referred to as formal equality, reflected the liberal notion of a level playing field.[7] The formal equality model was advocated, sometimes successfully, but often unsuccessfully, in the early equality cases at the beginning of this century,[8] as well as in the more recent cases under the *Canadian Bill of Rights* (discussed below). These fights for inclusion were largely waged by women who, with the exception of their gender, were from the dominant groups.[9] The feminist prototype became that of the white, Christian, non-disabled, middle-class, heterosexual woman. Many of the same assumptions and expectations that underlay the male prototype were unthinkingly transposed by white feminists to create the feminist prototype. Women of colour, Aboriginal women, non-Christian women, women with disabilities, lesbians, low income and poor women have been disregarded, not just by prototypical males, but by prototypical feminists as well. Multiple oppressions were ignored, as were the women from these communities who often were resisting and fighting for change at more fundamental levels than is possible under a formal equality model.

The Canadian Bill of Rights

In 1960, the *Canadian Bill of Rights*,[10] in some ways the precursor of the *Charter*, was passed. The *Bill of Rights* applies[11] to all federal laws to ensure that they do not 'abrogate, abridge or infringe' the rights and freedoms recognized in the *Bill*. Section 1 of the *Bill* provides, in part:

1 It is hereby recognized and declared that in Canada there have existed and shall continue to exist without discrimination by reason of race, national origin, colour, religion or sex, the following human rights and fundamental freedoms, namely, ...
    (b) the right of the individual to equality before the law and the protection of the law;

Despite the *Bill of Rights'* strong, and, from its wording, unequivocal statement of a pre-existing right to equality, the equality guaranteed thereby was, in application, so circumscribed and limited as to be virtually meaningless. The view, put forward in the committee discussion of section 1(b), prior to the passage of the *Bill*, by then Justice Minister Davie Fulton, that 'I do feel that the expression ... would not be interpreted by the courts so as to say we are making men and women equal, because men and women are not equal: they are different'[12] accurately foreshadowed the treatment that this equality guarantee was to receive at the hands of the Supreme Court of Canada.

By the 1980s, fewer than ten cases involving this equality section under the *Canadian Bill of Rights* had been decided by the Supreme Court of Canada. Two of these cases dealt with sex equality; two dealt with race equality; and five cases dealt with non-enumerated grounds, mostly in the context of criminal or quasi-criminal law.[13] The first Supreme Court of Canada decision on section 1(b) of the *Bill of Rights*, *R. v. Drybones*,[14] offered some promise that the equality guarantee might have a positive impact for oppressed groups in Canada.[15] However, *Drybones* was the only case in which the Supreme Court of Canada found the equality provision applied to the legislation under attack. In all of the other cases, the Court held that the law in question did not abrogate, abridge, or infringe the equality provision.

In *Drybones*, the accused, a First Nations man, was charged with being 'intoxicated off a reserve, contrary to section 94(b) of the *Indian Act*.' In a six-to-three decision, Justice Ritchie held that the *Bill of Rights* constituted a declaration of fundamental rights with the effect of rendering inoperative federal laws which conflicted with those rights. He interpreted section 1(b) to mean: 'No individual or group of individuals is to be treated more harshly than another under that law.'[16] Section 94(b) of the *Indian Act*, in making it 'an offence punishable at law on account of race, for a person to do something which all Canadians who are not members of that race may do with impunity,'[17] was found to infringe the equality provision of the *Bill of Rights*, and was thereby rendered inoperative. Recognizing the implications that such an application of the Bill of Rights might have (and should have had) for the *Indian Act* as a whole, and anticipating his own judgment in the *Lavell and Bedard* case two years later, Ritchie was careful to point out that, in his opinion, 'the same considerations do not by any means apply to all the provisions of the *Indian Act*.'[18]

The first *Bill of Rights* sex equality decision by the Supreme Court of Canada also involved a challenge to the *Indian Act*.[19] Two First Nations women, Jeannette Lavell and Yvonne Bedard, in two separate actions, argued that section 12(1)(b) of the *Indian Act* conflicted with section 1(b) of the *Bill of Rights*, and accordingly, was inoperative. Their cases were heard together at the Supreme Court of Canada, and a single decision was rendered which upheld section 12(1)(b) of the *Indian Act*. Under this provision of the *Indian Act*, a First Nations woman who married a non-Indian man lost[20] her Indian status and was struck from the Band list; conversely the non-Indian wife of a First Nations man gained Indian status as a result of the marriage. The children and further descendants of First Nations' women who were denied their Indian 'status' on this basis were, by extension, also denied their status.[21] In a five-to-four decision, the Court held that the distinction between the treatment of First Nations women and First Nations men did not constitute inequality under the Bill of Rights.

Writing for the majority, Justice Ritchie looked to old rule of law principles and defined equality before the law in the narrowest terms as meaning 'equality in the administration or application of the law by the law enforcement authorities and the ordinary Courts of the land.'[22] According to Ritchie, the *Indian Act* was 'a structure created by Parliament for the internal administration of the life of Indians on reserves and their entitlement to the use and benefit of Crown [sic] lands.'[23] According to Justice Ritchie, section 12(1)(b) was an essential component of this paternalistic structure. One could not, therefore, tinker with a piece of the *Act* for fear that the whole structure would come tumbling down, that the whole *Act* would be recognized as discriminatory. Justice Ritchie then distinguished his earlier decision in the *Drybones* case on the basis that it dealt with the 'behaviour of Indians *off* a reserve,' as opposed to 'the internal regulation of the lives of Indians *on* reserves.'[24]

The second and only other *Bill of Rights* sex equality case decided by the Supreme Court of Canada was *Bliss v. Attorney-General of Canada*,[25] decided in 1978, five years after *Lavell* and *Bedard*. The decision was again written by Justice Ritchie, but this time it was a unanimous decision of the seven-man Court. Stella Bliss, who had just had a baby, challenged the section of the *Unemployment Insurance Act* that disentitled a pregnant woman and new mother from regular unemployment insurance benefits for the period during which maternity benefits were available. However, to qualify for maternity benefits, the woman needed to have at least ten weeks of insured earnings whereas regular unemployment insurance benefits required only eight weeks of insured earnings. Bliss met the eight-week but not the ten-week requirement. In fact, she met all of the requirements for regular unemployment insurance benefits except that she fell within the period of pregnancy-based disentitlement. She argued that this disentitlement constituted sex discrimination resulting in denial of equality before the law. And she lost.

Applying the same narrow, rule-of-law definition of equality before the law as was applied in *Lavell* and *Bedard*, the Court held that 'the enforcement of the limitation ... does not involve denial of equality of treatment in the administration and enforcement of the law before the ordinary Courts of the land.'[26] The Court distinguished between qualifications for entitlement to benefits (*Bliss*) and differential harsh treatment (*Drybones*), as if denial of a benefit solely because a woman is pregnant does not constitute differential harsh treatment. However, the Court did not rely exclusively on the benefit/disadvantage distinction, their fallback position was to blame nature. In one of those supremely quotable displays of judicial sexism, Justice Ritchie stated: 'Any inequality between the sexes in this area is not created by legislation but by nature.'[27] He then proceeded to express his agreement with the following statement from Justice Pratte in the Federal Court of Appeal decision in this case: 'If s. 46 treats unemployed pregnant women differently from other unemployed persons, be they male or female, it is, it seems to me, because they are pregnant and not because they are women.'[28] Here we have a variation on the theme of the gender-neutral pregnant persons approach to the problem that was so popular in the United States at this same time[29] – just pretend that pregnancy is a factor unrelated to gender and your sex discrimination problems disappear. Such was the Supreme Court of Canada's response to sex discrimination.

The Advent of the *Charter*

This was the legacy of the equality decisions under the *Bill of Rights* – racism, sexism, and a lack of even the most basic understanding of discrimination and inequality that, even in its time, seemed incomprehensible. With this dismal history, it may be hard to imagine how and why feminists pursued the inclusion of equality rights provisions in the *Charter of Rights and Freedoms*. Certainly, the focus on the *Charter* and the hope placed in the entrenchment of equality rights were not shared by all, or even most, feminists in Canada. Many perceived the *Charter* project as hopeless or useless; some saw it as counterproductive; some saw it as co-optation. But others, unwilling to concede the territory to inequality, were determined to ensure that the *Charter* wording made it impossible to repeat the atrocities that had been inflicted under the *Bill of Rights*.

The initial wording proposed for section 15(1), the primary equality rights provision of the *Charter*, was exactly the wording of section 1 of the *Bill of Rights*. Feminists fought hard to have that wording expanded to avoid the restrictive interpretation of equality imposed by the Supreme Court of Canada on the *Bill of Rights*. In fact, one can see in the wording of section 15(1) the explicit attempt to address the decisions in *Lavell* and *Bedard* and *Bliss* and foreclose the possibility of their repetition:

15(1) Every individual is equal before and under the law and has the right to the equal protection and equal benefit of the law without discrimination based on race, national or ethnic origin, colour, religion, sex, age or mental or physical disability.

If one did not know the background of the *Bill of Rights* cases, this wording would no doubt appear redundant and excessive. However, in the context of those cases, the apparent excess makes perfect sense.

In a bid further to protect against the possibility of a restrictive interpretation of equality under section 15, feminists insisted on the inclusion of an additional equality provision directed exclusively to sex equality.[30] This was enacted in the *Charter* as section 28:

> 28 Notwithstanding anything in this *Charter*, the rights and freedoms referred to in it are guaranteed equally to male and female persons.

Although I understand and sympathize with the desperate desire to ensure that sexual equality would be taken seriously by the courts, I think this privileging of sex equality was itself a function of the privilege of those who were lobbying for it and constitutes an inappropriate and divisive singling out of one form of inequality.[31]

There was a flurry of academic writing at the time the *Charter* was enacted and shortly thereafter on the question of what, if anything, section 28 actually added in terms of sex equality protection. While section 28 was of huge symbolic significance at the time, and functioned as a major platform for organizing feminist support for the *Charter*, I think the sceptics have been shown to have been the more accurate in their assessment of the impact of section 28. Section 28 does not seem to have made any difference in terms of sex equality decisions under the *Charter* and is, at this point, rarely even referred to.

The feminists who advocated and worked so hard to have the *Charter* contain the strongest guarantees of sex equality possible were largely white, heterosexual, non-disabled, anglophone, middle- and upper-class women.[32] Many of them were lawyers, and as such no doubt had a tendency to overinvest in the law and legal routes as tools for social change. While this is a tendency about which we need to be vigilant, as similarly, the focus on legal strategies needs to be continuously questioned and challenged, it is, I think, simplistic to eschew law and law reform altogether. Whether or not the *Charter* is now considered beneficial for women, the political momentum in 1982 was such that the *Charter* was going to happen, with or without feminist input. Feminists did participate in the *Charter*-creating process, and their efforts made the *Charter* a better and more promising tool for oppressed groups. However, the *Charter* is by no means a feminist creation, and it would be unfair and inappropriate to blame those feminists, who fought for something better, for the shortcomings of the *Charter*, in its wording or in its application.[33]

Debates over whether the *Charter* is a good thing for oppressed groups or is simply another tool of domination were waged in the period when the *Charter* was negotiated and have continued relatively unabated to this day.[34] However interesting and important these discussions may be on a theoretical level, on the pragmatic level, they are somewhat anachronistic. Whatever else it may or may not be, the bottom line is that the *Charter* is. We cannot simply ignore it; and it seems to me that we would be foolish to concede the language of equality to those who seek to use it to maintain the status quo or even to roll back existing gains. Equality can be used to promote inequality, as easily as to address inequality. The challenge for feminist advocates and lawyers is to try to make the *Charter* more than a guarantee of the equal opportunity to participate in a prototype-defined world. And it is a challenge. The liberal roots of equality that tie it to an individualistic theory of rights and an assimilationist model of formal equality make this a difficult task. But the language of equality has the advantage of allowing us to focus on group-based inequality, on the specific, concrete, and often intersectional manifestations of women's oppression and on the systemic and intractable nature of that oppression. Equality to me is not a goal; I have no equality formula to offer; I do not know what equality would look like if we had it. Equality to me is a strategy and a process that we can use to try to address existing inequalities; the *Charter* equality provisions provide one vehicle through which we can make those arguments.[35]

(In)Equality after the *Charter*

The Andrews Case

The first Supreme Court of Canada decision applying section 15 of the *Charter* was *Law Society of British Columbia v. Andrews*,[36] decided in 1989, seven years after the advent of the *Charter*, four years after section 15 came into effect.[37] This case marked a clear turn away from the formal model of equality and a significant move towards the recognition of inequality as the starting point for analysis of the meaning(s) of equality.

Prior to this decision, most Canadian courts, in applying section 15 of the *Charter*, had tended to follow the equality jurisprudence of the United States in which equality was interpreted in the Aristotelian sense to require only that 'likes be treated alike' and 'unalikes be treated unalike.' The test for determining 'likeness' became known as the similarly situated test – persons who were similarly situated should be similarly treated. In applying this test, U.S. courts spent a huge amount of time and energy trying to determine whether a particular individual or group was similarly situated to the dominant group and, if so, what similar treatment might look like in the particular circumstances. In gender terms, this required women to try to prove that they were just like men in order to qualify for the same treatment as men. This was largely the substance of equality litigation under the similarly situated test; this was assimilation writ large.[38]

In the *Andrews* case, Mark Andrews and his co-claimant, Elizabeth Kinersly, were successful in their claim that the requirement of Canadian citizenship for admission to the bar of British Columbia contravened the equality guarantee of section 15 of the *Charter*. Mark Andrews, a British citizen, and Elizabeth Kinersly, a U.S. citizen, were both permanent residents in Canada and met all of the requirements for admission to the practice of law except that of Canadian citizenship. Although citizenship is not expressly included in section 15 as a prohibited ground of discrimination, the Court held that it is included as a ground analogous to the express grounds.[39] Non-citizens were found to fall within the type of 'discrete and insular minority' that section 15 was designed to protect, that is, 'those groups who suffer social, political and legal disadvantage in our society,'[40] a determination to be made by looking at the social context, not just the law being challenged.[41] These have become key words and concepts in section 15 jurisprudence, providing an important focus for the meaning of equality under the *Charter*, a focus on inequality, oppressed groups, and social context.

However, the wording of the test enunciated in *Andrews* is not without problems. 'Disadvantage' has become the primary word used to denote inequality. But, as First Nations scholar and activist Patricia Monture has explained, it is a word that is itself exceedingly problematic. Monture rejects the description of oppressed groups as disadvantaged:

> Generically I am speaking about racism and sexism and classism and all of the other isms of how individuals who fit those stereotypical classifications get qualified as disadvantaged. We are only disadvantaged if you are using a White middle class yardstick ... Disadvantage is a nice, soft comfortable word to describe dispossession, to describe a situation of force whereby our very existence, our histories are erased continuously right before our eyes. Words like disadvantage conceal racism.[42]

The characterization of the inequality as 'disadvantage' is from the perspective of the dominant group; from the perspective of the subordinated group it is oppression. The elision from oppression to disadvantage masks the harm, the animus, the systemic nature of the inequality. Hester Lessard, in her article on the decisions of Madam Justice Wilson, makes a similar critique of the term 'disadvantage' when she argues that 'we need to examine the cultural norms embedded in the concept of disadvantage which is increasingly presented as the benchmark of a social equality approach.'[43] Lessard goes on to raise the concern that what she calls the social equality model may rely on a single and dominant notion of social prosperity that is similarly, if less overtly, assimilationist as the formal equality model. These critiques of the language enshrined in the *Charter* and in *Charter* equality jurisprudence give rise to fundamental concerns about the potential of the *Charter* to facilitate social change – are the apparent shifts in the understanding of equality reflected in *Andrews* really shifts only on an abstract or linguistic level? Is equality forever trapped in a comparative assimilationist model, or is it capable of breaking free of dominant constructs, bringing oppressed people with it? The *Andrews* decision offers the hope of liberation and, at the same time, raises the fear that we will be unable or unwilling to move beyond assimilation.

Justice McIntyre, in a lengthy discussion of the meaning of equality, endorsed by the majority of the court in *Andrews*, firmly and unequivocally rejected the treating likes alike approach to equality. He recognized that such a test, applied literally, 'could be used to justify the Nuremberg laws of Adolf Hitler [in that s]imilar treatment was contemplated for all Jews'; or to justify the separate but equal doctrine of racial segregation in the United States; or to support the circular logic of the *Bliss* decision in Canada.[44] Justice McIntyre stated:

> [The] mere equality of application to similarly situated groups or individuals does not afford a realistic test for violation of equality rights. For, as has been said, a bad law will not be saved merely because it operates equally upon those to whom it has application. Nor will a law necessarily be bad because it makes distinctions ... Consideration must be given to the content of the law, to its purpose, and its impact upon those to whom it applies, and also upon those whom it excludes from its application.[45]

This was a much celebrated move by the Supreme Court of Canada and signalled the potential for section 15 to move beyond the assimilationist model of formal equality. However, even at the time of the *Andrews* decision, I feared that all may not be as positive as these words might indicate;[46] now as the section 15 jurisprudence develops, my fears increase. While the Court did reject the similarly situated test as a section 15 formula for determining the application of 'equality,' the actual result in the case seemed very much one of treating likes alike. From the limited information available in the *Andrews* decision, Mark Andrews and Elizabeth Kinersly seem very much 'like' the dominant image of both 'lawyer' and 'Canadian citizen.' It may be because of this 'likeness' that the Court was able to recognize that it was unfair to deny them the right to practise law accorded to Canadian citizens. It may be much harder to recognize an inequality as such when the claimants are less like the dominant group. It may be much easier to give up the treating likes alike approach in theory than it is to eliminate the unconscious application of the approach in practice.

While the *Andrews* decision was definitely a major step forward for equality in Canada, at the same time the seeds of possible future problems were sown. The characterization of the issue, by Justice McIntyre, as one pertaining to 'irrelevant personal difference'[47] and 'personal characteristics' has become a defining feature of the section 15 test of discrimination:

> ... discrimination may be described as a distinction, whether intentional or not but based on grounds relating to personal characteristics of the individual or group, which has the effect of imposing burdens, obligations or disadvantages on such individual or group not imposed on others, or which withholds or limits access to opportunities, benefits and advantages available to other members of society. Distinctions based on personal characteristics attributed to an individual solely on the basis of association with a group will rarely escape the charge of discrimination, while those based on an individual's merits and capacities will rarely be so classed.[48]

The recurring references to 'personal characteristics' and 'irrelevant personal differences' seem to me extremely unfortunate. When I try to apply them to myself as a white, non-disabled, middle-class, Christian, lesbian, I would say that in our highly gendered, lesbian-hating society, neither my gender nor my sexuality are irrelevant, either to me or to society. The point is that these characteristics are seen as relevant; they have been used as criteria for imposing burdens and denying benefits; they have been socially constructed as relevant, and that means they are relevant. The oppression comes from the characterization my being a woman and my being a lesbian as 'differences' from a perspective of dominance; and both of these 'differences' are considered as a relevant basis for differential treatment.[49] And, while both my gender and my sexuality are at one level deeply personal, in the larger social context neither is personal, that is, they are not really, or necessarily, about me. This is one of the ways discrimination works; it is, at the same time, all about the person being discriminated against and not really about that person at all.

Conversely, as a member of the dominant group with respect to race and disability, I have tended to view my race and absence of disability as irrelevant, that is, I take them for granted and do not really think about them. I accept the privileges and benefits they confer without recognizing them as such. Similar to the critique of disadvantage, the characterization of the focus of oppression as relating to 'irrelevant personal differences' comes from a position of dominance and privilege. The failure to incorporate notions of dominance into the definition of discrimination depoliticizes and individualizes the equality project. It becomes about mischaracterizations and disadvantage rather than oppression and dominance.

To move from personal characteristics to group-based claims, one has to read in the stereotypes that attach to members of that group.[50] Thus, the test itself perpetuates the stereotypes being challenged. Without apparently being aware of this problem of invoking the stereotype to challenge the stereotype, Justice McIntyre in *Andrews* seems to have been concerned with stereotyping as the primary issue of discrimination. Discrimination, according to Justice McIntyre, is about the attribution of personal characteristics based solely on group membership. But this notion of stereotyping as inaccurate attribution is only one of the problems of discrimination. Stereotyping involves much more than the question of its accuracy on either an individual or group basis. The larger and more systemic problem is the devaluation of those 'characteristics' traditionally assumed to belong to an oppressed group. Thus, consistent with the treating likes alike and unalikes unalike approach, the inequalities experienced by those who do fulfil the group-based stereotype are less likely to be recognized as such. Again, this is more about assimilation than it is about equality. Similarly, in asserting that distinctions based on an individual's merits and capacities would rarely be classed as discrimination, Justice McIntyre fails to recognize the systemically discriminatory nature of these concepts. 'Merit' and 'capacity,' defined in terms of the prototype model, have consistently been used to exclude those who do not fit that model – women, members of racialized groups, people with disabilities.[51] The less one fits the model, the less likely one is to be considered to have the required 'merit' or 'capacity.'

After *Andrews*

The Supreme Court of Canada section 15 equality decision that immediately followed *Andrews, R. v. Turpin*,[52] clarified and strengthened the (in)equality analysis in *Andrews*. According to Madam Justice Wilson in *Turpin*, 'A finding that there is discrimination will, I think in most but perhaps not all cases, necessarily entail a search for disadvantage that exists apart from and independent of the particular legal distinction being challenged.'[53] The decision in *Turpin* re-enforced the optimism with which *Andrews* had been greeted by oppressed groups[54] and their advocates. However, since the decision in *Turpin*, the meanings and direction of equality under the *Charter* have become increasingly uncertain and scattered. David Lepofsky has described the judicial approach to equality rights as a fast-moving accelerating roller-coaster.[55] He describes *Andrews* and *Turpin* as representing the promising heights of section 15 jurisprudence, which were followed by a dramatic plunge by the Supreme Court of Canada, particularly in their decisions upholding mandatory retirement.

I really like the image of the roller-coaster and the sense of risk and danger that it invokes. However, even with all of its ups and downs and sharp turns, I think that the analogy is still too linear and confined to accurately reflect *Charter* equality decisions. The decisions are all over the place and even to discuss them in terms of trends or directions is to impose an order that, to my mind, simply is not there. This makes it very difficult to talk about the cases and what is currently happening with equality under the *Charter*;[56] to focus on one or two cases is misleading; to generalize about anything is a problem. I am not sure how different the results actually are than they would have been under the application of the formal equality model, but the analysis can no longer be simplistically framed in terms of whether the assessment of likeness was accurate or framed as a critique of the likeness approach. Having moved away from a formulaic approach to equality, the Court has left behind the traditional framework for discussing the issues. While we have guidance provided by *Andrews* and *Turpin*, we do not have an accepted language of equality that would provide the base from which to analyse and critique what is happening. If we did a case-by-case assessment to determine how women and other oppressed groups are faring under the *Charter*, the picture presented would be bleak. And perhaps this is the answer – section 15 is not working to improve the situation of oppressed groups. However, I am stubborn and not willing to concede. There is still potential for strong and radical section 15 arguments to be made. The courts and judges are divided in their approach and analysis. It is, at this point, not possible to come up with a general picture or to describe in a coherent way what has happened or to predict the course the equality provisions might take and how effective they will be. There is still hope.

But some things can be said; some things have changed. In the early days of the *Charter*, the majority of the sex discrimination arguments under the *Charter* were put forward by men, as was the case with the equal protection clause under the U.S. *Constitution*.[57] Recently, the sex equality arguments are more frequently being made by women. However, something that makes an assessment of the effectiveness of section 15 for women even more difficult is that many of the *Charter* cases that most affect women and raise the most serious equality issues do not come forward as section 15 equality claims. Abortion,[58] pornography,[59] the relevance of the past sexual history of the woman who was raped in a sexual assault trial,[60] access to women's therapy and counselling records,[61] the incarceration of a pregnant woman in a 'treatment program' in order to protect her fetus[62] are all issues that have been decided in cases in which section 15 was not the central *Charter* provision, and the primary focus was not necessarily on women. It may be that equality arguments are not always presented in these types of cases and section 15 may or may not provide a basis for the decision; nonetheless, these cases are among the most significant sex equality decisions to date. Women and women's organizations need to be constantly vigilant about the cases that are being brought forward in which women have an interest that is not being represented. Section 15 does provide an important base from which women can demand to be heard by the court; and so far the courts have generally allowed women's groups to intervene to make their section 15 arguments.[63]

Section 15 provides the entry point through which a women-centred, intersectional analysis and argument can be made. It is, however, clear that the courts have not always, or not even usually, understood the arguments being put forward by women's organizations. In saying this, I am not equating understanding with agreeing with or supporting the section 15 sex equality analysis being presented to them (that would be the next step, hopefully). I am saying that, at a much more basic level, often the courts just do not seem to get it. Women's inequalities and the discrimination that is so interwoven into women's daily lives are largely unrecognizable and incomprehensible to those in dominant positions. It is the privilege of not knowing and the, often unconscious, resistance to finding out that are at stake here. Section 15 offers a place from which that privilege can be challenged and for this reason alone, it is an important tool. But whether the section 15 promise of equality will mean anything more than an opportunity to voice one's oppression very much remains to be seen.

I am not going to conclude with a review of recent cases because there are too many to canvass and it would feel too idiosyncratic to focus on one or two. I want simply to offer some of my thoughts on (in)equality under the *Charter*; I want to raise some concerns and questions (also idiosyncratic, but hopefully more interestingly so) and talk about a few cases, not as representative but as raising issues, and either offering promise or provoking fear. I do not offer a bigger picture because at the moment I cannot find one.

In terms of concerns, I want to come back to the issue of stereotyping that was central in McIntyre's discussion of discrimination in *Andrews*. The irony of the focus on stereotyping as the evil of discrimination is that frequently equality decisions explicitly, if unconsciously, reinforce and perpetuate stereotypes. Justice Linden, in his dissent at the Federal Court of Appeal in *Egan and Nesbit*, one of a number of gay 'spousal' benefit cases, alluded to this problem when he said: 'It would be paradoxical indeed if a decision under s. 15 were itself to be based on prejudice and stereotyping.'[64] The reliance on stereotypes in the name of equality is a central paradox of equality and one of the serious risks involved in raising or responding to a s. 15 argument. Stereotypes are inevitably a part of the analysis of discrimination, but unless the stereotypes are being critically unpacked, they are being perpetuated.

With respect to stereotypes and prejudices as the foundation of section 15 decisions, I think age discrimination cases produce some of the more overt examples, possibly because age discrimination is so unacknowledged and/or so accepted. It is seen as 'natural' and right to make distinctions based on age. The majority decision in *McKinney*,[65] one of the Supreme Court of Canada decisions upholding mandatory retirement, invokes, both implicitly and explicitly, the stereotyped correlation between aging and declining ability, accompanied by the paternalism of allegedly saving people over 65 from the embarrassment of performance reviews. At the other end of the age spectrum is the decision in *Lister and Lister v. The Queen*,[66] in which the Tax Court of Canada rejected a section 15 challenge to the refusal of a GST tax credit to persons under the age of nineteen. The court held that people under the age of nineteen are not members of a discrete and insular minority suffering stereotyping, historical disadvantage, or vulnerability to social and political pressure. In both cases, the court seems oblivious to the lived experiences of the members of the age groups involved and seems unwilling even to contemplate the possibility of discrimination as a factor.

The same point can be made about disability discrimination. For example, Justice McLachlin rejected out of hand the equality claim of Sue Rodriguez, saying: 'I am of the view that this is not at base a case about discrimination under s. 15 of the *Canadian Charter of Rights and Freedoms*, and that to treat it as such may deflect the equality jurisprudence from the true focus of s. 15 – "to remedy or prevent discrimination against groups subject to stereotyping, historical disadvantage and political and social prejudice in Canadian society."'[67] Sue Rodriguez, a woman with amyotrophic lateral sclerosis who was seeking the right to terminate her own life under conditions of her own choosing, met all of these criteria. The issues presented by this case are complex, and I do not think that there is a simple disability-positive conclusion, as is reflected in the fact that there were disability rights groups presenting arguments on both sides of the case. However, even though there may not be a clear-cut equality-based answer, the case is clearly about discrimination and equality rights. Whatever the results of the analysis, Sue Rodriguez's situation could only be fully understood in the context of an analysis of discrimination and equality. Yet this is what Justice McLachlin failed to recognize when she refused to apply an equality analysis to the complex issues before her. While there have been disability cases where the Supreme Court of Canada accepted that section 15 should be considered,[68] Rodriguez stands as an important reminder that disability is frequently not recognized as an issue of (in)equality.

Discrimination against people with disabilities and the systemic 'ablism' of all of our institutions and structures are so engrained, so understood as natural, that most of us are unable even to contemplate that they might be discriminatory. In the words of Simone de Beauvoir,[69] 'one of the ruses of oppression is to camouflage itself behind a natural situation since, after all, one cannot revolt against nature.'[70]

The *Rodriguez* decision also raises the problem that, despite the fact that the *Bliss* decision has been overruled by the Supreme Court of Canada, the logic of *Bliss* is still with us. In asking the question 'whether a claim by the terminally ill who cannot commit suicide without assistance can be supported on the ground that s. 241(b) [of the Criminal Code] discriminates against all disabled persons who are unable to commit suicide without assistance,' Justice Sopinka is asking a question akin to that which derailed *Bliss* – whether a claim by a pregnant woman can be supported as sex discrimination because the claim does not pertain to all women. The fact that the discrimination does not, or may not, apply, or apply in the same way, to all members of the oppressed group does not negate its discriminatory impact on a subset of that oppressed group.[71]

Other *Bliss*-type arguments are similarly resurfacing. The argument that only members of the oppressed group can be subject to disadvantageous treatment in order for the treatment to constitute discrimination is related to the *Bliss* argument that the discrimination has to affect all members of the oppressed group. The recurrence of this 'only the oppressed group' argument is truly surprising given that, even long before *Andrews*, the disparate impact on an oppressed group of an apparently neutral rule was clearly recognized in Canada as discrimination. Yet, the Federal Court of Appeal in 1994 in *Thibaudeau v. R.*[72] rejected the plaintiff's claim of sex discrimination based on the fact that the *Income Tax Act* provisions, requiring the inclusion of child support payments in taxable income, have an adverse impact on a small number of custodial fathers, as well as on custodial mothers who are the bulk of the people affected by this requirement.

A recent Supreme Court of Canada decision offers some hope that the courts are moving away from this myopic notion that because a gendered inequality does not affect only women or all women it is not sex discrimination. They may be returning to disparate impact with a more sophisticated analysis. In *British Columbia Government and Service Employees' Union v. Government of British Columbia*,[73] the Court used section 15 *Charter* analysis to eliminate the judicially created distinction between direct and indirect discrimination under human rights law, so as to allow for a more in-depth and critical analysis of job requirements that have the effect of keeping disproportionate numbers of women out of that form of employment. In this case it was women being excluded from being forest firefighters based on an aerobic standard that most women would have trouble attaining. In the absence of proof that this standard was reasonably necessary as a means to identify those who could perform the tasks of a firefighter safely and efficiently, the Court held that the standard did not constitute a bona fide occupational requirement. However, for some reason, the courts seem to be more receptive to recognizing the gendered nature and impact of job criteria than they have been in recognizing other gendered criteria such as that at issue in *Thibaudeau*. *Bliss* logic may resurface intermittently depending on the nature of the claim being made or the context of the discrimination being challenged.

The *Bliss* logic was employed in reverse to defeat the claim in the *Egan* case. Because an oppressed group (lesbians and gays) was a subset of a larger group (non-spouses) that experienced the same disadvantageous treatment (denial of access to the Old Age Security spousal allowance), the majority of the Supreme Court of Canada held that the oppressed group was not discriminated against by that denial. The Court held that lesbians and gays were simply treated the same as other non-spouses, that is the same as 'all sorts of other couples [sic] living together such as brothers and sisters or other relatives, regardless of sex, and others who are not related.'[74] The Federal Court of Appeal in this same case had explored this issue even further and more egregiously. Arguments by the plaintiffs distinguishing themselves from other non-spouses on the basis of their similarity to spouses[75] were rejected by the majority of the Federal Court of Appeal because such arguments invoked the similarly situated test repudiated in *Andrews*. This was a literal application of *Andrews* that totally undermined the intent of *Andrews*. *Andrews* did not transform the similarly situated test into a test of disentitlement, but simply recognized that the similarly situated test was not 'a realistic test for the violation of equality rights.'[76] The issues and questions are more complex and require deeper examination than a simple determination of similarity or not; in failing to look beyond the question of similarity, the majority of the Federal Court of Appeal did exactly what the court in *Andrews* had recognized as inadequate. The majority at the Supreme Court of Canada did not reproduce the illogic of similarity constituting the basis to deny an equality claim; instead they rejected the similarity argument, that is, they held that the distinction between heterosexual and gay and lesbian couples was relevant, on the basis of the erroneous assumption that [most] lesbians and gays do not and cannot have children.

Attempts to preserve reproduction (notwithstanding the copious evidence to the contrary) and marriage as exclusively heterosexual domains are at the root of the powerful and emphatic resistance to many of the equality claims that have been brought by lesbians and gays. Even when, as in *M. v. H.*,[77] the Court applied section 15 favourably to a lesbian claim, they were very careful to limit and circumscribe the decision to protect the illusion of heterosexual exclusivity with respect to reproduction and marriage. So in *M. v. H.*, while the court was willing to impose 'spousal' support obligations pursuant to the breakup of a lesbian relationship,[78] they were at great pains to repeat, at length, that this decision did not have any impact on marriage or even have any necessary consequences for the meaning of 'spouse' in any other context. Provincial and federal government responses to this case have certainly borne this out, with most governments going through incredible contortions to preserve the territory of marriage exclusively for heterosexuals.[79]

It is by now, and finally, accepted that sexual orientation is an analogous ground under section 15 of the *Charter*. It has been a long and difficult struggle for inclusion, and it remains to be seen how circumscribed the inclusion will be. The first time the Supreme Court of Canada dealt with a sexual orientation equality claim on its merits, the claim was rejected. Prior to that, a number of claims were rejected because, according to the Court, the applicant had failed to choose 'the right ground.'[80] It was a shell game, being played always at the expense of the claimants. *Vriend v. Alberta*[81] is the first time that the Supreme Court of Canada upheld a sexual orientation equality claim on its merits. The Court held that the omission of sexual orientation from the prohibited grounds in Alberta's human rights legislation was an unjustified breach of lesbian/gay section 15 equality rights. While this is an extremely important decision and a major victory in the face of vehement resistance from the Alberta government, it is to some extent an abstract victory. The decision recognizes the right of lesbians and gays not to be discriminated against, but it does not say anything about how the prohibition against discrimination is to be interpreted and applied. And it is in the application that many equality rights are severely circumscribed.

To some extent the reluctance of the courts to fully endorse and apply equality rights seems to be related to the overtness of the discrimination being challenged, coupled with the Court's discomfort, and unwillingness, to provide a remedy. It is also about the problems of compound discrimination and of multiple grounds of discrimination. In this regard, claimants are required, under section 15, to fit their experience(s) into the appropriate ground, that is pick the right shell or shells in the shell game; they have to present their experience(s) in terms of the shells in a way that does not allow their experience(s) to fall through the spaces between the shells; at the same time, they want to present their experience(s) under the different equality headings so that they are seen as integrally related, as a compound whole, not separate (un)grounded parts. It is a difficult, if not impossible task, for the claimants and a task that carries with it the risk of shattering their sense of self. And, even if claimants are able to present themselves and their claims in an integrated and interconnected way, the Court may simply pull them back apart, dissect them, and leave them in pieces.

Madam Justice L'Heureux-Dubé has for some time, although without success, been trying to get the Court to put an end to the shell game by adopting a more flexible and contextualized approach to equality that focuses less on the categories of discrimination and more on the discrimination experienced. Her approach moves away from the notion of grounds as discrete and severable boxes into which the claimant must contort her claim to an analysis in which social context is of prime importance and intersectionality is recognized and understood as creating potentially endless combinations and permutations of discrimination.

The Nova Scotia Court of Appeal decision in the *Sparks*[82] case offers some limited hope on the issue of intersectionality. In this case, an African-Canadian single mother on social assistance successfully challenged the reduced eviction notice requirements for public housing tenants on the basis of race, sex, and income. The court did not seem to have been overwhelmed by the different grounds, or to have felt obliged to pick a single ground as the 'real' ground, or, in confusion, to reject them all. However, the decision did not discuss the compound and interrelated nature of these oppressions. I am left wondering whether the judges were able to see Irma Sparks as a whole person or whether she was, for them, simply her discriminated-against parts.

Conclusion

Having broken free from the confines of the formal equality model according to which likes are to be treated alike, equality under the *Charter* has become an even more amorphous and uncertain concept.

Andrews, the first and most significant section 15 equality decision from the Supreme Court of Canada to date, offered a great deal of promise with respect to the direction and meaning(s) of equality, and the potential for improvements in the lives of oppressed people. At the same time, the *Andrews* formulation of equality contained the seeds of its own limitations and inadequacies. It is impossible to summarize where we are with 'equality,' in this country, at this time; we are everywhere and we are nowhere. The equality analysis is shifting and changing, such that both between and within decisions there are contradictions and inconsistencies. In many judgments the differences between dissent and majority, and even concurring, opinions are vast. They are often worlds apart in terms of approach and analysis, as well as result. In most cases I find the divergences disturbing, mostly because the results have not been good for women, and the predominant analysis is one that clearly rejects or fails to understand a systemic inequality analysis.

In its 1999 decision in *Law v. Canada*,[83] the Supreme Court of Canada went back to equality basics in an apparent attempt to extricate itself from the jurisprudential equality morass it had spawned and to reunite the Court under a single approach to section 15. In this case, a thirty-year-old, non-disabled woman without dependent children challenged the denial of survivor's benefits under the Canadian Pension Plan, arguing that this denial constituted age discrimination. Her claim was rejected by a unanimous Court, and most of the decision is devoted to setting down guidelines for the application of section 15. The focus is on a contextual and purposive analysis of section 15 and the concept of human dignity figures heavily and problematically in the Court's understanding of equality. The Court in *Law* draws extensively from *Andrews* and rearticulates much of what was said in that first Supreme Court equality decision. With some refinements and revisions, *Law* is largely a restatement of *Andrews*, with the same promise and the same limitations.

It would appear that the Court considered *Law* to be clear-cut, an easy case, and seized the opportunity of a non-contentious outcome to come to agreement on the basic principles that underlie section 15. But, of course, therein lies the problem – it is easy to agree on principles in the abstract or in the context of what is perceived to be a clear-cut case. It is in the hard cases, the ones that challenge dominant values or that raise the spectre of significant public expenditure or that demand fundamental realignment or rethinking of existing structures that the disagreements will arise. It is in the application to hard cases that shared principles become fragmented and the morass resurfaces. We can already see the fissures starting in the decision in *Corbière v. Canada*[86] released shortly after *Law*. Madam Justice L'Heureux-Dubé, in her concurring judgment in *Corbière*, tried yet again to move the Court to adopt a more flexible and contextualized approach that would be more responsive to intersectional claims of discrimination. But the majority rejected this approach and opted to decide the case on 'simpler grounds.' Although in *Corbière* the different approaches did not lead to different results, it would appear that the principled agreement in *Law* is abstract and tenuous. We may have a shared commitment to equality, but we do not have a shared understanding of what equality means, and we do not have a shared commitment to the elimination of inequality.

The equality issues being presented to the courts are complex and full of contradictions and arise in the context of deeply entrenched, widespread, and diverse inequalities. This raises the inevitable question of whether the legal forum, which is a place where issues tend to be simplified and where 'answers' are required, is an appropriate place to 'resolve' equality issues. My response to this question is that there is no place that is inappropriate for addressing equality issues; what happens to and with equality in the courts affects how equality issues are raised and fought in other forums; and vice versa – what happens on the streets, in the classroom, in the legislature, in the workplace, in the home, affects what happens in the court room. There is no right or best place to advocate or adjudicate equality. Equality is being negotiated, contested, defined, adjudicated – everywhere, all of the time.

Notes

1 This chapter was written for this book in 1995 and was revised in 2000. A lot has happened under s. 15 of the *Charter* in those intervening years. There have been a lot of cases that have invoked s. 15 of the *Charter*, and the courts' interpretation and application of s. 15 have shifted and changed dramatically from case to case and over time. I only make brief reference to some of the significant recent cases. Nonetheless, the dilemmas, questions, shortcomings, and possibilities that I raise in this chapter remain germane to current discussion of s. 15. The chapter draws from work that I have done previously on equality under the *Charter*. See 'Introduction,' *Report on the Statute Audit Project* (Toronto: Charter of Rights Educational Fund, 1985) I.20–I.36 (it was my work as director of this project that led me on to further work on the meaning(s) of equality

and inequality); 'Strategizing (In)Equality' (1987) 3 *Wisconsin Women's Law Journal* 169; 'Equality and Discrimination according to the Supreme Court of Canada' (1991) 2 *Canadian Journal of Women and the Law* (*CJWL*) 407.
2 For further discussion of this issue, see Elizabeth Spelman, *Inessential Woman: Problems of Exclusion in Feminist Thought* (Boston: Beacon Press, 1998); Nitya Iyer, 'Disappearing Women: Racial Minority Women in Human Rights Cases' (1993) 6 *CJWL* 25; Emily Carasco, 'A Case Of Double Jeopardy: Race and Gender' (1993) 6 *CJWL* 142; and Kimberly Crenshaw, 'Demarginalizing the Intersection of Race and Sex: A Black Feminist Critique of Antidiscrimination Doctrine, Feminist Theory and Antiracist Politics' (1989) *University of Chicago Legal Forum* 139.
3 Part I of the *Constitution Act, 1982*, being Schedule B of the *Canada Act 1982* (U.K.) 1982, c. 11 (hereinafter referred to as the *Charter*).
4 See for example, Mary Ellen Turpel, 'Aboriginal Peoples and the Canadian *Charter*: Interpretive Monopolies, Cultural Differences,' in Richard Devlin, ed., *Canadian Perspectives on Legal Theory* (Toronto: Emond Montgomery, 1991) 503.
5 See Constance Backhouse, *Petticoats and Prejudice: Women and Law in Nineteenth Century Canada* (Toronto: Osgoode Society, 1991); see also Mary Eberts, 'The Rights of Women,' in R. St. J. Macdonald and J.P. Humphrey, eds., *The Practice of Freedom* (Toronto: Butterworths, 1979).
6 See Susan Altschul and Christine Caron, 'Chronology of Some Legal Landmarks in the History of Canadian Women' (1975) 21 *McGill Law Journal* 467; see also T. Brettel Dawson, *Relating to Law: A Chronology of Women and Law in Canada* (North York, ON: Captus Press, 1990).
7 For a discussion of the concept of formal versus substantive equality, see Shelagh Day, 'The Process of Achieving Equality,' in Ryszard Cholewinski, ed., *Human Rights in Canada* (Ottawa: Human Rights Research and Education Centre, 1986) 83–115.
8 See, e.g., the famous persons case, *Edwards et al. v. Attorney General for Canada*, [1930] A.C. 124, in which five women challenged the exclusion of white women from sitting in the Senate; and *Re Mabel French* (1912), 1 D.L.R. 80 (N.B.S.C.); and *Dame Langstaff v. the Bar of the Province of Quebec* (1915), 46 Que. S.C. 131, in which white women challenged their exclusion from the practise of law.
9 The cases of *Attorney General of Canada v. Lavell; Isaac v. Bedard* (1973), 38 D.L.R. (3d) 481 (S.C.C.) brought by First Nations women are a notable exception to the dominance of white women as sex equality litigators in the pre-*Charter* cases.
10 *Canadian Bill of Rights*, R.S.C. 1970, Appendix III; hereinafter referred to as the *Bill of Rights*.

Women's (In)Equality before and after the *Charter*   127

11 I use the present tense in discussing the *Canadian Bill of Rights* because, even though, in practical terms, it has been superseded by the *Charter*, the *Bill of Rights* has not been repealed and continues as a valid, if obsolete, piece of federal legislation.
12 As quoted by Mary Eberts, 'Women and Constitutional Renewal,' in Audrey Doerr and Micheline Carrier, eds., *Women and the Constitution* (Ottawa: Canadian Advisory Council on the Status of Women, 1981) 10.
13 These were *R. v. Smythe* (1971), 19 D.L.R. (3d) 480 (S.C.C.), in which a hybrid offence under the *Income Tax Act* was challenged because of the harsher penalty if the charge proceeded by way of indictment; *Curr v. The Queen* (1972), 26 D.L.R. (3d) 603 (S.C.C.), in which the elimination of the right to refuse to provide a breathalyser sample was challenged; *R. v. Burnshine* (1974), 44 D.L.R. (3d) 584 (S.C.C.), in which regional disparities in provisions providing for the sentencing of young offenders were challenged; *Attorney-General of Canada v. Canard et al.* (1975), 52 D.L.R. (3d) 548 (S.C.C.), in which provisions under the *Indian Act* relating to the estates of deceased people of the First Nations were challenged; *Prata v. Ministry of Manpower and Immigration* (1975), 52 D.L.R. (3d) 383 (S.C.C.), in which the removal of the discretion to stay or quash a deportation order was challenged; and *Morgentaler v. The Queen* (1975), 53 D.L.R. (3d) 161 (S.C.C.) in which the system of preferred indictments was challenged because it denied the accused the opportunity of a preliminary inquiry.
14 (1969), 9 D.L.R. 473 (S.C.C.).
15 As I write this I am struck with horror by the potential parallel with the *Charter* – that is, that the first Supreme Court of Canada equality decision, or more accurately the first few decisions, under the *Charter*, showed lots of promise for oppressed peoples (see discussion infra) but that promise is being eroded by the courts through subsequent decisions. With the *Bill of Rights* the promise was immediately reneged. It is still early in *Charter* equality jurisprudence, and the meanings of *Charter* equality keep shifting. It is too early to give up on the *Charter* as a potential means to address inequalities. However, I fear that equality under the *Charter* may ultimately fare no better than equality under the *Bill of Rights*.
16 *Drybones*, 484.
17 Ibid., 486.
18 Ibid.
19 See *Lavell* and *Bedard*. Even though the case involved First Nations women fighting to retain their Indian status, it contains no discussion of racial discrimination. The interactive compound mix of race and sex was ignored and, in the face of the glaring significance of race, the case was decided exclusively on the basis of sex discrimination.

20 The Court refers to the claimants as having 'relinquished their status as Indians'; ibid., 485, thereby implying a degree of voluntariness and responsibility that stands in stark contrast to the reality of these women having had their status, and with it their right to live on a reserve, taken away from them by government fiat.
21 After a successful complaint against the Canadian government brought to the U.N. Human Rights Committee by Sandra Lovelace, as well as extensive and persistent activism by First Nations women across Canada, this situation has to some extent been rectified. However, reverberations from this egregious act continue to disrupt and divide First Nations communities. See Janet Silman, ed., *Enough Is Enough: Aboriginal Women Speak Out* (Toronto: Women's Press, 1987).
22 *Lavell* and *Bedard*, 495.
23 Ibid.
24 Ibid., 498–9.
25 (1978), 92 D.L.R. (3d) 417 (S.C.C.). *Bliss* was eventually overruled in 1989 in a human rights decision of the Supreme Court of Canada, *Brooks v. Canada Safeway Ltd.*, [1989] 1 S.C.R. 1219.
26 *Bliss*, 423.
27 Ibid., 422.
28 Ibid.
29 See Herma Hill Kay, 'Equality and Difference: The Case of Pregnancy' (1984) 1 *Berkeley Women's Law Journal* 1; and Wendy Williams, 'Equality's Riddle: Pregnancy and the Equal Treatment / Special Treatment Debate,' (1984–5) 13 *New York University Review of Law and Social Change* 325.
30 See Penny Kome, *The Taking of Twenty-Eight: Women Challenge the Constitution* (Toronto: Women's Press, 1983).
31 This is a view taken in hindsight as I have come to understand sex (in)equality in much more complex ways and come to recognize its connection and interconnection with other forms of oppression. Although I was not actively involved in the feminist negotiations around the *Charter*, I fully supported the efforts of my feminist colleagues, including the campaign for the inclusion of section 28 of the *Charter*.
32 See Sherene Razack, *Canadian Feminism and the Law: The Women's Education and Action Fund and the Pursuit of Equality* (Toronto: Second Story Press, 1991).
33 There is a belief held by some law reform advocates that if we just get the wording of legislation right, we will have solved the problem we are trying to address. This myth is tempting because it offers the possibility of actually effecting immediate and concrete positive change. However, to

subscribe to this myth is to overinvest in law and to ignore the reality of law and laws as social constructs mediated in the world by existing hierarchies, power dynamics, and systemic inequalities.

34 For an excellent discussion of the different perspectives on the role of the *Charter* in the context of social change, as well as the history of the *Charter*, see Radha Jhappan, '*Charter* Politics and the Judiciary,' in *Canadian Politics in the 21st Century*, 5th ed.; Michael Whittington and Glen Williams, eds. (Scarborough, ON: Nelson, Canada, 2000) 217–49. For a critique of the focus on equality, see Radha Jhappan, 'The Equality Pit or the Rehabilitation of Justice' in this volume.

35 For a fuller discussion of this approach, see my 'Strategizing (In)Equality.'

36 [1989] 1 S.C.R. 143.

37 Section 32(2) of the *Charter* delayed the implementation of section 15 for three years. The stated rationale for this moratorium on equality was to give the federal and provincial governments time to bring their legislation and policies into compliance with section 15. Not surprisingly, most governments ended up spending those three years desperately trying to catch up with the *Charter* provisions that were already in force, and spent very little, if any, time even thinking about section 15.

38 While exceedingly problematic in its assumptions and conception, this model of equality did allow for some progress for some women in the United States, and in Canada as well. Catharine MacKinnon makes this point: 'Its guiding impulse is: we're as good as you. Anything you can do, we can do. Just get out of the way. I have to confess a sincere affection for this approach. It has gotten women some access to employment and education, the public pursuits, including academic, professional, and blue-collar work; the military; and more than nominal access to athletics. It has moved to change the dead ends that were all we were seen as good for and has altered what passed for women's lack of physical training, which was really serious training in passivity and enforced weakness. It makes you want to cry sometimes to know that it has been a mission for many women just to be permitted to do the work of this society, to have the dignity of doing jobs a lot of other people don't even want to do' (notes omitted); 'Difference and Dominance: on Sex Discrimination,' in *Feminism Unmodified: Discourses on Life and Law* (Cambridge, MA: Harvard University Press, 1987) 35. What MacKinnon says here in relation to gender has been true for other oppressed groups as well. The doing of jobs that other people do not want to do has often been the only employment option for women and men who are disabled, immigrant, or from a racialized group. The work that racialized and immigrant women have been permitted to do is often

the work in the home that white women do not want to do. See Chrystos's powerful poem on this subject, 'You Can't Get Good Help These Daze,' in *Not Vanishing* (Vancouver: Press Gang, 1988) 2.

39 Unlike most human rights legislation in Canada, in which the lists of prohibited grounds are considered to be exhaustive (i.e., your claim must fit within one of the listed grounds), the wording of s. 15 has been interpreted to allow the argument that a ground of discrimination not expressly listed in s. 15 should be included because it is similar to the grounds listed. These grounds, incorporated into the *Charter* by way of analogy, are referred to as analogous grounds. The openness in s. 15 to analogous grounds is critically important; it is, e.g., the basis on which 'sexual orientation' has finally been included under *Charter* protection and no doubt will be the basis for the inclusion of other important grounds. I agree with Madam Justice Wilson's discussion in *Andrews*, supra 36, that s. 15 of the *Charter* does not reflect, nor do we even recognize, all of the varied and complex bases on which we subject groups to discrimination: 'The range of discrete and insular minorities has changed and will continue to change with changing political and social circumstances ... It can be anticipated that the discrete and insular minorities of tomorrow will include groups not recognized as such today. It is consistent with the constitutional status of s. 15 that it be interpreted with sufficient flexibility to ensure "unremitting protection" of equality rights in the years to come' (at 33). On the other hand, it is important to note that a large number of the s. 15 claims being made are on the basis of analogous grounds and, more frequently than not, the analogous grounds claimed flow from privilege not from oppression. These grounds include, e.g., a landlord seeking s. 15 protection from the stereotypes of landlords that deny their dignity and worth and are embodied in landlord/tenant legislation (*A&L Investments v. The Queen* (1993), 13 O.R. (3d) 799 (Div. Ct.); and a lawyer arguing that business taxes breach s. 15 in that they discriminate against business people based solely on occupation (*Scarborough v. Zwicker* (1992, Ontario Small Claims Court). The openness of s. 15 to analogous grounds encourages those with privilege to explore this new potential route to reinforce or add to their privilege. To date, the courts seem to be doing a good job of recognizing that these claims do not present grounds similar to those in the *Charter*, i.e., the claims are not being brought by members of 'groups who suffer social, political and legal disadvantage in our society.' Nonetheless, it is disconcerting to see the numbers and variety of these claims. Up to now, the negative decisions in these cases do not seem to be stemming the flood of privileged claims, and I fear that at any moment the courts' resolve may

crumble, and the s. 15 floodgates will be sprung to allow a flood of analogous grounds based on privilege.
40 *Andrews*, 34.
41 Ibid., 32.
42 Patricia Monture, 'Ka-Nin-Geh-Heh-Gah-E-Sa-Nonh-Yah-Gah' (1986) 2 *CJWL* 161. Monture is a member of the Mohawk Nation and the 'we' and 'our' to whom she refers in this quotation are First Nations people.
43 Hester Lessard, 'Equality and Access to Justice in the Work of Bertha Wilson' (1992) 15 *Dalhousie Law Journal* 59.
44 *Andrews*, 11–12.
45 Ibid., 12–13.
46 See my 'Equality and Discrimination According to the Supreme Court of Canada,' 425.
47 *Andrews*, 11. As Radha Jhappan pointed out to me, the characterization of citizenship, which was the basis of the discrimination being challenged in the *Andrews* case, as a 'personal difference' is inappropriate and inaccurate. Citizenship is a status conferred by the state to which a large number of benefits attach.
48 Ibid., 18.
49 This was the point made by Justice Robertson, but to the opposite effect, in the case of *Egan et al. v. The Queen* (1993), 103 D.L.R. (4th) 336 (Fed. C.A.) in which a gay male partner was denied access to the spousal allowance under the *Old Age Security Act*: 'The significance of the legal requirement that a distinction be based on an irrelevant personal difference cannot be ignored or dispensed with summarily ... The appellants have not argued discrimination because of a distinction based on an irrelevancy. Rather, they have identified the distinction in terms of differential treatment being accorded same-sex and opposite-sex couples and then deemed that irrele-vant. Consequently, sexual orientation remains highly relevant' (at 392). The logic here is incomprehensible to me, but the bottom line, I think, is clear – the more entrenched the oppression, the more relevant the 'difference' is perceived to be, and the less one is likely to get redress. The distinction has to be clearly irrelevant to the decision-maker in order for it to be recognized as discriminatory.
50 This concept of reading in the stereotype comes from Patricia Williams, 'The Death of the Profane,' in *The Alchemy of Race and Rights* (Cambridge, MA: Harvard University Press, 1991) in which she tells the story of an editor who had, in the name of racial neutrality, eliminated all references to her race such that the reader would have to read in racist stereotyping in order to understand her story.

51 See Margaret Thornton, 'Affirmative Action, Merit and the Liberal State' (1982) 2 *Australian Journal of Law and Society* 28; see also Anne Donnellon and Deborah Kolb, 'Constructive for Whom? The Fate of Diversity Disputes in Organizations' (1994) 50 *Journal of Social Issues* 139; and Iris Marion Young, *Justice and the Politics of Difference* (Princeton: Princeton University Press, 1990) 192–225.
52 [1989] 1 S.C.R. 1296.
53 Ibid., 1332.
54 I really dislike the expression 'equality-seeking groups' that is frequently used to describe oppressed groups who are trying to assert their rights under the *Charter*. To me this term has a supplicant connotation that I find demeaning. As well, it offers the illusion that equality exists out there simply waiting to be found, masking the reality that equality is both hard fought and vehemently resisted. There is nothing easy about equality, nor about the struggles to attain it.
55 David Lepofsky, 'The Canadian Judicial Approach to Equality Rights: Freedom Ride or Rollercoaster?' (1992) 1 *National Journal of Constitutional Law (NJCL)* 315.
56 For a comprehensive review of the Supreme Court of Canada s. 15 equality decisions up to 1995, see Andrea York, "The Inequality of Emerging *Charter* Jurisprudence: Supreme Court Interpretations of Section 15(1) (1996) 54 *University of Toronto Faculty of Law Review* 328.
57 See Gwen Brodsky and Shelagh Day, *Canadian Charter Equality Rights for Women: One Step Forward or Two Steps Back?* (Ottawa: Canadian Advisory Council on the Status of Women, 1989).
58 *R. v. Morgentaler*, [1993] 3 S.C.R. 463.
59 *R. v. Butler* (1992), 89 D.L.R (4th) 449 (S.C.C.).
60 *R. v. Seaboyer and Gayme*, [1991] 2 S.C.R. 577.
61 *R. v. O'Connor* (1995), 130 D.L.R. (4th) 235 (S.C.C.).
62 *Winnipeg Child and Family Services (Northwest Area) v. G.(D.F.)* (1997), 152 D.L.R. 4th 193 (S.C.C.).
63 The Women's Legal Education and Action Fund (LEAF), often in coalition with other groups, has probably been the organization that has intervened most consistently to raise women's equality issues. This is because this is what LEAF was established to do. See Razack, *Canadian Feminism*; see also LEAF, *Equality and the Charter: Ten Years of Feminist Advocacy before the Supreme Court of Canada* (Toronto: Emond Montgomery, 1996). Other groups intervene when the issues they work with – e.g., immigration, violence against women, reproductive rights – are before the court.

64 *Egan*, 359. I cannot help but think that Justice Linden made this statement in recognition of the prejudice and stereotyping underlying the majority decision in this case. This case dealt with the availability of the spousal allowance under the *Old Age Security Act* to a gay male partner. Having been denied the benefit at trial and by the Federal Court of Appeal, the plaintiffs appealed to the Supreme Court of Canada where the spousal allowance was again denied to them, *Egan v. Canada*, [1995] 2 S.C.R. 513.
65 *McKinney v. University of Guelph*, [1990] 1 S.C.R. 229.
66 (1994), 94 D.T.C. 6531 (Tax Court of Canada).
67 *Rodriguez v. Attorney General of Canada*, [1993] 3 S.C.R. 616.
68 In *Eaton v. Brant County Board of Education* (1997), 142 D.L.R. 4th 385 (S.C.C.), the Court held that s. 15 did not mandate a presumption of integrated schooling for children with disabilities and refused to overturn the tribunal decision that segregated schooling was in the best interests of this particular child. In *Eldridge v. British Columbia (Attorney-General)* (1997), 151 D.L.R. 4th (S.C.C.), the Court held that the failure to provide people who are deaf with sign language interpreters when they receive medical services was an unjustifiable breach of s. 15 of the *Charter*. I would describe these cases (simplistically) as a loss and a win respectively. *Eldridge* is a particularly important victory in that it is a decision that will cost the B.C. government money, something the courts tend to be reluctant to do.
69 For a current example, we need only look to the refusal of much of the Canadian public to recognize the killing of a child with cerebral palsy as murder. See *R. v. Latimer* (1997), 142 D.L.R. 4th 577 (S.C.C.).
70 Simone de Beauvoir, *The Ethics of Ambiguity* (New York: Citadel Press, 1948) 83.
71 This I would have thought was clear from the Supreme Court of Canada decisions in *Andrews*, *Brooks*, and *Janzen v. Pharos Restaurant*, [1989] 1 S.C.R. 1252 .
72 [1994] 2 F.C. 189 (C.A.). The challenge was successful in the Federal Court of Appeal under the analogous ground of being a separated custodial parent. See Ellen Zweibel, '*Thibaudeau v. R.*: Constitutional Challenge to the Taxation of Child Support Payments' (1994) 4 *NJCL* 305. The Federal Court of Appeal decision was overturned by the Supreme Court of Canada, [1995] 2 S.C.R. 627, on the basis that there was no s. 15 violation, on any ground, including sex.
73 (1999), 176 D.L.R. 4th 1 (S.C.C.).
74 Razack, *Canadian Feminism*, 535.
75 This is an assimilationist argument that, as a lesbian, I find particularly

worrisome. See Diana Majury, 'Refashioning the Unfashionable: Claiming Lesbian Identities in Legal Contexts' (1995) 7 *CJWL* 286–317.
76 *Andrews*, 11.
77 (1999), 171 D.L.R. 4th 577 (S.C.C.).
78 The courts appear more willing to recognize and remedy inequality when the economic costs of doing so fall on the shoulders of an individual rather than the state. This would offer some explanation for why M. and H. were recognized as spouses while Egan and Nesbitt were not.
79 I personally do not support the now large number of gay and lesbian challenges to the marriage prohibition. While I do agree that whatever is available should be available to any couple regardless of its gender configuration, I think the preferable route to attaining this equality is the abolition of marriage as a legal status. I am not aware of any reasons that justify the retention of marriage as a legally significant category and its meaning as such has already been seriously eroded. Marriage as a legal status has always been a proxy for the ascription of rights, benefits, duties, and responsibilities, and it has always been an inadequate proxy. In the absence of legal requirements relating to marriage, people would be free to marry whomever they choose in whatever forum would allow them to do so. The absence of state recognition, or state endorsement, of the relationship seems to me totally appropriate and a good thing.
80 For example, in *Mossop v. Attorney General of Canada*, [1993] 1 S.C.R. 554, the Court held that the claim should have been on the basis of sexual orientation, not family status.
81 (1998), 15 D.L.R. 4th 385 (S.C.C.).
82 *Dartmouth-Halifax County Regional Housing Authority v. Sparks* (1992), 12 N.S.R. (2d) 389 (C.A.).
83 [1999] 1 S.C.R. 497.
84 [1999] 2 S.C.R. 203.

CHAPTER FOUR

Towards a Democratic Practice of Feminist Litigation? LEAF's Changing Approach to *Charter* Equality

Lise Gotell

The new millennium is a time for reflection and for looking forward. As we enter the twenty-first century, many of us have begun to look back on some of the earlier arguments that we made about Canadian feminism and the *Canadian Charter of Rights and Freedoms*. With the benefit of more than fifteen years of feminist constitutional litigation to reflect on, we are in a position to craft more complex and nuanced analyses of the potential opportunities and constraints of legal strategy as feminist practice. There is no doubt that Canadian feminists must continue to engage in constitutional legal struggles. Rights-based claims that seek to undermine feminist political gains continue to proliferate, demanding defensive uses of the *Charter*'s equality provisions. This has been particularly evident in the area of sexual assault legislation where the legal rights sections of the *Charter* have been deployed to challenge protections for complainants and to subvert new statutory definitions of consent.[1] But in addition, the present is widely recognized as a time of decreased political opportunities for feminism. With the entrenchment of neoliberalism as the new norm of Canadian governance, feminist political campaigns are increasingly cast as the pursuits of a self-interested minority. As we witness equality-enhancing public policy being erased with the vestiges of the 'irresponsible' welfare state, rights-based and constitutional struggles assume new importance. They assume importance because it may be that the courts and constitution provide a forum for articulating the ongoing necessity of substantive equality projects when political actors are resistant and hostile.

At the time of this millennial re-evaluation, we need to recognize that there are diverse ways to approach the question of whether feminist litigation struggles have been successful. For many feminist legal scholars, this has meant careful scrutiny of Supreme Court decisions and their consequences. While this approach is important, and we can observe its usefulness in some of the articles in this collection, I have made the argument that on its own an evaluation of the results of feminist litigation is incomplete.[2] Indeed, as Judy Fudge wrote in an early consideration of the uses of the *Charter* for feminism, 'The impact of entrenching general and abstract rights in a constitutional document must be evaluated not only in terms of the actual results of litigation ... but also with reference to the form of political discourse constitutional litigation generates.'[3] Following from this insight, my past work has engaged in an interrogation of the manner in which Canadian feminists articulate their struggles and demands in legal discourse, highlighting the often difficult relationship between feminist politics and law.[4]

What is the relationship between feminist politics and law? This complex question is a central focus of this volume as a whole. But, of course, this is a question that can be approached in many ways. When we focus on how the courts respond to feminist demands, we ignore the prior and ultimately vexing question, 'What is a feminist demand?' This is left un-interrogated precisely because it is assumed that it can be answered simply. A feminist demand is one that issues from women's 'experience' of subordination and seeks to address gender domination. Feminism, in other words, is a political practice built from the ground of women's experience. But what happens when the foundations of this simple definition of feminist politics are challenged? What happens if we consider the category 'woman' as constructed? What happens if we consider women's experience as, in Joan Scott's words, 'always already an interpretation and always in need of interpretation'?[5]

Many feminists view these questions as a threat to the very existence of feminism as a political project; when we unhinge feminism from the subject women and from the authority of women's experience then, some assert, we leave it defenceless in a hostile climate.[6] If, in general, feminist anxieties about a post-foundational universe are acute, they are all the more acute in those versions of feminism that orient themselves towards law. It is, of course, well recognized that law as a discourse rests on the claim to 'Truth.' Law constitutes a powerful meta-narrative, assuming the guise of objectivity and promising to distinguish true from false. In this way, legal discourse is elevated above other discourses. The centrality of 'Truth' within legal discourse makes it resistant to complexity and contingency and responsive to demands that are both positivistic and categorical.[7] This is because law rests on a version of the subject that is universal, rational, and knowing. Consequently, as some feminist legal theorists have insisted, to refuse this subject and its 'Truth' within the domain of law may be nothing less than strategic suicide. As Jennifer Wicke has asked, 'How are feminist uses of law even possible if the subject which drives our efforts is incoherent and multiple?'[8]

The dilemmas posed by the demands of legal discourse are at the heart of this consideration of the relationship between feminist legal strategy and politics. In this chapter, I examine the evolution of a feminist litigation organization, the Women's Legal Education and Action Fund (LEAF). LEAF was formed in 1985 specifically to use the newly entrenched guarantees of constitutional equality to advance women's position in Canadian society. With its explicit focus on litigation as feminist strategy, an analysis of LEAF provides an excellent lens for bringing into focus some of the contradictions between what law seems to require of feminist actors and what we as feminists should demand of feminist politics. While law seems to demand that feminists speak in the unambiguous tones of 'Truth' in order to be heard, I suggest that a commitment to a democratic form of feminist politics demands that we relinquish such 'Truth' claims. In other words, we need to encourage within feminism an embrace of both respectful conversation and heated argument.[9] Feminist politics must be appreciated as encompassing far more than the conflict between feminism and its opposition; feminist politics is also and always necessarily marked by ongoing controversies about the meaning of feminism itself, it goals, and its strategies.[10] A politicization of feminism thus requires that we make spaces for differences among feminists that cannot merely be set aside by invoking universal 'Truth.' Accepting that feminism should never be understood as a finite theory and range of strategies is a tall order, particularly when juxtaposed against the modernist and foundational strictures of legal discourse. Nevertheless, what I argue here is that the costs of submitting to the foundationalist requisites of legal discourse may outweigh any gains, especially if we are committed to building a feminist politics based on participation and if we seek fuller legal recognition of the complexity of women's lives.

As I will demonstrate in this chapter, the character of LEAF's engagement with law and the discourse it has used to frame its claims have undergone profound shifts since its establishment. The first section of the chapter explores the essentialist and universalistic depiction of women's experience, which for many years provided the foundation for LEAF's equality litigation. Next, the chapter analyses how this approach appears to have given way to a far more complex understanding of women's lives, one capable of recognizing diversity and multidimensional inequalities. In spite of this, the epistemic assumption that women's experience (albeit particularized) provides an undisputed basis for knowledge and the blueprint for always correct jurisprudence has continued to influence LEAF's politics and practice. This attachment to 'Truth' claims lodged in experience may facilitate its engagements with law. At the same time, however, this foundationalism has tended to inhibit feminist politics, when politics is viewed as a space for arguing about feminist norms. In charting LEAF's discursive evolution and in evaluating the potential for a much more fully democratic feminist legal practice in the twenty-first century, the final section of the chapter examines how legalistic 'Truth' claims have silenced feminist conversations in the past, as well as some recent cases where the necessity of experiential foundations appears to have been challenged, thereby giving voice to more nuanced feminist legal positions. The conclusion will raise some thoughts on the future potential and perils of feminist constitutional litigation.

LEAF's Contextualized Approach to *Charter* Equality: 1985–1992

In contrast to the predictions of many *Charter* critics,[11] Canadian feminists working through LEAF very quickly developed an approach to the sexual equality provisions of the *Charter* that appeared to defy the decontextualizing impetus of rights discourse. This approach, first legally articulated in LEAF's intervention in *Andrews*,[12] has been labelled the 'contextualized approach to *Charter* sexual equality' (CASE). It is founded on the assertion that constitutional equality claims must be assessed from the standpoint of women's experience. The CASE approach attempts to frame sexual equality claims within the context of gendered relations of power and insists that adjudication be based on an evaluation of the impact for women's subordination. Quite clearly influenced by the work of American feminist legal theorist Catharine MacKinnon, who was active in LEAF in its early years,[13] this approach subverts the logic of abstract comparison underpinning the dominant liberal legalist approach to equality. It does this by challenging the narrow similarly situated test that had guided lower court interpretations of the *Charter*'s equality guarantees. In *Andrews*, LEAF argued forcefully that the purpose of section 15 was not merely to eradicate distinctions, but instead to promote the substantive equality of the 'powerless.'[14] The factum went on to lay out a test for section 15 that would focus on disadvantage rather than abstract comparison, requiring 'an applicant to explain his or her disadvantage, how it related to the legislation at issue and how the provision impairs his or her equality.'[15] In *Andrews* and in subsequent equality interventions, LEAF highlighted the systemic character of women's inequality, insisting on a purposive and remedial interpretation of section 15 as the proper legal understanding of the *Charter*'s equality guarantees.

In its stress on reconstructing equality from the perspective of women's subordination, CASE challenges the individualist ontology of liberal law and the masculine norm inherent in a comparative approach to sex equality. It contests the 'ruler's' top-down gaze on the question of equality, by arguing that the problem of inequality and the nature of social reality as a whole can only be seen from the bottom up – that is, from the ground of the 'different reality of women's lives,' a reality shaped by systemic patterns of 'dominance and subordination.'[16] CASE, in effect, represents a jurisprudential expression of feminist standpoint epistemology. Like MacKinnon's writings, the underlying premise of LEAF's approach to *Charter* equality is that within systems of social domination the 'ruler's' vision is especially limited; it is partial and perverse. Conversely, the vision of the oppressed captures the real relations between human beings because only it can escape from the distortions of power.[17] In LEAF's early litigation, the standpoint of women's subordination is embraced as the foundation for constructing a feminist *Charter* jurisprudence.

As I have argued elsewhere,[18] CASE, as elaborated in *Andrews* and in subsequent pre-1993 cases, represents a clear ontological prioritization of women's experience of subordination. And it shares with feminist standpoint theory two related tendencies. First, efforts to give voice to a 'women's perspective' in legal discourse, as in other discourses, tend to rely on the constitution of an essential women's experience. Expressions of feminist standpoint epistemology may acknowledge differences among women; yet as Kathy Ferguson contends, 'the logic of a search for a founding experience tends to elide difference nonetheless.'[19] In other words, the assumption that the experiences of all women can be subsumed under a single standpoint tends to universalize and abstract women's experience, much in the same way that liberal law has abstracted from and universalized men's experiences. Second, and perhaps more fundamentally, is standpoint feminism's tendency to accept unquestioningly the central promise of the Enlightenment – that is, the belief that 'Truth' will supplant power. The CASE approach invites the judiciary to 'come down among the women' because this is a site of powerlessness and powerlessness is 'truthful.' As Brown explains, this kind of feminist epistemic strategy seeks to legitimize its 'Truth' through its relation to worldly powerlessness, discrediting dominant 'truths' through their connection to power – 'Truth is always on the side of the damned or the excluded, hence truth is always clean of power, always reproaches power.'[20] While recognizing the distortions of the masculine perspective as it has been reflected in law, this approach seems incapable of admitting that its own vision may be restricted.[21]

In some of my early research on LEAF, I explored how the restricted vision of CASE resulted in a tendency to perceive women's experience as homogeneous; the lens produced by the 'bottom-up' gaze of this kind of feminist jurisprudence rendered gender subordination visible but obscured the construction, complexity, and diversities of women's experience. Of course, it is well recognized that within the discourse of sex equality, the difference between men and women is emphasized, differences among women are negated, the sameness among women is privileged, and the similarities between men and women are denied.[22] The inclination towards gender essentialism inherent in the discourse of sex equality is exacerbated when inserted within law. This is because law tends to hear feminists most clearly when they 'speak the univocal tones of the gen(d)eric woman.'[23] Indeed, essentialism has played an important role in constructing categorical legal claims on behalf of women. As Crenshaw's research in the United States and Duclos's research in Canada has demonstrated, the courts tend to resist assertions of complex and intersecting inequalities, preferring instead a model of 'simple, homogeneous categories of discrimination.'[24] Essentialist claims become a means of rendering gender domination comprehensible as a foundation for legal equality claims.

The problem of essentialism, a reliance on universalized and abstracted description of 'women's experience,' marked LEAF's litigation efforts in the period between its founding in 1985 and 1992.[25] Indeed, LEAF itself has acknowledged its earlier failure 'to address women's inequality in all its complexity and diversity.'[26] Some analysts have recently argued that this stress on gender as the only determining factor of women's experience, and the legal presentation of women's experience as unified, can be seen as a deployment of what Spivak has called strategic essentialism.²⁷ In other words, given the categorical nature of legal discourse, and the invisibility of women's subordination in legal decision-making, LEAF was simply trying to open law's eyes, a goal best achieved through a simple and pure representation. But my research on this period suggested that there was little that was consciously strategic about LEAF's essentialism. In attempting to analyse its construction of 'women' and 'women issues,' I undertook an extensive content/discourse analysis of LEAF literature including legal factums, litigation reports, and its newsletter *LEAFLines*.²⁸ Nowhere in this voluminous material was there evidence that alternative renderings of experience were recognized and yet discarded as too 'complex' for case arguments. It was not until the early 1990s that debates about race, ability, and sexuality emerged within LEAF (see below).

During its first seven years, LEAF was involved in approximately one hundred cases. In my analysis of this period, I found that by far the majority of these cases – some 74 per cent – are defined as having similar implications for all women, by virtue of their membership in the category 'women as a disadvantaged group.'²⁹ LEAF's legal arguments and case discussions most often failed to recognize how asymmetrical power relations based on race, class, sexual orientation, and ability structure the lives of women differently. Instead, an appeal to women's 'experience,' as if all women shared a similar experience of pregnancy, motherhood, work, and so on, grounded LEAF's analyses. In a 1990 article explaining its approach to *Charter* sexual equality, LEAF stated, 'While some have urged women to submerge any differences from men and argue sameness, and others have sought to value women's distinctiveness and argue difference, LEAF saw that neither approach made sense of women's experience. *Women suffer from social subordination: systemic abuse and deprivation of social power, resources and responsibility because we are women*' (my emphasis).³⁰ This theme of women's shared suffering emerges repeatedly within legal arguments made between 1985 and 1992. Any careful analysis of factums on such diverse issues as reproductive control, maternity leave, pregnancy discrimination, rape, sexual harassment, incest, pornography, or divorce, reveals a consistent effort to define 'women' in homogeneous terms.³¹

Implicit in the CASE approach is the critical importance of contextualization within a sexual hierarchy, and yet ironically, LEAF's arguments during this period often left women detached from other relations of power. There are two cases that provide an especially good illustration of this process of abstraction. In the first, *Baby R.*,³² a 'pregnant woman,' 'unmodified' (to borrow MacKinnon's language) by any other descriptor, underwent forced obstetrical intervention and ultimately fetal apprehension when she refused to undergo a Cesarean section. In this case, the B.C. Ministry of Social Services successfully argued that the fetus was a 'child in need of protection' within B.C. law. In the second case, *Norberg*,[33] a drug-dependent woman, induced by her physician to provide sex in exchange for painkillers, launched a civil suit claiming damages for sexual assault, professional negligence and breach of a doctor's fiduciary responsibility to a patient.

LEAF intervened in both cases, *Baby R.* at the B.C. Supreme Court and *Norberg* at the Supreme Court of Canada. In *Baby R.*, the thrust of LEAF's intervention was to underline the frightening implications for 'women' should the fetus be deemed a 'child' within law. In response to the assertion that the 'fetus' can be seen as an independent person with rights equal to and in conflict with a pregnant woman, LEAF sought to contextualize: first, to (re)place the fetus within the pregnant woman's body; next, to position the pregnant woman within a set of social relations in which women's childbearing abilities have been used to justify their subordination. As LEAF argued, to define the fetus as a rights-bearing 'person,' would be to sanction the most extreme regulation of pregnant women's lives, thus conflicting with the *Charter*'s guarantees of security of the person and sexual equality.[34]

In *Norberg*, in an effort to counter lower court decisions emphasizing Ms Norberg's 'consent' to the sexual advances of her doctor, LEAF similarly sought to contextualize. Drawing heavily on MacKinnon's writings, its factum argued that it was improper to 'reach conclusions as to the existence of consent without consideration of inequalities of sex, disability (chemical dependence) and the confidential relationship between doctor and patient.'[35] By ignoring power relationships between this woman and her doctor, the lower courts had failed to draw a distinction between 'consent freely exercised under conditions of equality' and 'forced submission' under conditions of domination.[36] In effect, LEAF's argument was that the constitutional guarantee of sexual equality requires appreciating power imbalances in determining sexual assault.

Presented in these ways, the circumstances of *Baby R.* and *Norberg* were defined as threats to women's equality and, therefore, of general relevance to all women.[37] In effect, Ms R. and Ms Norberg become symbols for all women in the ongoing struggle against reproductive and sexual coercion. Both women are primarily viewed through the lens of sex/gender, and gender subordination is presented as the essential explanation of their circumstances.

LEAF's one-dimensional construction of the problem of forced obstetrical intervention in *Baby R* stands as an example of how gender contexualization can strip social problems of complexity – the very kind of complexity that is necessary to construct useful feminist analyses and strategies. In an earlier article, I formed a critique of LEAF's intervention based on Brettel Dawson's published assertion that Ms R. was an Aboriginal woman, whose class and race were critical factors in explaining her lack of power in relation to the medical establishment, rendering her vulnerable to forced C-section and fetal apprehension.[38] LEAF's 'bleaching' of colour, class, and other relevant social relations from the story of Ms R., I suggested, was derived from its efforts to present issues as being of equal importance to all women. Based on Dawson's information, I argued that *Baby R.* represented a missed opportunity to illuminate the tangled web of gender, racial, and class interactions that together frame the problem of prenatal medical coercion. In 1998, I learned that Dawson was mistaken, that Ms R. was not an Aboriginal woman. This is the kind of mistake that can result from legal representations where generic litigants come to stand in for all women. As Majury has asked, emphasizing the incompleteness of contextualization within CASE, 'Should we have been told more of these women ... I would have liked to have been told more. I would have liked these women to be more than names to me, more than abstract pregnancies ... Does a contextualized approach require more information?'[39] More information would not only have prevented commentators from ascribing incorrect cultural/racial identities to Ms R., it would also have facilitated a deeper feminist analysis.

Even though Ms R. was not a Native woman, the problem of abstracted representation remains in LEAF's arguments, leaving many dimensions of prenatal coercion obscured. Research indicates that white, middle-class, English-speaking women are very unlikely to find themselves subject to forced medical intervention in pregnancy.[40] This was something that was quite clear in the existing research by the time LEAF wrote its factum in *Baby R.* in 1987. For example, Kolder et al.'s important U.S. study, published in 1987, found that 81 per cent of court-ordered interventions directed at pregnant women were for black, Asian, or Hispanic women; 44 per cent were unmarried, and none had private health care coverage.[41] The neo-eugenicism informing prenatal coercion constructs racialized women and women living in poverty as 'irresponsible,' incapable of making decisions that would lead to good pregnancy outcomes. LEAF's failure to draw out these interconnections results in an incomplete and possibly misleading story.

As for Ms Norberg, her vulnerability in relation to her doctor was rooted not only in her sex and 'disability,' as was LEAF's emphasis, but also in her Aboriginality, a factor surprisingly ignored in the factum. The systemic racism experienced by Aboriginal women at the hands of health care professionals has been extensively documented by the Royal Commission on Aboriginal Peoples and by the Aboriginal Panel of the Canadian Panel on Violence Against Women.[42] Horrific medical abuses, such as the denial of anesthetics during abortions, have been facilitated by cultural stereotypes of Aboriginal women as irresponsible and in need of discipline.[43] Language barriers and unfamiliar practices compound the vulnerability of Aboriginal women, often denying their voice and authority in interactions with the health care system.[44] Furthermore, the sexual assault of Aboriginal women by white men is not simply a practice of sexual domination, it is equally grounded in racist assumptions that construct Aboriginal women as less than fully human, as 'squaws,' incapable of withholding 'consent,' and lacking 'credibility.'[45] Just as LEAF erases Aboriginality and racism from the story of Ms Norberg, so too does it misrepresent her drug dependence as 'disability.' As Native men and women have insisted, the high rates of drug abuse among Canadian Aboriginal peoples are a function of cultural erosion and the breakdown of communities and families. It is a problem to be understood contextually and socially. Rooted in neither individual 'pathology' nor 'irresponsibility,' drug abuse is instead best understood as 'part of a circle of oppression, despair, violence, and self-destructive behaviour that must be addressed as a whole.'[46] In the words of the Aboriginal Circle of the Canadian Panel on Violence Against Women, Native women's drug dependence is a function 'low self-esteem, racism by the general population, social and economic conditions and the loss of Aboriginal social structures which were respectful to women.'[47] It is only within this many-sided context that we can begin to understand the complex power dynamics and issues at play in *Norberg*.

LEAF's arguments in *Norberg* could be seen as the result of an effort to squeeze multidimensional experiences through the prism of sex to be rendered compatible with the CASE approach. In the process of constructing a linear legal narrative of sexual domination, LEAF participated in a fragmentation of Ms Norberg's lived reality, a fragmentation, that as Monture Okanee has emphasized, constitutes an act of violence and a silencing of Aboriginal women.[48] Ms Norberg's story is appropriated; and like Ms R., she comes to stand in for 'all women.'

The recurrent oversimplification of complex experiences is evident in many other LEAF cases during the period between 1985 and 1992. In *Bezaire*,[49] a well-known and highly disturbing lesbian custody case, lesbianism lurks in the closet, ignored within LEAF's narrative.[50] In *Colgate Palmolive* (1990), the clearly racialized character of a black woman's workplace harassment is surprisingly absent from LEAF's initial legal analyses.[51] Here, as in *Baby R.* and *Norberg*, LEAF creates an essential woman's experience. During this period, sexual domination is highlighted as the only important aspect of women's context, even at the cost of oversimplification.[52]

LEAF's stress on women's shared experience of suffering during this period did not, however, mean that it completely ignored differences among women. Nevertheless, the attempt to encounter difference was relegated to a second level of cases in which LEAF focused on issues of concern to particular groups of women. Here the articulation of specificity was accomplished through a discourse of 'double disadvantage': '*in addition to being disadvantaged by sex, women are also subject to discrimination on the basis of race, religion, material status, age, disability, sexual orientation, economic status or other grounds.*'[53] In many ways, the double-disadvantage approach is deceptive. While appearing to acknowledge the complex conditions structuring women's lives, it in fact stresses commonality. Although 'double disadvantage' allows for some recognition of divergent experiences, it construes these as subsidiary to more basic similarities.

In LEAF's representation of 'difference' within this second level of cases we can observe a tendency to prioritize sexual inequality in the double-disadvantage equation – 'additional' forms of 'discrimination' became qualifiers, to be discussed in only the second instance. The following case discussions from *LEAFLines* seek to convey the importance of specific cases involving 'double disadvantage,' but issues are framed in ways that underline their significance for 'all women:'

- LEAF has undertaken cases challenging the inequitable treatment of *women prisoners, and in particular native women prisoners* ...[54]
- LEAF seeks to intervene to underline *the systemic nature of sex discrimi-*

nation in immigration policy, pointing to the ways in which *immigrant women* are disadvantaged. ... winning this case would help to address the problems of *sexism and racism* in immigration ...[55]
- *The eligibility criteria and their interpretation effectively deny women access to this programme* ... stereotypes about women and women's work and the context of women's lives result in women being screened out of the programme. *This raises fundamental equality problems that doubly burden women of colour* (my emphasis).[56]

Here 'sexism' is constructed as a first-order category, while 'other' forms of 'discrimination' are presented as distinct and secondary.[57]

In the period examined in my earlier research, there were repeated references to 'sex and race discrimination,' for example, in LEAF's case discussions and analyses; but until the initiation of its 'Inequality Project' in 1993 (see below), the interactions between sexism and racism were rarely explored. LEAF treated multidimensional issues as addition problems, and consequently, women of colour were viewed as being subject to sexism 'plus' racism, resulting in symbolic fragmentation. Women of colour, in effect, became reduced to what Harris has termed 'white women with an additional burden' or 'more than women.'[58] Paradoxically, while the discourse of 'double disadvantage' aims to emphasize 'differences' among women, it functions to reinforce the notion that we all share an essential 'womanhood.' The experience of 'womanhood' that is affirmed is, not surprisingly, the experience of the white, middle-class, able-bodied, heterosexual, woman.[59] This is because, when we 'subtract' all 'additional' forms of 'discrimination,' race, class, sexual orientation, ability, and so on, it is she who remains.

From Essentialism to Particularity: LEAF's Post-1992 Evolution

As I have stressed, for its first seven years LEAF's legal claims proceeded from foundational assertions about women's shared experience of oppression. By the 1990s, however, the essentialism that had grounded its earlier discourse was profoundly challenged, as LEAF underwent an 'internal struggle to be more responsive to the needs of all women.'[60] In 1990, in reaction to claims that its priorities and legal positions had failed to address the 'interests and experiences of diverse women,' an 'Outreach and Diversification Plan' was adopted.[61] This plan included: holding national consultations with Aboriginal women, women with disabilities, immigrant women, women of colour, and lesbians; steps to encourage the participation of women from these communities within LEAF; establishing liaison with diverse feminist organizations; holding racism workshops; establishing an employment equity plan; and attaching a new priority to cases 'which address heightened vulnerability of women on the basis of race, Aboriginal ancestry, disability, and sexual identity.'[62] As a result of these measures, LEAF began to evolve into an organization that was more representative of women's 'diversity' and with greater ties to community organizations. Inextricably linked with the Outreach and Diversification Plan, LEAF also began to participate in litigation efforts as part of broad-based coalitions. By 1996, six of its twenty-three Supreme Court interventions had been undertaken in coalition with other groups.[63] As an indication of the growing importance of this approach, six of the ten cases adopted by LEAF in 1998–9 were coalition-driven.[64] The 1990s also witnessed the adoption of a far more consultative approach to litigation. For example, before deciding to intervene before the Supreme Court in the *Little Sisters* case (on the issue of Customs' seizure of gay/lesbian material), LEAF both issued a discussion paper and held consultations.[65] These initiatives, taken together, most certainly enhance LEAF's legitimacy as a feminist litigation organization.

During the 1980s and early 1990s, LEAF had been dominated by a fairly elite group of women whose only experiences of exclusion were based on their gender.[66] As a result, they conceived women's context as being primarily shaped by gender domination. Changes in LEAF's composition and the involvement of other extra-legal organizations in its litigation efforts have helped to complicate the essentialized construction of women's experience that underpinned the CASE approach. In other words, greater representation has led to the 're-presentation' of women's contexts as complex. Over the past ten years, LEAF's rhetoric about 'women's' equality has undergone a profound shift, with new attention to women's 'variety' and 'diversity.' In 1992, LEAF sponsored a major symposium on 'women's constitutional equality rights,' the central themes of which were an exploration of 'women's diversity' and the need to 'widen the circle.'[67] This symposium provided a space within which Aboriginal women, women of colour, and women with disabilities could demand a feminist equality theory that would ensure that 'issues of race, heritage and disability are never "add-ons" to the experience of sexism.'[68] The often difficult conversations that emerged revealed deep dissatisfaction with and alienation from the feminist legal project as it had been constructed by LEAF. The multiple concerns voiced underlined the narrowness of feminist struggles built on an abstracted women's experience. While critiques of essentialism may have been old news within the academy by the early 1990s, struggles for inclusion and diversity were only just occurring within LEAF.

By LEAF's own account, the symposium was both 'invigorating' and 'exhausting.'[69] In the effort to construct a positive response, a working group of the National Legal Committee, the 'Inequality Project,' was established, charged with developing 'a comprehensive equality theory that accommodates women's differences.'[70] In 1996, LEAF cautioned that such a theory may be 'elusive,' that 'the issues raised are uniquely difficult,' as is the task of incorporating into legal work 'the conflicting insights that accompany the recognition of women's difference.'[71] Perhaps owing to these challenges, by June 1999 the Inequality Project had been classified as 'inactive.'[72] Nonetheless, efforts such as this project foreshadowed an unravelling of the notion of women's shared suffering that had been at the heart of LEAF's approach to *Charter* sexual equality.

The nature of LEAF's participation in a broad-based feminist lobby for the 1992 sexual assault law stands as one of the first indications of this transition. After the Supreme Court struck down Canada's rape shield legislation, LEAF (along with other national feminist groups and groups representing lesbians, Aboriginal women, women with disabilities, immigrant women, sex trade workers, and women of colour) was centrally involved in feminist struggles to draft a new law. Moving away from the gender essentialist construction of sexual violence which had framed many of its prior interventions, LEAF argued strongly for law which would: specifically recognize 'the role of inequities based on race, class and ability' in sexual assault; establish new categories of assault based on racism and bigotry; and encompass a recognition of multiple power inequalities in the statutory definition of consent.[73] LEAF's participation in this coalition signalled its embrace of a multidimensional understanding of equality, as well as a willingness to submit itself to the scrutiny of diverse extra-legal organizations.

In successive cases since the mid-1990s, an emphasis on particularity and interacting power relations has replaced the homogeneous and essentialist construction of women's experience that previously grounded LEAF's conception of feminist jurisprudence.[74] I will focus my comments on two cases that provide a clear contrast to *Baby R.* and *Norberg*: *G. (D.F.)* (1997) concerning the court-ordered drug treatment and confinement of a pregnant Aboriginal woman; and *O'Connor* (1995)[75] involving the sexual assault of Aboriginal women at a residential school and the disclosure of confidential records.[76] When analysed alongside *Baby R.* and *Norberg, G. (D.F.)*[77] and *O'Connor* appear to be models of contextualization.

The *O'Connor* factum, for example, clearly built on positions that had been debated and negotiated during the 1992 sexual assault lobby and its analysis stands in contrast to the abstracted narrative of *Norberg*. Like *Norberg*, *O'Connor* (1995) was a case involving the sexual assault of Aboriginal women. The central issue at stake in *O'Connor* was the constitutionality of defence counsel's requests for third-party disclosure of the complainant's private records, a tactic that has escalated in the wake of legislative restrictions on past sexual history evidence.[78] This defence tactic, as LEAF insisted, has been used to discredit the stories of complainants and is founded on the myth that women are uniquely likely to fabricate rape allegations.[79] To assess disclosure requests only in relation to the fair trial rights of those accused, as the factum stated, is to decontextualize, ignoring 'social, historical, political and legal conditions of inequality in which sexual violence occurs; out of which legal principles and practices emerge; and under which records sought to be disclosed are generated.'[80]

In an effort to draw attention to the equality interests of complainants, LEAF, in coalition with the Aboriginal Women's Council, the DisAbled Women's Network, and the Canadian Association of Sexual Assault Centres, emphasized sexual assault as a practice of domination that is simultaneously raced and gendered. The factum described the 'heightened vulnerability' of Aboriginal women to sexual violence, the result of the 'breakdown of family (and community) structures' within Aboriginal communities and 'degrading and dehumanizing stereotypes' of Aboriginal women present within Canadian society.[81] Significantly, the arguments made by LEAF in *O'Connor* also break away from the quantitative logic (more vulnerable than white women) inscribed in the discourse of double discrimination. While recognizing that the disclosure of personal records infringes on the personal security and equality rights of all women complainants, the factum situates the experiences of these Aboriginal women within the specific context of assimilationist policies and racist practices. In *O'Connor*, the accused was a white man, the priest, employer, and principal at a residential school where the complainants had attended and later worked. The critical importance of this context is emphasized in LEAF's factum. The factum describes residential schools as the Canadian state's 'primary vehicle of forced assimilation.'[82] It cites well-documented evidence of widespread sexual and physical abuse of Aboriginal students and in this way inextricably links sexual exploitation and practices of cultural assimilation.[83] LEAF also emphasizes the likelihood of extensive and coercive documentation of Aboriginal students. At the same time, it calls attention to the character of records obtained in circumstances where children were punished for speaking their own language and frequently adopted silence as a strategy of resistance.[84] LEAF concluded by arguing that, '[a] justice system animated by equality principles would not have allowed records generated by state policies designed to eradicate an entire culture to be canvassed for potential information discreditable to survivors of such policies. Nor would it have authorized virtually unlimited access by the accused to the complainants' entire history of sexual abuse and their attempts to recover therefrom as the purchase price of access to white justice.'[85]

Continuing in the carefully situated footsteps of LEAF's intervention in *O'Connor*, the *G. (D.F.)* factum brings into focus that which is erased from the opaque arguments of *Baby R*. Most certainly, if courts are able to enforce the medical treatment of pregnant women against their will, all women's liberty and autonomy is dangerously threatened. As in *Baby R.*, when fetuses are viewed as separable from the wombs of their mothers and when the maternal–fetal relation is conceptualized as competitive and antagonistic, there is wide scope for intrusion into the lives of pregnant women.[86] But as LEAF failed to recognize in *Baby R.*, not all women are equally vulnerable to coercive legal intervention.[87] In the United States, legal sanctions against maternal drug use have been adopted by thirty states since the mid-1980s. In cases where race is identified, 70 per cent of those criminally charged have been women of colour.[88] Roberts argues that this punitive approach perpetuates the devaluation of black mothering and diverts attention away from the social ills of poverty and racism, identifying black women as individually blameworthy for pregnancy outcomes.[89] Rather than occluding this complex form of oppression, that as Roberts contends is 'more than the sum of its parts,'[90] in *G. (D.F.)* LEAF draws attention to the racial and class specificity of 'good mothering.' It points out the manner in which the discursive construction of Aboriginal women as 'bad mothers' has functioned historically as a mechanism for the destruction of Aboriginal communities and families, first through the residential schools policy and then through the removal of native children by child welfare authorities.[91] And it identifies the regulation of pregnancy as 'the next phase of control over Aboriginal mothering.'[92] LEAF's central argument here is that substantive equality demands a recognition of specific context, including the likelihood that Aboriginal women, who are already often carefully regulated through interactions with social welfare authorities, will be among those most likely to experience court-ordered coercion.

In *O'Connor* and *G.(D.F.)*, LEAF approaches the objective of ensuring that the experience of Aboriginal women is never 'simply an add-on' to the experience of white women. A recognition of the dangers to 'all women' flowing from the disclosure of personal records in sexual assault trials and from prenatal coercion stands beside an intricate explanation of cultural assimilation and racism. In this way, these factums bridge gaps between Aboriginal women and non-Aboriginal women, encouraging an understanding of common interests, while educating about differences and the historical context from which these differences arise. The appropriation of voice and experience that had occurred in *Norberg* and the simplified overgeneralization of *Baby R.* here give way to the articulation of Aboriginal women's stories and to a far more complex and contextualized sociolegal analysis of forced disclosure and of coercive approaches to prenatal drug abuse. This shift is accomplished as an effect of LEAF's recent self-reflection and coalition work.

Opening feminist legal strategy and argument to participation and critique by extra-legal feminist actors has had the effect of complicating the picture of women's experience(s) that lies at the heart of LEAF's contextualized approach to equality. Coalition-driven litigation erodes the automatic privileging of those with legal expertise and requires the accommodation of many organizations whose viewpoints, in LEAF's words, 'are diverse and often conflicting.'[93] But the barriers that stand in the way of a more participatory form of feminist litigation are significant. At the level of practical politics, coalition-directed litigation requires both extensive funding and commitments of time. Against the overly optimistic visions of LEAF's founders, most feminist *Charter* litigation has taken place on the defensive, in contexts where quick responses are demanded and possibilities for coalition work and even consultation are foreclosed.[94] *Charter*-based 'counter-claims' to women's equality (mounted by 'pro-life' and antifeminist organizations, men's rights activists, and men accused of sexual assault, among others) quickly came to dominate the agenda of the courts.[95] In fact, it is the case that nearly half of LEAF's Supreme Court interventions have concerned sexual violence, rooted in the extensive use of the legal rights sections of the *Charter* to attack protections for complainants.[96] There are indeed significant obstacles that litter the pathways of participatory feminist litigation.

By the end of the 1990s, however, it seemed clear that the momentum created by diversification initiatives and by LEAF's commitment to an 'intersecting equality analysis' had led to a definite movement away from essentialism. As LEAF attempts to tell more complicated stories, more women listen. The impact of multidimensional equality analysis on *Charter* jurisprudence has been far less resounding. In fact, we might say that it has been like the sound of one hand clapping. Majority opinions have, by and large, failed to respond to intersectional forms of analysis.[97] In *O'Connor* (1995), for example, LEAF's efforts to situate sexual violence within racism and records production within the context of residential schools policy went completely unnoticed in a majority decision that also gave short shrift to the equality rights of the complainant. The *G. (D.F.)* (1997) decision affirmed the live birth rule and emphasized the potential for serious restrictions on women's liberty when the courts are able to direct pregnant women's choices. Despite this positive outcome, LEAF's careful framing of prenatal coercion within racism, colonization, and poverty failed to influence the majority decision. A discussion of Aboriginality appears in the dissent, but in a paternalistic narrative, highlighting the seriousness of fetal alcohol syndrome as a 'Native' problem and the consequent need for authoritative and 'disciplinary' action.[98]

As Jhappan comments, 'It is not clear whether [the failure to respond to intersecting analyses] is because the judges do not understand the analysis, do not agree with it, because it is too complex, because they prefer to stick to technical issues wherever possible, because the equality frame is simply too limited or because of something else.'[99] Whatever the source of judicial resistance, the necessity of telling complex stories is clear. If feminist litigants do not repeatedly make intersectional arguments, unilinear and categorical models of equality/inequality will continue to frame judicial decisions, preventing true contextualization. Moreover, without venues for extra-legal participation in feminist litigation and without the intersectional arguments that have arisen from this, the project of democratizing feminist litigation would be halted. Telling complicated stories and achieving some positive legal recognition of the interwoven web of relations producing differences of situation is no easy task; but as I have stressed, the embrace of diversity is necessary to democratize feminist litigation. Eroding the abstraction of generic womanhood, however difficult in law, is an essential first step in the process of creating a feminist legal praxis which is more fully grounded in feminist politics.

Experiential Truth versus Politics: *Butler* and Beyond

Despite the unhinging of the essentialism that had framed LEAF praxis until the early 1990s, the foundational attachment to experiential 'Truth' has lingered on. With the exception of some recent and extremely interesting cases (that I will discuss below), LEAF's approach to equality has remained rooted in the premise that experience, albeit particularized, provides the standpoint for correct jurisprudential direction. This was strikingly apparent in some of the output of LEAF's 'Inequality Project.' In a *LEAFLines* article on the work of this project, one participant emphasized how we must build from black women's 'experience'; because it is located at the crossroads of race and gender, and she claimed, it constitutes black women as 'experts' and gives their voices 'authenticity.'[100] While recognizing specificity and posing a more complex understanding of 'experience,' this argument fails to acknowledge the political act of naming and interpreting experience. As Scott cautions, 'When experience is taken as the origin of knowledge ... questions about the constructed nature of experience, about how subjects are constituted as different in the first place, about how one's vision is structured – about language [or discourse] and history – are left aside. The evidence of experience then becomes evidence for the fact of difference, rather than exploring how difference is established, how it operates in the world, and in what ways it constitutes subjects who see and act in the world.'[101] By embracing particularized experience as the foundation for knowledge and action, the standpoint epistemology of CASE is reaffirmed, thus reinforcing LEAF's claim to 'Truth.' This 'Truth' is nearly always rooted in the encoding of legal identities based on injury and on the affirmation of victimization.

In the effort to account for the prevalence of foundationalist arguments in law, Smart observes, 'It is as if law's claim to truth is so legitimate that feminists can only challenge it and maintain their credibility ... by positing an equally positivistic alternative.'[102] For many years LEAF justified its positions by invoking women's experience(s) as a site of epistemic privilege. While the assertion of 'Truth' rooted in experience may have the effect of empowering our claims in law, this

154   Lise Gotell

foundationalist strategy is not without its perils for feminist politics. 'Truth' claims authorize feminist legal voices and can be deployed to silence feminist debate. The belief that experience provides an indisputable basis for feminist action (in this case, legal action) obscures the constructed character of all experience, as well as the normative content of feminist politics. In this manner, feminist 'Truth' forecloses feminist politics, and democratic debate within feminism is discouraged.

As I have argued elsewhere,[103] LEAF's intervention in the controversial *Butler* case (1992)[104] provides perhaps the clearest example of this process in which 'Truth' trumps politics. Despite the existence of marked divisions within Canadian feminism on pornography and censorship, LEAF made the decision to support criminal obscenity legislation in its *Butler* intervention without the benefit of outside consultations,[105] and the tone of its factum was unequivocal.[106] When viewed from the standpoint of women, LEAF argued, the impact of pornography is clear; it is degrading, dehumanizing, subordinating, and dangerous.[107] Given that pornography contributes to the social context of women's disadvantage, the factum insisted that it does not merit constitutional protection as expression; its restriction through the *Criminal Code* is instead constitutionally mandated by the equality provisions of the *Charter*. But LEAF also argued that the legal definition of obscenity must be recast to encompass the perspectives of women victimized through pornography. The court was encouraged to abandon the conservative moral discourse that has long framed the definition of obscenity, in favour of an approach based on the harms pornography causes women. Under this test, obscenity would be defined as material which is 'dehumanizing' and 'degrading' for women.[108]

LEAF's position in *Butler* was presented in the most categorical of terms, as if it were revealing a singular feminist 'Truth' to the judiciary – *prohibiting pornography promotes equality*. This factum embodied the characteristic narrative style of legal argument. It was closed and unequivocal; it refused complexity and contingency. The factum was, in effect, marked by what Yeatman refers to as generic closure – the assertion of an 'impersonal voice of authority, where propositions appear as features of fact, formal principles of order are fundamental to shaping the text, and there are no indications of process, uncertainty, or contest.'[109] This unequivocal tone in a context of multiple and competing feminist positions erects an artificial and misleading certainty that is also evident in the literalist approach to pornography underpinning the *Butler* factum. In LEAF's view, the pornographic possesses a singular and universal meaning, readily apparent to anyone. The importance of context and subjectivity in the interpretation of sexual imagery is thus effectively denied. The task of defining what is 'degrading and dehumanizing' is seen to be open to objective legal determination. In this manner, legal objectivity is reified, and the 'Truth' claims of law are bolstered.

The factum also employed social science research to make the claim that pornography promotes sexual violence. LEAF contended that 'it is uncontroversial that exposure to such materials causes aggression towards women in laboratory settings.'[110] This research is, however, extremely controversial.[111] It has been plagued by methodological problems and inconclusive results, and many key researchers on pornography and sexual aggression acknowledge that the existing data are very contradictory.

Finally, and reflecting the epistemic foundations of its discourse of equality, LEAF presented subordination as a position of 'Truth.' Underlying this factum is a view of sexuality as domination and of pornography as being about the domination of women by men.[112] Within this repressive view of power, women are constructed as victims, passive objects, who have been completely constructed by male sexual domination. By constituting women as thoroughly victimized, we become 'innocent' of power and thus capable of apprehending 'Truth.' And by constructing women as silent victims, devoid of agency, LEAF's authority to speak for women is symbolically confirmed.

LEAF's claim that degradation is the 'Truth' of pornography did carry some force in the Supreme Court. In *Butler*, the Supreme Court upheld existing obscenity legislation and made overtures towards a feminist 'harm-based' definition of pornography. Yet as Cossman has demonstrated, informing this decision was a traditional 'moralistic' sexual subtext, which sees sex as dirty and construes representations of sex as antisocial.[113] While somewhat persuasive in the courts, LEAF's unequivocal 'porn as violence and degradation position' also produced an intensification of the feminist porn wars in Canada as artists, academics, writers, lesbians, bookstore and media workers, and sex trade workers, reacted with outrage to the presentation of antipornography feminism as feminist orthodoxy.[114] Far from constituting a feminist legal victory, these critics argued forcefully, *Butler* merely provided a new feminist language to legitimize what is really a conservative moral agenda. And they sketched the post-*Butler* landscape as a time of repression marked by: the restriction of gay/lesbian materials by judges employing the notion of porn as 'harm'; the increased targeting of lesbian/gay materials by Canada Customs; the harassment of sex trade workers; and the increased self-censorship of cultural workers.[115] In effect, against LEAF's embrace of *Butler* as a 'victory,' critics contended that state censorship merely thwarts feminist attempts to re-map the terrain of sexuality, operating to silence those voices who challenge dominant sexual norms.

This construction of women – as 'agents' with 'voice' – contrasts sharply with the 'passive, silent victim' that grounded LEAF's anti-pornography stance. Ironically, it was this 'victim' who was called on to insulate LEAF's position from the criticisms of anticensorship feminists. At a 1993 meeting, LEAF attempted to respond to charges that its argument in Butler was not 'representative,' through invoking the vantage-point of 'victimization.' As one member of the National Litigation Committee insisted, LEAF had attempted to 'represent' the needs of 'victims' of male violence, of 'battered' women, of those women 'most marginalized' and not present to defend their concerns.[116] It was on the basis of this vantage-point that LEAF defended its position; from the perspective of 'victims,' pornography is 'harm,' and the Supreme Court's decision in *Butler* a 'feminist' victory. In this way, the *Butler* factum became unassailable, placed beyond the push and pull of feminist contestation.[117] In the context of its 1999 decision to intervene in *Little Sisters*, LEAF was again called on to reconsider *Butler*, this time in relation to the targeting of gay and lesbian materials by Canada Customs.[118] In a discussion paper entitled 'Revisiting Butler,' LEAF argues that its stance in *Butler* was specifically anti–hetero-pornography and argues against homophobic interpretations of the 'degrading and dehumanizing' standard.[119] This more recent effort to distinguish hetero- from lesbian porn, a distinction that nowhere appears in its 1992 sweeping condemnation of 'pornography' (as singular and unified), enables LEAF to at once hold onto its *Butler* position, while condemning the courts' and Customs' tendency to define gay and lesbian materials as 'degrading.'[120]

The insertion into law of feminist positions that assume the mantle of 'Truth' obscures the normative and politically constructed nature of all feminist positions. Because pornography is a site of such clear contestation, LEAF's intervention in *Butler* serves as a stark illustration of how the equation of experience and 'Truth' erases decision and political struggle from legal argument. Making feminist legal strategy more consistent with democratic norms requires an unhinging of experience from 'Truth,' and this is something that seems to contradict the kind of feminist jurisprudential project embraced by LEAF. The risk of admitting contingency and complexity within legal argument may be reduced persuasiveness in the courts. The tensions between inclusion and making feminist politics visible in law, on the one hand, and constructing categorical claims compatible with the foundationalism of legal discourse, on the other, are, in my view, among the central challenges faced by feminist litigation in the new millennium.

A tentative and yet promising effort to achieve some balance between feminist politics and legal persuasion is evident in at least two recent LEAF factums. These arguments made in *M. v. H* (1999)[121] and in *Vriend* (1998) suggest some movement away from the feminist foundationalism that has characterized LEAF's legal interventions for the past decade. Both of these cases concern lesbian inequality. It may well be that the conspicuous socially constructed character of lesbian identity opened greater possibilities for contingent legal argumentation. As Foucaultian-inspired feminist theorists convincingly argue, the category 'lesbian' emerged only at the end of the nineteenth century, born out of the taxonomical efforts of sexologists.[122] Before this time, it was virtually impossible to make the claim 'I am a lesbian' – even though same-sex erotic behaviour between women has no doubt always existed, the sexual identity 'lesbian' is a recent invention. Unlike identity categories built on visible bodily markers – skin colour, ability, genitalia – lesbian identity is perhaps more transparently and obviously socially and discursively constructed. This, in turn, may impede the unreflexive equation of experience and strategy that has been at the heart of standpoint epistemology and its jurisprudential cousin, CASE.

Most certainly all lesbians experience oppression, and indeed it is the case that direct legal discrimination on the basis of sexual identity categories remains prevalent at a time when most discrimination against women/people of colour, for example, is indirect and systemic. Nonetheless, there have always been marked differences of opinion among lesbian activists on both the essence of lesbian oppression and appropriate strategic directions.[123] These divisions are evident in the issues raised by both *M. v. H.* and *Vriend*, the first cases concerning lesbian identity in which LEAF intervened. Rather than obscuring the complexity of diverse points of view, these factums make an effort to reveal political and normative differences, thus implicitly challenging the premise that 'Truth' resides in experience.

M. v. H. involved a *Charter* equality challenge to the heterosexual definition of spouse in the support provisions of the *Ontario Family Law Act* and thus engaged the extremely controversial strategic question of are we or are we not family? Debates on the question of whether lesbians should seek spousal status have been longstanding and continue to raise many contentious issues. In this case, the Respondent M. had challenged the legal exclusion of lesbians from the definition of spouse by deploying an assimilationist argument – homosexual relationships are 'just like' heterosexual ones in terms of commitment, longevity, and fidelity.[124] Many lesbian (and gay) activists have supported 'sameness' arguments because they are strategic; they are rooted in and grow out of a liberal comparative model of equality, and they are thus highly consistent with dominant legal norms and political values. At the same time, however, as critics have warned, sameness arguments can quickly slide into containment, as normative heterosexuality is reinforced. As Boyd asks, 'Isn't it problematic that the normative model of heterosexual coupledom is taken for granted and affirmed, in this assessment – that "a strategy of inclusion, recognition, containment, and control that reinforces 'family' values and inevitably draws lines between good homosexuals (middle class, monogamous, double income) and bad homosexuals (gays who cruise the bars, baths and parks, and dykes who ride motorcycles topless)" is reinforced?'[125]

Rather than endorsing the simple and strategic 'sameness' argument in *M. v. H.*, LEAF's factum departs significantly from the position of the respondent. The 'sameness' position relies on the similarly situated test that LEAF has long sought to displace and, as its factum argued, asserting sameness is unnecessary, as successive Supreme Court decisions have accepted that similarity is not a measure of entitlement to *Charter* equality.[126] More significantly, however, LEAF directly engages in the extensive lesbian literature that critiques assimilationist strategies. As the factum acknowledges, the claim that 'we are just like hetero couples' fails to challenge normative heterosexuality and risks devaluing lesbian and gay relationships that 'least resemble heterosexual ones.'[127] At the same time, however, the outcome sought in this case is one that implicitly supports the argument that lesbians (and gays) should be entitled to be defined as spouses with the same rights and benefits as heterosexuals. As LEAF contended, the continued exclusion of lesbian relationships from legislative protection reinforces disadvantage. This exclusion not only denies lesbian women who are financially dependent on partners the bare right to apply for economic support on relationship breakdown; it also deprives lesbians of social recognition and respect, challenges the formation of lesbian relationships, and reinforces homophobia.[128] In effect, LEAF made the complex argument that exclusion promotes lesbian disadvantage, while at the same time cautioning that a demand for inclusion should not be interpreted as a plea for assimilation into heterosexual norms.[129]

As some participants have acknowledged, the LEAF case committee for *M. v. H.* was a site of intense debate. Differences arose not only on the question of assimilation, but also on the related consequences of making an argument for privatized support obligations between gays and lesbians. As Boyd, Gavigan, Cossman, and many others contend, endorsing privatized obligations is perfectly consistent with a central underlying premise of neoliberal public policy, that is, the privatization of social reproduction.[130] Increasing familial support obligations is one way in which governments have pushed forward the erosion of the welfare state; in this context, feminist litigators must think very carefully about whether their strategies may exacerbate such trends. However, grappling with the structural implications of privatization proved a far more difficult challenge for LEAF than the reconciliation of spousal support and a resistance to heteronormativity. The *M. v. H.* factum recognized the intensity of lesbian concerns about privatizing social responsibilities – 'the more that private remedies for economic disadvantage are created for some, the less responsibility the government may accept for the economic well-being of some individuals.'[131] Yet the thrust of this critique is then blunted by LEAF's next point – 'in the current era of restructuring by government, these concerns may be somewhat moot.'[132] What results, then, is at best a hesitant recognition of deeper strategic problems of the struggle for spousal recognition or, at worst, as Boyd suggests, an implicit endorsement of the privatizing rationale of family law.[133] Nonetheless, dissent is quite clearly brought to the fore in *M. v. H.* in a way that stands in contrast to the univocal tones of *Butler* – generic closure is replaced by greater attention to contestation, and the factum even refers to the issue of spousal status as a 'controversial' one among lesbians. The existence and experience of lesbian disadvantage is thus no guarantee of political, strategic, or normative coherence. As the factum emphasized, 'Lesbian reservations about the risks of assimilation within the family law system have been voiced by the same constitutionally relevant group whose interests are coextensive'; but, as LEAF underlined, 'To the degree that differences of opinion exist, they turn on how best to promote lesbians' equality interests in an unequal society, not whether to promote them at all.'[134]

The nuances of the argument in *M. v. H.* did not appear to reduce the persuasiveness of LEAF's position that the exclusion of lesbians from spousal support provisions infringed on the equality guarantees of the *Charter*. In a decision widely hailed as a victory by gay and lesbian activists, the Supreme Court struck down the opposite-sex definition of spouse in the impugned provision of the *Ontario Family Law Act*, delaying the declaration for six months to allow the Ontario government time to amend its legislation and consider the impact of the decision for other laws. The majority reasoning did not rest on a necessary assertion of similarity between the hetero-norm and same-sex relationships, although it did emphasize that broadening the definition of spouse in support laws would have the benefit of reducing the burden on the public purse. In this sense, LEAF's hesitant cautioning about the privatization of social responsibility fell on deaf ears, and the decision as a whole is one that is consistent with neoliberal strategy.

Perhaps the visibility of normative and strategic difference in the *M. v. H.* factum was made less risky by the fact that there were other intervenors, including the Foundation for Equal Families and Equality for Gays and Lesbians Everywhere (EGALE), asserting a set of liberal, sameness-oriented rationales – the we are 'family' position.[135] In other words, creativity, contingency, and nuance in feminist legal argument may be facilitated in situations where LEAF intervenes alongside many others, all arguing for the same outcome but in different voices. This was also the case in *Vriend* where LEAF was one among a number of intervenors contesting the exclusion of sexual orientation as a prohibited ground of discrimination in Alberta human rights legislation.[136]

As Young has observed, while of tremendous symbolic importance, especially in a province in which the government's back bench is so vocal in its embrace of a right-wing and explicitly homophobic 'family values agenda,' the issue at stake in *Vriend* was not one likely to rock the boat of hetero-patriarchy.[137] Including 'sexual orientation' in human rights law enables sexual minorities to make complaints about discrimination in housing, employment, and commercial relationships; but recognizing a right not to be discriminated against is not the same as measures that might support and encourage gays and lesbians to live openly and freely. In effect, antidiscrimination laws fall clearly on the less radical 'compassion' side of the compassion/condonation dichotomy identified by Ryder.[138] By the time the Supreme Court heard the *Vriend* case, seven provinces had already embraced the 'compassion' approach by including sexual orientation in their human rights legislation. Nevertheless, an equality-affirming decision was by no means predictable in this case, partly because it invoked the difficult issue of what constitutes state action for the purposes of the *Charter* – that is, can legislative inaction (or 'neutral silence' as the attorney-general of Alberta asserted this was) infringe on *Charter* equality?

LEAF's intervention in *Vriend* was intended to combat the erasure of lesbians from the legal category 'sexual orientation,' to render 'lesbian experience' visible, while at the same time contesting the blanket denial of human rights protection to gays and lesbians in Alberta.[139] In this case, LEAF went a step further than in *M. v. H.* in severing the foundationalist equation of identity, experience, and strategy. This is because in *Vriend* the categorical nature of antidiscrimination law is challenged and disrupted. In constructing its argument, LEAF was forced to confront the complexity of the identity category 'lesbian,' as well as debates about the essence of lesbian oppression. Some lesbian analysts have taken the position that lesbian disadvantage is grounded in sex/gender. In this view, because compulsory heterosexuality is central to gender domination, protection against lesbian discrimination is already available through inclusion of sex as a prohibited ground of discrimination.[140] In *Vriend*, LEAF sought to challenge what it referred to as the 'watertight' compartments view of grounds of discrimination and contended that, properly interpreted, the ground 'sex' (or race) could encompass lesbian experience;[141] at the same time, the factum argued that 'lesbian oppression cannot always be conceptualized either as a matter of 'sex' or 'sexual orientation.''[142] As Pellatt notes, there were marked divisions on the case committee with respect to conceiving the discrimination to which lesbians are subject and defining it in law for strategic purposes.[143] While as a short-term measure, the LEAF factum advocated the inclusion of sexual orientation in Alberta human rights legislation, it also critiqued the necessity of exclusive grounds and recommended that equality interpretation move towards a 'groundless' purposive approach.

LEAF's factum, in effect, mirrored Nitya Iyer's influential critique of antidiscrimination doctrine. Iyer argued that laws that address inequality have been structured so that claimants must attempt to fit themselves into narrowly defined, rigid, and prefabricated categories. Grounds of discrimination are treated as pockets of identity separable from one another so that interactive oppressions fall between the cracks. Claimants who cannot simplify their story, so that it accords with the dominant group's narrow understanding of the category grounding their claim will fail.[144] As an example, the majority of Supreme Court justices in *Mossop* (1993),[145] a case involving the inability of a gay man to claim bereavement leave on his partner's father's death, defined the relevant ground of discrimination as 'sexual orientation,' a category which at that time was not protected in the *Canadian Human Rights Act*. While Mossop had claimed 'family status' discrimination, the majority constructed this category as heterosexual, so as to cover variations in heterosexual family forms. Thus, family status was heterosexualized, and Mossop was defined solely by his sexual orientation. Reliant on an oversimplified image of 'difference' (as different in one respect from a silent background norm), antidiscrimination law projects uniformity onto groups/identities/grounds of discrimination.[146] As LEAF tried to convey to the Court in *Vriend*, homogeneous grounds will always fail to capture the complex and inherently intersectional character of lesbian identity.

The *Vriend* factum represented not only a fundamental critique of the category-based and comparative nature of antidiscrimination doctrine; it also, I would suggest, expressed a movement away from the experientially based foundations of the CASE approach. This was evident in the factum's near silence on the specific character of 'lesbian experience.' As I have emphasized, LEAF's approach to equality has rested on an enunciation of experiences of disadvantage as grounding for feminist 'Truth' claims before the court. By contrast, the *Vriend* factum is unique in the sense that it does not include any extensive effort to document lesbian oppression. Pellatt attributes this to the dearth of credible studies on lesbian-specific discrimination and to a reluctance by case committee members to employ a more anecdotal approach.[147] It is also possible, however, that once one moves away from grounds and categories as a way of conceptualizing inequality it becomes difficult, and perhaps impossible to fix or rigidly define experience. In turn, it would seem that this radical and complex shift in thinking about antidiscrimination in law leads to far more transparently politically informed legal strategies and arguments. In effect, the progression of CASE, from identity to experience to 'Truth,' is disrupted and the positions that are advanced become more reflective of *decision*.

As with *M. v. H*, LEAF's complex argument in *Vriend* did not seem to have a resounding impact on what was at the same time an extremely positive Supreme Court decision. An eight-member majority of the Court did articulate a ringing condemnation of discrimination on the basis of sexual orientation and chose to 'read in' protection on this basis into Alberta human rights legislation. The Court was also unanimous in defining deliberate legislative inaction as 'state action' and thus properly scrutinized under the *Charter*. Ultimately LEAF, along with the many other interveners supporting the appellant, can claim responsibility for this important decision. The majority opinions also included 'lesbians,' at least at the level of terminology. Unlike earlier decisions that have used the descriptor 'homosexual,' *Vriend* deploys the more inclusive gays and lesbians' (bisexuals and transgendered people, not surprisingly, appear to be missing from the Court understanding of sexuality). Even so, this change in language could hardly be seen as the recognition of 'lesbian specificity' that LEAF had hoped for. But more critically, LEAF's carefully articulated 'groundless' and purposive approach to equality in *Vriend* was not referred to at all in the majority decision. It was only in L'Heureux-Dube's concurring decision, in which she too critiques an equality test overly focused on 'grounds,' that we can see an echo of LEAF's position.

In successive judgments beginning with *Egan* (1995),[148] L'Heureux-Dubé has developed an approach to equality interpretation that would focus on the impact, not the ground of discrimination – 'to determine whether the impact was unfair it is necessary to look not only at the group who has been disadvantaged but at the nature of power in terms of which the discrimination was effected and, also at the nature of the interests which have been affected by the discrimination.'[149] As Majury observes, this approach 'de-emphasiz[es] the categories and arguably introduc[es] the potential for a more flexible and complex analysis that would be less prone to stereotype and essentialism and would more easily accommodate interactive discrimination.'[150] Shifting legal emphasis away from categories of identity and towards the nature of power not only undermines essentialism, it also opens the way for equality argumentation more explicitly rooted in normative decision. If approaches to inequality become less focused on identity, then 'experience' becomes more visibly constructed and strategy more overtly political. It has been a premise of CASE that 'experience,' as held by members of a disadvantaged group, is the appropriate jurisprudential standpoint for discerning 'correct' action; once identity is removed from a privileged position in the equality equation, politics, not 'Truth' becomes the basis of feminist claims before the courts. In LEAF's factum in *Vriend* and in the approach to equality articulated by L'Heureux-Dubé, we can observe the beginnings of a challenge to the categorical nature of legal thought and the creation of an opening (however narrow it may be) for the development of feminist litigation that is more fully and explicitly grounded in feminist politics.

Conclusion

It is not clear whether the *Vriend* factum represents a fundamental turning-point in LEAF's approach to equality away from foundations and the truth of experience. This chapter has, however, charted a series of critical changes in LEAF's discourse – from essentialist notions of women's shared suffering to the recognition of the specificities of experience, from univocal positions that correspond with the 'Truth' tones of legal discourse to more nuanced, incoherent, and at the same time more democratic legal arguments. I began this chapter by insisting on the ongoing necessity of feminist litigation and specifically, feminist *Charter* litigation. As LEAF has succinctly argued, 'the women's movement cannot abjure the *Charter*. The *Charter* will not abjure us.'[151] While it is certainly true that feminists cannot ignore *Charter* litigation, neither should they ignore the often difficult questions underlying feminist legal strategy. The importance of LEAF's work should never mean that it be insulated from feminist criticism. The effect of feminist criticism is very often productive. As I have demonstrated, critiques of LEAF's once homogeneous construction of women's experience have produced a fundamental shift in its equality discourse. A recognition of particularity has paved the way for a practice of feminist litigation grounded in an embrace of women's differences from one another, as well as their common interests. Nevertheless, to the extent that the equation 'experience = Truth' remains the central premise of LEAF's praxis, feminist debates and challenges will continue to be silenced.

Law's preference for categorical and foundational discourses poses strategic dilemmas for actors such as LEAF whose primary function is litigation, but who must, at the same time, seek legitimation among extra-legal feminist actors. Law may listen most closely to authoritative narratives, yet in conforming to the discursive requirements of law feminist legal actors deny the always normative content of their positions. I have argued that foundational claims collapse spaces for normative contestation and are, therefore, inherently hostile to democratic feminist politics. Law as it currently exists does indeed rest on foundations; but perhaps feminist legal strategy should seek to unsettle these foundations. The positions articulated in *M v. H.* and *Vriend* could be viewed as the tentative beginnings of this more complex future.

As Smart has argued, feminists must attempt to disrupt law at its heart, including its privileging of objectivity and abstraction, in order to make way for multiple and diverse feminist discourses.[152] At the level of practice, perhaps this means that feminist litigators of the twenty-first century should make it explicit that legal arguments are always the product of politics and normative assertion, rather than 'Truth.' Perhaps it means that feminist legal argument should attempt to reflect complexity, contingency, and contending feminist positions. Perhaps it also means that we should encourage multiple and sometimes competing feminist interventions in law. Coherent subject positions and 'Truth' do enable feminist uses of law; but foundational claims may also inhibit legal recognition of the full texture and complexities of social relations. This contradiction and the dilemmas it presents will remain central for feminist legal strategy. For LEAF and other feminist legal actors, risks, but also possibilities, accompany this contradiction.

Notes

1 See McIntyre, this volume.
2 Lise Gotell, 'Litigating Feminist "Truth": An Anti-foundational Critique,' (1995) 4 *Social and Legal Studies* 100.
3 Judy Fudge, 'The Effect of Entrenching a Bill of Rights on Political Discourse: Feminist Demands and Sexual Violence in Canada' (1989) 17 *International Journal of the Sociology of Law* 450.
4 See Gotell, 'Litigating Feminist "Truth"'; and Gotell, 'Shaping *Butler*: The New Politics of Antipornography,' in Brenda Cossman, Shannon Bell, Lise Gotell, and Becki Ross, eds., *Bad Attitude/s on Trial* (Toronto: University of Toronto Press, 1997) 48–106.
5 Joan Scott, 'Experience,' in Judith Butler and Joan Scott, eds., *Feminists Theorize the Political* (New York: Routledge, 1992) 37.
6 Nancy Hartsock, 'Foucault on Power: A Theory for Women?' in Linda Nicholson, ed., *Feminism/Postmodernism* (New York: Routledge, 1990) 171–2.
7 Carol Smart, *Feminism and the Power of Law* (London: Routledge, 1989) 71; Toni Williams, 'Re-Forming "Women's" Truth: A Critique of the Royal Commission on the Status of Women' (1990) 22 *Ottawa Law Review* 751.
8 Jennifer Wicke, 'Postmodern Identity and the Legal Subject' (1991) *University of Colorado Law Review* 759.
9 Wendy Brown, 'Feminist Hesitations, Postmodern Exposures' (1991) 3, 1 *Differences* 69.

166 Lise Gotell

10 Kirstie McClure, 'The Issue of Foundations,' in Butler and Scott, *Feminists Theorize*, 343.
11 Fudge, 'The Effect of Entrenching'; Michael Mandel, *The Charter of Rights and the Legalization of Politics in Canada* (Toronto: Thompson, 1994).
12 *Andrews v. Law Society of British Columbia*, [1989] 1 S.C.R. 143.
13 The first mention of MacKinnon was in LEAF, '*Litigation Works: A Report on LEAF Litigation Year Two*,' 30 June 1987, 12. After this she appears frequently in LEAF's literature. Gillian More ('Towards a New Conception of Equality: The Canadian Approach,' paper prepared for the British Association of Canadian Studies Conference, April 1991, 17) also stresses MacKinnon's influence on LEAF's approach.
14 LEAF, 'Factum of the Intervenor, Andrews v. Law Society of British Columbia, [1999] S.C.C.,' as reproduced in LEAF, 'Introduction,' in *Equality and the Charter* (Toronto: Emond Montgomery, 1996) 10.
15 Ibid., 18.
16 Ibid., 15.
17 Nancy Love, 'Politics and Voice(s): An Empowerment/Knowledge Regime' (1991) 3, 1 *Differences* 92.
18 Gotell, 'Litigating Feminist "Truth."'
19 Kathy Ferguson, *The Man Question* (Berkeley: University of California Press, 1993) 5.
20 Brown, 'Feminist Hesitations,' 76.
21 Ibid., 73; Donna Haraway, *Simians, Cyborgs and Women* (New York: Routledge, 1991), 191.
22 Zillah Eisenstein, *The Female Body and the Law* (Berkeley: University of California Press, 1989), 2.
23 Williams, 'Re-Forming,' 751.
24 Kimberle Crenshaw, 'Demarginalizing the Intersection of Race and Sex,' (1989) 169 *University of Chicago Legal Forum* 139; Nitya Duclos, 'Disappearing Women: Racial Minority Women in Human Rights Cases' (1993) 6, 1 *Canadian Journal of Women and the Law* 25.
25 Gotell, 'Litigating.'
26 LEAF, 'Introduction,' *Equality and the Charter*, xxi.
27 Gayatri Spivak, 'Criticism, Feminism and the Institution – an Interview with Gayatri Chakravorty Spivak' (1984–5) 10, 11 *Thesis Eleven* 175; Anna Pellatt, 'Equality Rights, Litigation and Social Transformation: A Consideration of the Women's Legal Education and Action Fund's Intervention in *Vriend*' (2000) 12, 1 *Canadian Journal of Women and the Law*.
28 For a fuller discussion, see Gotell, 'Litigating.'
29 Ibid., 107.

30 Catharine MacKinnon, 'LEAF's Theory of Equality: Breaking New Ground' (1990) 3, 2 *LEAFLines*, 1.
31 Factum of the Intervenor, LEAF, *Butler v. Her Majesty the Queen* 1991 (S.C.C.); Factum of the Intervenor, LEAF, *Sullivan/Lemay v. Her Majesty the Queen* 1990 (S.C.C.); Factum of the Intervenor, LEAF, *Albrecht v. Albrecht* 1990 (O.S.C.), court file no. 1135/89; Factum of the Intervenor, LEAF, *Brooks/Allen/Dixon v. Canada Safeway Company* 1989 (S.C.C.); Factum of the Intervenor, LEAF, *Daigle v. Tremblay* 1989 (S.C.C.); Factum of the Intervenor, LEAF, *Borowski v. A.G. Canada* 1988 (S.C.C.); Factum of the Intervenor, LEAF, *Canadian Newspapers Company Ltd. v. Her Majesty the Queen* 1988 (S.C.C.); Factum of the Intervenor, LEAF, *Janzen/Govereau v. Platy Enterprises* 1987 S.C.C.; Factum of the Intervenor, LEAF, *Andrews v. the Law Society of British Columbia* 1987 (S.C.C.); Memorandum of Argument of LEAF, *Re: Pirjo Margit Roininen* 1987 (B.C.S.C.), court file no. 192; Factum of the Intervenor, LEAF, *Seaboyer/Gayme v. Her Majesty the Queen* 1991 (S.C.C.) 1996; Factum of the Intervenor, LEAF, *Her Majesty the Queen and the Canada Employment and Immigration Commission v. Schacter* 1992 (S.C.C.). All of these are reproduced in LEAF, *Equality and the Charter*.
32 *Re: 'Baby R.'* [1988] 15 R.F.L. (3d) 225.
33 *Norberg v. Wynrib*, [1992] 2 S.C.R. 226.
34 Memorandum of Argument of LEAF, *Re: Pirjo Margit Roininen*, 32.
35 Factum of the Intervenor, LEAF, *Norberg v. Wynrib* (S.C.C.), as reproduced in LEAF, *Equality and the Charter*, 230.
36 Ibid., 230.
37 For example, LEAF would later explain the significance of *Baby R.* and of its other reproductive rights cases: 'Let us be clear, what is at stake in cases deciding who has control over reproduction is a woman's right to sexual equality – to freedom from discrimination that exploits women's role as childbearers, actual and potential, and as mothers'; 'LEAF and Reproductive Rights' (1989) 3, 1 *LEAFLines* 5.
38 Gotell, 'Litigating,' 110–1; T. Brettel Dawson, 'Re *Baby R*: A Comment on Fetal Apprehension' (1990) 4 *Canadian Journal of Women and the Law* 265.
39 Diana Majury, 'Equality and Discrimination According to the Supreme Court of Canada' (1990–1) 4 *Canadian Journal of Women and the Law* 428.
40 Those most vulnerable to prenatal coercion have been Aboriginal women, women of colour, and immigrant women with limited English skills; the few white women who have shared this experience have been poor, sometimes transient, often with a history of drug or alcohol abuse (Dawson, 'Re: *Baby R.*, 271).

168   Lise Gotell

41 Veronica Kolder, J. Gallagher and M. Parsons, 'Court Ordered Obstetrical Interventions' (1987) 19 *New England Journal of Medicine* 1192.
42 Royal Commission on Aboriginal Peoples, *Gathering Strength: Report*, vol. 3 (Ottawa: Minister of Supply and Services, 1996), chap. 3; Canadian Panel on Violence Against Women, *Changing the Landscape: Ending Violence, Achieving Equality* (Ottawa: Canadian Panel on Violence Against Women, 1993) 178–9.
43 Canadian Panel on Violence Against Women, *Changing the Landscape*, 178.
44 Ibid.
45 A.C. Hamilton and C.M. Sinclair, *Report of the Aboriginal Justice Inquiry of Manitoba*, vol.1, *The Justice System and Aboriginal People* (Winnipeg: The Inquiry, 1991) 481–2; Canadian Panel on Violence Against Women, *Changing the Landscape*, 156–7.
46 Royal Commission on Aboriginal Peoples, *Gathering Strength*, 161–2.
47 Canadian Panel on Violence Against Women, *Changing the Landscape*, 180.
48 Patricia Monture-Okanee, 'The Violence We Women Do: A First Nations Perspective,' in C. Backhouse and D. Flaherty, eds., *Challenging Times* (Montreal and Kingston: McGill-Queen's, 1992), 194.
49 *Bezaire v. Bezaire* (1980), 20 R.F.L. (2d) 361 (Ont. C.A.). For a discussion, see Katherine Arnup, 'Mothers Just Like Others: Lesbians, Divorce and Child Custody in Canada' (1989) 3 *Canadian Journal of Women and the Law* 18.
50 After being denied custody and fearing the abuse of her children, Ms Bezaire abducted her children and was criminally charged. While LEAF was not directly involved in these legal proceedings, it did provide funding for her defence. For this reason, her case was discussed once in a LEAF litigation report and once in *LEAFLines* (*Litigation Works: A Report on LEAF Litigation Year Two*, 30 June 1987, 16; 'Bezaire' (1987) 1, 3 *LEAFLines* 4). LEAF's marginalization of lesbian issues extends beyond the *Bezaire* case. While LEAF was briefly involved in another lesbian case involving the exclusion of lesbian families from provincial health coverage, here again it constructed this case as an issue of benefits for 'same sex partners' ('Karen Andrews: Health Benefits for Same Sex Spouses' (1988) 2, 2 *LEAFLines* 8). It was not until 1991, in fact, that the word 'lesbian' first appeared in a LEAF newsletter ('Outreach Meetings Held in Maritimes' (1991) 4, 3 *LEAFLines* 10). Moreover, LEAF's wholehearted endorsement of state censorship in the *Butler* case has, in the view of many lesbians, precipitated the targeting of lesbian sexual materials and contributed to the repression of lesbian voices. (Interview with Elaine Carol, Censorstop, 6 June 1993).

LEAF's Changing Approach to *Charter* Equality 169

51 *Re: 'Colgate Palmolive'* [1990] Decision of Hearings Officer, Workmen's Compensation Board, 29 June 1990. LEAF defined the complainant's experience solely in terms of its gendered dimension – as 'sexual harassment,' an 'injury experienced almost exclusively by women' (see LEAF, *Litigation Works*, 16–17; and LEAF, 'New Cases' (1987) 1, 4, *LEAFLines* 1–2). It was not until four years later that LEAF began to highlight the 'racist and sexist' character of this black woman's experience (see LEAF, 'Colgate Palmolive' (1992) 4, 4 *LEAFLines* 6).

52 While these cases stand out as stark examples of abstraction, they suggest a more extensive pattern. It is, however, most often impossible to know which kinds of relevant factors have been erased from other cases that LEAF identifies as being of significance to 'all women.' This is because we frequently do not know very much about those who are at the centre of LEAF cases other than that they are women.

53 LEAF, *Litigation Works*, 3.

54 LEAF, 'Daniels' (1991) 4, 3 *LEAFLines* 10.

55 LEAF, 'Smart: LEAF Seeks Leave to Intervene in Immigration Case' (1990) 3, 2 *LEAFLines* 7.

56 LEAF, 'Immigrant Women's Organization Joins Challenge of Language Training Programme' (1990) 3, 3 *LEAFLines* 4.

57 This tendency to privilege 'sex disadvantage' in the first instance was also apparent in LEAF's legal construction of cases involving multiple oppression. In the *Daniels* case, e.g., LEAF challenged the incarceration of a Native woman in the Prison for Women (P4W), stressing 'the inadequacies of P4W which render *women's* confinement there unconstitutional.' Again we can discern a prioritization of sex inequality. In its written submission before the Saskatchewan Court of Appeal, the thrust of LEAF's first three arguments was to identify the inadequacies of P4W for 'women,' while the 'absence of adequate facilities to meet the particular needs of native women' was raised as a final and subsidiary argument (LEAF, 'Daniels,' 9).

58 Angela Harris, 'Race and Essentialism in Feminist Legal Theory' (1990) 42 *Stanford Law Review* 589.

59 Ibid., 603.

60 LEAF, 'Introduction,' *Equality and the Charter*, xxi.

61 Ibid.

62 LEAF, 'LEAF's Policy of Outreach and Diversification' (1993) 5, 3 *LEAFLines* 3; LEAF, 'Introduction,' *Equality and the Charter*, xxii.

63 For a discussion of these efforts, see LEAF, 'Introduction,' *Equality and the Charter*, xxi–xxii.

64 LEAF (1999) 'Cases Adopted 1998–1999.'

170 Lise Gotell

65 LEAF (1999) 'Special Projects.'
66 Sherene Razack, *Canadian Feminism and the Law* (Toronto: Second Story Books, 1991) 53.
67 LEAF, 'Widening the Circle: LEAF Sponsors Major Symposium on Equality Rights' (1992) 5, 1 *LEAFLines* 2.
68 Ibid., 3.
69 Ibid., 2.
70 LEAF, 'Introduction,' *Equality and the Charter*, xxii.
71 Ibid., xxi–ii.
72 As of 30 June 1999, this project was inactive, in part because of the lack of funding (LEAF, 'Special Projects,' 1999).
73 Sheila McIntyre, 'The Consultations which Shaped Bill C-49,' in J. Roberts and Renata Mohr, eds., *Confronting Sexual Assault* (Toronto: University of Toronto Press, 1994) 304–5.
74 Radha Jhappan, 'The Equality Pit or the Rehabilitation of Justice' (1998) 10, 1 *Canadian Journal of Women and the Law* 78.
75 *R. v. O'Connor*, [1995] 4 S.C.R. 411.
76 Other central examples are: LEAF's intervention in *Eldridge v. British Columbia* (1997), a case involving a province's failure to provide sign language interpretation as a part of health services, in this specific case to a deaf woman giving birth (Factum of the Intervenor, LEAF, *Eldridge v. British Columbia (Attorney General),*' 1997); LEAF's intervention in *R.D.S v. R.* (1997), a case in which the Court of Appeal had determined that an African-Canadian woman judge's comments concerning racism in police practice constituted a reasonable apprehension of bias (see LEAF, 'Factum of the Intervenor, LEAF, *R. v. S. (R.D.)*, 1997); and LEAF's intervention in *Vriend* (1998), discussed below (Factum of the Intervenor, LEAF, *Vriend v. Alberta*, 1998).
77 *Winnipeg Family and Child Services v. G. (D.F.)*, [1997] 3 S.C.R. 925.
78 LEAF, 'Submissions to the Standing Committee on Justice and Legal Affairs: Review of Bill C-46,' 1997, 11.
79 Factum of the Intervenor, LEAF, *O'Connor v. The Queen* (S.C.C.), 1995, as reproduced in LEAF, *Equality and the Charter*, 432.
80 Ibid., 431.
81 Ibid., 434.
82 Ibid., 439.
83 Ibid., 439.
84 Ibid., 440.
85 Ibid., 440.
86 T. Brettel Dawson critiques the prevailing model of individual legal subjec-

tivity and contends that this model has prevented law from developing legal principles that could encompass the maternal–fetal relation ('First Person Familiar: Judicial Intervention in Pregnancy, Again: *G. (D.F.)*' (1998) 10, 1 *Canadian Journal of Women and the Law* 213).
87 Factum of the Intervenor, LEAF, *Winnipeg Family and Child Services v. G. (D.F.)* 1997, 16–17.
88 Susan Boyd, *Mothers and Illicit Drugs* (Toronto: University of Toronto Press, 1999) 23–4.
89 D. Roberts, ' Punishing Drug Addicts Who Have Babies: Women of Color, Equality and the Right to Privacy,' Adrien Wing, ed., *Critical Race Feminism* (New York: New York University Press, 1997) 130.
90 Ibid., 128.
91 Factum of the Intervenor, LEAF, *Winnipeg Family and Child Services v. G. (D.F.)*, 1997, 4–5.
92 Ibid., 5.
93 LEAF, 'Introduction,' *Equality and the Charter*, xxii.
94 Ibid., xxi.
95 Razack, *Canadian Feminism*, 62; John McInnes and Christine Boyle, 'Judging Sexual Assault Law against a Standard of Equality' (1995) 29, 2 *University of British Columbia Law Review* 341.
96 LEAF, 'Submissions to the Standing Committee on Justice and Legal Affairs: Review of Bill C-46,' 1997, 1.
97 Jhappan, 'The Equality Pit,' 78.
98 *Winnipeg Family and Child Services v. G. (D.F.)*, per Major J. at para. 88.
99 Jhappan, 'The Equality Pit,' 78–9.
100 LEAF, 'LEAF's Race, Culture, Religion and Gender Inequality Project' (1993) 5, 3 *LEAFLines*, 9.
101 Scott, 'Experience,' 25.
102 Smart, *Feminism*, 71.
103 Gotell, 'Litigating' Gotell, 'Shaping *Butler.*'
104 *R. v. Butler* [1992] 2 S.C.R. 452.
105 At a meeting between LEAF representatives and the Ad Hoc Coalition of Anti-Censorship Activists, Sheila McIntyre, a member of LEAF's National Legal Committee, indicated that national consultations had not taken place on *Butler* because LEAF was responding to a three-week time-line. Notes of Meeting, 21 June 1993.
106 'Factum of the Intervenor, LEAF, *Butler v. Her Majesty the Queen* (1992) (S.C.C.), as reproduced in *Equality and the Charter*, 201–21.
107 Ibid., 207, 214.
108 Ibid., 207–9.

109 Anna Yeatman, *Bureaucrats, Technocrats and Femocrats* (London: Allen and Unwin, 1990) 167.
110 Factum of the Intervenor, LEAF, *Butler v. Her Majesty the Queen* (1992) (S.C.C.),' as reproduced in *Equality and the Charter*, 213.
111 Alison King, 'Mystery and Imagination: The Case of Pornography Effects Studies,' in A. Assiter and A. Carol, eds., *Bad Girls and Dirty Pictures* (London: Pluto, 1993) 57–87.
112 For a critique of this view, see Mary Jo Frug, *Postmodern Legal Feminism* (New York: Routledge, 1992) 151–3.
113 Brenda Cossman, 'Feminist Fashion or Morality in Drag?' in *Bad Attitude/s on Trial*, 107–51.
114 According to artist Elaine Carol, anticensorship feminist activists in groups such as the Ontario Coalition Against Film and Video Censorship (OCAFVC) and Censorstop reacted with shock to the *Butler* decision and to the position LEAF had taken in it. These women formed a task force charged with contacting LEAF to voice criticism. Ultimately these anticensorship feminists formed an Ad Hoc Coalition of Anti-censorship Women which drew together representatives from OCAFVC, Maggies (a group of sex trade workers), the Lesbian and Gay Film Festival, *Fireweed* (feminist periodical), Toronto Women's Bookstore, Playwrights Union of Canada, York University Centre for Feminist Research, Glad Day Bookshop, lawyers, and academics. Interview, Elaine Carol, 6 June 1993. Minutes of meeting, Ad Hoc Coalition of Anti-censorship Women, 17 June 1993.
115 For a discussion, see Cossman et al. *Bad Attitude/s on Trial*.
116 Remarks of Karen Busby, Minutes of meeting between Ad Hoc Coalition of Anti-censorship Women and representatives of LEAF, 17 June 1993.
117 A news release was produced at the end of this meeting. In it, anticensorship feminists and LEAF together criticized the targeting of gay and lesbian materials by police, customs officials, and the courts. Moreover, they agreed to move from this common position to further discussions on pornography and censorship. To my knowledge, these further discussions have not taken place.
118 LEAF, '*Little Sisters Book and Art Emporium et al. v. Canada (A.G.)*: discrimination in the Enforcement of Obscenity Laws' (1999) 9, 1 *LEAFLines* 7.
119 LEAF, 'LEAF and the Little Sisters Case,' http://www.leaf.ca/DisButler.htm.
120 It is not the *Butler* standard that needs to be rethought, according to a recent article in *LEAFLines*; it is instead a problem of 'discriminatory enforcement,' LEAF, '*Little Sisters Book and Art Emporium*,' 7.

121 *M. v. H.*, [1999] 2. S.C.R. 3.
122 Kathleen Martindale, 'What Makes Lesbianism Thinkable? Theorizing Lesbianism from Adrienne Rich to Queer Theory,' in Nancy Mandell, ed., *Feminist Issues: Race, Class and Sexuality*, (Scarborough: Prentice-Hall Canada, 1998) 58.
123 Diana Majury, 'Representing Gays and Lesbians in Law,' in Janice Ristock and Catherine Taylor, eds., *Inside the Academy and Out* (Toronto: University of Toronto Press, 1998) 328–93.
124 Factum of the Intervenor, LEAF, *M. v. H.* [1999] S.C.C. 14.
125 Susan Boyd, 'Best Friends or Spouses? Privatization and the Recognition of Lesbian Relationships in *M. v. H.*' (1996) 13 *Canadian Journal of Family Law* 326.
126 LEAF, 'Factum,' *M. v. H.* 14.
127 Ibid., 13.
128 Ibid., 4.
129 Ibid., 15.
130 Susan Boyd, 'Family, Law and Sexualiity: Feminist Engagements' (1999) 8, 3 *Social and Legal Studies* 369–90; Shelley Gavigan, 'Paradise Lost, Paradox Revisited: The Implications of Familial Ideology for Feminist, Lesbian and Gay Engagement with the Law' (1993) 31 *Osgoode Hall Law Journal* 589–624; Brenda Cossman, 'Family Feuds: Neo-Liberal and Conservative Visions of the Reprivatization Project,' paper prepared for Gender, Sexuality and Law Conference, Keele University, England, 1998.
131 LEAF, 'Factum,' *M. v. H.*, file no. 25838, 13.
132 Ibid.
133 Boyd, 'Family, Law and Sexuality,' 380.
134 LEAF, 'Factum,' *M. v. H.*, 13.
135 The other interveners supporting this equality challenge were the Foundation for Equal Families, Equality for Gays and Lesbians Everywhere (EGALE), the Ontario Human Rights Commission, and the United Church. *M. v. H.* [1999] S.C.C.
136 These included: the Attorney General of Canada, the Attorney General of Ontario, the Alberta Civil Liberties Union, EGALE, the Foundation for Equal Families, the Canadian Human Rights Commission, the Canadian Labour Congress, the Canadian Bar Association, the Canadian Association of Statutory Human Rights Associations, the Canadian AIDS Society, the United Church, and the Canadian Jewish Congress. The appellant, Delwin Vriend, undertook this appeal with the Gay and Lesbian Awareness Association, the Gay and Lesbian Community Centre of Edmonton, and Dignity Canada. *Vriend v. Alberta*, [1998] 1 S.C.R. 493.

137 Margot Young, 'Change at the Margins: *Eldridge v. British Columbia (A.G.)* and *Vriend v. Alberta*' (1998) 10, 1 *Canadian Journal of Women and the Law* 260–1.
138 Bruce Ryder, 'Equality Rights and Sexual Orientation: Confronting Heterosexual Family Privilege' (1990) 9 *Canadian Journal of Family Law* 39.
139 Pellat, 'Equality Rights,' 18 and 26; LEAF, 'Factum, *Vriend v. Alberta*' 1998 at para. 4.
140 Diana Majury, 'Refashioning the Unfashionable: Claiming Lesbian Identities in a Legal Context' (1994) 7, 2 *Canadian Journal of Women and the Law* 286–318.
141 LEAF, 'Factum,' *Vriend v. Alberta*' (1998) para. 56.
142 Ibid., para. 33.
143 Pellatt, 'Equality Rights,' 31.
144 Nitya Iyer, 'Categorical Denials: Equality Rights and the Shaping of Social Identity' (1993) 19 *Queen's Law Journal* 179.
145 *Canada (Attorney General) v. Mossop*, [1993] 1 S.C.R. 554.
146 Iyer, 'Categorial Denials.'
147 Pellatt, 'Equality Rights,' 33.
148 *Egan v. Canada*, [1995] 2 S.C.R. 513.
149 As quoted in Hon. Madame Justice Claire L'Heureux-Dubé, 'The Changing Face of Equality' (1999) 19, 1–2 *Canadian Woman Studies / Les cahiers de la femme* 32.
150 Majury, 'Representing Gays and Lesbians in Law,' 318.
151 LEAF, 'Introduction,' *Equality and the Charter*, xxiv.
152 Smart, *Feminism* 88–9.

CHAPTER FIVE

The Equality Pit or the Rehabilitation of Justice?[1]

Radha Jhappan

Many years ago, I heard an account of a creative approach to problem-solving that concerned complaints about the slowness of the elevators in a very tall office building that accommodated thousands of employees of various businesses. The architects and engineers consulted about the problem proposed solutions (such as installing extra elevators on the outside of the building) that would have cost millions of dollars. Eventually, the owners called in the well-known psychologist and virtuoso problem-solver, Edward de Bono, who had made 'lateral thinking' famous and rather trendy in the 1970s.[2] De Bono solved the problem for a few thousand dollars by installing large mirrors beside the elevators on each floor. He reached this solution by identifying the problem, not as the speed of the elevators, but as the fact that people were *complaining* about the *wait*, and so he gave them something to do while they were waiting (attend to their grooming, observe others, and so on). I have no way of knowing how successful this solution ultimately was (though apparently the number of complaints dropped substantially), but the story does address the critical point that the way in which we define a problem will ultimately determine the kinds of solutions we look for.

In Canada as elsewhere, women, racialized peoples, lesbians and gay men, people with disabilities, and other oppressed groups have for some time been complaining about the wait *and* the speed (or rather slowness) in the coming of the liberty and equality promised by liberalism and its progeny, liberal democratic constitutions. In addition to a wide range of political strategies, some of the social movement organizations associated with these collectivities have engaged, to varying degrees, in contestation of public policies and laws through such strategies as lobbying legislators, participating in the drafting of laws, and, since the passage of the *Canadian Charter of Rights and Freedoms* in 1982,[3] challenging the constitutionality of various laws through litigation.

The litigation strategies of oppressed groups have been strenuously criticized, not only, predictably, by the ideological right, but also by Canadian legal scholars on the left, who have singled out women's legal strategies in particular because since 1985 women's organizations in Canada, and especially the Women's Legal Education and Action Fund (LEAF), have been the most active in intervening to present equality analyses in constitutional litigation. As noted in the 'Introduction' to this volume, left legal scholars have proffered some very weighty critiques of law, the legal system, legal culture, the courts, rights discourse, and the *Charter*, critiques that understand law as a key instrument for the maintenance of relations of power and, as such, as brimming with perils for those hoping to use it to transform those relations. I argued there, however, that although I find these critiques theoretically compelling, there are many practical reasons why women and other subordinated collectivities are nevertheless obliged to wage at least part of their struggle for social justice on legal terrain. My answer to the question raised in the 'Introduction' of whether women should persevere with the legal project despite its manifest perils is therefore, 'yes,' because I see law as simply too important a site of political struggle to avoid for fear of failure. The focus in this chapter, however, turns away from the 'to engage or not to engage' debate, towards the question of what we can learn from the strategies pursued to date and how they might be improved in future struggles. As the essays in this volume collectively demonstrate, the feminist constitutional litigation record in the area of sex equality has been a mixed bag of breakthroughs and setbacks, and assessments of 'successes' and 'failures' vary with the perspectives and interests of diverse groups of women. Hence, my concern in this chapter is to analyse, in a friendly way, the strengths and weaknesses of the kinds of analyses and claims feminist intervenors have advanced in constitutional litigation, and to ask whether it might be worth considering alternative strategies.

Feminists are, of course, acutely aware of the dangers of engaging with law, as is evidenced by an extensive body of feminist legal scholarship critiquing the patriarchal nature of contemporary liberal legal systems and rights instruments. Much of this literature has been self-reflectively critical of what has come to be the core discourse and objective in feminist legal strategy, namely, equality rights. This chapter therefore outlines some of the pitfalls associated with equality that have been identified by feminist thinkers, including the problem of the sameness/difference dichotomy. Compounding these difficulties are the more recent developments in critical race theory and deconstructions of antidiscrimination laws by black feminists, Aboriginal women, and women of colour that have revealed the forced essentialism and assimilationist demands of those laws and their inability to address intersecting axes of discrimination.[4] Taken together, I argue, these bodies of literature seem to point to the impossibility of equality both as a theoretical and as a practical enterprise for women, people of colour, and other subjugated collectivities. I have come to the view that the discourse of *legal* equality as an overarching goal and strategy is an idea whose time may have passed. This is not to deny its utility in certain circumstances (as a key to open the door to constitutional litigation, for example) or to advocate its wholesale abandonment; but at the very least, its position at the core of feminist legal discourse and strategy needs to be defended, not merely assumed.

If social movement organizations, such as LEAF, *are* going to intervene in constitutional cases, frequent re-evaluations of their litigation strategies are needed, including questions about the nature of their legal discourse, definition of the 'problems' to be addressed through litigation, and the issue of which constituencies of women are being represented by whom, for what purposes, and (from time to time) at whose expense. This task has been undertaken in various ways by feminist theorists and activists who are constantly critiquing, updating, re-assessing, strategizing, reworking, and learning from women's diverse experiences. This essay is a small contribution to this collective effort.

My main argument is that the definition of the 'problem' as an equality/inequality problem has led to a search for equality 'solutions,' which, however, are neither capable of transcending the problems inherent in the liberal comparative model nor ultimately what women or other oppressed groups are truly asking of law. In my view, women's and other progressive social movement organizations that are acting as intervenors in constitutional litigation might be better served by a much more flexible concept that can avoid many of the problems with equality – that is, justice. Therefore, after outlining some of the reasons why justice has not been a major element in legal feminist theorizing, I offer a critique of Carol Gilligan's justice/care distinction and an elaboration and adaptation of Iris Young's mission to rescue justice from the liberal abstract rights model of material distribution.[5] I argue that Young's approach provides an excellent foundation for the development of feminist approaches to justice and suggest that instead of equality, contextualized approaches to justice might both speak more accurately to what we are really asking of the law and yield more satisfactory results.

There are, of course, very good reasons why feminist and other justice-seeking litigators have focused on constitutional equality – among them are its historical power as an organizing and mobilizing concept and, importantly in Canada, its enshrinement in section 15 of the *Charter*. Section 15 has, in fact, become the key that gives a wide range of groups access to the Constitution and to the courts as claimants or intervenors. Because feminist legal theory and strategy in particular have been seized of the equality maxim (albeit with an acute awareness of its limits), so much has been invested in it that many individuals might find it difficult to divert legal strategies in other directions. Certainly, women's organizations have struggled vigorously against perceived threats to sections 15 and 28, and have mobilized significant opposition to the (ultimately defeated) Meech[6] and Charlottetown accords[7] of 1987 and 1992. In addition, it is possible that in the future the courts themselves would present further obstacles, especially since justice approaches by women and others would initially be novel; that is, feminist approaches to justice would be principally outcome-oriented, in contrast to the predominantly process-oriented understanding courts have typically applied. That such approaches would be contested seems inevitable, so that it would take time for the courts to settle on preferred interpretations. Nevertheless, it might still be worth pursuing new approaches in view of the constrictions revealed in those cases in which equality-based strategies have been pursued.

The chapter concludes with a discussion of the possibilities for the strategic use of justice in Canadian *Charter* litigation. By way of example, I briefly analyse a number of past and recent Supreme Court of Canada decisions that have represented serious losses for the equality-seeking claimants. I do not claim that these cases capture the range and tenor of the many equality decisions that have issued from the courts, nor are they presented as representative of any trend. I use them merely as illustrations of the formidable obstacles associated with the common law system, the *Charter*, rights, and the equality strategy deployed to date. More specifically, they speak to my point about how the essentialist definition of the 'problem' of gender (race, sexual identity, or disability) as an equality/inequality problem constrains the search for broader remedies to injustice. The discussion concludes with some tentative examples of how recasting the issues in a justice frame offers hope of escape from the pitfalls of the equality approach.

Feminist Critiques of Law

Feminist critical analysis of law has generated a substantial literature that often anticipated the sorts of positions taken by the predominantly male legal Left and critical legal studies (CLS) scholars as well as postmodernists, and has identified a crucial dimension unseen by the former group, that is, the patriarchal nature of law – the notion that law is male. Feminist legal theorists, in many cases before the legal left, have done with gender what the left did with class in their analysis of the power of law. This body of literature has unpacked the treatment of women in law and charted the multiple subtle ways in which law has been modelled on men's world views, behavioural patterns, needs, and interests, to the exclusion of those of women.

In view of this body of work, it is quite remarkable that even the most critical feminists generally and usually reluctantly take the position that women cannot avoid resorting to law. Indeed, some of these individuals are of the view that feminist engagement with law can yield net benefits even in the face of high costs. Of course, feminist thought is diverse, and its main strands have distinctive ideological anchors. Yet, most feminists writing about law seem to accept the inevitability of engagement: from liberal feminists, whose commitment to legal reform implies a conviction that law *can* be used to pursue equality; through socialist feminists, who see liberal rights as an impediment to social transformation; to radical feminists, such as Catherine MacKinnon, who point out the impossibility of equality within patriarchy, but who nevertheless regard legal activism as a necessary evil. Even those from communities that have been most severely oppressed through law, including black feminists and critical race theorists, do not advocate boycotting law entirely but argue the need for rights despite their limitations.[8] In fact, most would appear to agree with Carol Smart – a leading legal feminist, who is quite heavily influenced by postmodernist thought – who argues that women should be extremely cautious of resorting to law because it disqualifies women's knowledge and experience; that we should be aware of its 'malevolence,' its congruence with 'masculine culture,' but that we should continue anyway to focus on and challenge law because it is 'such an important signifier of masculine power.'⁹ Most of the feminist legal literature, then, shows that generally, feminists are acutely aware of the hazards of law, but aim, as Sherene Razack notes, 'to put a notion of community back into law, and to further characterize the community women inhabit as one that is oppressed.'¹⁰

At the same time, as Smart notes, in the past decade or so, much feminist analysis has become more deconstructionist, and thus deeply sceptical of the 'naturalistic, over-generalized and abstract assumptions about the social world' associated with malestream theories.¹¹ The unpacking of the assumptions of liberal legal regimes has revealed their tendencies to disguise particularism as universalism, and to conceal law's functioning in the interests of certain (male) elites within a series of 'master narratives' of fairness, impartiality, the rule of law, and its disinterested application to all. The new feminist analysis thus rejects grand theorizing as much within feminist thought as within the male canon. And yet, while feminist legal theorizing and strategizing have sought to demystify law's hollow promises, they seem to have fallen prey to at least one component of the 'master narrative' of western liberal law – one overarching concept into which an enormous range of women's aspirations, needs, and interests have been squeezed – equality.

The Equality Pit

There can be no doubt that in European states and their settler satellites, since the French and American revolutions, equality has been a particularly powerful political principle. It is a Circean concept that promises to nullify hierarchies of status (and associated rights and privileges), and, as used in a general sense (especially by oppressed groups), it is understood as meaning that we are all 'equally human,' 'equally worthy,' and 'equally deserving.' Even the Supreme Court of Canada understands it in this way. In *Egan v. Canada*,¹² for example, Justice L'Heureux-Dubé stated in her dissenting reasons that 'at the heart of s. 15 is the protection of, and respect for, basic human dignity ... [equality means being] equally worthy of recognition or value as a human being or as a member of Canadian society, equally deserving of concern, respect, and consideration.'¹³ The idealist notion of equality is especially appealing to those who have been excluded from the benefits, rights, and privileges enjoyed by the few who hold political, social, cultural, and economic power.

It should be noted that the ascendancy of equality discourse among social movements is a relatively recent development. In the Canadian context, for example, it was preceded by broad visions of social justice among early feminists – albeit visions that few feminists would espouse today. In her study of the evolution of feminist perceptions of fair laws for women in Canada, Sandra Burt notes that in the nineteenth and early twentieth centuries the 'first-wave' (Euro-Canadian) feminists' vision was based on a 'common interest' model that encompassed 'a stable, moral community grounded in religious convictions and committed to the preservation of the family.'[14] Although Burt notes that the 'concept of justice *per se* did not figure largely in the deliberations of most feminist groups active in the pre-*Charter* days,'[15] it has not been much in evidence in post-*Charter* days either. Instead, over the past couple of decades, 'equal rights thinking has come to dominate the discourse of organized feminism in English Canada ... [and] perceptions of fairness have shifted away from a broad definition of social justice based on a vision of the 'good society' to a much narrower focus on group rights.'[16]

There are several explanations for this reliance on equality – principal among them is the fact that the women's movements in the Anglo-American and European democracies have been dominated by middle-class women of western and northern European descent, who, based on their own experiences, believed that patriarchy was the chief source of oppression of women and that they could somehow be 'equal' to 'men' (or in reality, certain white men). After the achievement of formal political equality in the form of the extension of the franchise in liberal democratic states to adults regardless of sex, race, and other 'personal characteristics' (though many refused the franchise to inmates of mental institutions and prisons, for example), it did not seem too far-fetched to demand civil rights and equality in the law. These beliefs produced an equality analysis that translated into a demand for legal equality rights, which took the form, in the United States, of the unsuccessful campaign for an Equal Rights Amendment,[17] and, in Canada, of sections 15 and 28 of the *Charter*.

In the Canadian context, in particular, the pull of equality was especially strong in the late 1970s and early 1980s, when the federal Liberal government of Pierre Trudeau proposed a charter of rights as part of the package to repatriate the Canadian constitution from Britain. Since equality was on the constitutional bargaining table from 1978 to 1981, Canadian women's organizations resolved to make sure that it would serve women and thereby avoid the fate of the very limited equality section of the *Canadian Bill of Rights*.[18] Consequently, the understanding of equality proffered by women's organizations went somewhat beyond the formalism of liberal civil and political rights.[19]

The main problem with 'equality' in Canada, as in other European and white settler societies, however, has been how to operationalize it. It is a problem, principally, because the powerful have had radically different ideas from the powerless of what 'equally worthy' implies in terms of civil and human rights and state responsibilities regarding the redistribution of wealth and opportunity. It was hard enough for established institutions of political control to extend formal *political* equality as a minimal condition of citizenship, let alone to conceive of putting it into practice in hundreds of discrete areas of law, even assuming they had wanted to. Feminists have also had a very difficult time with equality both in theory and in practical application. Adopting equality as an overarching goal as well as political/legal strategy has seemingly trapped women into an ultimately irresolvable debate over whether equality entails the same or different treatment and over the nature of formal versus substantive equality.

Intergender Essentialism: Same versus Different Treatment

The picture that has emerged from recent sociohistorical feminist research suggests that early western (white, middle-class, heterosexual) feminist movements tended to demand limited formal political and social rights for women of their class and racial/ethnic ilks, while accepting and even promoting the racialist ideologies and policies that excluded all indigenous peoples, people of colour, and even poor and working-class whites of less-preferred ethnicities.[20] Yet even after the overtly racist and class biases of the early formal equality claims had dissipated somewhat, as liberal states extended formal political equality to more (though not all) groups, the new claims of the so-called second wave of feminism for equality of all women regardless of race and class produced what has become a critical problem for western feminist movements – gender essentialism.

The equality model that has been traditionally relied on in the Anglo-American democracies is essentialist in a number of senses. First, it assumes the reference group is men as a class – an assumption that denies significant differences between, and assumes identical experiences and interests among, men, and which thereby essentializes men.

But then, oddly enough, women using the formal equality approach deny any politically significant differences between women and men – they argue that women are the same as men, or in legal language, that they are similarly situated *but for* this one issue of their gender, which is irrelevant. Consequently, feminists who rely on this strategy present an essentialist and gender-neutral model of the liberal citizen who, as it turns out, is an essentialized man. An additional problem with the formalist claim, however, is that gender *is not* irrelevant; it is deeply relevant, although in varying degrees, depending on context. Finally, this equality model is essentialist in the sense that, as in the case of its assumptions about male identity, it relies on a construction of an essential and generic female identity that denies significant differences between women (such as race, ethnicity, class, sexuality, and so on) and, hence, assumes identical experiences and interests among them.

While I do not wish to reiterate the terms of a debate that is widely reported in feminist literature, I will briefly outline some of the major problems with the formal equality or same treatment model by way of preparation for my subsequent argument. First, although the model is appropriate for some claims involving straightforward comparisons of the treatment of women with that of men (the vote, property ownership, and especially pay equity, for example), it is clearly inappropriate in a wide range of areas of law, for example, in the regulation of pregnancy and maternity benefits in which women are generally *not* similarly situated to men.[21] Second, many feminists have pointed out that the same treatment doctrine assumes that maleness is the norm and that 'the goal is assimilation to an existing standard without questioning the desirability of that standard ... thus [limiting] the debate to what policies will best achieve the assimilation.'[22] Third, as Lucinda Finley points out, equality theory provides no guideline as to how we should identify what is a relevant similarity and what is a relevant difference in any particular situation.[23] Fourth, and ironically, the same treatment approach that succeeded in winning facial neutrality in many laws has ended up repeating many of the consequences of liberal law's male-defined abstractions.[24] Finally, I would add that the core problem underlying the same treatment model is the whopping male supremacist assumption that women have to prove that they are the same as men in order to qualify for the benefits and privileges of citizenship.

The limitations of the formal equality or same treatment model have led to an intense debate among feminists about whether women should instead demand different treatment to account for women's unique situations and interests.[25] The difference approach aims at advancing women's overall equality by arguing that because of their unique reproductive capacity, and associated socially prescribed roles, women should demand special accommodations for those of their needs that differ from those of men. Special treatment is justified to the extent that same treatment in law and policy produces adverse impacts and because asking for same treatment does not make sense if a benefit (such as pregnancy leave and maternity benefit) is not provided for men.

From my reading of recent feminist literature, it would seem that for most feminists same treatment has been more or less abandoned in favour of the difference approach, although in the Canadian context the latter has been reworked and refined into a somewhat more sophisticated model, which is discussed later in this chapter. The difference model, however, is not without its problems. Chief among them is the fact that it provides biological alibis for legislatures and courts that are bent on justifying different, and often unequal, treatment of women. In addition, the difference model does not manage to transcend the male-as-norm problem any more than its predecessor. As Catharine MacKinnon has noted, 'Being the same as men or being different from men are just two ways of having men as your standard.'[26] However, either approach is infinitely complicated by the fact that many of the conditions women contest in litigation do not apply exclusively to women. It is not only women who are raped, battered, sexually harassed, or who face barriers and disadvantages as custodial parents, for example. As the discussion of case examples below will show, the non-exclusivity of certain conditions undercuts essentialist claims with a strong counter-position that not only does the given situation not apply to *all* women, [27] it also applies to some men as well. In part because of these factors, I shall argue below that this essentialist construction of all women compared against all men is neither desirable nor possible. In fact, both approaches to equality are problematic; as Carol Smart concludes, 'The difference approach ultimately nourishes a crude sociobiology, the equality approach can be used as easily by men as by women and often to the detriment of women.'[28] The Canadian experience in *Charter* litigation certainly confirms this analysis.

Learning from the American experience, as well as the pre-*Charter* jurisprudence, Canadian feminist lawyers and activists working through LEAF have attempted to sidestep the sameness/difference dilemma by developing a results-oriented approach to equality litigation. As Sherene Razack, Lise Gotell, and Sheila McIntyre each show,[29] LEAF's brilliant

The Equality Pit or the Rehabilitation of Justice? 185

innovation has been to develop a contextualized approach to equality that rejects the purely formalist model and recognizes that substantively equal outcomes may require different treatments. Yet this is not the mere adoption of a straightforward difference model; it is a considerably more sophisticated and historically grounded understanding of *inequality* as being rooted in *gendered social relations*, not in women's similarity to, or difference from, men in any naturalistic sense.[30] The core of LEAF's litigation strategy to date has been premised on Catherine MacKinnon's critique of liberalism's sameness/difference dichotomy. She displaces this dichotomy with a dominance/subordination analysis that insists that courts begin, not from the liberal assumption that the law applies equally to all save for the odd deviation from the norm, but rather from the assumption of women's experience of subordination. The courts should then look at the manner and extent to which specific laws reinforce this subordination. Equality for MacKinnon, and thus LEAF, means dismantling domination and overturning subordination.

The contextualized approach to (in)equality,[31] developed by LEAF, is liberating in that it avoids some of the problems of the sameness/difference dichotomy, namely, that women need not argue that they are really the same as men and so deserve the same treatment, nor are they different from men and so deserve different treatment. They can point out that it is not nature that has created their 'inequality,' but rather that their *subordination* has been socially constructed and legally enforced. The focus is then switched from individual to systemic discrimination. The task for courts is to help tear down, piece by piece, the legal edifice fabricated to ensure male dominance / female subordination.

LEAF's successes using the contextualized approach are extraordinary,[32] especially since the approach challenges some of liberalism's key assumptions, as well as the legal system's abstract and decontextualized methodologies. Since the landmark *Andrews v. Law Society of British Columbia*[33] decision of 1989, in which the Supreme Court of Canada substantially accepted LEAF's results-oriented contextualized approach, the sameness/difference, likes alike, similarly situated language seems to have been virtually expunged from *Charter* jurisprudence, at least among the higher courts. In fact, a few Supreme Court decisions since then have explicitly adopted LEAF's analysis of women's subordination and substantive equality.[34] And yet, these 'successes' notwithstanding, two latticed questions arise in my mind. First, has the change in terminology really amounted to a shift in the courts' understanding of equality away from the formalist, similarly situated model across a range of areas of law? Second, has the contextualized, substantive approach in itself managed to avoid the sameness/ difference logic of the equality frame at the theoretical level?

The appropriate response to the first question seems to be 'no.' For example, in her assessment of the equality jurisprudence in this volume, Diana Majury notes that the actual result in *Andrews* struck her as being pretty much about treating likes alike (the two litigants fit the sociodemographic profile of the 'advantaged,' except for their citizenship) and that the post-*Andrews* decisions are rife with contradictions and inconsistencies. By and large, Majury notes, the courts either reject outright or simply do not comprehend systemic inequality analysis, and the results have not been good for women.[35] Further, as *Egan* (discussed below) amply demonstrates, courts even reject straight forward formalist / similarly situated / likes alike arguments, even when such arguments would help dismantle the historic systemic oppressions visited on groups by law and social practices.

I would submit that the answer to the second question is also 'no,' albeit a qualified 'no.' As already noted, the contextualized approach means that women can avoid arguing either that they are really the same as men or that they are different, but that they can instead point out that the asymmetry of their social position as a group relative to that of men is accounted for by a large range of socially constructed practices and ideologies and not by nature. What has changed, then, is that instead of making the old formal equality argument that women are essentially similarly situated, in effect, women now argue that they are *not* similarly situated because of their socially constructed inequality. Yet in a way, this does not appear to be significantly at variance with the difference approach and could be seen as a reconstructed articulation of it because, in practice, it still ends up as an argument for either same or different *treatment*, depending on the nature of the objection to the specific law at issue. And, of course, the underlying claim of not being similarly situated and therefore of requiring different treatment to bring up women's overall equality is still a claim in relation to the putative position of 'men.'

LEAF's contextualized approach is still gender essentialist, therefore, to the extent that it has not managed to avoid the sameness/difference logic of the gender equality frame. Such essentialism may be unavoidable in constitutional terms: section 15 of the *Charter*, for example, is structured in such a way as to require claimants to identify themselves by a characteristic, implicitly contrasted to that of the dominant 'advantaged' group (such as race, national, or ethnic origin, colour, religion, sex, age, or mental or physical disability). Equality means always having to say who you are equal to, always comparing one group against another, almost invariably on one axis, and for this reason, it will not let claimants out of the similarly situated, likes alike, sameness/difference traps, regardless of the new language used. Sameness/difference is a function of essentialism and vice versa.

LEAF's contextualized approach remains gender essentialist on the issue of *who* is constructed as dominant/subordinate. For LEAF, 'contextualized' has meant the context of the subordination of 'women' to 'men,' not the specific contexts in which various aspects of ascriptive identity shape experience. LEAF's approach has rarely accounted for the conflicting experiences women *and* men can have based on factors other than gender, that is, the fragmented aspects of experience people can have in different contexts. It has not accounted for the fact that, for example, white women or women of colour of certain class positions may exercise more privileges in different aspects of their lives than white men and men of colour from socioeconomically deprived classes, notwithstanding that the latter may exercise/experience privileges in some aspects of their lives vis-à-vis women, racialized groups, and others. Yet the equality frame demands that the undifferentiated category of 'women' be measured against the undifferentiated category of 'men,' as if there is some great plateau full of privilege on which all men psychically reside and to which all women aspire. In these ways, then, sameness/difference casts a long shadow over LEAF's approach to equality.

Intragender Essentialism: Problems with Intersections and Antidiscrimination Models

As mentioned earlier, sex equality theory has fallen prey to a second form of essentialism that assumes a generic female identity in the sense of identical experiences and interests *among women*, regardless of any differences or relations of power between them (such as those based on race, ethnicity, religion, culture, class, sexuality, and disability). This form of essentialism has recently come under severe criticism from black and Aboriginal women, women of colour, lesbians, and women with disabilities, who have elaborated a number of critiques of feminist legal theory. These critiques generally point out that the latter's analysis of law as an oppressive practice and discourse has been principally modelled on the situations of white, socioeconomically privileged, heterosexual women (though this has rarely been explicitly recognized in white feminists' theorizing),[36] and has aimed at achieving equality for them with white men. This analysis has scarcely acknowledged, let alone incorporated, the intersections of gender, race, and class, and has tended also to overlook 'the economic and symbolic structures that perpetuate the oppression of women and minorities.'[37] Sherene Razack attributes this exclusive focus on gender to white, middle-class women's closeness to their male counterparts, so that '[they] did not personally notice how coercive, racist and economically exploitative the state and law were.'[38] Their failure to deal with intersections appears to be an inevitable consequence of the essentialist gender constructions that have driven the sameness/difference debates and even the contextualized approach to women's equality to men. Such essentialist constructions reinforce, as they are, in turn, reinforced by, legal equality provisions.

Since equality claims in the Anglo-American democracies tend to be cast in terms of discrimination, a number of black feminists working in law in the United States have analysed major problems with antidiscrimination doctrine. Although some progress has been made in this area (most notably the shift from claimants having to prove discrimination was intentional to having only to show adverse impact of policies), the doctrine is still riddled with deficits. Kimberle Crenshaw's germinal work in this area, for example, has exposed the silent assumption of the antidiscrimination doctrine that recognizes only one axis of discrimination at a time and, hence, fails to register the possibility of compounded factors. In her analysis of a U.S. case in which five African-American women brought suit against General Motors on the grounds that the employer's seniority system perpetuated the effects of past discrimination against black women, Crenshaw argues that the courts' refusal to acknowledge that black women suffer combined race and sex discrimination suggests that 'the boundaries of sex and race discrimination are defined respectively by white women's and black men's experiences.' Black women will be protected only to the extent that their experiences coincide with one or other of the two groups.[39] Black women are therefore marginalized, not just by the courts, but also by the traditional feminist and civil rights approaches that adhere to the *'either race or sex'* model of discrimination.

Aside from the either/or dilemma, a further problem with the antidiscrimination doctrine identified by Crenshaw is its tendency to generate remedies tailored to those who are privileged *but for* one aspect of their social identities, that is, but for their race *or* their sex. Hence, in race discrimination cases, discrimination tends to be viewed in terms of sex- or class-privileged blacks, while in sex discrimination cases, it is defined in terms of race- and class-privileged women.[40] This observation is consistent with studies of affirmative action policies that show the chief beneficiaries to be white, middle-class women or otherwise middle-class black men (or other men of colour) rather than working- or middle-class black women and women of colour.[41] In Crenshaw's view, antidiscrimination doctrine should aim to address the situations of the least privileged, a focus that would automatically include the situations of those otherwise privileged but for one aspect of their social identities.

If the 'either/or' and 'but for' problems were not serious enough, Crenshaw also identifies the key escape offered by traditional antidiscrimination doctrine: by essentializing individuals within a given category, the doctrine maintains the fiction that a discriminator will treat everyone within a race or sex category similarly, so that if she or he does not treat them all in the same way, then there is no discrimination against any. This flaw in doctrinal logic means that discriminators can easily immunize themselves against charges of discrimination by treating one or a few women or people of colour in a non-discriminatory manner. Meanwhile, antidiscrimination doctrine fails to take into consideration the possibility that seemingly neutral policies may act to confer advantages upon the already privileged who fit the traditional profile of preferred racial/ethnic and gender groups. Instead, '[r]ace or sex ... become significant only when they operate explicitly to *disadvantage* the victims; because the *privileging* of whiteness or maleness is implicit, it is generally not perceived at all.'[42]

Following the lead of U.S. black legal feminists, Nitya Iyer has discovered that the same problems of antidiscrimination doctrine plague Canadian law. In her investigation of all *Canadian Human Rights Reporter* decisions up to 1992 in which race or sex discrimination was alleged, Iyer describes how racial minority women 'disappear' in the either/or frame because the race of minority women is usually omitted from Canadian case descriptions as if it is not a factor. Antidiscrimination doctrine, she observes, has been so narrowly construed that it cannot deal with the problem of intersecting axes and it 'appears almost entirely oblivious to the fact that a complainant alleging race discrimination also has a gender [or vice versa].'⁴³ Antidiscrimination laws are actually structured so as to make claimants fit themselves into narrowly defined categories – they must present a caricature or cartoon of themselves that distorts individual and communal experience into an oversimplified image of 'difference.'⁴⁴ This difference becomes the salient group identifier that is then taken to be the key aspect of the group's social identity, and any differences between members of the group (such as class) become irrelevant for the purposes of antidiscrimination law.

If these problems with antidiscrimination law do not make equality claims difficult enough, there remains the problem of the state's response to past claims of discrimination. As noted above, in the Canadian context (as in most of the Anglo-American democracies), this response has included not only eradicating the most overtly discriminatory laws, but also making remaining laws facially neutral by deleting race- or gender-specific language. Yet, that the law's face is not neutral but is, in reality, a male face and a white face is apparent, as Iyer points out, from the very language of antidiscrimination laws: 'We can ascertain the social characteristics of the dominant social identity by contemplating what we do *not* imagine when we think about the superficially neutral characteristics listed in anti-discrimination laws: race is 'not white,' sex is 'not male,' sexual orientation is 'not heterosexual,' disability is 'not able-bodied.'⁴⁵

It is nigh impossible, however, to convince judges that the law's face (not to mention their own face) is anything but neutral. There is no place in legal provisions, procedures, or rules of evidence even to offer such analyses. Instead, the ostensible neutrality of contemporary legal language has cultivated the yarn that law is no longer implicated in maintaining the institutionalized racism and sexism that authorize social inequality.⁴⁶ The courts are seemingly as charmed by the mythology of law's neutrality as is the general public. This mythology is continually reinforced in the area of racial equality, especially since the erasure of explicitly racist classifications makes it difficult to advance *any* legal claims, even when law does have adverse effects on racialized peoples. This goes some way towards explaining why there have been very few race equality claims under the *Charter*.

To be fair, I should note that LEAF has in recent years taken to heart the strong criticisms (voiced by women of colour, women with disabilities, lesbians, and others) of its essentialist approaches, as well as of the undemocratic nature of its practice of assigning a little clique of lawyers and academics to fashion arguments to win within the current operating parameters. LEAF's responses to these criticisms have included holding various consultation processes with social movement organizations, individuals, and front-line workers, and cultivating coalitions or partners-in-litigation efforts. With the process of democratization, LEAF's equality analysis since 1992 has become somewhat more complex and less essentialist, with recent factums beginning to articulate intersectional modes of analysis. For example, LEAF's factum in *R. v. O'Connor* (developed in conjunction with the Aboriginal Women's Council, the DisAbled Women's Network of Canada, and the Canadian Association of Sexual Assault Centres) presented the Supreme Court with a sophisticated account of the heightened vulnerability of Aboriginal and black women and women with disabilities to sexual assault and violence, the forced assimilation of the residential school system imposed on indigenous peoples, and the 'racist stereotyping [that] has been shown to infiltrate sexual assault proceedings involving aboriginal complainants.'[47] The Court, however, has not responded to the intersecting equality claims advanced in *O'Connor* and several other cases. It is not clear whether this is because the judges just do not understand the analysis, because they disagree with it, because it is too complex, because they prefer to stick to more technical issues whenever possible, because the equality frame is simply too limited to contain it, or because of something else. Nevertheless, despite the array of possible causes, I would still emphasize the latter argument, that is, that the equality frame is simply too narrow to contain complex intersectional analysis because it is *by nature* comparative (one group compared against another) essentialist, and as I shall argue presently, impossible.

The Impossibility of Equality

As already noted, women of colour have criticized feminist legal practice and discourse for its unstated but overwhelming focus on the situations of white, socioeconomically privileged, heterosexual women. They have questioned the reference group that is implicitly targeted by those women, for although their gender essentialist positions have pitted all women against all men, in reality they crave equality with only *certain* men. As bell hooks puts it: 'Most people in the United States think of feminism ... as a movement that aims to make women the social equals of men ... Since men are not equals in white supremacist, capitalist, patriarchal class structure, which men do women want to be equal to?'[48] It is obvious that for the white, socioeconomically privileged, heterosexual women who pioneered, and today still dominate, feminist theory and politics, equality with white, socioeconomically privileged, heterosexual men is the ultimate destination. It is not necessarily, however, the ultimate destination for many oppressed peoples. In the Canadian context in particular, Aboriginal people rarely identify equality as a political goal, and some reject it outright. Mary Ellen Turpel, for example, has argued that the idea that women should enjoy equal opportunities with men within their communities is conceptually and culturally inappropriate for First Nations women: 'First Nations communities, and in particular the communities of my heredity, the Cree community, are ones which do not have a prevailing ethic of equal opportunity for men and women ... [Equality] is frequently seen by our Elders as a suspiciously selfish notion, as individualistic and alienating from others in the community ... We are committed to what would be termed a 'communitarian' notion of responsibilities to our peoples, as learned through traditional teachings and our life experiences.'[49]

It must be noted that this issue has been more than contentious in indigenous politics, as evidenced by the position of the Native Women's Association of Canada that the patriarchy that has been imported into their communities under colonialism requires that First Nations women have access to the gender equality guarantee of the *Charter*.[50] However, aside from the issue of gender relations *within* First Nations communities, Turpel's view of gender equality between Aboriginal women and non-Aboriginal men is a much larger indictment of the values of non-Aboriginal society. It rejects gender equality with white men for the acceptance of *cultural* values such a goal implies, a proposition that is far less contentious within Native political discourse:

> My interpretation of the objective of ensuring equal opportunity with men as expressed in the Royal Commission [on the Status of Women] mandate implies equal opportunity for First Nations women with non-aboriginal (so-called White) men ... I do not see it as worthwhile or worthy to aspire to, or desire, equal opportunity with White men, or with the system that they have created. The aspirations of White men in the dominant society are simply not our aspirations. We do not want to inherit their objectives and positions or to adopt their world view. To be perfectly frank, I cannot figure out why non-aboriginal women would want to do this either.[51]

Quite apart from such cultural critiques, in my view, the inability of feminist legal theory and practice to deal with the complexities of intersectionality stems from a much more profound problem with equality discourse than white feminists' failure consciously to incorporate race, sexuality, and disability into their equality analyses – that is, the absolute impossibility of the claim to equality with privileged white men. The claim is impossible because, just as the African proverb (recently appropriated by Hillary Rodham Clinton) observes, 'it takes a village to raise a child,' I would maintain that it takes a whole world – an international political economy featuring racialized and gendered divisions of labour and distributions of wealth, and a domestic economic, political, and social structure that actually *requires* First World/Third World, racial/ethnic, gender, and class hierarchies – in order that *certain* white men can enjoy the particular rights, privileges, and benefits they have distributed to themselves. As I have argued elsewhere, the positions of power and privilege enjoyed by certain white men have only been made possible by racism, imperialism, and sexism – they depend on inequality, skewed power relations, and the subjugation of people of colour and white women, the majority of people in the world.[52] Therefore, white women's equality with privileged white men *may* be possible assuming the preservation of the current race and class hierarchy, but people (and especially women) of colour cannot be 'equal,' since white men preside at the apex of a racially stratified socioeconomic system. Equality with white men is thus not conceivable in an unreconstituted political economy and social system.

Curiously, the goal of the reformist equality strategies used to date by Euro-Canadian feminists has been access to the power and privileges of the very political economy and social system for which the inequality or oppression of people of colour and white women is a prerequisite. The claim to equality is fundamentally contradictory, therefore, and it is no wonder the courts cannot deliver it. It is impossible for subjugated groups such as women, people of colour, and lesbians and gays to demand and get what privileged white men have. They cannot aspire to that kind of equality, and not just because, with the current retrenchment of the redistributive policies of the welfare state, we are told that the resources are not there, and, therefore, the material equality and the many non-material benefits and privileges that would go with it are not on offer. In fact, subjugated groups cannot, and, in my view, should not, want to aspire to equality with white men in their current positions of power and privilege both nationally and internationally because those positions are contingent upon the oppression of various groups both historically and in the present.

In the end, the equality oppressed groups and individuals are pursuing through legal claims is a phantom anyway – both a theoretical and a practical impossibility. This fact may explain why we have so much trouble with the idea of equality beyond the normative principle that we are all equally human and equally deserving of fundamental human rights, especially political and civil rights.

All things considered, it seems to me that if equality were a house, it would be the sort of house realtors euphemistically call a 'fixer-upper,' in other words, a money pit. Aside from a few minor problems, it looked almost perfect when you decided to buy it, but the day you move in the wiring fritzes, the next day, the plumbing backs up, and no matter what you do the back door always seems to be open. Then it turns out the foundations were laid on a fault line, the façade crumbles, and the roof caves in. By the time all your energy and resources are spent and you realize you bought a dud, the bank will not foreclose on your loan because it wants you to keep paying for it in perpetuity.

Why Gals Don't Do Justice, But Should

If equality has been revealed (by legal decisions as much as by anything) as a conceptual, strategic, and practical hazard, why are women and other oppressed collectivities still using it in their litigation strategies? If it is not really what we mean to be asking of the law, what *is*? In my view, equality is but a subset of a much larger normative principle, a principle that has been the key preoccupation of western political philosophy, and which, in theory at least, is the background assumption of law itself – justice. Yet curiously, feminists have rarely cast their legal claims as justice claims. Instead, they have almost invariably attempted to squeeze all issues into the equality box, even when equality is not necessarily what is missing or wanted, and even when it has meant distorting the concept beyond recognition. Of course, as discussed earlier, there are good reasons why equality has come to dominate theory and strategy in various countries, but the question is whether it should continue to be deployed as the central political and legal objective of oppressed groups.

The hegemony of the equality idea has led to the neglect of justice as a developmental discourse or as a litigation strategy among feminist legal scholars and practitioners. Indeed, apart from the odd appearance in titles of articles or books, general references to the criminal justice system, or the occasional allusion to women's quest for 'equality and social justice,' few feminist legal scholars and activists even mention the term 'justice' in their discourses of equality. In the very occasional references to 'social justice,' the term itself is never the focus of analysis and is never seen as a strategic possibility; rather, it appears as a background value to the *real* goal, equality. To my knowledge, the only exception to this is in the writings of people of colour, and especially in the discourse of Aboriginal scholars and activists, who characterize the multiple facets of their dispossession as a question of justice/injustice. But in the bulk of feminist legal work, it appears that the whole field of justice has been ceded to male political theorists, and relatively little work has been done by any feminist scholars, let alone legal ones.

This apparent cession of justice to male theorists may be not be so surprising given that for more than two and a half millennia, justice theory in the European-derived democracies has been dominated by the Aristotelian paradigm and has largely been a discourse justifying *in*equality. Neither is it surprising that Aristotle caught the imaginations of western men given that he regarded women merely as the incubators of the male seed (carrier of the true human form), and, thus, as creatures to whom justice was simply inapplicable.[53] On the other hand, however, Aristotle also monopolized the field of equality (treat equals equally and unequals unequally) and made it male in the western mind, but that has not prevented modern feminists from trying to decolonize equality.

Although justice has been largely abandoned to male theorists, in recent years some feminist philosophers have produced critiques of (male) theories of justice, in particular, the widely celebrated neo-Kantian social contract model advanced by John Rawls in 1971.[54] Some have even tried to redeem such theories by 'unveiling' their gendered nature and reworking them to see what they might look like ungendered.[55] However, these analyses have been more or less confined to exchanges between philosophers, and they have been conspicuously absent from legal feminists' theorizing or strategizing.

In the meantime, other feminist scholars have argued that even if theories of justice did not assume male subjects, justice discourse is inappropriate anyway to the extent that it aims to identify abstract principles in the form of rules that can be applied on a universal basis. In this regard, the work of the American developmental psychologist Carol Gilligan has been enormously influential among many feminists. Gilligan's work has unmasked the supposition that male ways of thinking about justice are definitively human ways as simply an assumption arising from the androcentric ideology of a profoundly gendered society. This insight elicited a distinction between what she calls 'an ethic of justice' and 'an ethic of care.'[56]

Briefly, Gilligan regarded the selection of all-male samples in psychological studies of 'moral development' as a critical deficiency in their conclusions about how people approach morality and justice.[57] Like that of the studies she questions, Gilligan's focus is on personal constructions of morality, or how individuals go about solving (usually hypothetical) moral dilemmas, such as whether Heinz, whose wife will die without an extremely expensive medicine, should steal it from the pharmacist who will not lower his price. Her research with female and male children and adult subjects led her to conclude that instead of one universal model, there are two basic moral orientations. The justice orientation is associated with thinking, egoism, and theoretical reasoning,[58] and involves abstracting moral situations from interpersonal relationships, weighting competing rights and values, and 'finding in the logic of fairness an objective way to decide who will win the dispute.'[59] In the Heinz scenario, Gilligan found that a person with a justice orientation would consider whether there are any permissible exceptions to the general rule against stealing, and would justify departures from it by ranking competing values or rights (e.g., the woman's right to life is more important than the pharmacist's right to property in the life-and-death scenario).

In contrast to the justice orientation, the care orientation is associated with feeling, altruism, and practical/contextual reasoning,[60] and involves framing moral dilemmas more in terms of 'a network of connection, a web of relationships that is sustained by a process of communication.'[61] In the care frame, the question is heard, not so much as whether Heinz *should* steal the medicine, but whether he should *steal* the medicine (bearing in mind the network of relationships and how they would be affected by theft), or whether he should try to find some other solution (borrowing the money, making a deal with the pharmacist). For Gilligan, 'the moral injunctions, not to act unfairly toward others, and not to turn away from someone in need, capture these different concerns.'[62]

Gilligan has been criticized on methodological and various other grounds, and not least for her exclusive focus on class-privileged, well-educated, white children, and adults – a selection that leaves her observations bereft of race, culture, caste, consciousness, and class analysis.[63] Nevertheless, as Cass Sunstein points out, much feminist work since Gilligan has challenged or rejected 'approaches that purport, for normative or explanatory purposes, to treat people as self-interested maximizers of private or [prepolitical] existing desires.'[64] Positions like this one dovetail easily with those that reject the legal system's adversarial, win/lose, aggressive approach to dispute resolution and argue instead for mediation methods involving negotiated compromises between parties. In fact, whether it was Gilligan's intention or not, much of this work seems to take the justice/care distinction as more oppositional than she perhaps intended, and adopts certain bifurcated 'justice bad/care good' assumptions which have made many suspicious of the justice frame.

Gilligan's work may indeed have done a disservice to justice and impeded the development of a feminist jurisprudence that avoids some of the snares of equality by deploying justice strategically. My critiques are as follows. First, the implicitly negative evaluation of the justice approach in the justice/care dichotomy has been somewhat overdrawn. Certainly, the traditional liberal model of justice characterizes the current positivist system of supposedly universal, neutral legal rules and principles much more than does care. However, the either/or position assumes that justice cannot include, or even be defined by care, and vice versa. While it does not follow that care could not at least survive in a fundamentally unjust society, it is difficult to imagine justice prevailing in a fundamentally uncaring one. Second, the care orientation's conservative commitment to preserving the giant web of relationships in which each person is involved seems somewhat suspect to the extent that it assumes those relationships are more or less egalitarian, benevolent, and thus deserving of preservation, rather than unequal, malevolent, exploitative, and thus deserving of transformation. The extant web of relationships is surely grounded in power relations, and their preservation needs to be justified, not assumed.[65]

Notwithstanding the implicit egalitarian assumption, the care orientation is perhaps better suited than justice to the realms of personal, family, friend, and small community networks of connection where face-to-face relationships allow for the negotiation of compromise settlements of conflicts. It is not at all clear, however, that the care approach is well suited to the larger realm of modern society where we are connected through impersonal structures and institutions and where technology further erases our relation to others as organic (rather than virtual) beings. In fact, the very persistence of relations of oppression between the dominant and subordinated racial/ethnic/class/gender groups suggests that we cannot rely on the assumption of care.

It is not clear, therefore, that the care approach negates the need for justice. We need justice, in my view, precisely because of the nature of the economic, political, and social structures and institutions of modern capitalist, liberal society. These institutions create, and are created by, a discursive and material competition for relatively scarce resources, and they are embedded within a culture and ideology that indulge more self-interestedness than altruism. We need justice because the size, diversity, and segregation of the communities comprising the populace do not permit face-to-face negotiation of moral or distributive contestations, and even if they did, such communities or groups are very differently situated in terms of their social, economic, and political power. In other words, they exist within complicated relations of domination and oppression and cannot negotiate as equals. This point is not insensible of the fact that the traditional liberal construction of justice has been key to both the endurance and legitimation of these relations, but as I will argue presently, rather than abandon justice, we should aim to reconstruct it to address domination and oppression.

The above observations about the nature of our socioeconomic and political institutions and the relations of domination and subordination between social groups point to another dimension in which the justice/care division seems unsatisfactory. The care approach assumes both familiarity and good will, a large assumption even for face-to-face relationships, let alone for impersonal group-to-group ones; justice applies precisely when these conditions do not hold, when care is absent, and especially when material scarcity means that some gain at the expense of others. For these reasons, public policy cannot simply assume care, but must be founded on principles of justice that, in the distributive dimension, are based on fairness, and in non-distributive matters, respect the values of self-development and self-determination for oppressed groups as for others.

In posing these arguments, I do not mean to assign justice exclusively to the public realm and care to the 'private.' As I suggested above, justice (usually construed as fairness) is a critical issue within families, especially between parents and children, as well as within other types of non-public relationships. However, a fundamental commitment to some form of care seems essential to many public policies, such as health and welfare programs. My point is that a requirement of care instead of, and to the exclusion of, justice is not a recipe for good public policy.

Finally, proponents of the care approach rarely, if ever, address the question of how it could be pressed into practical, strategic service given the actually existing constitutional provisions and legal system we have. It is certainly a powerful argument for changing the legal system from an adversarial to a mediatory one. Until such a change is affected, however, care seems of less immediate strategic help. It may be more appropriate to areas of law with a distributive focus (employment, property, and social programs) than to those with non-distributive aims (rape and assault law, reproductive freedom, and criminal law). In particular, the care approach, with its emphasis on personal constructions of morality, does not seem geared towards addressing the needs of oppressed groups (such as racial/ethnic minorities, lesbians and gay men, women, people with disabilities) for recognition and respect within the polity and society of their differences, self-development, and self-determination.

In highlighting some of the limitations of the care approach, I do not mean to endorse the liberal notion of justice that assumes unconnected, atomistic individuals exercising their pre-political 'preferences,' subject only to a system of rational rules for the settlement of disputes when rights clash. On the contrary, I wish to endorse the efforts of those who have recently begun to explore the possibility of reframing the concept of justice towards encompassing the claims of oppressed groups. Iris Marion Young, for example, has made some critical observations in her mission to wrest justice back from the liberal abstract rights model. Her key aim is to displace that model that regards justice as concerned with the distribution of benefits and burdens in society, particularly in the form of material goods (things, resources, income, wealth) and social positions (especially jobs).[66] She argues that this distributive paradigm, which drives most theories of justice, is partial in that it ignores the social and institutional contexts (and, one might add, the national and international political economy) that shape the pattern of distribution. It is also reductionist in that it fails to consider social goods, such as rights, opportunity, power, and self-respect.[67]

Just as Catharine MacKinnon proposed that equality be understood in terms of dominance and subordination,[68] Young argues that the notion of justice should begin with the concepts of domination and oppression, defined as situations in which a group is one or more of the following: exploited (the benefits of their work and energy go to others without proportionate reciprocity); marginalized (excluded from participation in major social activities, such as certain occupations); powerless (they live and work under the authority of others with little autonomy); subjected to cultural imperialism (stereotyped as a group with little opportunity or audience for the expression of their experience and perspective on social events); and targeted for violence and harassment motivated by group hatred or fear. Young considers that in the United States, groups oppressed in one or more ways include women, African, Native, and Asian Americans, Chicanos, Puerto Ricans, and other Spanish-speaking Americans, lesbians and gay men, working-class people, poor people, old people, and people with mental and physical disabilities.[69]

Following this, Young points out that many claims about justice and injustice in society are claims for things other than the distribution of income, resources, or positions. They may instead be concerned with the organization of government institutions; decision-making rules and procedures; the social division of labour in which certain occupations are allocated to certain groups, and are valued or devalued along with the racial/ethnic or gender groups to which they are allocated; or they may be concerned with 'the cultural imperialism which marks and stereotypes some groups at the same time that it silences their self-expression.'[70] For Young, these justice issues are beyond arguments about end-state distributions of wealth and positions (or how the given pie ought to be apportioned between competing members of society); they are instead about the extent to which institutional conditions support people's ability to develop and exercise their capacities and express their experience, as well as their ability to participate in determining their actions and conditions of action.[71] These are values that Young sees as universalist and as corresponding to 'two social conditions that define injustice: oppression, the institutional constraint on self-development; and domination, the institutional constraint on self-determination.'[72] The opposite of oppression and domination would be 'thorough social and political democracy.'[73] Beyond distribution, justice is therefore about 'enabling.'

Young's analysis is helpful in several ways. First, the concepts of domination and oppression express the dynamic social relations between dominant and subjugated groups far more accurately than equality/inequality. They are process – rather than status- or end-state-oriented. Equality/inequality is a static-state dyad that could just as well describe intrinsic qualities of the equal/unequal. Of course, it suggests they are equal or unequal *in relation to* each other, but it does not convey the active sense of a *process* of domination and oppression of one group (or individual) by another. Together with all the other problems with equality outlined throughout this chapter, I would consider this a good reason to discard the language of equality/inequality, except in specific, circumscribed contexts and for specific, circumscribed purposes.

Second, Young's list of five criteria for recognizing dominated and oppressed collectivities is useful for determining when injustice is present in particular as well as general contexts. The list is not exhaustive; it can be extended or fine-tuned to cover the micro-situations of specific groups in specific circumstances. As well as exploitation, marginalization, powerlessness, subjection to cultural imperialism, and targeting for violence and harassment, other criteria would include dispossession (of indigenous peoples, for example), or the exclusion of particular groups from the benefits or protections of specific laws. Young provides a sound basic framework, then, on which feminist approaches to justice in practical terms can be built.

Third, Young's observation that justice is not only about distribution is also on-point for my purposes: I would extend it to argue that equality, as it generally has been construed, likewise rests on a distributive assumption, and like justice, equality is not only about distribution. In practical terms, the distributive underpinning of equality means that courts have at least been able to *understand* legal claims for equal access to state benefits and positions when they have been called upon to decide whether classes of persons have been excluded from them on the basis of 'irrelevant' criteria (in areas such as pay and employment equity, prisoners' voting rights, landed immigrants' rights to practice law, criminal procedures, variations in provincial laws, paid parental leave, social and family benefits, and so on). Ironically, the extent to which courts are driven to compose heroically inventive *legal* rationales for denying some of them (for essentially *political* reasons) can be taken as indicative of their basic comprehension of the distributive nature of the claims for same treatment.

Courts have found it much more difficult, however, to comprehend non-formalist equality claims that cannot be satisfied by the extension of a simple benefit or position and that ask for different treatment. For example, petitions for remedy for offences against women that arise out of relations of domination, and oppression (rape and sexual assault, violence against women, pornography, sexual harassment, men's attempts to control women's reproduction), which patently do *not* require same treatment do not fit easily into the distributive framework of equality. They will not be fixed by giving women what men have.

They are indirect claims that, if the remedies sought were granted piece by piece, they might contribute to women's overall status of equality in society. However, as legal remedies in themselves, they do not call for symmetrical treatment of women and men. In fact, to the extent that the remedies called for would promote women's physical integrity, self-respect, self-determination and autonomy, they need not be characterized as equality claims at all, but rather as justice claims.

Young's framework is useful for my purposes in a fourth sense, therefore: despite the fact that the legal/constitutional system obliges groups and individuals to funnel their petitions through the narrow aperture of equality, many claims made by oppressed groups are not for equality per se, but for justice in the senses that Young identifies, among others. I do not mean to argue that equality is not a part of justice, or that justice is not a part of equality, but rather that equality analysis that is not anchored in a justice frame does not always capture what it is that we are truly seeking through law.

Feminist Approaches to Justice

It has long been a basic tenet of feminist thought that theory should be grounded in women's diverse experiences rather than in methodologies of pure abstraction that assume a generic subject. Thanks, in part, to postmodernism, most feminists recoil from 'totalizing' theories pretending to universality. In her reworking of justice from the distributive paradigm, for example, Iris Marion Young is careful to disavow any notion of constructing a theory of justice per se on the grounds that such a theory 'typically derives fundamental principles of justice that apply to all or most societies, whatever their concrete configuration and social relations, from a few general premises about the nature of human beings, the nature of societies, and the nature of reason.'[74] As a scholar deeply influenced by postmodernist thought, Young regards with suspicion any theory that claims comprehensiveness and universal application independently of particular social situations, institutions, or practices. Such theories cannot be very helpful in evaluating actual institutions and practices, and must be illusory.[75] I would enlarge Young's point to observe that most, if not all, theories of justice within the western canon seem insensible of the fact that justice is a concept that is relative to specific cultures and periods and that therefore varies radically across cultures. It is certainly no accident that the understandings and practices of justice of non-European cultures have not been represented in European-derived legal systems, or that justice conceived as fidelity to black letter law and legal process rather than to outcome has accompanied the dispossession of indigenous peoples, among others.

In view of the need for culturally specific notions of justice and the fact that justice will require different analyses and remedies in different social, economic, and institutional contexts, I am not attempting to advocate a universalist theory of justice. Indeed, as Mari Matsuda notes, feminism is 'a theory-in-progress, collectively formed,' so that 'it would be somewhat unfeminist for one woman to write a book called *The Feminist Theory of Justice.*'[76] Similarly, in rejecting 'grand theory' (though not spurning theorizing as an attempt to make sense of experience or the social order),[77] Carol Smart observes that 'feminist work has a growing affinity with the idea of analyzing the micro-politics of power, and the everyday oppressions of women which are invisible to the grand theorist.'[78] We need to develop feminist *approaches* to justice, not as totalizing or overarching theories applicable to all times, places, and issues, but on a context-sensitive, issue-by-issue basis. In other words, we need to comb through each area of family law (property, marriage, divorce, child custody, spousal support, and so on), criminal law (assault, domestic violence, and rape laws), labour law, contract law, tax law, welfare laws, laws regulating Aboriginal peoples, and so on, to develop fully integrated historical and contemporary analyses of how they penalize particular women (indigenous women, poor women, women of colour, lesbians, women with disabilities, and so on) and offer solutions as to what would best serve their needs and interests in their social situations – not on an 'equal' basis, but on a just basis. We need situational approaches to justice that take domination and oppression into account, as well as the idea of redress, as in rebalancing. In some cases, this approach will mean arguing for just solutions for men as well, insofar as they are subject to the same injustices because of their race, ethnicity, disability, class, sexual identities, or other constructed bases of subordination. In other cases, the justice approach would mean recognizing that women too are differently situated according to these and other bases of subordination and that some women are implicated in the subjugation of others.[79]

The approach I am suggesting does not require an overarching grand theory of justice. Indeed, sometimes we should advocate justice in its distributive dimension, at other times it might be retributive, at others recognition-oriented, sometimes it should be about process (though more usually about substantive outcomes), sometimes about autonomy, in other contexts about community, sometimes requiring equality as same treatment, sometimes different treatment. In this endeavour, feminists might borrow a time-worn problem-solving technique, which is, to work backwards from the solution by constructing what a just society would look like and then what the specific area of law would look like in such a society. Naturally, just as the meaning of equality has been disputed within and outside feminist movements, so constructions of a 'just society' will be contested. Nevertheless, justice, in my view, is a concept both citizens and courts would be better able to cope with since it allows difference, releases us from essentialist and assimilationist imperatives, lends itself much more to situational, rather than to abstract, analysis, and appeals to a sense of fairness, of treating people well, as worthy and deserving of respect.

In advocating situational approaches to justice, I am not suggesting that we abandon equality discourse altogether. Nor am I denying that equality, like liberty, is still a revolutionary idea in many areas of the world. It is certainly ironic that while many members of progressive, liberationist movements in other countries are risking their lives for those ideas, many European-derived societies are reaching the outer limits of their usefulness. This is not sufficient reason, however, to maintain their psychic hegemony in those societies that have the luxury of exploring the terra incognita beyond them.

The Strategic Use of Justice

As noted earlier, the psychic hegemony of the equality idea has been reinforced in Canadian constitutional law in the form of section 15 of the *Charter*, for historically oppressed groups perhaps the most obvious point of entry into constitutional litigation. Yet, there are at least two keys that can open the door to *Charter* challenges using a justice approach – the first is contained in section 7 and the second in section 1. The most obvious key is found in section 7, which guarantees everyone 'the right to life, liberty and security of the person and the right not to be deprived thereof except in accordance with the principles of fundamental justice.' Not surprisingly, the principles of fundamental justice tend most often to be invoked in criminal cases in which an accused challenges some aspect of the criminal law as violating those principles while depriving her or him of liberty and security of the person. It is thus primarily in the context of criminal law, and particularly in the massive body of common law dedicated to protecting the rights of accused criminals, that 'the principles of fundamental justice' have been honed. In part because of their location in the legal rights section of the *Charter*, fundamental justice principles have been viewed predominantly (though not exclusively) as procedural guarantees.

However, although legislative history suggests that the *Charter's* framers understood the principles of fundamental justice in the procedural sense,[80] the higher courts have shown some willingness to construe them as substantive guarantees as well. In the 1985 case, *Reference Re Section 94(2) of the B. C. Motor Vehicle Act*,[81] the Supreme Court of Canada found a breach of substantive justice in a provincial act that gave an automatic prison sentence to anyone found driving a car with a defective licence, whether or not they knew of any defect. Thus, among other things, the case stands for the proposition that principles of fundamental justice should not be limited solely to procedural guarantees. Generally, the court held that 'the principles of fundamental justice are to be found in the basic tenets of our legal system.'[82]

The question of what are the basic tenets of our legal system is obviously a function of point of view, and looks quite different to all the Aboriginal people, people of colour, women, lesbians and gays, people with disabilities, and other marginalized groups that have been dispossessed and oppressed by these tenets. There is a pressing need for groups historically and currently oppressed through law to articulate the fundamental tenets of the legal system in ways that promote substantive or just outcomes, and the Supreme Court has opened up the space for such approaches.

In addition to the development of just outcomes interpretations of the principles of fundamental justice, our analyses should articulate the principles in specific contexts and *read them into* other *Charter* rights. It would take an extraordinarily pendantic positivist reading of the *Charter* for any Crown attorney or other intervenor to argue that the principles of fundamental justice should not govern the whole *Charter* but are confined to the section in which the words appear. Nor is it easy to imagine the courts accepting such an argument given that justice is supposed to be the hallowed ground on which the legal system is built, and given that the Supreme Court has held that the *Charter* should be given a large and liberal interpretation.

Justice Bertha Wilson's concurring reasons in *R. v. Morgentaler*[83] are particularly useful to the substantive/just outcomes approach. In that case, she asserted that the principles of fundamental justice encompass not only the rights and freedoms contained in the legal rights section but also those found elsewhere in the *Charter*. In *Morgentaler*, according to Wilson J., the apposite principle was that of conscientious freedom, which underlies section 2 of the *Charter*. Thus, she expanded the range of values and commitments embedded in section 7 beyond those that pertain narrowly to the trial process or the administration of the penal justice system.[84]

Section 7 of the *Charter*, therefore, can be used in at least two ways. First, it can be used as a key to provide entrance into *Charter* litigation in and of itself, as it already has been used for a variety of issues (including abortion, apprehension of the fetus, fetal rights, assisted suicide, and immigration and refugee claims). Second, and perhaps more significantly, the 'principles of fundamental justice' clause can be *read into* other *Charter* rights, and vice versa, to argue for substantive just outcomes.

The latter strategy could be used in conjunction with, or to complement, analysis of section 1 – the second entry point for a feminist justice analysis – which states that the *Charter* 'guarantees the rights and freedoms set out in it subject only to such reasonable limits prescribed by law as can be demonstrably justified in a free and democratic society.' To my knowledge, feminist legal theoreticians have not to date been much engaged in the construction of feminist visions of a free and democratic society, even in their section 1 arguments in various cases. The focus has instead been on the 'reasonable limits' aspect, specifically on whether the particular objectives of laws found to infringe *Charter* rights are of a pressing and substantial nature and whether the means used are rationally connected to these objectives. In fact, section 1 analysis has been constrained by the *Oakes* test as set out by the Supreme Court,[85] which merely assumes without interrogation that Canada *is* a free and democratic society. The latter should be the focus of women's section 1 analyses; constitutional litigation using the justice frame would question whether a free and democratic society could be described as such if it were not just. Unmasking an injustice will unmask also the ways in which our society is *not* free and democratic, to the extent that the groups that have been excluded from state-level political decision-making will be forced consumers of the unjust policies and laws that have contributed to their marginalization, exploitation, dispossession, and so on. Having said all this, I am not suggesting that feminists should try to funnel all litigation through section 7. As a strategic matter, section 15 (or other sections) could be used as the initial key with which to enter into a *Charter* challenge, and thereafter, the emphasis would be switched to an analysis of the principles of fundamental justice that are being violated in a supposedly free and democratic society – in other words, the emphasis would be on reading the principles of fundamental justice into other sections of the *Charter* so that those principles frame equality, and vice versa.

Finally, the substantive/just outcomes approach would be buttressed by the remedies provision of the *Charter*, namely, section 24(1), which provides that '[a]nyone whose rights or freedoms, as guaranteed by this Charter, have been infringed or denied may apply to a court of competent jurisdiction to obtain such remedy as the court considers appropriate and *just in the circumstances*' (emphasis added). In reading the latter phrase, it would seem that justice had already been understood by the framers of the *Charter* to be not only contextually bound, but outcome- rather than merely process-oriented.

Justice versus Equality Approaches

Framing legal claims in terms of justice rather than equality offers several ways of avoiding the equality pit, depending on the issue or area in question. For example, as we have seen, one of the major problems with gender equality claims is that the reference group is always men. This circumstance leads to narrow analyses of issues that do not reduce simply to gender. By way of illustration, the oft-cited *Canadian Bill of Rights* decision in *Lavell v. A.G. Canada* is a case in point.[86] The case involved a challenge to the *Indian Act*,[87] which (to use the language of the statute) provided that an 'Indian' woman who married 'a person who [was] not an Indian' (or a 'non-status Indian') lost her status under the Act (as did any children of the union) and hence access to certain 'benefits,' such as the right to live on her reserve, inherit property thereon, and claim the benefits of the *Indian Act*, such as they were. In contrast, 'Indian' men who married 'non-Indian' women did not lose their status; in fact, their 'non-Indian' wives and offspring gained status under the Act. The majority of the Supreme Court of Canada had found that this was not a case of sex discrimination on the grounds that equality before the law was not a substantive requirement of the *Canadian Bill of Rights*. Instead, it meant 'equality of treatment in the enforcement and application of the laws ... whereas no such inequality of treatment between Indian men and Indian women flows as a necessary result of the application of s. 12(1)(b) of the Indian Act.'[88] In other words, the law was applied equally to all those in a category defined by the Act: it stripped *all* 'Indian' women who married 'non-Indian' men of their status, but left intact the status of all those who did not marry 'non-Indian' men.

Now, standard feminist analyses tend to scorn the *Lavell* decision on the grounds that the court's effective comparison of the treatment of other 'Indian' women was absurd and that obviously the appropriate reference group was Indian men. Hence, it is construed as a simple case of sex discrimination.[89] In contrast, a justice approach would recognize that the treatment of indigenous peoples in Canada is the quintessential and foundational model of domination and oppression. As well as having been dispossessed, indigenous peoples have been, in Young's terms, exploited, marginalized, rendered politically 'powerless,' subjected to cultural imperialism, and targeted for violence and harassment. A justice approach could not ignore the overall context of oppression of Aboriginal women *and* men. In a justice frame, then, the context is colonization, and the appropriate reference group is non-Aboriginal men and women since *they* did not have their legal and social status or their rights to live in their communities revoked according to the *racial/ethnic identity* of their spouses.[90] A justice approach would ask: What is it that made it acceptable to non-Aboriginal Canadian society that white men in Parliament should determine, not only what rights, benefits, and burdens should accrue to Aboriginality, but who should qualify for membership in indigenous communities? The legal regime Parliament created to govern 'Indians' was fundamentally based on racism, and in enshrining the particular sexism of the Victorian era, it created a racialized form of patriarchy that is not captured by a generic gender equality axiom.[91]

The justice approach would further ask: By what principles of fundamental justice is Parliament authorized to abrogate Aboriginal women's Aboriginal rights and exile them from their communities? In effect, the simple gender equality analysis accepts the legitimacy of colonial law and would be satisfied if 'Indian' women were treated like 'Indian' men. As such, it ends up arguing that as long as all members of the oppressed group are treated in the same way *regardless of their sex*, there is no discrimination. It is hard to see how this is more satisfactory than the Supreme Court's formal equality position.[92] A justice approach would hold that Aboriginal men, who are themselves subjugated by Canada's racist history, constitution, policies, and social practices should not be under that regime either. That the case turned on the question of whether the *Bill of Rights* would make the entire Act discriminatory and hence inoperative[93] shows that the Supreme Court judges knew very well what they were keeping in place in *Lavell*, and the narrow gender equality analysis they were offered up helped them to do it.[94]

As noted earlier, as well as assuming that the reference group is men, a related problem of gender equality claims is that they tend to be essentialist in their implicit assumption that women are equally subjugated by men, and cannot or do not subjugate each other. Even when feminist legal theorists have acknowledged other axes of oppression such as race, sexuality, disability, and class, the law itself allows for only one ground of discrimination, and this tends to reinforce essentialist and ultimately assimilationist assumptions.

In contrast to the essentialist and assimilationist logic of equality claims and provisions, the justice approach switches the focus from the gender (or race or class, etc.) *identity* of the claimant to the *relationship* in which the claimant is oppressed. Justice is more flexible therefore in forwarding intersecting claims, as it is unencumbered by narrow comparisons of ascribed identities. Justice can take account of the many and intricate relations of domination in various areas of the economy and society, including those in which white women and men dominate and subjugate women and men of colour, with the law's express permission. The situations of foreign domestic workers and migrant farmworkers illustrate the point well as each group, in Young's terms, has been exploited, marginalized, rendered politically powerless, targeted for violence and harassment, and in different ways subjected to cultural imperialism.

Although foreign domestic workers are clearly in a profoundly gendered labour market, gender equality claims do not capture the reality of their positions. First, there is no comparable male reference group against which to make the claim. Second, they are also in a fundamentally racialized labour market structured by an international political economy that puts many women from poorer countries in the position of leaving their own families to work for affluent employers in richer countries, usually without the minimal employment standards and protections against exploitation that are applicable to other workers. In other words, these workers are not exploited and marginalized *only* because of their gender, but also because they are poor women from poorer countries. As such, they are at the mercy of an international political/economic system in which affluent states negotiate their exploitation with their countries of origin. As Bakan and Stasiulis (in this volume) show, among other things, access to citizenship and other rights has become more and more restricted for these migrant workers as the source countries have changed from Britain/Europe to Asia and the Caribbean.

In the case of agricultural workers, both men and women are oppressed by their employers who benefit from the workers' outright exclusion from or under-inclusion (depending on province) in minimal health, safety, working hours, and pay standards mandated by labour codes. A recent constitutional challenge to the exclusion of agricultural workers from the benefits of association under the statutory labour relations regime of Ontario illustrates well the limitations of the equality frame in this context. In *Dunmore v. Ontario (A.G.)*, both the lower court and the Ontario Court of Appeal held that the act in question violated neither the freedom of association nor the equality rights of agricultural workers.[95] The equality rights argument was dismissed on the grounds that agricultural workers were not being discriminated against because of their individual traits, as they were not all of the same race or gender or age, for instance. In other words, they did not share an *identity*. The *occupational* category of agricultural workers as a *class* could not, in this view, attract *Charter* protection. Indeed, in the appeal heard and reserved by the Supreme Court of Canada on 19 February 2001 (attended by the author) much of the judges' oral questioning of counsel for Dunmore and the United Food and Commercial Workers International Union revolved around the issue of whether agricultural workers could claim equality rights under section 15 (given that they do not share a single immutable racial, ethnic, age, or gender identity) or whether occupational status that is associated with disadvantage and powerlessness in society constitutes discrimination on a ground analogous to those listed in s. 15(1) of the *Charter*. If previous jurisprudence is anything to go by, although they may well find a violation of the s. 2(d) freedom of association right, the Court (with the probable exception of Justice Claire L'Heureux-Dubé) is unlikely to accept an essentially economic definition of a class of workers as being analogous to the immutable identity criteria set out in section 15. According to this logic, if we cannot say that agricultural workers are being discriminated against because of their race or another 'personal' characteristic, and if membership in the group is fluid, then the most we can say is that they are being discriminated against because they are in a particular occupation, which is economic and not itself immutable. With no uniform immutable identity, it is difficult to find an appropriate comparison group for the purposes of the equality frame of s. 15.

This is where a fundamental justice approach would be more helpful. By focusing on relations of domination supported by a particular political economy rather than on ascribed biological and social identities, the justice frame is better able to avoid essentialism than the equality frame. We would ask the question: What principles of fundamental justice are served by the exclusion of these categories of workers from the benefits of those minimal standards in labour laws in a way that sanctions their exploitation? It is a very different way of regarding the problem than trying to decide whether members of the group share an immutable identity, or which other group is the 'correct' reference group to which claimants must compare themselves and argue that they are similarly situated (or not). Feminists should be prepared to stick up for men's interests too, particularly those from subordinated groups, if only because their emancipation will contribute to the health and welfare of all of our families and communities.

A series of significant losses for equality-seeking groups before the Supreme Court of Canada amply illustrates some of the deficits of the equality approach, suggesting that more than a decade of so-called substantive (rather than formal) equality analysis has had only a marginal effect on judges' thinking, and a sporadic and unpredictable effect at that. The Supreme Court of Canada's 1994 decision in *Daviault v. The Queen*[96] is a case in point. Among other things, it demonstrates the dangers of the procedural or due process view of the principles of fundamental justice, and it is a compelling argument for women to develop just outcomes analyses to displace this view where appropriate. The decision provoked something of a public outcry, especially among women, for the sheer absurdity of its reasoning. Henri Daviault, a man in his sixties, had raped a 65-year-old disabled woman after allegedly drinking forty ounces of brandy over nine hours. He claimed that his extreme intoxication meant that he could not have formed the *mens rea* (guilty mind or intent) to commit sexual assault. Daviault thus challenged the rule previously established by the Court that the *mens rea* of a general intent offence cannot be negated by drunkenness, and claimed that it violated his section 7 right to 'fundamental justice' and his section 11(d) right to the presumption of innocence. The Supreme Court majority (including both women justices) accepted his defence, finding that 'the substituted *mens rea* of an intention to become drunk cannot establish the *mens rea* to commit the assault.'[97]

It is difficult to see how the Court could have concluded this since, by its own account of the facts of the case, Daviault's actions showed not only intent, but considerable *commitment*, not just to get drunk but also to rape the woman; he wheeled her into the bedroom in her wheelchair, manoeuvred her out of it, got her onto the bed, took her clothes off, and then raped her. It seems that such a sequence of actions requires a fairly high level of commitment, not to mention an unusual physical constitution, as extreme intoxication generally produces certain mechanical problems; if the word of a poet is anything to go by, alcohol in large quantities 'provokes the desire, but ... takes away the performance.'[98] The Supreme Court majority nevertheless felt that his state of mind was more important than such considerations: 'To deny that even a very minimal mental element is required for sexual assault offends the *Charter* in a manner that is so drastic and so contrary to the principles of fundamental justice that it cannot be justified under section 1 of the *Charter* ... [and] it would equally infringe section 7 of the *Charter* if an accused who was not acting voluntarily could be convicted of a criminal offence.'[99]

Daviault is a perfect example of how sexual assault law measures guilt according to what the accused says was going on in his mind. In most cases, this means his perception of whether or how the victim consented, whereas what was going in *her* mind and in her actions, *her* word that she refused consent, or *her* experience of violation and assault is secondary. What counts is what he thought (or says he thought) or chose to believe. In Daviault's case, he claimed that what was going on in his mind could not have included an intent to rape since the alcohol distorted his ability to intend, which effectively ends up as a claim that he had raped her accidentally – and the Court believed him. The Court's reasoning then went from bad to worse as the majority held: 'It is only the accused who can give evidence as to the amount of alcohol consumed and its effect upon him.'[100] Thus has the Court endorsed the ideal defence for rapists ('I had a skinful, your Honour, so I couldn't have formed an intent to rape her – the drink made me do it'). Even Alcoholics Anonymous takes the position that although alcoholism is a disease that is treatable, you choose to take the first drink and those that follow, and are therefore fully responsible for any actions committed when drunk. Yet, the majority put Daviault's right to be 'presumed innocent' above all else: only the three dissenting justices refused to admit extreme (or indeed any) intoxication as a defence.[101]

It should be noted that there were no intervenors in *Daviault*, so no equality analysis confronted the court. Obviously, neither LEAF nor any other social movement organization is in a position to intervene in each of the thousands of cases (of which criminal cases comprise the single largest component) in which equality or other *Charter* rights are at stake. The decision shows, nevertheless, what little effect equality analysis has had on the overall attitudes of judges. They are free to discard it even if intervenors are in court contesting each and every case, and they are free to ignore it entirely when they are not. Thus, decisions like *Daviault* push the issue of victims' rights into the law and order discourse of the ideological right, whose approach is *not* based on a gendered analysis of power relations between women and men.

On the other hand, because feminists have not been developing or offering up to the courts feminist interpretations of 'the principles of fundamental justice,' criminal lawyers and judges are almost always able to restrict the phrase to a guarantee of procedural justice that favours accused criminals – in this case, principally male assaulters of women. A justice approach to *Daviault* would have begun by asking: What principles of fundamental justice allow a man to escape responsibility for his *admitted* criminal sexual assault actions against a woman by choosing to drink himself to the point of loss of self-control or memory? What principles of fundamental justice award him the presumption of *innocence* (not just lack of criminal responsibility) even when he does not contest having committed the offence? What principles of fundamental justice dictate that women in such situations (or children or, indeed, other men) must accept without recourse, reciprocity, or retribution such violations of their security of the person? Violence, harassment, and sexual assault of women by men occur within particular social relations of domination and oppression, which the law condones and even encourages by allotting the principles of fundamental justice to the rapist who has admitted his action but refuses to accept the call to accountability for it. Even the federal government recognized this fact when it acted quickly to amend the *Criminal Code* to redress some of the damage done by the Supreme Court's decision (another example of a 'bad' decision leading to legislative change).[102]

The principles of fundamental justice come into play in a wide array of areas other than the criminal law but, particularly, in those areas in which the operative principles have typically been cast in equality terms. Equality was the core analysis offered the Court in the *Egan v. Canada* case, which was decided in 1995, for example. In a five-to-four decision, the Supreme Court majority rejected a claim by two gay men to spousal benefits by finding the definition of 'spouse' in the *Old Age Security Act*[103] constitutional, even though they agreed that the law makes a distinction that results in a disadvantage and that denial of the benefit is based on a personal characteristic that falls 'within the ambit of s. 15 protection as being analogous to the enumerated grounds.'[104] The justices divided in complex ways that should be noted: while five of the nine (Justices Claire L'Heureux-Dubé, Peter Cory, Beverly McLachlin, Frank Iacobucci, and John Sopinka) found a section 15 violation, Sopinka J. thought the offending provision was saved by section 1 of the *Charter*. He, therefore, agreed in result with Chief Justice Antonio Lamer and Justices Gerard LaForest, Charles Gonthier, and John Major, who found no violation and ruled against Egan.

Lesbians and gay men in Canada, as in many other countries, fit Iris Marion Young's definition of oppressed collectivities subjected to unjust treatment; they have been marginalized, subjected to cultural imperialism (in the form of heterosexism and silencing/concealment of their identities and experiences), targeted for violence and harassment, and excluded from the benefits and protections of various laws as well as institutions (such as marriage). Nevertheless, like many gay male and lesbian claims, *Egan* was cast as a classic formal equality question. This approach is perhaps not surprising, as lesbians and gay men are among the few groups left (along with people with disabilities and immigrants, for example) that still do not enjoy formal legal equality and against whom various laws are still allowed explicitly to discriminate. Once more we see the similarly situated, likes alike approach, beyond which the Supreme Court had supposedly gone in *Andrews*. Yet, the *Egan* case still yielded both reasoning and results that would not have looked out of place in the battery of Supreme Court decisions under the *Canadian Bill of Rights*, of which only one recognized the equality claim.

In *Egan*, the minority on the rights violation issue considered whether the characteristic ('homosexuality') was a relevant distinction that would justify unequal treatment, and, in order to decide the issue, they looked at 'the functional values underlying the law.' LaForest J., writing for the majority, found that Parliament's intent was to 'accord support to married couples (and common law couples) who were aged and elderly [*sic*] for the advancement of public policy central to society.'[105] The ultimate raison d'être of marriage, the minority decided, transcends legal, philosophical, and religious traditions, being 'firmly anchored in the biological and social realities that heterosexual couples have the unique ability to procreate, that most children are the product of these relationships, and that they are generally cared for and nurtured by those who live in that relationship. In this sense, marriage is by nature heterosexual.'[106] They admitted that it might be possible to amend the law to include same-sex couples, but, in their view, 'this would not change the biological and social realities that underlie traditional marriage.'[107] LaForest J et al. thus justified the exclusion of gay men and lesbians from the benefits of the Act by claiming that none of the couples excluded from benefits under the Act was capable of meeting 'the fundamental social objectives' promoted by Parliament.[108]

From a purely common sense point of view, LaForest J's construal of the issues is, to be charitable, startlingly ignorant of the current realities of social and family life. The claims that heterosexual couples have the unique ability to procreate and that most children are the product of these relationships miss the glaring fact that many lesbians and gay men have children, some via heterosexual intercourse and relationships, but others by means of low- and high-tech reproductive technologies that do not require heterosexual relationships or sexual intercourse at all. LaForest J's claim that children are generally cared for and nurtured by those who live in heterosexual relationships is likewise oddly oblivious to the statistics on single parenthood and the many different family forms that have preceded and succeeded the Euro-Canadian nuclear family. Following from this, his claim that none of the couples excluded from benefits under the Act was capable of meeting the fundamental social objectives promoted by Parliament (procreation and the nurture of children) is patently false. The minority failed to establish the necessary connections between marriage and biological reproduction, and between heterosexuality and parenthood.

The analysis presented by LaForest et al., of course, misses the obvious point that Egan's claim was for old age security, which is a public policy designed for people not currently capable of procreation. Even so, not only did the analysis not recognize that many lesbians and gay men have children, it also disregarded the fact that many heterosexuals have either not had children or have had their children as a result of a relationship prior to the one in which they find themselves in old age. In neither case are heterosexuals penalized in the social system. According to LaForest J, then, Parliament can be taken to be rewarding heterosexuals for their entire lifetimes simply for the *possibility* that they may have procreated, or could have if they had wanted to (no proof required), either with the spouses or common law partners that they find themselves with in old age, or with anybody else in their lifetimes. The minority did not suggest withdrawing the benefits from those heterosexual couples *included* in the scheme who, for whatever reasons, had not procreated and who, from the minority's reasoning, had not therefore met 'the fundamental social objectives' promoted by Parliament.

The reasoning of the minority in *Egan* startled many lesbians and gay men, lawyers, and legal activists, particularly in view of the fact that the Court had not long before suggested that Brian Mossop might have succeeded in *his* claim for same-sex benefits under a sexual orientation claim rather than a family status claim.[109] In *Egan*, however, the minority suggested that it would not think much of extending family benefits to lesbians and gay men even if they were allowed to marry, because of the allegedly pivotal social and biological functions of procreation, which is presumed to be exclusively applicable to heterosexuals. It is significant that gay men and lesbians could not claim even one win at the Supreme Court level until 1998,[110] even though that Court *had* declared in the *majority* reasons in *Egan* that 'sexual orientation' is an analogous ground falling under section 15, and even though their formal equality claims had played into the whopping heterosexist assumption that lesbians and gay men have to be the same as heterosexuals, that is, similarly rather than differently situated to qualify for equality before, under, and for equal protection and equal benefit of the law.

Obviously, a justice approach to *Egan* would have cast the question in a different light than the similarly situated frame deployed. It would have demanded from the Court an account of the principles of fundamental justice that, among other things, force lesbians and gay men to pay the costs of citizenship (including paying into social programs) but oblige them to forgo the benefits unless they conform to an alien sexuality and lifestyle.

Finally, the *Thibaudeau v. Canada* decision, which was released in May 1995, represented another legal blow to gender equality rights. The all-male Supreme Court majority (the two women justices dissenting) found no discrimination in the sections of the *Income Tax Act*[111] which allowed non-custodial parents (98 per cent of whom are men) to deduct child support payments from their taxable income, while custodial parents (98 per cent of whom are women) were obliged to add the sum of the support payments to *their* taxable income. The majority seemed oblivious of the fact that the custodial parent also contributes to the support of the children. Not only was her contribution subject to regular income tax, but she was also obliged to pay tax on *his* contribution (effectively, a proportion of his income), resulting in an 'upside down subsidy.' Although this legislative device resulted in a clear denial of equal benefit of the law, even if only because the *Income Tax Act* does not require any other category of individuals to pay tax on other individuals' income, this fact evaded the majority.

The gender equality approach is complicated, in cases like *Thibaudeau*, by the facts that not all custodial parents are women and that the law's facial neutrality means that it applies in the same way to male custodial parents. In fact, at the Federal Court of Appeal, Justice James Hugessen found that there was no sex discrimination, since the *Income Tax Act* rule had the same adverse effect on male custodial parents (2 per cent) as on female ones (98 per cent).[112] The majority at the Supreme Court level did not address the adverse impacts arguments of the Coalition of Intervenors.[113] That majority disposed of the sex equality claim in more inventive ways. First, they construed the appropriate comparators neither as women versus men nor custodial versus non-custodial parents, but instead as divorced versus non-divorced 'couples.' This construction was accomplished by appealing to the putative purpose of the law – in this case, to 'minimize the tax consequences of support payments, thereby promoting the best interests of the children by ensuring that more money is available to provide for their care.'[114] Rather than suggesting that Parliament find some other way of accomplishing this objective other than by rewarding the non-custodial while penalizing the custodial parent, the majority simply made the comparison group non-divorced parents, arguing: 'If anything, the inclusion/deduction régime confers a benefit on the post-divorce "family unit."'[115] From there, it was an easy step to assert: 'The fact that one member of the unit might derive a greater benefit from the legislation than the other does not, in and of itself, trigger a s. 15(1) violation, nor does it lead to a finding that the distinction in any way amounts to a denial of equal benefit or protection of the law.'[116]

The majority's insistence on continuing to treat two divorced people living separately, with separate sources of income and separate expenses (other than those associated with children) as a 'couple' or a 'family unit' is a legal sleight of hand that enabled the majority to find inequality *within* the 'unit' acceptable. Its conclusion was predicated on a series of assumptions – all disputed on the basis of the evidence by the two women justices, Justice Claire L'Heureux-Dubé and Justice Beverly McLachlin, that the family law system will do the right 'grossing up' in child support awards to offset the custodial parent's tax liability, that the tax saving to the non-custodial parent will be shared with the custodial parent, and that the custodial parent's marginal tax rate is always lower than that of the non-custodial parent so that her tax liability will be lower. In all of this reasoning, there is no acknowledgment that the vast majority of custodial parents are women, or that women's incomes generally decline dramatically after divorce while men's increase substantially. Only the two women judges in dissent even mentioned gender, let alone found it significant as an equality issue.[117]

The *Thibaudeau* case (along with many others decided by the Supreme Court and lower level courts) is illustrative of some of the critiques outlined in this chapter of law, in general, and the *Charter*, in particular, and it shows what we are still up against after so many years of struggle for equality on the legal front. It also shows how vulnerable the notion of equality is, how simple it is for the courts to put other considerations above it or swap the comparators, and how easily it is overwhelmed by competition.

Conclusion

In view of the overall record of equality rights litigation under the *Charter* since 1985, it has become more and more difficult for equality-seeking groups to suspend their disbelief in seeking legal remedies to social relations of dominance and subordination. Nevertheless, along with almost all feminists working in and around law, I have argued that (notwithstanding critiques of how law maintains relations of domination and oppression, critiques of rights discourse, legal culture and process, the liberal individualist cast of *Charter* rights, problems of access, law as an instrument of class/male/white power, and its patriarchal origins, values, and practices), women cannot and should not abandon law altogether. I have argued, however, that women's *Charter* litigation strategies have been hampered by their sole reliance on equality – a salutary concept in the general sense of the equal worth of all, but one as difficult to operationalize in law as in life.

Since 'the problem' for women has been defined as one of inequality, not surprisingly, the 'solution' has been defined in equality terms. Yet equality is rife with deficiencies: among other things, it tends towards essentialism and assimilationism, is difficult for courts to apply differentially according to context, and is susceptible to hostile takeover by the privileged. Given the myriad problems with the concept both theoretically and practically, it seems that women who aspire to equality with men lack ambition. In my view, we should aim higher: for justice.

In advocating the development of feminist approaches to justice, I am not suggesting that justice is the only virtue or goal. Nor do I imagine that merely swapping one old concept for another, or changing the *word*, will do the trick. Rather, I am suggesting that reclaiming justice from the traditional liberal, abstract, universalist, rule- and process-oriented 'malestream' interpretations that have dominated in theory and in law, will, at the very least, enable women to fashion gendered but non-essentialist claims and so avoid some of the snares of the equality approach.

Of course, I would not wish to overestimate justice or to suggest that feminist readings of and claims for it will not be contested by those who have all along contested equality claims. We could certainly expect vehement opposition from the usual groups, plus more of the ilk of the men's organization, In Search of Justice, whose main goals have been to fight for custody rights for men and the 'rights' of sexual assaulters, and to oppose abortion, affirmative action, and anything else demanded by women. Nor would I be surprised if judges had no more difficulty justifying injustices (in their own minds, at least) than they have had justifying inequalities. My position is not rooted in a delusion that justice will be a fix-all. It may not produce any more 'wins' than the equality strategy, but then, it is not as if we would be giving up a winning streak.

In fact, from my reading of various studies, it seems that one of the key problems with litigation strategies pursued to date is that women, lesbians and gay men, people of colour, and people with disabilities have been trying to *win* cases within law's narrow, categorical terms – trying to fit large, complex issues into small simplified categories that judges can understand as abstractions. This strategy sacrifices the development of more accurate, contextualized, intersectional race, gender, and class analysis for legal argument as well as the mobilization of political action. Yet, if we recognize that often, specific case outcomes are not definitive anyway (some 'successful' cases have led to worse public policies, while some supposedly unsuccessful cases led to 'better' policies, depending on point of view), then the definition of wins or losses changes. As a strategic matter, test cases might be better used as slingshots aimed at unsatisfactory policies to prompt particular public policy actions (much like *Thibaudeau*, as it turns out) than as 'solutions' in and of themselves.

As pointed out earlier, the substantive contextualized equality strategy LEAF pioneered and the organization's post-1992 attempts to develop more complex and less gender-essentialist equality analysis have been theoretically brilliant. To the extent that the courts have occasionally subscribed to LEAF's approaches, they have been practically brilliant as well, contributing to substantial and historic breakthroughs. However, although much progress has been made, LEAF has not yet developed a fully integrated and non-essentialist intersectional analysis (it is still trying to 'win' cases). In my view, this problem stems from LEAF's, and legal feminists' fidelity to the equality/inequality discourse that has proved so ineffective so often for so many reasons.[118] It may well be that we are locked into the comparative model of equality. However, it could perhaps be used in more creative ways, as part of a multipronged strategy that includes, but is not limited to, the equality frame.

Having argued enthusiastically for justice approaches, I must admit the probability that, just like equality, substantive justice is not possible under liberalism either, and for the same reason – the current system of privileges for the minority relies on a massive web of injustices of which inequalities are only a subset. Just as I argued earlier that equality-seeking groups are inevitably trapped by the contradictions and uncertainties intrinsic to the attempt to expand the meaning of equality, possibly beyond the ken of the liberal paradigm, the same may be true of attempts to expand the liberal model of justice much beyond the habitual process-orientation of the legal system. There is bound to be political and judicial resistance to recognizing the harms and injustices for which women seek legal redress, whether they are conceptualized as substantive equality or substantive fundamental justice issues.

Yet, in spite of it all, I take heart from the Supreme Court's willingness to move from process to a substantive just outcomes approach in cases such as *Reference Re Section 94(2) of the B.C. Motor Vehicle Act*[119] and *Morgentaler*,[120] which appear to open the space for a feminist reformulation of section 7's 'principles of fundamental justice.' In light of this, I have come to the view that if feminists are going to engage in constitutional litigation, a political economy of justice approach that demonstrates the ways in which liberalism is fundamentally unjust in practice is a better bet than an essentialist gender equality frame. I have tried to point out some of the concrete differences between the two models, including justice's move out of equality's comparative framework and its potential for escaping essentialism and assimilationism.

The task of constructing such an approach is likely to be everlastingly laborious. But even if true justice is equally impossible under current conditions, even if this is nothing but a conceit on my part, and even if it turns out to be little more than something to do while we are waiting for the elevator, at least women would be asking for what is truly wanted and needed in and from the law.

Notes

1 Although originally written for this book, a shorter version of this chapter appeared as 'The Equality Pit or the Rehabilitation of Justice' (1998) 10 *Canadian Journal of Women and the Law* 60. It has benefited from the kind critical comments of Susan Boyd, Brettel Dawson, Diana Majury, Daiva Stasiulis, Jill Vickers, and the anonymous reviewers for the journal and for this book, as well as those of the editorial board of the *Journal*, especially Hester Lessard, who together have helped me to avoid some embarrassing errors of commission and omission, but none of whom may be held liable for its remaining flaws or final texture.
2 Edward de Bono, *Lateral Thinking: Creativity Step by Step* (New York: Harper, 1970).
3 *Canadian Charter of Rights and Freedoms*, Part I of the *Constitution Act, 1982*, as enacted by the *Canada Act 1982* (U.K.), 1982, c. 11.
4 Readers will note that the terms 'black feminist/s' and 'women of colour' are occasionally used interchangeably in this essay. The term 'black feminist' is used to refer to those writers and activists of African descent, living in the United States, Canadian, and British diasporas, who have been instrumental in the development of critical race approaches to politics and law (and who write in English). The body of critical analysis created by these women is built on their specific experiences in different countries, with the U.S. history of slavery, e.g., shaping in distinct ways the enormous contribution of 'African American' women. The term 'women of colour' generally refers to racialized women who trace their lines of descent from Asia, Central and South America, the Caribbean, Pacifica, and the Middle East. These women bring their very heterogeneous experiences of racialization in white-majority, as well as 'Third World,' societies to the project of deconstructing Eurocentric social and political theory and praxis. The essay also refers to indigenous or Aboriginal women of Canada as those descended from the original, pre-European-settler nations of the 'Americas,' who again bring the distinctive perspectives of their histories

and experiences of colonization by Europeans. I have tried to use each term specifically, especially when individual women are named. However, on occasion, when referring to a position or body of ideas that is common to feminists of each of the groups I use the generic term 'women of colour.' I am aware that each and every one of these terms is problematic for a variety of reasons, but they are still nevertheless used in various literatures and in movements, and alas, I have none better to offer.

5 Carol Gilligan, *In a Different Voice* (Cambridge: Harvard University Press, 1982); Iris Marion Young, *Justice and the Politics of Difference* (Princeton, NJ: Princeton University Press, 1990).
6 The Meech Lake Constitutional Accord was made at Meech Lake, Quebec, on 30 April 1987. The text is set out in Peter Hogg, *Meech Lake Constitutional Accord Annotated* (Toronto: Carswell, 1988).
7 The Charlottetown Accord was made on 28 August 1992. The text of the accord is set out in the appendices to Kenneth McRoberts and Patrick Monahan, eds., *The Charlottetown Accord, the Referendum and the Future of Canada* (Toronto: University of Toronto Press, 1993).
8 Kimberle Crenshaw, 'Race, Reform and Retrenchment: Transformation and Legitimation in Anti-Discrimination Law' (1988) 101 *Harvard Law Review* 1370. Crenshaw argues that while formal equality claims actually function to legitimate the legal system as well as systemic inequalities, they nevertheless mobilize social actors and affirm marginalized identities.
9 Carol Smart, *Feminism and the Power of Law* (London: Routledge, 1989) 2.
10 Sherene Razack, 'Using Law for Social Change: Historical Perspectives' (1992) 17 *Queen's Law Journal*, 32.
11 Smart, *Feminism and the Power of Law*, 68.
12 [1995] 2 S.C.R. 513.
13 Ibid., 545. Indeed, Christine Boyle notes that in her experience the term 'feminism' itself is often used to refer to the doctrine of equality between the sexes in 'A Feminist Approach to Criminal Defences,' in Richard F. Devlin, ed., *Canadian Perspectives on Legal Theory* (Toronto: Emond Montgomery, 1991) 274.
14 Sandra Burt, 'What's Fair? Changing Feminist Perceptions of Justice in English Canada' (1992) 12 *Windsor Yearbook of Access to Justice* 338–9.
15 Ibid. 338–9.
16 Ibid., 341.
17 Proposed *Amendment XXVII* (proposed by U. S. Congress on 22 March 1972). For an analysis of the Equal Rights Amendment campaign, see Deborah L. Rhode, *Justice and Gender* (Cambridge, MA: Harvard University Press, 1989), esp. chap. 4.

18 S.C. 1960, c. 44.
19 As Burt notes, the demands of the Ad Hoc Committee on the Constitution conference in October 1981 were for 'women's right to equal economic opportunities and reproductive freedom; the inclusion of marital status, sexual orientation, and political beliefs on the list of prohibited grounds of discrimination; and a statement of purpose in the *Charter* which would guarantee ... the declared rights and freedoms ... equally to men and women, with no limitations.' See Burt, 'What's Fair,' 344.
20 As Carol Lee Bacchi's account of 'English-Canadian' suffragist history shows, 'first-wave' feminists typically demanded the vote using maternal feminist, 'separate spheres,' superior moral character arguments to buttress their claims that their voices were needed in the public domain as 'moral arbiters for the nation,' as well as to exclude 'undesirable foreigners.' One of their chief strategies was 'capitalizing on the anxiety over the deterioration of the [Anglo-Saxon] race,' which, however, tied them to domestic and reproductive roles, and 'they did not question the limitations they imposed on women's attitudes and activities.' See Carol Lee Bacchi, *Liberation Deferred? The Ideas of the English-Canadian Suffragists, 1877–1918* (Toronto: University of Toronto Press, 1983) 116. These dynamics are also traced, e.g., in Daiva Stasiulis and Nira Yuval-Davis, eds., *Unsettling Settler Societies: Articulations of Gender, Race, Ethnicity and Class* (London: Sage, 1995). See esp., Daiva Stasiulis and Radha Jhappan, 'The Fractious Politics of a Settler Society: Canada,' 106–16; Wendy Larner and Paul Spoonley, 'Post-Colonial Politics in Aotearoa / New Zealand,' 46; and Jan Jindy Pettman, 'Race, Ethnicity and Gender in Australia,' 72.
21 These areas include family law (alimony, child support, child custody, and divorce), reproductive rights, social welfare policy, child care, sexual and domestic violence, tax law, and employment policy. In each of these areas, and in many others, treating women identically to men actually exacerbates the real-world inequality of women.
22 Lucinda M. Finley, 'Transcending Equality Theory: A Way Out of the Maternity and the Workplace Debate' (1986) 86 *Columbia Law Review* 1118–82. Finley presents an excellent synopsis of the same vs special treatment debate in the United States.
23 Finley argues that the assessment of whether two parties are similarly situated depends on the characteristic selected, and this selection is a highly political, value-laden choice, determined by one's world view and perspective. Ibid., 1122. Patricia Williams, in *The Alchemy of Race and Rights: Diary of a Law Professor* (Cambridge, MA: Harvard University Press, 1991) 98–9, makes a similar point by noting that it is rare that two people

are absolutely equally qualified (in the sense that they both went to Harvard, graduated in the same class, tied for number one, took all the same classes), and given the myriad of factors that might affect assessments (marking according to the bell curve, personal preferences, or prejudices of assessors) the judgment of equality is usually fairly subjective anyway. See also Sherene Razack, *Canadian Feminism and the Law: The Women's Legal Education and Action Fund and the Pursuit of Equality* (Toronto: Second Story Press, 1991) 21–5.

24 Judy Fudge notes that the abolition of 'rape' in favour of 'sexual assault' was being reconsidered by feminists because the expunging of gender specificity in sexual assault offences meant that women could not really address the gendered relations of social power that are manifested in sexual assault. See Judy Fudge, 'The Effect of Entrenching a Bill of Rights upon Political Discourse: Feminist Demands and Sexual Violence in Canada' (1989) 17 *International Journal of the Sociology of Law* 454.

25 Much of this debate in the Anglo-American democracies has revolved around the question of pregnancy and maternity benefits, clearly an area in which equality patently could not be satisfied by giving women the same rights or benefits that men have.

26 Catharine MacKinnon, quoted in Finley, 'Transcending Equality Theory,' 1156.

27 For example, in *Brooks v. Canada Safeway Ltd.*, [1989] 1 S.C.R. 1219, Safeway argued that the exclusion of pregnant women from the company's disability plan was not sex discrimination because not all women are or will be pregnant (at 1247), and in *Janzen v. Platy Enterprises Ltd.*, [1989] 1 S.C.R. 1252, the employer of two women who had been sexually harassed by a male employee argued that sexual harassment is not sex discrimination because not all women employees had been harassed. These arguments were rejected by the Supreme Court in these cases, but that does not guarantee their future rejection by that court or lower courts.

28 Smart, *Feminism*, 84.

29 See Razack, *Canadian Feminism*, passim; and chaps. 2 and 4 of this volume.

30 See Diana Majury, 'Equality and Discrimination According to the Supreme Court of Canada' (1991) 4 *Canadian Journal of Women and the Law* 416–20, in which she outlines the two key planks of contextualization and the stress on the current situation of *inequality* in which women find themselves.

31 This term is borrowed from Diana Majury's chapter in this volume.

32 LEAF was on the 'winning' side in a number of important constitutional cases, including: *Andrews v. Law Society of British Columbia*, [1989] 1 S.C.R.

143; *Canadian Newspapers v. Canada*, [1988] 2 S.C.R. 122; *Borowski v. Attorney-General of Canada*, [1989] 1 S.C.R. 342; *Brooks*, 1219; *Janzen*, 1252; *Daigle v. Tremblay*, [1989] 2 S.C.R. 530; *Taylor and the Western Guard Party v. the Canadian Human Rights Commission et al.*, [1990] 3 S.C.R. 892; *R. v. Keegstra*, [1990] 3 S.C.R. 697; *R. v. Sullivan and Lemay*, [1991] 1 S.C.R. 489; *Butler v. The Queen*, [1992] 1 S.C.R. 452; *Norberg v. Wynrib*, [1992] 2 S.C.R. 318; *R. v. M.L.M.*, [1994] 2 S.C.R. 3; *Moge v. Moge*, [1992] 3 S.C.R. 813; *Conway v. The Queen*, [1993] 2 S.C.R. 872; *M.(K.) v. M.(H.)*, [1992] 3 S.C.R. 6; *Whitley and Mowers v. The Queen*, [1994] 3 S.C.R. 830; *Goertz v. Gordon*, [1996] 2 S.C.R. 27; *Winnipeg Child and Family Services v. G.(D.F.)*, [1997] 3 S.C.R. 925; *Eldridge v. British Columbia (A.G.)*, [1997] 3 S.C.R. 624; *R. v. S.(R.D.)*, [1997] 3 S.C.R. 484; *Vriend v. Alberta (A.G.)*, [1998] 1 S.C.R. 493; and *M. v. H.*, [1999] 2 S.C.R. 3. LEAF has been on the 'losing' side in fewer constitutional cases, including *Seaboyer and Gayme v. The Queen*, [1991] 2 S.C.R. 577; *Canadian Council of Churches v. The Queen*, [1992] 1 S.C.R. 236; *R. v. Thibaudeau*, [1995] 2 S.C.R. 627; *and O'Connor v. The Queen*, [1995] 4 S.C.R. 411. All of LEAF's Supreme Court of Canada factums up to 1996 have been published in Women's Legal Education and Action Fund, *Equality and the Charter: Ten Years of Feminist Advocacy before the Supreme Court of Canada* (Toronto: Emond Montgomery, 1996). I qualify the terms 'winning' and 'losing' because LEAF's positions have been contested within the women's movements; for example, LEAF's pro-censorship position in *Butler* has been reviled by anticensorship feminists. I should also note that even though it turned out that LEAF was on the 'winning' side, the Supreme Court did not necessarily endorse LEAF's analysis, and often decided cases on quite different grounds.

33 See Majury's analysis of the case, this volume.
34 See, e.g., several pornography/obscenity cases including *R. v. Red Hot Video Ltd.*, [1985] 45 C.R. (3d) 36 (B.C.C.A.), and the more contentious *Butler* case, in which the Court held that violent pornography was degrading and dehumanizing, and thus harmful to women and their equality rights. Some individuals have argued that the courts merely deployed the systemic equality analysis to disguise and justify their morally conservative antipornography agendas. See Brenda Cossman, 'Feminist Fashion or Morality in Drag?' in Brenda Cossman, Shannon Bell, Lise Gotell, and Becki Ross, eds., *Bad Attitude/s on Trial* (Toronto: University of Toronto Press, 1997) 107–51.
35 Majury, this volume.
36 Angela P. Harris, 'Race and Essentialism in Feminist Legal Theory,' in

D. Kelly Weisberg, ed., *Feminist Legal Theory: Foundations* (Philadelphia: Temple University Press, 1993) 348. See also Archana Parashar, 'Essentialism or Pluralism: The Future of Legal Feminism' (1993) 6 *Canadian Journal of Women and the Law* 328; and Sherene Razack, 'Speaking for Ourselves: Feminist Jurisprudence and Minority Women' (1990–1) 4 *Canadian Journal of Women and the Law* 440; and Razack, 'Using Law for Social Change.'
37 Razack, 'Using Law for Social Change,' 32–3.
38 Ibid., 39.
39 Kimberle Crenshaw, 'Demarginalizing the Intersection of Race and Sex: A Black Feminist Critique of Anti-discrimination Doctrine, Feminist Theory and Anti-racist Politics,' in D. Kelly Weisberg, ed., *Feminist Legal Theory*, 385. The Title VII case was *DeGraffenreid v. General Motors* 558 F. 2d (8th Cir. 1977).
40 Crenshaw, 'Demarginalizing the Intersection,' 383.
41 See, e.g., William Julius Wilson, *The Truly Disadvantaged: The Inner City, the Underclass and Public Policy* (Chicago: University of Chicago Press, 1987) 115–18; Anthony Cortese, 'Affirmative Action: Are White Women Gaining at the Expense of Black Men?' (1992) 25, 2–4, *Equity and Excellence* 77–89; and Bruce Hare, 'On the Desegregation of the Visible Elite: or Be-ware of the Emperor's New Helpers; He or She May Look Like You or Me' (1995) 10, 4 *Sociological Forum* 673–8.
42 Crenshaw, 'Demarginalizing the Intersection,' 386.
43 Nitya Duclos (now Iyer), 'Disappearing Women: Racial Minority Women in Human Rights Cases' (1993) 6 *Canadian Journal of Women and the Law* 25, 41.
44 Nitya Iyer, 'Categorical Denials: Equality Rights and the Shaping of Social Identity' (1993) 19, 1 *Queen's Law Journal* 179, 191–2.
45 Ibid., 190.
46 I would exempt heterosexism and ableism from this point as various laws clearly and deliberately, by admission and express permission of the courts, discriminate against lesbians and gay men, and people with disabilities.
47 See 'Factum of the Aboriginal Women's Council et al.,' in LEAF, *Equality and the Charter*, 434.
48 bell hooks, 'Feminism: A Movement to End Sexist Oppression,' in Anne Phillips, ed., *Feminism and Equality* (Oxford: Basil Blackwell, 1987) 62.
49 Mary Ellen Turpel, 'Patriarchy and Paternalism: The Legacy of the Canadian State for First Nations Women' (1993) 6 *Canadian Journal of Women and the Law* 179–80.
50 See Teressa Anne Nahanee, 'Indian Women, Sex Equality, and the Charter,'

in Caroline Andrew and Sandra Rodgers, eds., *Women and the Canadian State* (Montreal and Kingston: McGill-Queen's University Press, 1997) 89–103.
51 Turpel, 'Patriarchy and Paternalism,' 184.
52 Radha Jhappan, 'Post-Modern Race and Gender Essentialism or a Post-Mortem of Scholarship' (1996) 51 *Studies in Political Economy* 25.
53 See Shadia B. Drury, 'Aristotle on the Inferiority of Women' (1987) 7, 4 *Women and Politics* 51–65.
54 John Rawls, *A Theory of Justice* (Cambridge, MA: Harvard University Press, 1971). Rawls's key assumption is that rational adults hypothetically deciding on the principles of justice to govern their society would try to balance the maximum amount of liberty for all. They would tolerate only that level of inequality that would benefit the least advantaged, *provided that*, in what he calls 'the original position,' such adults were behind a 'veil of ignorance' so that they would not know their gender, racial, or class identities, or their physical and mental attributes, idiosyncratic desires and interests, or social rank in the society. Many feminist theorists, while admiring Rawls's general approach, have criticized it for being rooted in rational choice theory, and for the abstraction of the original position that erases real sociopolitical contexts. It is also regarded as fundamentally androcentric since (among other things) the original position assumes male heads of households and does not assume justice *within* the family. See, e.g., Mari J. Matsuda, 'Liberal Jurisprudence and Abstracted Visions of Human Nature: A Feminist Critique of Rawls' Theory of Justice' (1986) 16 *New Mexico Law Review* 613; and Susan Moller Okin, 'Are Our Theories of Justice Gender-Neutral?' in Robin K. Fullinwider and Claudia Mills, eds., *The Moral Foundation of Civil Rights* (Totawa, NJ: Rowman and Littlefield, 1986); and Seyla Benhabib, 'The Generalized and the Concrete Other,' in Eva F. Kittay and Diana T. Meyers, eds., *Women and Moral Theory* (Totawa, NJ: Rowman and Littlefield, 1987).
55 See Susan Moller Okin, who, in 'Reason and Feeling in Thinking about Justice,' (1989) 100 *Ethics* 229, wants to save Rawls by claiming that his theory is not wholly rationalist but requires caring for others. See also Taina Bien-Aime, 'The Woman behind the Blindfold: Toward a Feminist Reconstruction of Rawls' *Theory of Justice*' (1990–1) 18 *Review of Law and Social Change* 1125; and Janet Moore, 'Covenant and Feminist Reconstructions of Subjectivity within Theories of Justice' (1992) 55, 3 *Law and Contemporary Problems* 159.
56 Gilligan, 'In a Different Voice,' 24–39.
57 Carol Gilligan, 'Moral Orientation and Moral Development,' 21.

58 Ibid.
59 Gilligan, 'In a Different Voice,' 31.
60 Gilligan, 'Moral Orientation,' 21.
61 Gilligan, 'In a Different Voice,' 31.
62 Gilligan, 'Moral Orientation,' 21. The relationship between the two orientations is not entirely clear. Gilligan is at times careful to point out that 'justice and care as moral perspectives are not opposites or mirror-images of one another, with justice uncaring and caring unjust' (ibid., 23). Yet at other times, she claims they are 'fundamentally incompatible' (as quoted in Will Kymlicka, *Contemporary Political Philosophy: An Introduction* [Oxford: Clarendon, 1990], 294). And, although Gilligan finds that men and boys are more likely to take the justice approach, while girls and women are more associated with the ethic of care, she does acknowledge that across six different studies she conducted 'most people, male and female [an average of 65 per cent of 200 people], represent[ed] both voices in defining and resolving moral problems.' Still, she noted 'an overwhelming tendency in men to focus on justice and only minimally to represent caring' (and vice versa for women). See the conversation with and reported by Isabel Marcus and Paul Speigelman, 'Feminist Discourse: Moral Values and the Law, A Conversation' (1985) 34 *Buffalo Law Review* 42–3.
63 See Carol Stack, 'The Culture of Gender: Women and Men of Colour,' (1986) 11 *Signs* 321. In my view, Gilligan's work assumes the cultural values of certain European and North American dominant societies based on capitalist and liberal ideological norms of self-interest. This model does not fit the thousands of cultures of indigenous peoples of the world, as well as other cultures of Asia, South and Central America, Africa, Australasia, and the island cultures of Pacifica, which, to the extent that they have managed to resist capitalist liberal individualism, seem to organize morality and justice precisely within webs of social relationships and responsibilities that Gilligan associates with femaleness in western contexts. Of course, I am guilty here of aggregating and generalizing about all non-western cultures in a way that negates their considerable specificities and differences from one another, but my point is simply to challenge Gilligan's view that the different approaches are attributable to gender rather than to a specific mode of production/distribution, superstructural ideology, and culture that happens to be ascendant in the west.
64 Cass R. Sunstein, 'Introduction: Notes on Feminist Political Thought,' in Cass R. Sunstein, ed., *Feminism and Political Theory* (Chicago: University of Chicago Press, 1990), 2.
65 Catharine MacKinnon argues that the female voices Gilligan heard are the

voices of the subordinate and cannot be regarded as women's authentic voices until their subordination ends. See Katherine O'Donovan, 'Engendering Justice: Women's Perspectives and the Rule of Law' (1989) 39 *University of Toronto Law Journal* 134.

66 Young, *Justice*, 15.
67 Ibid., 9.
68 Catharine A. MacKinnon, 'Making Sex Equality Real,' in Lynn Smith et al., eds., *Righting the Balance: Canada's New Equality Rights* (Saskatoon: Canadian Human Rights Reporter, 1986) 37–42.
69 Iris Young, 'Polity and Group Difference: A Critique of the Ideal of Universal Citizenship' (1989) 99 *Ethics* 258.
70 Young, *Justice*, 22–4. Although a thorough critique of Young's approach is beyond the scope of this chapter, I find some of her criticisms of the distributive model somewhat overdrawn. For instance, she claims that it is focused on property and positions, yet acknowledges that many justice theorists include non-material goods, such as rights, decision-making, power, opportunity, citizenship, authority, honour, and self-respect (24–5), and even that some are concerned with the institutional relations that produce distributions (at 30). Her criticism is that they conceive of such goods as things that can be possessed by specific agents in specific amounts. However, in my reading, distributive justice can be just as much about the *process* by which material and non-material goods are allocated as about end-state allocations – which also happens to be what democratic theory is about.
71 Nancy Fraser, in 'From Redistribution to Recognition? Dilemmas of Justice in a "Post-Socialist" Age' (1995) 212 *New Left Review* 68–70, has criticized Young's framework on the grounds that it fudges the distinction between groups whose demands for justice are principally political–economic in nature (such as class-defined groups) and would be satisfied by a range of redistributive remedies, groups whose justice demands are more culturally rooted (such as lesbians and gay men) and who would be satisfied by recognition remedies, and groups whose struggle for justice requires both redistribution and recognition (such as women and racialized groups). Ultimately, she regards Young's emphasis on the politics of identity/difference and recognition rather than on redistribution as ill-advised as in her view 'virtually every struggle against injustice ... implies demands for both redistribution and recognition' (at 70). See also Nancy Fraser's book, *Justice Interruptus* (New York: Routledge, 1997) 189–206.
72 Young, *Justice*, 37.
73 Ibid., 37–8.

74 Ibid., 3.
75 Ibid., 4–5.
76 Matsuda, 'Liberal Jurisprudence,' 621–2.
77 Smart, *Feminism*, 71.
78 Ibid., 68.
79 Sherene Razack has argued, e.g., in 'Speaking for Ourselves,' 455–6, that feminism needs to develop a broader analysis of oppression based on the interlocking of all systems of domination. Such analysis would require white women to examine their own white skin privilege. For example, with regard to foreign domestic workers, the analysis would describe the economy and work structure in which both white men and white women may have secured their positions by hiring women of colour to assume their household and child care responsibilities.
80 Peter Hogg, *Constitutional Law of Canada*, 3rd ed. (Toronto: Carswell, 1992) 1032. See also Christopher Manfredi's discussion of the process vs substance approaches to the principles of fundamental justice in *Judicial Power and the Charter: Canada and the Paradox of Liberal Constitutionalism* (Toronto: McClelland and Stewart, 1993) 94–100.
81 (1985) 23 C.C.C. (3d) 289 (S.C.C.).
82 [1985] 2 S.C.R., 503.
83 (1988) 44 D.L.R. (4th), 482–500 (S.C.C.).
84 I am grateful to Hester Lessard for this point. It could also be argued that in the *O'Connor* decision, the Supreme Court moved the principles of fundamental justice beyond s. 7 to apply, not just to all of the legal rights in ss. 8–14, but also to 'rights' not even mentioned in the *Charter*, yet, according to the Court, adhering to alleged victims or witnesses of crimes. Although ultimately the majority upheld the accused's claim for access to the therapeutic records of the complainants/victims of sexual assault (subject to a judge's assessment of the salutary or deleterious effects and a test of the relevance of the record for the accused's defence), they commented that the witnesses 'are not to be deprived of their reasonable expectation of privacy except in accordance with the principles of fundamental justice' (429–30). It is significant that the court thus recognized the privacy rights of the witnesses attached to the principles of justice in s. 7, especially since privacy is not explicitly mentioned anywhere in the *Charter*.
85 *R. v. Oakes* (1986), 26 D.L.R. (4th) 20 (S.C.C.). In *Oakes*, the Court set out the following analytical framework for determining whether a law constitutes a reasonable limit on a *Charter* right. First, the objective of the legislation must be pressing and substantial. Second, the means chosen to attain this legislative end must be reasonable and demonstrably justifiable in a free

and democratic society. To satisfy the second requirement, three criteria must be met: (1) the rights violation must be rationally connected to the aim of the legislation; (2) the impugned provision must impair the *Charter* guarantee minimally; and (3) there must be a proportionality between the effect of the measure and its objective so that the attainment of the legislative goal is not outweighed by the abridgement of the right.

86 *Lavell v. A. G. Canada*, [1974] S.C.R. 1349.
87 R.S.C. 1970, c. I-6.
88 Justice Roland Ritchie wrote for Chief Justice Gérald Fauteux and Justices Ronald Martland and Wilfred Judson. See Peter Russell, Rainer Knopff, and Frederick L. Morton, *Federalism and the Charter: Leading Constitutional Decisions* (Ottawa: Carleton University Press, 1989) 368. They were supported by Justice Louis-Philippe Pigeon (at 373), who reiterated his earlier contention in *R. v. Drybones*, [1970] S.C.R. 282, now concurred in by Ritchie J. et al., that 'the enactment of the *Canadian Bill of Rights* was not intended to effect a virtual suppression of federal legislation over Indians.'
89 See, e.g., Mary Eberts, 'Sex-based Discrimination and the Charter,' in Anne Bayefsky and Mary Eberts, eds., *Equality Rights and the Canadian Charter of Rights and Freedoms* (Toronto: Carswell, 1985) 198.
90 This point is not to deny that until relatively recently, under Canadian law a married woman's citizenship was derived from her husband's. My point, however, is that in the case of Aboriginal women, they actually *lost* rights for having married non-Indians on the explicit basis of racial/ethnic identity.
91 There is no question that s. 12(1)(b) of the *Indian Act* served a variety of functions from the federal government's point of view, including: the reduction of the number of people who could claim rights under the Act and hence a reduction in the 'Indian' population for the purposes of land claims, treaty, and government spending obligations; forced assimilation of the women and children expelled from their communities and, hence, a dilution of their cultural identities; and the introduction of Euro-Canadian culture and values to the reserves via the 'non-Indian' women granted rights under the Act via marriage to registered 'Indian' men, and hence, a further biological/racial, as well as cultural, dilution.
92 In dissent, Justice Bora Laskin (supported by Justice Abbott) found that s. 12(1)(b) effected 'a statutory excommunication of Indian women from [their] society but not of Indian men.' Justice Laskin's analysis recognized the racist context in which the sex discrimination claim was being made, though this analysis was lost on the majority: '[I]t appears to me that the contention that a differentiation on the basis of sex is not offensive to the

Canadian Bill of Rights where that differentiation operates only among Indians under the Indian Act is one that compounds racial inequality even beyond the point that the *Drybones* case found unacceptable.' See Russell, Knopff, *Federalism*, 372, 371.

93 See the discussion in Douglas Sanders, 'The Renewal of Indian Special Status,' in Bayefsky and Eberts, *Equality Rights*, 545–6.

94 It should be noted that 'status Indian' organizations opposed the case and several other similar cases, not because the *Indian Act* satisfied their needs or aspirations, but on the grounds that if it were struck down, there would be absolutely no legal recognition of the nation-to-nation relationship between First Nations and the Crown, and since the government was not offering self-determination, the alternative would be assimilation. Other complicated issues included the fact that the influx of newly registered or reregistered 'Indian' women and children would further strain already inadequate reserve housing and social resources, which the government had no plans to improve. See Mary Ellen Turpel, 'Aboriginal Peoples and the Canadian Charter: Interpretive Monopolies, Cultural Differences,' in R. Devlin, *Canadian Perspectives*, 525.

95 *Dunmore v. Ontario (A.G.)* 155 D.L.R. (4th) 193; 37 O.R. (3d) 287 (1997), O.J. No. 4947. The Ontario Court of Appeal dismissed the workers' appeal in (1999), O.J. No. 1104, thus upholding Mike Harris's Progressive Conservative government's Labour Relations and Employment Statute Law Amendment Act (1995. S.O. 1995, c. 1) which had repealed the New Democratic Party government's legislation extending protection of the act to agricultural workers.

96 [1994] 3 S.C.R. 63.

97 Ibid., 65.

98 William Shakespeare, *Macbeth* (II, 3: 25–31). The scene involves a porter talking about carousing all night, who makes the following observation about the effects of alcohol: 'Lechery, sir, it provokes and unprovokes: it provokes the desire, but it takes away the performance. [It makes a man] stand to and not stand to.'

99 *Daviault*, 65, 66.

100 Ibid.

101 The dissenters were Justices John Sopinka, Charles Gonthier, and John Major, who took the view that: 'society is entitled to punish those who of their own free will render themselves so intoxicated as to pose a threat to other members of the community ... Individuals who render themselves incapable of knowing what they are doing through the voluntary consumption of alcohol or drugs possess a sufficiently blameworthy state of

mind that their imprisonment does not offend the principle of fundamental justice which prohibits imprisonment of the innocent.' Ibid., 66–7. This seems to me to be a sensible approach, although of course, it is within narrow parameters, and does not in any way address the asymmetrical power relations implicated in the sexual assault, especially in view of the victim's disability. Nevertheless, the minority's reasoning is consistent with that in other areas of law, most notably impaired driving laws, so that we could not imagine a drunk driver who, having killed someone while driving under the influence, then defends himself by claiming, 'your Honour, I was too blind drunk to form an intent to run that person over.' Indeed, so committed is the legal system to deterring drunken driving, offenders are punished for it whether they harm anyone else or not; the rule is simply, if you drink and drive, you are already committing a criminal offence, *and* you are responsible for any harms you cause while doing so. Would that we had such commitment to stamping out sexual assault.

102 See Bill S-6, *An Act to Amend the Criminal Code (dangerous intoxication)*, S.C. 1995, c. 32.
103 R.S.C., 1985, c. 0–9.
104 *Egan*, 514.
105 Ibid., 515.
106 Ibid.
107 Ibid.
108 Ibid., 516.
109 *Canada (Attorney General) v. Mossop*, [1993] 1 S.C.R. 554.
110 *In Vriend v. Alberta (A.G.)*, [1998] 1 S.C.R. 493, the Supreme Court of Canada ruled in favour of Delwin Vriend's claim that Alberta's *Individual Rights Protection Act* violated s. 15 of the *Charter* by excluding sexual orientation from its list of prohibited grounds of discrimination. The court criticized the 'cruel historical omission' that plundered homosexuals' sense of self-worth and implicitly encouraged others to discriminate against them. See 'Court Protects Gays,' *Globe and Mail*, 3 April 1998, A1.
111 S.C. 1970–71–72, c. 63.
112 *Thibaudeau v. Canada*, [1994] 2 F.C. 189.
113 See Claire F.L. Young, '(In)visible Inequalities: Women, Tax and Poverty' (1995) 27, 1 *Ottawa Law Review* 125. This evasion of the complexities of discrimination is a good example of Kimberle Crenshaw's point about the ways in which antidiscrimination doctrines let discriminators off the hook if the impugned effect does not apply to each and every member of the group, or if it applies to some members of other groups. See Crenshaw,

234 Radha Jhappan

'Demarginalizing the Intersection.' Only L'Heureux-Dubé J in *Thibaudeau* addressed this point directly: 'A denial of equality does not necessarily require that all members of a group be adversely affected by the distinction. It suffices that a particular group is significantly more likely to suffer an adverse effect as a result of a legislative distinction than any other group.' See *Thibaudeau*, 636.
114 *Thibaudeau*, [1995] 2 S.C.R. at 629.
115 Ibid.
116 Ibid.
117 See McLachlin J's comments, ibid., 632 and L'Heureux-Dubé J's comments, ibid., 636. Gonthier J's reasoning was even more interesting and reads like a throwback to the formal equality as administrative application days of *Lavell*: '[T]he right to equal benefit of the law does not mean that each taxpayer has an equal right to receive the same amounts, deductions or benefits, but merely that he or she has a right to be equally governed by the law.' Ibid., 629.
118 As one of the anonymous reviewers for this book has pointed out, in the Canadian context, the pull of equality is also partly determined by the fact that the federal government's Court Challenges Program, as the only significant funder of litigation (paying for disbursements and a significant portion of legal expenses), affects the ways in which organizations structure their litigation approaches. Because the program only funds constitutional equality and language rights challenges to federal laws, there are strong incentives for organizations to choose federal cases and to structure their interventions around equality claims.
119 (1985) 23 C.C.C. (3d) 289 (S.C.C.)
120 *Morgentaler*, 482–500.

PART THREE
Race and Citizenship

CHAPTER SIX

Negotiating the Citizenship Divide: Foreign Domestic Worker Policy and Legal Jurisprudence[1]

Daiva Stasiulis and Abigail B. Bakan

The first case concerning live-in caregivers and equality rights under the *Canadian Charter of Rights and Freedoms*[2] ever to reach the Supreme Court of Canada was decided in 1993 in *Symes v. Canada*.[3] Beth Symes, a self-employed lawyer, litigated for the right to deduct the full salary of her live-in nanny as a business expense, rather than the much smaller annual child care deduction allowed under the federal *Income Tax Act*.[4] While the Federal Court of Canada had ruled in Symes's favour in 1989,[5] two years later, the Federal Court of Appeal reversed that ruling.[6] In 1993, Symes lost the Supreme Court appeal in a seven-to-two decision. The two dissenting judges, the only female justices in Canada's highest court, supported Symes's claim that the *Income Tax Act* was discriminatory against women. Maintaining that the Act was designed by men for men, they submitted that it failed 'to recognize the reality of business women.'[7] Madam Justice Claire L'Heureux-Dubé further argued that the cost of a nanny should be regarded at least as legitimate a business expense as cars, private club memberships, 'and the wining and dining of clients and customers.'[8] But the majority of justices rejected this argument, contending that the responsibility for paying for child care is shared by both parents. In the words of Justice Frank Iacobucci, 'proof that women incur social costs is not sufficient proof that they incur child care expenses.'[9] A disappointed Symes retorted: 'If it's clear to the court that women are paying the social costs of child care, who do they think are paying the actual cost? ... We don't all have a benefactor behind us.'[10]

This chapter addresses the question of 'who pays the actual cost' of the care of children, the elderly, and the infirm in the many Canadian households employing migrant women as live-in caregivers. A full answer to this question entails broadening the analysis of the social reproduction of Canadian families beyond relations of gender, and beyond the geojuridical borders of the Canadian nation-state. It involves consideration of the forces that compel poorer women from underdeveloped nations to endure years of hardship ministering to the personal needs and conveniences of the families of upper- and middle-class strangers, while separated from their own families. It also involves examining how the laws in receiving states such as Canada do not merely reflect, but also create and reproduce the 'citizenship divide' between populations of the North and the South.

Other authors, such as Anthony Richmond, have flagged the significance of something similar to the concept of the 'citizenship divide' as we understand it in viewing wealthy countries' current preoccupation with border control, state security, and the preservation of their sovereignty as 'global apartheid.'[11] In other words, by creating more restrictive immigration and refugee policies, the more economically developed and affluent countries have banded together to prevent populations from the poorer countries from gaining access to their territories and citizenship resources. We use the term 'citizenship divide' to characterize the processes that produce minimal access to First World rights and entitlements for Third World, impoverished migrant women, and that make their domestic labour available to first world, more affluent families, who are secure in their rights attached to First World citizenship.[12] In this chapter we are particularly concerned to reveal the roles that Canadian immigration policy and judicial decisions in domestic worker cases have played in reproducing (or mitigating) the glaring division in rights and burdens of citizenship between marginalized non-citizen domestic workers and their citizen–employers.

The irony of the *Symes* case is that while the issue of child care provided by live-in nannies made it to the Supreme Court, the case did not address the multifaceted discrimination experienced by this non-citizen segment of the Canadian workforce. Rather, it emphasized the sex discrimination in the *Income Tax Act* against the self-employed and socioeconomically advantaged female employers of live-in nannies. The nanny, and her dire legal, social, and financial circumstances, were rendered invisible in this case, appearing only, as Joanne St Lewis (in this volume) pointedly suggests, in the commodified guise of 'tax write-offs.' This irony was marked further by the fact that although the leading feminist advocacy group established to forward women's constitutional equality, the Women's Legal Education and Action Fund

(LEAF) did not intervene in the case, Beth Symes and her lawyer, Mary Eberts, are both founding members of LEAF.

It is notable that the Canadian Day Care Advocacy Association had explicitly rejected the approach to subsidizing child care through income tax deductions adopted in *Symes*, as that scheme favoured middle- and upper-income earners and thus reflected a class bias.[13] In her discussion of the case, Susan Phillips points out that the *Symes* case did not receive a great deal of media coverage and did not 'serve as a rallying point for the women's movement and childcare advocates because they do not see the tax system as the appropriate vehicle for implementing a national strategy.'[14] This muted response, and LEAF's non-participation in the case, however, might equally reflect the unease felt by at least some feminists, who were mindful of the racialized and class-based power relations such cases generally involve. *Symes* assigned to the unnamed, low-paid nanny only the passive roles of business expense and appendage to her professional employer, rather than an active role of plaintiff seeking justice for the discrimination routinely visited upon her as a modern-day foreign indentured servant.[15] In bringing to the highest court a discussion of Beth Symes's 'nanny problem,' no one thought to inquire into Beth Symes's nanny's problems. In legal, financial, and social terms, the latter were surely more pressing and more severe than the former.

Since the *Symes* case, the legal injustices and abrogation of basic human and worker rights of female migrant live-in caregivers have still not become the focus of a Supreme Court case. There have been some efforts to raise issues before lower courts concerning facets of the discriminatory treatment inherent in the administration of the federal government's foreign domestic program. But to date there has not been a comprehensive legal challenge to the 'special program' within Canadian immigration policy that imports poor migrant Third World women to work as live-in caregivers. This is despite conditions of work and life established by the program that are considered unacceptable to citizen–workers, and that subject 'women entering Canada as domestic workers to state scrutiny, monitoring and control not evident in any other area of immigrant or temporary worker selection.'[16]

This chapter examines the Canadian jurisprudence involving domestic workers and the efforts made by Canadian domestic workers and their associations to win fairness in immigration policies and labour rights for migrant domestics through the courts. Unlike the communities of women described in other chapters in this volume, this chapter is concerned with women who do not have access to equality-based legal entitlements per se. The chapter discusses the limitations of using standard legal strategies to improve the oppressive conditions of foreign domestic workers, including difficulties in applying rights strategies (whether through the courts or human rights commissions) to immigration policy. *Charter* challenges to immigration policy confront the hegemonic uses of border control by more affluent states to limit poor Third World migrants' access to First World citizenship. The denial of many fundamental human and labour rights, generally associated with citizenship in industrially advanced countries, to foreign domestic workers by receiving states – such as Canada – and the efforts of these workers to (re)claim[17] these rights, can fruitfully be viewed as battles over citizenship.

The Citizenship Divide

Ann Oakley has drawn an analogy between 'women's' historical exclusion from citizenship and the non-citizenship status of 'the most completely ignored social group in European history ... the servant class.'[18] Oakley's comparison between the disenfranchised lot of paid domestic workers and housewives went as follows: 'Servants are the counterparts in the market economy of housewives – ubiquitous and essential, but working in the coerced silence of a double oppression as women and as secret agents maintaining the all-important cultural boundary between personal and public life. It is not coincidental that servants, like women, were defined as the dependents of men (property-owners) and were the last social group to receive enfranchisement as citizens.'[19]

The analogy is not an exact one. The domestic servants Oakley speaks of were presumably both men and women and, rather than international migrant workers, they were usually born in the European countries where they were employed. It is nonetheless significant that Oakley singled out private domestic servants in terms of their status at the very bottom of the citizenship hierarchy. What is striking in the global context of the contemporary employment of migrant domestic workers is the near universal extent to which this social group is excluded from entitlement to many, most, or indeed, sometimes all, citizenship rights associated with their employing states. At the same time, they are compelled to take on citizenshiplike responsibilities, yet, through the process of migration, they relinquish most of the citizenship rights attached to their labour-exporting states.[20]

Citizenship is much more dynamic and multidimensional than simply a formal, legal status. It involves a broad spectrum of rights and obligations related to membership within nation-states, but constructed from the positioning of individuals and groups within a grid of intersecting power relations that often cross-cut national boundaries. While citizenship is usually defined in terms of membership of a nation-state, the ideologies about the criteria for legitimate membership are also articulated within civil society. Our conceptualization of citizenship is similar to that offered by Richard Falk, who argues that 'citizenship can be understood both formally as a status and, more adequately, existentially as a shifting set of attitudes, relationships, and expectations with no necessary territorial delimitation.'[21] Thus, while some groups (e.g., indigenous peoples, racial, ethnic, and religious minorities) may have formal access to sets of political, social, and civil entitlements within a given nation-state, their histories of discriminatory treatment within these states may mean that they are not identified by others (and, in some cases, even by themselves) as citizen-members of those states. Other groups, including labour migrants, may reside for long periods of time within a nation-state, while being denied access to the 'right to have rights' within the labour-importing state.

In contemporary conditions of global crisis and restructuring, states' tendencies to grant nominal or partial recognition of universal human rights have coincided with increased restrictions on the rights of migrants and refugees. States regulate different individuals' and groups' access to various forms of rights and obligations, and they impose various responsibilities and hardships upon them. How favourably or unfavourably particular individuals or groups are positioned with respect to border control policies depends partly on their class position or relative wealth, and partly on their positions within hierarchies constructed out of the intersection of other social relations, including colonialism, race, ethnicity, gender, and sexuality.

Citizenship and non-citizenship – and various intermediary categories such as non-citizen residency – emerge simultaneously, defined and redefined according to dynamic processes of struggle and negotiation. Labour migrants and refugees, particularly those of poor Third World origins, are compelled to strive for even minimal citizenship rights from reluctant host states and among populations encouraged by national receiving governments to scapegoat migrants who are seeking permanent resident status and full equality. Citizenship is thus a relational phenomenon, resulting in an unstable set of negotiated statuses for individuals and social groups, and reflecting a hierarchy among states in the world system. Moreover, the extensive damage wrought by the global crisis of capitalism has increased economic and social disparities between the North and the South.[22]

Nowhere are the struggles for inclusion within nation-state citizenship and new trans-border forms of citizenship more apparent than in the movement to claim rights among foreign domestic workers. The employment of female migrant domestic workers from Third World countries in the Canadian family household presents in microcosm the relationship between citizens and non-citizens. It also indicates a matrix of mutually determining social relations that intensify the citizenship divide between worker and employer. As discussed below, the (usually) citizen–employers hire (usually) female migrant non-citizen workers whose entry status into Canada through a 'special' foreign domestic worker program offers only limited and conditional access to Canadian citizenship rights and entitlements. In addition, these migrant women are low-wage earners employed by middle- and upper-class Canadians. They are also likely to be judged racially and ethnically inferior to their employers in a domestic labour market where racial and ethnic preferences are accepted as job-relevant criteria in meeting the demand for live-in caregivers and other household workers.[23]

The campaigns of domestic workers and advocacy groups to win reforms in immigration and labour legislation can thus be viewed as movements to win national and trans-border citizenship rights for female, foreign domestic workers. These women workers are globally constructed by labour-importing states as commodified surplus labour and expendable non-citizens. They are also politically and administratively constituted by Canadian immigration policy as non-citizens / non-permanent residents, and as on probation for the more desirable landed status and the coveted status of Canadian citizen. As a result, further legal restrictions are imposed on their job and residency mobility, as well as on their standards of employment.

The Canadian Live-in Caregiver Program in a Global Context

In Canada, foreign domestic workers face a labyrinth of regulations that govern the federal Live-in Caregiver Program (LCP) and the provincial employment standards and regulations for domestic workers. A number of writers have argued that these restrictions define the status of foreign domestics as feudal-like, or akin to slavery or indenture, and, hence, as antithetical to the basic tenets of liberal democracies.[24] And yet, in apparent contradiction, the Canadian LCP is frequently lauded both internationally and by its proponents at home for the assistance it provides in the admission of Third World women into Canada and their treatment upon arrival.[25]

To make sense of these contradictory responses to the LCP and the conditions established through shared federal and provincial jurisdiction, it is necessary to understand Canada's treatment of foreign household workers in a global context. This context supports a sexualized, racialized, international economy of highly exploited migrant household workers. Our contention is that Canada's domestic worker program appears positive only because the legal statuses and conditions elsewhere for migrant domestics are at the lowest point in the labour rights spectrum of any given country. Since the international consensus condones various degrees of oppression of migrant female workers who provide domestic labour in private households, any departure from this pattern that accords foreign domestic workers *some* rights, including those commonly enjoyed by most other categories of workers or immigrants, takes on a progressive appearance.

In the majority of receiving countries, domestic workers are specifically excluded from the ambit of most labour legislation.[26] 'Labouring outside protective legislation,' Elize Delport notes, 'these domestic workers enter into a highly personalized and socially invisible working relationship with an employer, without enjoying the benefits of collective bargaining and the entitlements of ordinary workers' rights.'[27] Among labour migrants, only female migrant workers in the entertainment industry / sex trades experience a comparable level of politically induced vulnerability to extreme exploitation and abuse.[28]

In part, such abuse continues because the supply of potential migrant domestic workers is immensely supple. This situation is created by conditions of poverty and underdevelopment, the spiralling external debt of poor countries, and the willingness of governments in the South to export women workers as a central plank of their debt management strategies. Governments send their female nationals abroad despite negative publicity regarding their maltreatment and despite the presence of strong moral norms opposing such migration in some of these societies.[29] There is growing competition among sending countries to penetrate foreign labour markets in order to earn foreign exchange through remittances from workers deployed overseas. This competition has had the effect of creating a downward trend to the already substandard wages and working and living conditions of foreign domestics. Yet for prospective migrant domestic workers, the wages they can earn as domestic workers abroad are often several times higher than female professionals earn in their home countries.[30] Many of these migrants are the sole supporters of landless parents, unemployed husbands, and financially dependent children.

The sheer volume of female migrants from developing countries seeking domestic service jobs in developed and newly industrializing countries has rendered contemporary domestic work an international business, with profits siphoned off at every phase of recruitment and migration.[31] This transnational business has many stakeholders, including the International Monetary Fund (IMF); the governments that 'deploy' their workers abroad and those that receive them; and a host of non-state intermediaries, including recruitment and placement agencies, training centres, and loan institutions, which often operate illegally or at the margins of legality.[32] Various parties that benefit from this coerced labour in receiving countries disguise the inherent servitude of migrant domestic labour by discursively representing domestic worker migration as mutually beneficial for employers and workers.

While the worldwide treatment of migrant domestic workers can generally be characterized as harsh and abusive, entailing minimal entitlements and major obstacles to their exercising the few existing rights permitted to foreign domestics, not all countries treat overseas household workers equally. Domestic workers from the Philippines who have prior experience working under very exploitative conditions in Saudi Arabia, Singapore, or Hong Kong, for instance, express a clear preference for working in Canadian households.[33] Employers also praise the Canadian program because of its support for the labour-force participation of educated women with children through the creation of a specialized program for the migration of child care workers.[34]

The Canadian government has had a long history of involvement in importing household workers from other countries, dating back to the state's beginnings in Confederation in 1867.[35] Although Canadian government recruiting schemes have frequently been aided by groups within civil society, the state itself has played an interventionist role in migrant domestic worker schemes. The current federal government program for recruiting foreign domestic workers is the Live-in Caregiver Program (LCP), which came into effect in April 1992. The LCP itself replaced the Foreign Domestic Movement (FDM) which was initiated in 1981. These programs constitute a hybrid between 'regular' immigration schemes that bring in 'landed' immigrants, or permanent residents – who enjoy most of the benefits of Canadian citizenship[36] – and temporary employment immigration schemes, whose purpose is to import foreign workers to fill specific labour shortages.

The LCP is the latest in a series of immigration programs meant to respond to the chronic child care crisis by resorting to the historical solution of importing household workers from abroad. The increase in the number of Canadian women with children entering the paid labour force, the trend towards irregular hours of work, the high cost of regulated care, and the difficulty of securing subsidized day care have all created a pressing need for affordable and flexible child care arrangements.[37] Despite these trends, successive federal governments have refused to honour a long-standing policy commitment to implement a national child care program.[38] In an effort to appease the more affluent segments of the electorate, programs such as the LCP (and its precursors the FDM, 1981–92, and the Temporary Employment Authorization Program for domestic workers, 1973–81), responded to the child care needs of middle- and upper-class Canadian parents. With the aging of baby boomers and funding cuts to health care and hospitals, the LCP also has increasingly been used to import foreign workers to care for the elderly and chronically ill.[39]

The LCP requires that foreign domestic workers have a valid offer of full-time, live-in employment to enter the country. Eligibility criteria include: successful completion of the equivalent of a Canadian grade 12 education; either six months' full-time training in the specific caregiving occupation sought (child care, elderly care, and so on) or twelve months' practical job experience;[40] and English or French language competency. As under the FDM, following completion of two years of live-in caregiving employment, participants have the right to apply for permanent residence in Canada.

The LCP differs from the FDM in the following ways. First, unlike the FDM, which required that applicants provide evidence of 'upgrading' and self-sufficiency as criteria for landing, the LCP has more or less made equivalent the criteria for acceptance into the LCP and the criteria for landing. The significant distinction is that proof must be provided for landing of two years of live-in employment as a domestic worker in Canada within three years of being admitted into the country.[41] Second, the LCP abolished the FDM's requirement that domestic workers obtain 'release letters' from their employer prior to changing work situations within the domestic work industry.[42] The letter of permission to leave, with its connotation of bondage, had been an odious symbol of the indentured relationship of the domestic to the employer under the FDM. Nonetheless, it should be noted that under the LCP, domestic workers continue to have to notify a Canadian Immigration Centre of their intentions to change employers, a requirement that deters many employees from leaving even abusive situations.

Third, the education requirement had been raised from the equivalent of Canadian grade 10 under the FDM, to the equivalent of Canadian grade 12 under the LCP. Domestic advocates decried the new educational criterion on the grounds that it revealed the hidden intention of immigration policy-makers concerning the LCP – the deliberate exclusion of women of colour from developing countries. Immigration authorities' rationale for this change was their concern with the integration into the 'general labour market' of foreign domestics who leave in-home care, assuming that '65% of new jobs created over the next ten years will require grade 12.'[43] However, domestic worker groups rejected this argument and viewed the Immigration Department's motivations with scepticism. They pointed out that the link between subsequent success in the Canadian labour market of former domestic workers and the possession of grade 12 qualifications had not been substantiated by immigration officials. The publicity generated by immigrant women's lobby groups and foreign professionals about the problems of obtaining recognition for overseas qualifications, even among highly educated immigrants, further fueled the suspicions of domestic workers.

For domestic worker associations such as the Toronto-based INTERCEDE and Vancouver-based West Coast Domestic Workers Association (WCDWA), the new education and formal training requirements indicated a move on the part of immigration authorities to shut the door on all but white applicants. As expressed in a group discussion of WCDWA community advisers, 'The overriding concern of Immigration has been that there were too many Filipinas entering through the program.'[44] The assertion by immigration authorities that 'raising the education requirement ... would not adversely affect any world areas,'[45] including the Philippines, 70 per cent of whose entrants into the FDM were said to have grade 12 equivalency, was directly challenged by domestic worker groups.[46] Thus, a 1992 survey of the education level of INTERCEDE members indicated that fully 70 per cent would have been ineligible to enter Canada under the admission criteria of the LCP.[47]

A clear impetus for the new education and training criteria was the decision of the Federal Court (Trial Division) in *Pinto v. Minister of Employment and Immigration*.[48] *Pinto* was instigated by the refusal of a visa officer at the Canadian High Commission in New Delhi, India, to issue a visa with an employment authorization to Ms Renny Quadros, a schoolteacher who wished to become employed as a domestic worker in the Canadian household of Joachim Pinto. The decision of the visa officer was based on Ms Quadros's lack of 'experience' as a domestic worker. This decision was quashed by Mr Justice McKay, who concluded that the visa officer had imported a 'rigid and ... undue notion of specialization' in assessing Ms Quadros's experience. The ruling claimed that the visa officer ignored the caregiving qualifications the applicant had gained from sixteen years of primary school teaching, and her experience as a single mother of a teenaged daughter. However, as importantly, the court in *Pinto* observed that the selection criteria for the FDM program were ultra vires insofar as they had no specific authority in the *Immigration Act* or the *Immigration Regulations, 1978*.[49] Thus, the visa officer was judged to have fettered his discretion by using the FDM guidelines and was ordered to reconsider Ms Quadros's application only in accordance with the less stringent criteria for the issuance of employment authorizations to visitors set out in the *Immigration Act* and *Regulations*. This meant that visa officers were required to base their assessments of prospective domestic workers on the actual qualifications to perform the job offered, in the same manner of assessment as for foreign workers entering Canada to accept temporary employment in any other occupation. This requirement would have the effect of eliminating the more onerous admission criteria that underpinned the FDM. The only route by which the minister could legally overcome the *Pinto* decision was to fix admission requirements to the LCP in the *Immigration Regulations*.[50] Thus, the purpose of the new legislative basis of the program was clearly not to provide enhanced legal protection for foreign domestics. Instead, it was to retain fairly onerous criteria pertaining to participants' education, training, and language skills before their application for an employment authorization could be considered.[51]

A fourth change introduced in the LCP, and one directly influenced by the *Pinto* decision, was an alteration in the legal status of the program. It became a regulatory program, rather than one established by policy.[52] Several scholars had pointed out the legal tenuousness and ambiguity of the FDM and previous domestic worker policies,[53] which had existed in a series of revised policy decisions, and a 'myriad of little rules ...

applied to monitor and control' foreign domestics.[54] While the impact of the FDM had been extremely coercive and punishing of the behaviour of foreign domestics, the rules and regulations of the FDM program had no legal authority by virtue of their inclusion in the *Immigration Manual*, rather than the *Immigration Act* itself and the *Immigration Regulations*.[55] Barbara Jackman argued that the new regulatory status of the LCP would benefit foreign domestics insofar as 'it provides a more fixed legal basis upon which statutory rights may be asserted before an immigration official or a court.'[56] In addition, the landing process for women already accepted into the LCP would at least be facilitated administratively, since landing is now 'pursuant to regulation, rather than by a case by case exemption from the requirements of the Act,' which states that landing take place outside of Canada.[57]

In contrast, Audrey Macklin maintained that the LCP might in fact become *more* disadvantageous for applicants for landed status. This argument was based on the fact that the LCP made commensurate criteria for entrance into the program and those for landing, thus shifting the locus of decision-making on landing decisions from immigration officials in Canada to visa officers abroad. Recourse to legal strategies such as judicial review of administrative decisions is less available to applicants overseas than to foreign domestics in Canada, unless pursued, as in *Pinto,* by other parties in Canada. Moreover, even where immigration visa decisions made abroad have been judicially reviewed, the Federal Court has denied *Charter* protection to visa applicants abroad.[58] Macklin also argued that there was a greater likelihood that 'bureaucratic arbitrariness and unfairness may go unchecked in Canadian visa offices overseas than in Canada, a prospect which can only redound to the detriment of the persons subject to the ... LCP.'[59]

The 1992 introduction of the Live-in Caregiver Program was met by a storm of protest by domestic advocacy groups. Domestic advocates and legal advisers have viewed the policy as racist insofar as it disqualifies many domestic workers from Third World countries who are unable to meet the increased education and training requirements.[60] Even though the initial training requirement was amended under pressure to allow for relevant job experience, the fears of these groups have been borne out in recent statistics. While the percentage of entrants into the LCP from the Philippines has remained high (between 61 and 75 per cent of total entrants in the 1990s), the overall numbers of domestics entering under the LCP have been drastically reduced. Thus, the number of entrants into the LCP in 1997 (1,606) was less than one-fifth of the number of entrants in 1991, the last year of the FDM (8,630) and only 15 per cent of the 1990 figure (10,739).[61] The precipitous drop in numbers of migrants entering through the LCP reflects the choking off of an important means of legal entry into Canada and acquisition of Canadian residence and citizenship for Third World women.

The increased difficulty of working legally as foreign domestics has forced many female migrant workers to work in undocumented statuses (e.g., entering as visitors, asylum seekers, or students, and remaining to work illegally). Although there are no accurate estimates of the numbers of undocumented foreign household workers, anecdotal sources suggest that the numbers are large and growing. The results of our questionnaire survey of fifty domestic workers in Toronto conducted in 1994 and 1995 suggest that for groups of particular national/regional origins facing barriers to legal entry as domestic workers, entry as visitors and unlawful work in a shadow economy are already well-established practices.[62] Workers' undocumented status further increases the asymmetrical power of employers over employees in personal domestic service. Employers may utilize the real threat of the employee's deportation to enforce arbitrary demands. They are particularly apt to do so in a context where the Canadian state feels no obligation to offer labour and human rights protections to undocumented workers.

Despite its new regulatory status and other changes, the LCP retained two fundamental features of the previous migrant domestic policy, features that define its anomalous nature in comparison with other Canadian immigration programs. These are, first, the temporary nature of the visa, or alternatively, the denial of landed status to foreign domestics.[63] As with the FDM, the visa provided to LCP migrants places them in the 'technically non-existent category of "visiting immigrant."'[64] As Macklin argues, 'In practice, a domestic worker bears the burden of both immigrants and visitors, yet receives the benefits of neither.'[65] Foreign domestics are subjected to more stringent entrance criteria than 'visitors,' and to greater constraints in occupational mobility and greater vulnerability to removal from the country than 'immigrants.'[66]

Second, proceeding on the unsubstantiated assumption that there is no shortage of live-out caregivers and that a labour market need exists only for live-in care,[67] the LCP continued to make living in the home of the employer a mandatory feature of the program. As elaborated later in this chapter, these two features of the domestic worker program bear the greatest responsibility for structuring the isolation and vulnerability to exploitation of migrant women in the program.

The 'contract' between a worker and the Canadian employer under the LCP (and formerly under the FDM) reveals the unequal rights of the two parties. As a condition of receiving a temporary employment authorization under the FDM, the domestic worker and her employer signed a 'Domestic Worker / Employer Agreement,' witnessed by one or more Canada Employment and Immigration officials, which stipulated wages, as well as working and living conditions of the employee.[68] Although the agreement was signed by both the employer and the employee, the employee agreed to 'accept the terms and conditions as outlined,' whereas the employer signed a statement that merely 'certifie[d] that the information is accurate.'[69] As stated in a 1987 article in the WCDWA newsletter: 'If an employer refuses to live up to the terms of the employment contract, there is nothing [the domestic worker] can do to make her employer change. Employment and Immigration will not investigate a complaint and make the employer behave properly. The contract is not binding on the employer. The Immigration Department pretends that employment contracts are serious documents but only takes action if domestics are at fault.'[70] There is no record of enforcement of the provision of the agreement which states that employers failing to abide by the terms of the contract will be denied further requests for domestic workers.[71]

The enforceability of the contract/agreement had not been (and remains) untested in the courts. The WCDWA therefore recommended that domestic workers 'treat the agreement as a contract ... Since the employers themselves do not know whether the agreement is a contract or not, do not tell them it isn't. Instead, try to convince them that it is a contract to which they are legally bound.'[72] In the current program, the LCP, ambiguity as to the status of the contract continues. If anything, the clarification Citizenship and Immigration Canada has given to the matter of contracts in the LCP information currently distributed to employers and domestics alerts employers to the fact that 'Citizenship and Immigration Canada is not a party to, nor does it bear responsibility for, the enforcement of this contract.'[73] In the guise of a neutral party, the federal government reinforces the power employers wield over domestic employees by giving them implicit permission to violate contractual provisions. It is a fundamental principle of contract law that both parties are bound by a contract. Hence these 'contracts' cannot be defined as such. Yet, the foreign domestic worker is bound on pain of deportation by Immigration Canada.

The non-enforcement of the 'Domestic Worker / Employer Agreement' against employers is simply one aspect of the domestic worker policy that highlights the 'employer's almost complete immunity from government regulation, monitoring and enforcement.'[74] There are no sanctions mandated by Immigration Canada against abusive employers, and Immigration authorities do not keep statistics on complaints they have received from workers.[75] The *Immigration Manual* does, however, instruct immigration officers to investigate domestic workers dismissed for serious cause – such as child abuse, theft, and gross neglect.[76]

The one-sided enforcement of the employer–foreign worker agreement reinforces the propensity of domestic employees to refrain from reporting breaches of the employment agreement, including gross abuse, to Immigration authorities or to provincial authorities. This reluctance stems from fear induced by a perpetual threat of deportation through employer-initiated reprisals. The LCP requirement that women entering the program live in their employer's place of residence reinforces submission to the employer's dictates. Live-in workers are dependent on the good will of their employer for a 'shot at the prize of landed status.'[77] They are also dependent on the employer's graces simply for a roof over their heads. As elaborated below, there is plenty of evidence to show that employers are ready to take advantage of the state-imposed constraints on their domestic employees to disregard the rights to which foreign domestic workers are legally entitled.

Canadian Indentured Servitude

Practices associated with servitude, such as imprisonment in the employer's home, or physical and sexual abuse, are less common in Canada than in countries in the Gulf Region and East Asia. In the latter regions, legal rights of domestics are scarce or non-existent. But such practices do occur in Canada, a function of specific mandated conditions of the federal government's foreign domestic worker policies, and the ideological conditions that globally rationalize the abuse of foreign domestics. The potential for abuse is heightened for workers who are women of colour from another culture, unfamiliar with Canadian law and practice, and isolated from friends and family – conditions that characterize the majority of migrant live-in caregivers in Canada.[78] The precarious legal–immigration status of foreign domestic workers means that abusive practices are rarely revealed to, or reported by, the mass media.[79] The case files of domestic advocacy groups,[80] court and human rights records, surveys of domestics' conditions, and community and academic research all indicate a pattern of systematic violation of domestic worker rights. While no one study can produce statistically representative results, the overall effect of this information is to convey a pattern of widespread injustice and discrimination against women from the Philippines and other Third World countries who are imported to Canada to provide personal domestic service.

The mandated live-in condition of the government's domestic worker policies has created particular hardships for migrant domestic workers. While living in the midst of the employer's family, live-in caregivers are not members of these families. Typically their relations with other household members involve a dialectic of 'intimacy and depersonalization.'[81] Among the difficulties experienced by workers as a result of the mandatory live-in requirement are: non-payment of wages earned, especially regarding overtime; inadequate accommodation; insufficient and poor quality food; lack of privacy; the use by employers of workers' living space as guestrooms; the inability to have visitors, especially male visitors; the inability to take sick leave; isolation and loneliness; the tendency never to feel at home; sexual and racial harassment; and vulnerability to false accusations of theft.[82]

The live-in requirement renders domestic workers especially susceptible to sexual and racial harassment, as well as physical and emotional abuse from employers and household members.[83] A serious problem for live-in workers is the danger of unwanted sexual advances from (usually male) members of the household. Given the general reticence of all harassed women to report sexual harassment and abuse, augmented in the case of foreign domestic workers by the fear of imperiling their immigration status, the actual incidence of sexual harassment is unknown. Researchers have warned that the topic of sexual harassment is too sensitive and complex to be meaningfully handled in questionnaire surveys.[84] Sexual abuse, however, is a recurrent theme in the narratives of foreign domestic workers in Canada.[85] In one complaint heard in the B.C. Council of Human Rights, a live-in domestic worker Leonida Guzman won her case against her employers Dr and Mrs T., who were found to have failed to provide the complainant with a working environment free of sexual harassment.[86] In this instance, the employer's thirteen-year-old son had engaged in 'very aggressive and violent' sexual harassment of the complainant, including stalking her, destroying her property, and 'criminal incidents of sexual assault.' The complainant was awarded lost wages plus $6,500 as 'compensation for the injury to her feelings, dignity and self-respect.'[87]

In another sexual harassment case, *Singson v. Pasion and Moore*,[88] also brought before the B.C. Council of Human Rights, the council ruled in favour of the complainant who had worked as a live-in nanny for several months in 1992 for the respondents. Ms Singson quit her job after having been subjected to several incidents of sexual harassment by her male employer Mr Moore, who threatened her with deportation in an attempt to silence her. The council ordered Ms Singson's former employers to recompense her for four months of wage loss, plus $3,500 'to compensate her for injury to her dignity, feelings and self-respect.' The council's assessment of the quantum of damages in this case took into account the complainant's vulnerability as a migrant from the Philippines who had been in Canada for fewer than four months, and who was 'adapting to a new culture and lack[ing] an understanding of her legal rights.' Specifically, the council mentioned the serious limitations on Ms Singson's mobility imposed by the conditions of her employment authorization and position as a foreign live-in worker. It also drew attention to the psychological impact of the harassment in a context where the complainant had concerns that her immigration status would be jeopardized if she left her abusive employment situation.[89]

The privacy and autonomy of live-in domestic employees are compromised by their living conditions. According to a 1997 survey of B.C. nannies by the West Coast Domestic Workers' Association, about half of the 100 nannies surveyed reported having no locks on their rooms; 16 per cent did not have a separate bedroom; and 4 per cent reported even lacking a bed.[90] While the quality of accommodation varies markedly, ranging from unventilated basement laundry rooms and attics to separate suites with kitchens and bathrooms, the living space for the majority of live-in domestics in Canadian middle-class homes was not designed to provide privacy and separation for live-in workers from employer's families.[91] The resulting lack of privacy and constant intentional or unavoidable employer (and employing family member) surveillance inhibits domestic workers from having any private life of their own.[92] These restrictions include intimate friendships and familial and sexual relationships, creating conditions that are in direct contradiction with the ideals of adulthood and personal freedom in Canadian society.

Overwork and undercompensation are among the most common employer transgressions of the employment rights of live-in domestic workers in Canada.[93] The mandatory live-in condition makes long, excessive, and unremunerated hours of work a standard feature of the working conditions of foreign domestics. In the live-in situation, the worker is unable to draw a clearly defined boundary between her 'private' space and the 'public' workplace. This ambiguity tends similarly to prevail over what is and is not recognized as 'real work' by employers. Employers frequently do not recognize as work: activities that do not involve tangible effort, such as watching over sleeping children, playing with children, staying at home to oversee repairs, or receiving deliveries.[94] Employers take advantage of their live-in employees by demanding services during these workers' agreed-upon off-work hours and by assuming that these workers are perpetually available.

The extent to which workers are entitled to minimum wage, compensation for overtime work, and other worker benefits varies by province and territory. Labour legislation coverage across the country varies significantly. Alberta, Saskatchewan, Nova Scotia, New Brunswick,[95] and the Northwest Territories exempt live-in domestic workers from minimum wage, hours of work, and overtime provisions altogether. Newfoundland, Prince Edward Island, Quebec, and Manitoba[96] have separate and lower minimum wage provisions for domestics and/or longer work weeks. Only British Columbia and Ontario[97] guarantee domestics minimum wage, overtime, and most employee benefits within the prevailing provincial employment standards.

Quebec labour standards exclude 'employees whose main duty is the care in a dwelling, of a child, or of a disabled, handicapped, or aged person, even when they perform household tasks that are directly related to the immediate needs of that person, and that work does not serve to procure profit to the employer.'[98] In-home caregivers for the elderly, disabled, or children are thus exempted from minimum wage and employment standards. As of February 2001, Quebec workers and live-out domestic workers were paid a minimum wage of $7.00 an hour and overtime after forty-three hours. However, live-in domestic workers were only guaranteed a minimum of $271 per week, and were to work forty-nine hours to be eligible for overtime. Also, as of 1 October 1998, Quebec law disallowed any employer deductions for room and board.[99]

In Ontario, since 1993, full-time live-in domestic workers have been entitled to receive at least the minimum wage (currently $6.85 an hour) and overtime pay for work performed over forty-four hours per week. Ontario Employment Standards permits employers to give workers time off in lieu of pay for overtime worked, although it specifies that such an arrangement must be agreed upon by the employee. Live-in domestics are also entitled to equal pay for equal work, pregnancy leave, paid public holidays, parental leave, regular payment of wages, vacation, free periods, termination notice, and work details in writing.[100]

Domestic workers in British Columbia have been fully covered by the *Employment Standards Act*[101] since 1995. This includes minimum wage ($8.00 as of November 2001), hours of work, and overtime provisions. In the B.C. legislation, 'a domestic is an employee who resides and works at an employer's residence, providing cooking, cleaning, child care and other services.' One provision specifies the guarantee of a 'written contract setting out the terms of employment [including] job duties, hours of work, wages, and charges for room and board. Charges for room and board cannot exceed $325 per month.'[102] An employer registry kept by the Employment Standards Branch was introduced in 1995 to assist in the enforcement of the Act.

While it is certainly a gain to have formal rights for foreign domestic workers recognized in labour law, neither permanence nor enforcement of such laws are assured. That certain rights granted after protracted worker struggles could be easily withdrawn was evidenced in the Ontario Conservative government's 1995 amendments to the *Ontario Labour Relations Act*,[103] which reversed the right won by domestic workers to organize in the preceding New Democratic government's labour policies.[104] Moreover, despite the existence and broad coverage in a couple of provinces of employment standards for live-in domestic workers, employer non-compliance with these standards is the rule rather than the exception among employers. Provincial governments allocate few resources for enforcement, and whatever enforcement does occur is through investigation of complaints rather than more proactive strategies. The laxity of state enforcement of standards also reflects provinces' reluctance to intervene in households based on concern for the sanctity and privacy of homes and of families. As Macklin observes, 'Privileging a definition of the household as private and thus immune from both market behaviour and state intervention effectively effaces the domestic worker's identity as an employee in a workplace.'[105]

Employer compliance with provincial employment standards is usually not investigated unless inspectors receive complaints from nannies who are frequently afraid to risk their chances of obtaining landed status by reporting their employers' breaches of the law. Thus, where provincial labour legislation has existed governing overtime work, as in Ontario and British Columbia, it has proven difficult to enforce; the domestic worker lives in the home of her employer and 'is present and "available" to do extra tasks during her "offtime" hours.'[106] According to a survey by the West Coast Domestic Workers Association of 158 foreign caregivers, conducted in Vancouver from June 1992 through February 1993, the average working day in 237 job situations was 9.9 hours; the average number of hours worked per week was 50.6.[107] In the most recent (1997) survey by the WCDWA of about a hundred B.C. nannies, the average work week had increased to 51.4 hours. Despite the full inclusion of domestic workers in the 1995 *Employment Standards Act*, eight out of ten respondents reported that they were not paid the provincial minimum wage of $7 an hour plus overtime.[108] Moreover, few employers upheld their legal obligation of registering their employment of a nanny, prompting the WCDWA to call for fines of $500 for recalcitrant employers.[109]

The possibility of legal entry to Canada through an immigration program that offers the hope of landed status contrasts favourably with migrant domestic workers' undocumented status in much of the rest of the world. The inclusion of domestic work in the employment standards of some provinces provides foreign domestic workers legitimacy as real workers. It signals a respect for their entitlement to certain rights in Canada, which is otherwise obscured by the isolated and invisible nature of their working conditions.

The liberal democratic and multicultural dimensions of Canadian governance and civil society are easily critiqued for their inability to deal with structural inequities and injustice. Nonetheless, they also provide a set of norms against which different marginalized groups have demanded, and sometimes won, better conditions than have comparable groups in societies lacking such norms. Notwithstanding such arguments for 'Canadian exceptionalism,' there is a good case to be made that Canadian conditions are different in degree rather than kind from those that prevail globally for migrant household workers. The federal government's foreign domestic worker policies institute a form of indentured labour and patterned discrimination and thus resolutely resist principles of fairness, human rights, and equity. The mandatory live-in condition of the LCP is itself an abrogation of certain fundamental human rights for domestic workers – to privacy, autonomy, family life, mobility – and lends itself to further employer abuses. Arguably, the most relevant point of comparison in assessing the conditions and rights of domestic workers in Canada working under Canadian law should be the conditions of other Canadian workers, rather than the conditions of domestic workers globally. In such a comparative framework, migrant live-in household workers fare poorly. This is precisely why there is, as the Canadian government euphemistically phrases it, 'a shortage in live-in workers' in the Canadian labour market.

Domestic Worker Jurisprudence

To date, most jurisprudence involving domestic workers has consisted of cases brought by the state against individual foreign domestic workers, rather than cases initiated by domestic workers to press for their legal rights, or legal challenges to the foreign domestic worker program. Despite their reactive rather than proactive nature, some of the cases have afforded migrant domestic workers opportunities to seek some semblance of justice in face of the demeaning and seemingly arbitrary practices of a hostile bureaucracy administering a policy rife with class, racist, and sexist biases. For those household workers willing and able to assert their rights, the Canadian courts have primarily offered an avenue to obtain redress against decisions by Immigration authorities who have applied the most narrow and detrimental interpretations of immigration procedures.

Individual domestic workers have used the courts to stay deportation orders brought against them in order to remain in Canada to work, and/or to be eligible for permanent residence. Several cases focus on issues of misrepresentation by domestic workers of marital and family status, identity, and occupational background. Several concern domestic workers' failure to meet the regulations of the LCP, breaches that are then regarded by immigration authorities as just cause for denying permanent residence to these workers. Some of the mandatory conditions of the LCP, the contravention of which has led the Department of Immigration to reject workers' applications for permanent residence include: the condition that caregivers not take additional work outside their caregiving duties, the compulsory live-in requirement, mandatory successful medical examination of family members, and the requirement that foreign caregivers work twenty-four months in a three-year period.

The decisions by the Federal Court, in particular, tend to show a fairly sympathetic stance insofar as they overturn Immigration and Refugee Board decisions, and urge compassion for foreign domestic workers considering their highly constrained circumstances. They invoke the view that one of the purposes of the foreign domestic worker program is to facilitate the attainment of permanent resident status for migrant workers. Several of the judgments admonish the Immigration Department for failing to facilitate the fulfilment of this goal and for its use of technical grounds to issue deportation orders against domestic workers who have breached LCP or FDM regulations.

Transgressions by employers of foreign domestic worker rights have come before human rights commissions, as mentioned above, but have rarely been the subject of reported court cases as such. In our analyses below, we include a couple of cases that were decided by the Immigration and Refugee Board, including its Appeal Division, to illuminate the underlying assumptions of the Canadian foreign domestic worker policy about the appropriate treatment of migrant household workers.

The recent Supreme Court decision in *Baker v. Canada*,[110] while not directly involving the Canadian foreign domestic worker program, has enormous significance for migrant domestic workers and other non-citizens and will be discussed here. This case raises issues concerning the rights of a woman who established a life in Canada, and gave birth to Canadian-born children, while working illegally for several years as a live-in domestic worker. One of the major issues *Baker* invokes is the relevance of international human rights standards as applied to immigration law.

Misrepresentation

A number of cases that came before the Canadian courts in the late 1970s and 1980s involved the issue of marital and familial misrepresentation. These cases reveal the manner in which state policies of both receiving and sending states criminalize migrant women in a dual strategy of importing cheap household labour and inhibiting permanent migration. The emergence of cases involving misrepresentation of marital status and family obligations is a legacy of the Caribbean Scheme of the 1950s and 1960s, and the 1973 Temporary Employment Authorization Program. These earlier programs explicitly disqualified married women, women in common-law relationships, and/or women with dependent children from coming to Canada as domestic workers.[111] Immigration authorities could forestall the settlement and reproduction of families and communities of colour through the legal fiction that Third World domestics imported to look after Canadian families had no family attachments themselves. The Foreign Domestic Movement retained the incentive to conceal marital status and family commitments.

It linked the presence of 'dependent family members residing outside of Canada who may be coming to Canada to join the applicant' to the assessment of the future ability of the low-income applicant to become 'self-sufficient.'[112] A failure to demonstrate self-sufficiency would prevent the applicant from successfully obtaining landed immigrant status in Canada.

In the 1979 case, *Lodge v. M.M.I*,[113] the Federal Court of Appeal ruled that it had no jurisdiction to prevent the removal of the 'seven Jamaican mothers' previously admitted as landed immigrants while their complaints of discriminatory treatment were pending before the newly established Canadian Human Rights Commission.[114] The grounds for deportation were that the women had misrepresented their marital status and family commitments when applying to enter Canada. The familial relations of the seven women were subsequently revealed when they sought to sponsor their spouses and children and bring them to Canada as permanent residents. This case became a rallying point for a major campaign publicizing the Canadian government's racist and sexist policies against foreign domestics. It drew the support of domestic advocacy associations, the black community, and anti-racist organizations. While unsuccessful in their litigation, the sympathetic publicity the case attracted ultimately won the Jamaican women readmission to Canada and landed status through the provision of Minister's Permits. The latter is an exceptional intervention available to cabinet ministers, in cases such as these, on humanitarian grounds. Such intervention does not alter the nature of the law in general.

In the 1989 case, *Fernandez*, reported on by Macklin, 'an inquiry under the Immigration Act was ordered to investigate the allegation that Ms Fernandez, qua visitor, was in violation of section 27(2)(g), which speaks of 'fraudulent or improper means or misrepresentation of any material fact.'[115] The adjudicator in *Fernandez* ruled that misrepresentation of marital or family obligations are 'material' only in the evaluation of immigrants, not, as in Ms Fernandez's case, of visitors. Ms Fernandez's order of deportation was consequently overturned.[116] *Fernandez* was a victory for foreign domestics who felt pressured to conceal their marital and family ties, and who were often actually counselled to conceal them by employment agencies in their respective countries,[117] but for whom such disclosure is ultimately a condition for immigration to Canada.

Notwithstanding the legal victory for foreign domestics in *Fernandez*, the institutionalization of the right to remain in the LCP, and thus in

Canada, despite having misrepresented one's marital and/or family status, occurred only as the product of persistent lobbying and pressure by domestic worker associations. Thus, the West Coast Domestic Workers Association reported in October 1989 that divergent practices of dealing with marital misrepresentation occurred in the Vancouver and Toronto immigration offices. In Vancouver, domestics with misrepresented marital status were taken to immigration inquiries and ordered to leave Canada. In Toronto, immigration officials permitted domestic workers to write to the federal government to disclose their true marital status. The change in the Toronto policy was reported to result from meetings between domestic worker advocates and immigration representatives.[118] Following a meeting between WCDWA representatives and immigration authorities in Vancouver, the practice of handling misrepresentation in that office was made consistent with that of the Toronto office. Subsequently, misrepresentation of marital and family status by foreign domestics was to become relevant only at the time of application for landed status.[119]

Despite the shift in policy to refrain from removing those women in the FDM who had made misrepresentations concerning their marital status, *Mitra v. Canada*[120] revealed that immigration authorities do not always comply with policy in practice. In 1991, Anita Mitra had applied for a visa pursuant to the Foreign Domestic Workers Movement. In order to meet the requirements to enter Canada as a domestic worker, she made misrepresentations concerning her age, marital status, and whether she had children. Ms Mitra was admitted and subsequently lived and worked in British Columbia as a domestic worker. When she was made aware of the policy shift whereby marital misrepresentation would no longer be grounds for deportation, Ms Mitra informed the manager of the Immigration Centre in Prince George that she had made misrepresentations. The manager advised her that if she obtained a divorce from her husband in the Philippines, she would be landed. Ms Mitra retained counsel working with the West Coast Domestic Workers Association to assist her with her immigration matter. The immigration manager decided to proceed to an inquiry where the adjudicator issued a departure order against Ms Mitra.

The judge in the Federal Court of Canada (Trial Division) ruled in favour of Ms Mitra, granting her an application for judicial review. Mr Justice Rouleau argued that the immigration manager had acted in bad faith and that the decision to order an inquiry was made because the applicant had retained counsel to assist her. The judge stated further that 'it is incumbent on the [Immigration] Minister to apply [the] policy to all concerned in an even-handed and consistent manner.'[121]

The uneven process by which the new policy on misrepresentation came into practice and has been administered reveals two essential aspects of the foreign domestic worker policy specifically, and immigration policy more generally. First, immigration policy involves a very wide berth of discretion on the part of individual immigration officials. This allows for the exercise of many arbitrary and prejudicial biases that systematically disfavour constituencies who do not fit the ideologically constructed notions of 'real' and 'desirable' immigrants. Second, as Deborah Cheney describes it, 'immigration law, which consists of both legislation, non-statutory rules, and administrative practice, is less an entity in or of itself that can be fixed and "read" than a shifting array of expressions which confuse and disorientate.'[122] Foreign domestic policy in particular has developed as a mutating patchwork of administrative rules and regulations. Given this fact, immigration officers who are asked to administer such policy both in Canada and abroad have acted with inconsistent understandings of the policy. The inclination to turn to stereotypes and past practices rather than to a standardized body of legally accountable criteria is endemic.

Eugenio v. Canada (Minister of Citizenship and Immigration)[123] involved a case of misrepresentation of the domestic worker's identity. Edith Mabini Eugenio had applied from the Philippines to be a domestic helper in Singapore. While boarding the plane to Singapore, she noticed that the passport provided by her recruiting agent was not in her name but under the name of Erlinda Angeles Ullero. The agent explained that he had arranged for her to take the place of another nanny who had been approved but could not then travel. The financial survival of her family (her husband and four children) was a major motivating factor for Ms Eugenio to accept overseas work under a false identity. Approximately two years later, in 1990, still using the false passport, Ms Eugenio successfully applied from Singapore to enter Canada under the FDM. While in Canada, she continued to use her false identity to acquire official documents including employment authorizations, a driver's licence, a passport, U.S. visas, and a social insurance number. In 1993, she was granted landed status under the assumed name. After being injured in an accident that prevented her from visiting her family in the Philippines, the appellant decided to reveal her true identity to immigration authorities.

When an immigration inquiry was conducted, an adjudicator ordered Ms Eugenio deported. It was determined that Ms Eugenio was a person described in section 27(1)(e) of the *Immigration Act*, that is, a person 'who was granted landing by reason of possession of a false or improperly obtained passport, visa or other document pertaining to his [sic] admission or by reason of any fraudulent or improper means or misrepresentation of any material fact whether exercised or made by himself [sic] or by any other person.' Ms Eugenio's appeal contended that the issuance of the deportation order under section 27(1)(e), which applies to permanent residents, stopped the minister from denying that the appellant was a permanent resident. The minister, relying on section 27(2)(g) of the Act, contended that Ms Eugenio was not landed, did not have status as a permanent resident, and thus had no right to appeal. Mr Teitelbaum, the adjudicator at the Appeal Division hearing, deemed immaterial the arguments of the appellant's counsel that an agent, rather than Ms Eugenio herself, had concocted the false identity, and also disregarded the accomplishments of Ms Eugenio during her five years in Canada. 'No amount of sympathy or taking into account her contribution to Canadian society alters the fact that Ms Eugenio does not exist in Canada.'[124] The Appeal Division adjudicator also represented Ms Eugenio as a criminal, who 'once having started in the cloak of another... perpetuated the fraud by obtaining a variety of documents to sustain the charade.'[125] In the view of the adjudicator, she had 'committed an act of impersonation punishable under the Criminal Code' and was 'liable to imprisonment for a term not exceeding fourteen years.'[126]

The reasoning of the immigration adjudicators in *Eugenio* is premised on a liberal model of individual autonomy and responsibility. Such a perspective is blind to the international political economy that drives Third World women to leave their families and endure years of servile labour overseas in isolating and fearful circumstances. The citizenship divide requires these women to become enmeshed in various layers of restriction, regulation, and inevitably deceit, in the process of obtaining even minimal rights within Canada. But deceit is itself treated by differential criteria depending on which side of the citizenship divide is affected. Domestic worker migration is compelled by broader socioeconomic and political forces, and it operates largely through the coercive and often fraudulent practices of intermediaries such as recruitment and placement agencies. These aspects of the domestic worker business are ignored in immigration hearings where domestic workers are treated as individuals assumed to exercise judgments within a liberal framework of freedom and choice. Alternatively, Third World women who seek redress in their quest to obtain citizenship rights are treated with suspicion, as individuals wilfully breaking the law. Appellants become criminalized as persons who commit indictable offences, rather than being seen as 'emotionally complex human beings trapped and manipulated within the pressures of a wider socio-political framework,' the international political economy, and the restrictions of particular state policies.[127] The fear among foreign domestics of disclosure of a fraudulent identity imposed by a recruitment agent is the same fear that inhibits workers from seeking redress against employers whose employment practices are in violation of federal immigration and provincial employment standards laws. Domestic workers often accurately perceive that they, rather than their employers, will be punished for failing to observe immigration regulations and policy. This perception was challenged in the ruling made in *Bernardez v. Canada*.[128]

Other Worker Transgressions of Immigration Regulations

Bernardez involves a case of a Filipino woman who was admitted to Canada as a live-in caregiver and who was required by her employer to work in the employer's family business, a variety store some distance from the employer's home. She was asked to clean, attend to customers, and perform other chores associated with maintaining store operations. Ms Bernardez did not receive additional payment for her work at the store, but acquiesced to the extra work in the belief that her refusal would lead to her removal back to the Philippines. A deportation order was issued against Ms Bernardez following the finding of an immigration adjudicator that her employment in the store was not a legitimate extension of her domestic duties, but rather unauthorized employment in a completely different job. In his decision, the adjudicator reasoned that Ms Bernardez's behaviour was reasonable under the circumstances given to 'obedient domestic servants.' He also exonerated the employers from blame, arguing that they made an understandable error in regarding their business as an extension of their home. Nevertheless, the domestic worker was issued a deportation order while the employer's actions were not penalized. The adjudicator characterized Ms Bernardez in the following way:

> *You are an obedient domestic servant.* The employer asked you to work in their place of business as well as the home and you in pursuit of the

objectives which are readily apparent to everyone were obedient and carried out these duties. It may very well be and probably is that the employers were acting in good faith. They probably considered this place of business to be an extension of their home, but nevertheless they [sic] are quite separate. It would be perhaps a little different if the household, as *often is in ethnic situations* [sic] is located in the same building, perhaps above the store and things like this might get fuzzy, but here it's a quite clear-cut difference.[129]

The value of obedience is reinforced here and in other parts of the adjudicator's decision as a proper attribute displayed by Third World, female domestic servants towards their employers. Yet, because this obedience led the servant, Ms Bernardez, to carry out unauthorized employment contrary to section 27(2) (b) and (e) of the *Immigration Act*, the adjudicator issued a deportation order. The decision was overturned, however. In the judgment of Jerome ACJ at the Federal Court of Canada (Trial Division), the immigration adjudicator had neglected to take into consideration the exploitation of Ms Bernardez who was compelled 'to submit to her employer's reasonable demands to clean their family store.'[130] The judge argued that the question of the employment under section 2 of the *Immigration Act* depends on the 'circumstances in which it is performed' which in this case included the 'lack of collusion with the employer, the fact that no surplus money or benefits were received by the applicant, and the fact that this foreign domestic feared potential dismissal and was ignorant of her right to refuse the unauthorized work.' Associate Chief Justice Jerome also brought attention to the coerced nature of work performed by foreign live-in workers in suggesting that it is questionable that the work of 'a domestic who is coerced or compelled to perform duties for her employer can truly be considered to be employed in that capacity.' In failing to consider these issues, Mr Justice Jerome concluded that the adjudicator committed an error of law. He also argued that fairness was lacking in the Immigration Department's failure to advise the applicant that she was engaged in unauthorized conduct in order to afford her 'opportunity to correct the impugned behaviour prior to being expelled from Canada.' Citing his own previous judgment in *Turingan v. Canada*[131] (discussed below), Jerome J in *Bernardez* argued that 'the purpose of the Live-in Caregiver Program is to facilitate the attainment of permanent resident status for foreign domestic workers and, therefore, it is incumbent on the Immigration Department to adopt a flexible and constructive approach in its dealing with the program's participants. Failure to do so undermines the purpose of the program.'[132]

In *Turingan*, the court was asked to rule in the case of Marissa Turingan, a Filipino domestic worker in the FDM who had had her application for permanent residence status turned down by an immigration admissions officer. The reason given for the denial of application and order for departure was Ms Turingan's failure to live-in full-time for the required twenty-four months prior to her application. While Ms Turingan resided with various employers for most of the time, she departed from this pattern when she developed abdominal pains and began cooking and staying over at a friend's apartment. Associate Chief Justice Jerome allowed Ms Turingan's application for permanent residence, on the grounds that her explanation about her living arrangements was very credible. He chastised the Department of Immigration's harsh stance and breach of basic principles of fairness in drawing only on technical grounds in the interpretation of the criteria for landing under the LCP. Instead, argued Jerome J, '[t]he primary purpose of the Live-in Caregiver Program ... is to encourage people to come to Canada to fill a void which exists in Canada's labour market. As consideration for this commitment to work in the domestic field, the program's participants are virtually guaranteed permanent residence status provided that they work the required 24-month period.'[133]

In granting applications for reconsideration of removal orders of foreign domestic workers in other cases, the court held the Immigration Department to the duty of fairness, and the obligation to adopt a 'flexible and constructive approach' in dealing with FDM/LCP participants. In *Caletana v. Canada*[134] the matter before the court was the application for permanent residence of Ligaya Gadot Caletana, a former participant in the Live-in Caregiver Program. Although her application for permanent residence was provisionally accepted, it was subsequently refused by the Immigration Department when two of her infant children failed to pass their medical examinations. Ms Caletana was seeking an order staying the execution of the departure notice in order to contest the medical evidence. The judge, Jerome ACJ, took the facts of the case and especially 'the unique nature of the foreign domestic program ' into account in his judgment to grant the applicant a stay of execution of the departure notice pending the outcome of a leave application for judicial review. He also argued that there is a duty of immigration authorities to 'encourage and assist' participants in the foreign domestic worker program with their applications for permanent residence, rather than to ignore worker intentions and to use breaches of regulations to deport them.

Similarly, in *Peje v. Canada*[135] the Federal Court's initial ruling set aside the Immigration Department's decision to disqualify the applicant from the domestic program on the grounds that she had worked only seventeen months, rather than the required twenty-four months, in a three-year period, because of illness. As the Immigration Department refused work authorization for Ms Peje once she had recovered her health, the court argued that Citizenship and Immigration 'must bear some portion of the responsibility for her failing to meet the conditions of the program.' The coerced circumstances stemming from the program, which places participants in a Catch-22 position, are also acknowledged in the judge's observation that 'this applicant appears to have been trapped in a situation where she was afraid to work without the required authorization and yet unable to obtain the necessary permit from the Minister.'[136] The judgment reflects the court's understanding of the manner in which foreign domestic workers are 'trapped' by the need to adhere to conditions established within the FDM/LCP so as not to jeopardize their tenuous legal status in Canada. Nevertheless, this decision was overturned the following year by Justice McDonald, who deferred to the immigration adjudicator's legal positivist assessment that Peje had violated the statutory provisions, and that neither humanitarian and compassionate grounds nor the question of whether the minister had met his obligation to the applicant under the domestic program could be considered.[137]

The Application of International Human Rights to Immigration Decision-Making

Baker differs from the other domestic worker decisions considered thus far in that the appellant did not enter Canada under the foreign domestic worker program and the case does not refer specifically to the obligations of the Canadian Immigration Department to participants of such programs. Mavis Baker, a Jamaican citizen and already a mother of four children, came to Canada in 1981. She supported herself illegally as a live-in domestic worker for eleven years. Ms Baker entered Canada as a visitor and took up domestic work, as have many tens of thousands of Caribbean women, at a time when legal entry as domestics from this region had been foreclosed by Canadian immigration authorities. She had four more children in Canada. Following the birth of her last child, she suffered from post-partum psychosis and was diagnosed with paranoid schizophrenia. While Ms Baker was receiving treatment, two of her children were placed in the custody of their father and the other two went to foster care, though these two children were returned to her when her health improved. Her 1993 application under section 114(2) of the *Immigration Act* for leave to make an internal application for landing was dismissed on the basis of insufficient humanitarian and compassionate (H & C) grounds. A deportation order was issued and served Ms Baker in May 1994. Notes made by the subordinate reviewing officer (Lorenz) and subsequently used by a senior officer (Caden) when reaching the decision to deport Ms Baker included the following passages:

> PC is unemployed – on Welfare. No income shown – no assets. Has four Cdn.-born children – four other children in Jamaica – HAS A TOTAL OF EIGHT CHILDREN ... This case is a catastrophy [sic]. It is also an indictment of our 'system' that the client came here as a visitor in Aug. '81, was not ordered deported until Dec. '92 and in APRIL '94 IS STILL HERE!

> ... The PC is a paranoid schizophrenic and on welfare. She has no qualifications other than as a domestic. She has FOUR CHILDREN IN JAMAICA AND ANOTHER FOUR BORN HERE. She will, of course, be a tremendous strain on our social welfare systems for (probably) the rest of her life. There are no H&C factors other than her FOUR CANADIAN BORN CHILDREN. Do we let her stay because of that? I am of the opinion that Canada can no longer afford this kind of generosity.[138]

The Federal Court of Canada (Trial Division) ordered the stay of the deportation order. Justice Rouleau cited the argument of the applicant's counsel that Ms Baker's removal would be in violation of the *Canadian Charter of Rights and Freedoms* (presumably of section 7, 'life, liberty and security of the person,' although the specific section was not cited). However, the Federal Court of Appeal dismissed Ms Baker's application for judicial review. The motions judge also certified a question concerning the international *Convention on the Rights of the Child*. At issue was whether Ms Baker's deportation order should be stayed given the interests of her four Canadian-born children, who were citizens in Canada.[139]

The Supreme Court overturned Ms Baker's deportation order and accepted her appeal, which meant that the matter would be returned to the minister for redetermination by a different immigration officer. The Supreme Court justices concluded that the principle of procedural fairness had been violated in this case insofar as there was a reasonable apprehension of bias in the making of the decision. Justice L'Heureux-Dubé pointed out that given the great importance to the individuals affected by the decisions taken by immigration officers, a special sensitivity and openness to diversity is required of these officers. Instead, the immigration officer's notes reveal a predisposition to stereotypes regarding Baker's mental illness, her training as a domestic worker, and her status as a single mother with several children. The officer's frustration with the 'system' was also noted to have interfered with his duty to act impartially.

The lower courts in the *Baker* case had forwarded the question of the approach to be taken to the interests of children when reviewing an H & C decision. The Supreme Court found that the decision to deport Ms Baker was unreasonable insofar as the immigration officer had been completely dismissive of the interests of Ms Baker's children. The immigration officer had failed to take a contextual approach to statutory interpretation of section 114(2) of the *Immigration Act* governing H & C considerations, which requires close attention to the interests and needs of children. The court held: 'Children's rights, and attention to their interests, are central humanitarian and compassionate values in Canadian society.'[140] The ruling thus recognizes that non-citizens with children born in Canada have human rights in Canada.

While the Supreme Court decision to overturn the deportation order of Ms Baker was unanimous, judges were divided as to whether international conventions ratified by Canada had any legal effect if they had not been incorporated into domestic law. The view of the majority (Justices Claire L'Heureux-Dubé, Charles Gonthier, Beverly McLachlin, Michel Bastarache, and Ian Binnie) was that the values reflected in international human rights law 'may help inform the contextual approach to statutory interpretation and judicial review,' whereas a minority (Justices Peter Cory and Frank Iacobucci) disagreed. Justice Iacobucci argued that the Court should not give 'force and effect within the domestic legal system to international obligations undertaken by the executive alone that have yet to be subject to the democratic will of Parliament.'[141] Given that the *Convention on the Rights of the Child* was not part of the law of Canada, Justice Iacobucci argued that it had no application to this case. This interpretation suggests that even where international rights conventions offer a greater range of rights to migrants, the doctrines of state sovereignty and parliamentary supremacy might be invoked by Canadian judges to limit the application of international norms, rights, and obligations.

Nevertheless, the majority in *Baker* accepted that international law constitutes 'a part of the legal context in which legislation is enacted and read.' Insofar as is possible, therefore, 'interpretations that reflect these values and principles are preferred.'[142] The *Baker* case thus raises important questions about the strategic uses of international conventions in Canadian courts to broaden access of foreign domestic workers to certain rights, including the right to remain within the country legally. It is notable that immigration and refugee legislation introduced by the Liberal government in April 2000 (which, however, died on the Order Paper with the federal election call in October of that year) did indeed, state the need for immigration policy to take into account the children's rights convention. As discussed below, one of the international conventions for which domestic advocates have vigorously sought Canada's signature and compliance has been the *International Convention on the Protection of the Rights of All Migrant Workers and Members of Their Families*.[143]

Baker also indicates that the courts can serve to render visible the complex human dimensions of the migration of Third World female workers to Canada. These workers may remain for many years, bear children who establish ties with Canada, and then, like any individual, become ill and incapacitated – all costs to the Canadian state which a 'temporary worker' program such as the FDM/LCP were designed to prevent.

Employer Abuses

The cases considered thus far, with the exception of the two sexual harassment cases, pertain to purported worker transgressions of the domestic worker program's rules and regulations, with its attendant consequence of deportation from the country. That very few reported cases involve employer abuses of their institutionalized power over non-citizen, live-in caregivers, is in itself significant. One exception is *Mustaji v. Tjin and Tjin*[144] which was decided by the B.C. Supreme Court, and unsuccessfully appealed by the defendants. This case involved an extreme instance of exploitation of Sarmini Mustaji, a domestic worker virtually held prisoner in the Vancouver home of her employers, Khi Yeong and Rosna Elly Tjin. After working for the Tjins as a nanny for their four children in Indonesia and Singapore, in 1989 Ms Mustaji accompanied her employers to Vancouver, as a participant in the FDM program. Ms Mustaji and Khi Yoeng Tjin signed a document provided by Immigration Canada outlining Ms Mustaji's work duties, her monthly wages of $883 for a forty-hour week, and room and board deductions of $225 per month. The plaintiff testified that after her arrival in Vancouver she worked for the Tjins as their live-in servant and nanny for three years and three months, over fifteen hours a day, seven days a week, and 365 days a year. For this work she was paid $40 or $50 every two or three months.

Her employers kept Ms Mustaji a virtual prisoner, denying her use of the telephone, the freedom to go out on her own, or the opportunity to invite friends home. Her isolation was aggravated by her inability to speak or read English and her lack of both friends and money. By approaching a stranger, Ms Mustaji was placed in contact with the West Coast Domestic Workers Association, which appointed a lawyer for her and assisted her in fleeing her employers. With the assistance of WCDWA, Ms Mustaji filed a claim for wages with the B.C. Employment Standards Branch, and recovered $5,000 for the last six months of her employment. The B.C. Supreme Court ruled that the Tjins had a duty not to exploit Ms Mustaji and upheld a jury award totaling $250,000 – the highest amount ever awarded in a domestic worker case.[145] The Tjins lost their appeal of the B.C. Supreme Court decision. They were ordered by the court to pay Ms Mustaji about $75,000 in lost wages and $175,000 in damages for breach of fiduciary duty.

Mustaji serves as a warning to employers that limitless exploitation of foreign-born household workers may result in hefty monetary damages ordered to be paid to their extremely exploited domestic employees. It also shows that Canadian courts and juries regard the enslavement of foreign domestic workers as an unacceptable practice. Aspects of this case, however, such as the extreme nature of reported abuse, the exceptional wealth of the employers, and the fact that the employers were, like their domestic employee, also foreign-born Asians, may limit the beneficial aspects of this legal victory for other domestic workers. The *Mustaji* case could be read as an isolated case of a notoriously bad, and not incidentally foreign, employer. Yet as discussed earlier, the majority of live-in nannies in British Columbia, and in Canada more generally, continue to be paid less than is legally required and continue to work and live under substandard conditions working for (usually) white Canadian employers. The Canadian government's liability for establishing these conditions for domestic worker exploitation, and for failing to protect the limited rights available to these vulnerable workers, was never raised in *Mustaji*. Indeed, there has never been a legal challenge to the 'special' immigration program, which establishes the Byzantine labyrinth and numerous obstacles that migrant domestic workers must negotiate in their protracted process of seeking Canadian immigrant, worker and citizenship rights.

Constitutional Challenges to Immigration Policy

Courts have generally been sympathetic to upholding domestic workers' procedural rights on an individual basis to stem the unjust deportation of these workers from Canada. Litigation has challenged the unfairness and restrictive technical reasoning deployed in immigration hearings to deny continued legal presence in the country, or permanent residence, to individual foreign domestic workers who have done their time in the purgatory of live-in domestic service. Yet there has hitherto been no judicial review of the federal domestic worker program(s). The absence of legal challenge to the federal government's LCP and past domestic worker programs must be questioned given the long-standing consensus among domestic worker associations regarding the unfairness and discrimination inherent in the temporary status and mandatory live-in condition. Abolition of these coercive conditions within immigration policy has widely been recognized to be 'a key precondition to the realization and vindication of all other rights.'[146]

Immigration lawyers have tied the absence of legal challenge, particularly *Charter* challenges to foreign domestic worker policy, to immigration policy more generally, and to characteristics of the legal establishment. These include the relatively recent development of specialization in immigration and refugee law among lawyers; the heavy demands of immigration legal practice which militate against taking up costly and time-consuming *Charter* challenges; and the absence of principled legal scholarship supporting *Charter* litigation in the immigration field.[147] Macklin additionally sees the dearth of judicial challenge to domestic worker policy as reflecting a self-interested position among lawyers who 'are among the major employers of domestic workers.'[148] The fact that *Symes*, in which the plaintiff herself was a lawyer, was the first case involving nannies to be brought to the Supreme Court by feminist lawyers lends substance to this occupational and class-based argument.

Lawyers with feminist, antiracist sensibilities have, however, been actively involved in cases that launched *Charter* challenges to exemptions of domestic workers from provincial employment standards in Ontario and British Columbia.[149] If progressive lawyers are willing and able to challenge the discriminatory treatment of foreign domestic workers in labour laws, why has there been a reluctance to pursue legal challenges to foreign domestic worker immigration policies?

Part of the explanation for this absence of a constitutional challenge lies in the reticence of domestic worker associations. Until recently, these organizations had decided strategically to attack the objectionable conditions of the programs, especially the temporary visa and the mandatory live-in requirement, rather than the programs themselves. Domestic advocates had feared that openly arguing for the abolition of the program would jeopardize an important means for legal entry of women from Third World countries such as the Philippines. An important deterrent was the question of available remedies should the court have found the LCP to be in violation of the *Charter* (section 15, perhaps). Asking the court to replace the LCP, or certain offensive parts of the policy, would be beyond its jurisdiction. Domestic worker legal advocates may therefore have refrained from legally challenging the LCP and past domestic worker immigration policies because they feared the consequences of the entire shut-down of the program. The desire to maintain a legal means for the entry of foreign domestic workers was reflected in the submissions of domestic worker groups during the federal review of the FDM. Rather than recommending the outright abolition of the LCP, these submissions generally spoke of the need to provide workers with permanent residency status on landing, and to make 'living-in' optional.[150]

During the last few years, however, domestic worker associations have been more openly calling for the elimination of the program, while legal feminists have continued to endorse a reformed temporary worker program that would mitigate (though not remove) the worst aspects of the program. The Philippine Women Centre of British Columbia, for instance, has been especially outspoken against the program for its racism and antiwoman biases. The centre has argued that women from the Philippines who are trained as nurses, teachers, and other professionals should be permitted to enter as landed immigrants and thus be permitted to practise in their professions, rather than be chained to the deskilled and exploited conditions of live-in domestic service.[151] The Association des Aides Familiaux du Québec has made similar arguments.[152] The National Action Committee on the Status of Women (NAC) also stated its support for the elimination of the program during a brief consultation process held by the Immigration Department in spring 1998. INTERCEDE's submission on Bill C-31, the Liberal government's proposed *Immigration and Refugee Protection Act*, clearly recommended that domestic workers and caregivers 'be admitted as permanent residents in accordance with experience, educational and skills criteria that are appropriate and practical to their occupation.'[153] And, while supporting the admission of foreign domestic workers as landed immigrants, a coalition led by more legally inclined feminist groups, which included the National Association of Women and the Law, West Coast Domestic Workers Association, La Table féministe francophone de concertation provinciale de l'Ontario, and the National Organization of Immigrant and Visible Minority Women of Canada, offered legislative amendments to Bill C-31 that would continue to permit caregivers to enter under temporary employment authorizations.[154]

A second problem in mounting a constitutional challenge is that of finding plaintiffs, given that foreign domestic workers are among the most vulnerable groups in Canadian society. While they may be willing to stand up in court when they are being threatened with deportation as individuals, they may be less willing to jeopardize their future chances in Canada for the sake of challenging the program that brought them there.

The absence of a constitutional challenge to foreign domestic worker policy also reflects the unique character and importance of immigration policy as a gatekeeper to citizenship rights, which in part has been shaped and reproduced by judicial rulings. One prominent immigration lawyer aptly characterizes immigration law as 'unnecessarily arbitrary, unfair and discriminatory.'[155] Immigration law 'has the reputation among people interested in administrative law as a sort of wasteland in which judges have been loath to apply the legal principles we normally associate with a sense of justice in Canadian public administration.'[156] Immigration law is compared with the Hydra, the monstrous serpent of Greek myth. This Hydra 'turns a number of faces toward those who come before it,' but, when successful court cases or legislative amendments 'strike off one of the heads[,] new heads replace it.'[157]

The issue of whether reliance on law, including constitutional litigation, is a liberatory or depoliticizing strategy as it pertains to domestic worker rights must thus include consideration of the specific limitations of immigration law, which place low priority on human rights, and high priority on defending the territorial sovereignty of the state.[158] Immigration law is based on the fundamental belief that sovereign states can accord 'aliens' access to mere 'privileges' rather than 'rights' (such as the privilege of entering and remaining within a nation-state's territory) and that such 'privileges' exist at the pleasure of the state. While states may make available a share of the bounty to 'guests' that they more readily provide to their citizens, they hold to the belief that they alone decide which guests have access to their territory and to which of the state's resources.

State governments are generally loath constitutionally to enshrine claims for rights to 'guests' who are imported to provide labour in 'menial,' low-paid jobs. The assumption that immigration control and broad exclusionary powers are central to state sovereignty is tenacious – states have shown little willingness to limit these powers. The doctrine of strong national, territorially based sovereignty that underpins the international order, and the strengthening of movements supporting ethnic, racial, and nationalist exclusivism, have not augured well for the extension of immigration and refugee rights to vulnerable non-citizen populations such as asylum seekers or labour migrants.[159]

There appears to be a high level of judicial discomfort over the idea of bringing the administration of the Canadian immigration system under scrutiny using any section of the *Charter*.[160] The exceptions have tended to be in refugee cases. In these cases, section 7 of the *Charter* has been invoked and, in contrast to other immigration cases, the right to liberty and to security of the person could be seen to be at stake in the decisions made by Canadian immigration officials.[161] In contrast, the federal courts have refused to apply the *Charter* to immigrant selection decisions by visa officers, the major representatives of the Immigration Department abroad.[162]

At the heart of the courts' reluctance to challenge even the most blatantly discriminatory parts of immigration policy, such as those presented by foreign domestic worker policy, is the deference of the judiciary to the sovereign power of the Canadian state to assert control over its borders. As Barbara Jackman points out, the common law position that no alien has the right to enter the country except by leave of the Crown, and that the Crown can refuse leave without giving any reason, is entrenched in Canadian judicial history.[163] It is not, however, a uniquely Canadian position. The courts in many other countries – including Britain, the United States, and Australia – have also been reluctant to interfere in immigration decisions. This deference to the sovereign power of the state translates readily into a justification for exclusionary powers to withdraw human rights protection from non-citizens and expendable new migrants. In a context where immigration policy is increasingly slanted towards the importation of business and highly skilled migrants, the citizenship divide is likely to widen. Those on one side of the divide will be disproportionately disadvantaged, including Third World, poorer, female migrants, whose distance from the ideal citizen is defined through racialized, Eurocentric, gendered, and class-bound norms. Canada, like other developed states, which regard immigration liberalization as an invitation to the unwashed and criminal Third World hordes, is guarding its borders with increasing jealousy.

The gap between immigration policy and rights legislation and instruments is reflected in the stance taken by Canada and other labour-importing states towards international conventions and treaties on migrant worker rights. International conventions reflect compromises, which leave large gaps in safeguards for non-citizen rights. These compromises are evident in the *International Convention on the Protection of the Rights of All Migrant Workers and Members of Their Families*. Adopted by the U.N. General Assembly in 1990, this convention introduced important innovations in basic human rights accorded without distinction to all migrants and members of their families, documented and undocumented. It supports such rights as family reunification, recourse to consular or diplomatic protection, information regarding working conditions, political rights, and equality with nationals in educational, social, and health services. Nonetheless, Article 79 of this convention affirms that sovereign states legitimately have broad exclusionary power and the power to determine the criteria governing admission of migrant workers and members of their families, which might also extend to questions of residence and expulsion.[164] According to Bosniak, the debates leading up to the controversial inclusion of article 79 in the convention attested 'to the enormous, almost talismanic power that assertions of state sovereignty have had ... in the area of human rights for aliens.'[165]

A sign of the resistance of migrant-receiving countries, including Canada, to cede sovereignty on matters of border control and the migrants' rights is their unwillingness to support this convention. Thus, the convention has not entered into force as international law given that the small and insufficient number of signatories to it have been migrant-sending countries (e.g., Philippines and Pakistan), while migrant-receiving countries have assiduously forestalled its ratification. The reason provided by Canadian officials for non-ratification of the U.N. and International Labour Organization (ILO) conventions on rights of migrant workers (such as Convention No. 97) is that their definition of 'migrant workers' is not relevant to the situation in Canada. This reasoning reinforces the invisibility of paid domestic labour and the plight of migrant domestic workers.

Recent Developments

At the time of writing, the question of the use of *Charter* challenges or other litigation strategies to dismantle or reform the LCP is probably moot. The government may well abolish the LCP. In any case, it has been rendered so restrictive that it is now far less frequently utilized as a means of entry into Canada for migrant Third World women than it has been in years past. In April 2000, the Canadian government introduced new and extensive reforms to immigration policy following consultations with interested parties in 1994, a consultants' report titled *Not Just Numbers*[166] issued in late December 1997, and a further brief consultation process in spring 1998. Bill C-31, the legislative proposals introduced by Immigration Minister Elinor Caplan in April 2000, contained a mixture of measures, enhancing and restricting potential immigration flows and immigrant rights. These included: assigning more weight to education, flexible skills, and knowledge of official languages for independent immigrants; reducing the length of sponsorship requirements from ten to three years; speeding the deportation of illegal immigrants; and offering refugees increased protection while, paradoxically, creating additional bars on access to the refugee determination system. The Canadian Council for Refugees voiced its concern over the negative rhetoric used by the government in announcing the bill, which focused on issues of border control and the 'criminal abuse of our immigration and refugee protection systems,' thus following the example of so many countries in scapegoating foreigners.[167]

The precise shape of future immigration policy for migrant domestic workers is as yet unknown. The crucial provisions concerning domestic worker policy were to be in the Regulations rather than the Act, and thus shielded from parliamentary oversight. Bill C-31 died on the order paper with Prime Minister Chrétien's election call in October 2000, and the intentions of the newly elected majority Liberal government in the immigration field are as yet unknown.[168]

Regardless of whether the LCP is to be abolished, reformed, or retained, it is clear that the dwindling numbers utilizing this program means that a growing proportion of all migrant household workers are now entering Canada with other temporary or undocumented statuses. Like Mavis Baker, they work in the shadow economy and face even less security regarding their conditions and futures in Canada. This trend towards undocumented status for household workers has further deepened the citizenship divide within Canada – even between a middle class that has increasingly experienced declining incomes and reduced public services and migrant Third World women. The latter are counted on to compensate through practices such as nanny-sharing which cut down on Canadian families' child care costs, and yet which penalize caregivers when they are assessed for permanent resident status by immigration authorities.[169] A major challenge for those wishing to reform the laws regulating domestic workers will be to slash and burn the heads of the Hydra of immigration law,[170] which have provided such formidable barriers to the acquisition of citizenship rights for foreign Third World women.

Conclusion

Insofar as they embody the cross-border dynamics of a globalized economy, the situation of foreign domestic workers throws a searchlight on the citizenship divide that exists between populations of the North and the South. Canada's Live-in Caregiver Program and past domestic worker immigration programs have played on and reproduced this global disparity, while offering a means for individual Third World migrant women to scale the border's fences in order to attain the rights associated with First World citizenship. Review of jurisprudence concerning domestic workers reveals that the courts have generally been sympathetic to individuals who have failed to meet certain requirements of the LCP, but who have endured the sacrifices and hardships entailed by the program and made invaluable contributions to the Canadian economy and Canadian families in caregiving occupations. Individual domestic workers have seen their rights to procedural justice affirmed by the courts. It remains fair to say, however, that the judiciary's rulings have neither expanded the substantive rights of domestic workers as a class nor forced immigration officials to give up any of their traditional absolute power over the immigration process. To date, there has been no constitutional challenge to the foreign domestic worker policy, in spite of the program's obvious discrimination against its participants as both immigrants and workers. In the absence of such a challenge, the courts have affirmed the hegemonic belief in the uncontested control of Canada's borders by the Immigration Department. The discretionary power vested in the Immigration Minister and Department, and the attendant discriminatory uses of that power, offer potent means for maintaining the 'integrity' of Canadian citizenship, by limiting access to 'deserving' citizen–recipients of a diminished pool of social rights. Those deemed deserving are less likely to include those poorer, Third World women of colour who, for several decades, have provided migrant household labour in Canadian households.

Notes

1 We gratefully acknowledge the research assistance of Dr Godwin Friday and Ms Claudette Breault, and the translation of French language legal material by Ms Breault. We are also indebted to the Association des Aides Familiaux du Québec, INTERCEDE, the Philippine Women Centre, and the West Coast Domestic Workers Association for their generosity in giving us access to their files and documents. The research for this paper was supported by the Social Sciences and Humanities Research Council and Queen's University Advisory Research Committee.
2 *Canadian Charter of Rights and Freedoms*, Part I of the *Constitution Act, 1982*, as enacted by the *Canada Act 1982* (U.K.), 1982, c. 11 (hereinafter *Charter*).
3 *Symes v. Canada* (1993), 110 D.L.R. (4th) 470 (S.C.C.) [hereinafter *Symes*]. Later in this chapter we examine *Baker v. Canada (Minister of Citizenship and Immigration)*, [1999] 2 S.C.R. 817 (hereinafter *Baker*). That case involved a deportation order against a Jamaican woman who worked illegally as a live-in caregiver. Interestingly, the nature of her occupation is not mentioned in the report of the Federal Court of Appeal hearing or the preliminary report of the Supreme Court of Canada hearing of her case.
4 S.C. 1970–72, c. 63.
5 *Symes v. Canada*, [1989] 3 F.C. 59 (F.C.T.D.).
6 *Symes v. Canada*, [1991] 3 F.C. 507 (F.C.A.).
7 David Vienneau, 'Woman can't claim her nanny's salary as business expense,' *Toronto Star*, 17 December 1993, A1. In this case, the gender divide on the Supreme Court is significant, particularly since the minority's justification for dissenting was based on gendered criteria. However, we do not want to imply that such a correlation extends to rulings generally, as it clearly does not.

8 Ibid.
9 Ibid.
10 Ibid.
11 Anthony H. Richmond, *Global Apartheid: Refugees, Racism, and the New World Order* (Toronto: Oxford University Press, 1994).
12 We are aware of the over-simplifications involved in the use of such dichotomies as First World/Third World, North/South, developed/developing, to designate the economic status of given states in the global economy. Our use of these crude dichotomized terms in no way suggests that we accept a ranking of states according to ethical or cultural criteria. Nor do we endorse a static evolutionary schema of development, with a teleological goal of a 'modern state.' In the absence of more acceptable terms which are less apt to 'flatten heterogeneities, mask contradictions, and elide differences,' we make use of these dichotomized categories in the knowledge that they retain heuristic value in signaling protracted geopolitical structural domination. See Ella Shohat and Robert Stam, *Unthinking Eurocentrism: Multiculturalism and the Media* (London: Routledge, 1994) 26. In particular, our use of these terms reflects our understanding that the development of Third World states such as the Philippines has been blocked as a result of their economic relations with 'developed' imperialist states and through an international system of economic and military competition that forces external priorities on the internal management of human and material resources.
13 Sherene Razack, *Canadian Feminism and the Law: The Women's Legal Education and Action Fund and the Pursuit of Equality* (Toronto: Second Story Press, 1991) 58; Nitya Iyer, 'Categorical Denials: Equality Rights and the Shaping of Social Identity' (1993) 19, 1 *Queen's Law Journal* 199–203. In a recent article, Rebecca Johnson states that 'both Symes and [her nanny] Mrs Simpson were white,' and that, therefore, the questions of race privilege and disadvantage were rarely raised in public discussion of the case. See Rebecca Johnson, 'If Choice Is the Answer, What Is the Question? Spelunking in *Symes v. Canada*,' in Dorothy E. Chunn and Dany Lacombe, eds., *Law as a Gendering Practice* (Don Mills: Oxford University Press, 2000) 203. The fact that Symes's live-in nanny was atypically white, rather than Filipino or from the Caribbean, does not, however, detract from our critique regarding the perilous precedent that would have been set had Symes been successful. As a feminist legal strategy, *Symes* privileges the interests of more affluent white women at the expense of those typically racialized migrant women who provide in-home care to their children and who do their housework.
14 Phillips, this volume.

15 Symes's 'nanny expenses' were reported to be between $10,075 and $13,359 per year during 1982–5. For a live-in nanny, these costs would presumably include salary, room, and board. Vienneau, 'Woman can't claim.'
16 Barbara Jackman, 'Admission of Foreign Domestic Workers: An Overview of the Program,' January 1993 (on file with authors), 13.
17 Some of the rights for which migrant domestic workers are currently struggling – such as the right to enter Canada with landed status – were accessible historically to earlier waves of foreign domestic workers. Daenzer argues that the right to enter as a permanent immigrant was withdrawn when European sources of domestic worker immigration gave way to Caribbean sources. Patricia Daenzer, *Regulating Class Privilege: Immigrant Servants in Canada, 1940s–1990s* (Toronto: Canadian Scholars' Press, 1993).
18 Ann Oakley, *Subject Women: Where Women Stand Today – Politically, Economically, Socially, Emotionally* (New York: Pantheon Books, 1981), 182.
19 Ibid.
20 Labour-exporting governments generally lack the political will to forcefully demand fair treatment of their overseas workers because of their fears of jeopardizing their markets for labour export and foreign investment in their economies. Their capacity to protect their migrant workers is limited by the tendency for the labour, criminal, and other laws of the labour-importing country to override those of the sending society. For an elaboration of these arguments, see Daiva K. Stasiulis and Abigail B. Bakan, 'Regulation and Resistance: Strategies of Migrant Domestic Workers in Canada and Internationally' (1997) 6, 1 *Asian and Pacific Migration Journal* 31–57.
21 Richard Falk, 'The Making of Global Citizenship,' in Jeremy Brecher et al., eds., *Global Visions: Beyond the New World Order* (Boston: South End Press, 1993) 39.
22 See Abigail B. Bakan, 'Capitalism, Marxism and the World Economy: APEC and the MAI,' in Abigail B. Bakan and Eleanor MacDonald, eds., *Critical Political Studies: Debates and Dialogues from the Left* (Montreal: McGill-Queen's University Press, forthcoming).
23 See Abigail B. Bakan and Daiva Stasiulis, 'Making the Match: Domestic Placement Agencies and the Racialization of Household Work' (1995) 20, 2 *Signs* 303–35.
24 For instance, Jennifer Aitken maintains that 'in an era of collective bargaining and legislated labour protections, the relationship between a domestic and her employer remains almost feudal.' Jennifer Aitken, 'A Stranger in

the Family: The Legal Status of Domestic Workers in Ontario' (1997) 45, 2 Toronto Faculty of Law Review 391–418. See also Sedef Arat-Koc, 'In the Privacy of Our Own Home: Foreign Domestic Workers and the Definition of Citizenship in Canada' (1989) 28 *Studies in Political Economy* 33–58; Abigail B. Bakan and Daiva Stasiulis, 'Foreign Domestic Worker Policy in Canada and the Social Boundaries of Modern Citizenship' (1994) 58, 1 *Science and Society* 7–33; Audrey Macklin, 'Foreign Domestic Worker: Surrogate Housewife or Mail Order Servant?" (1992) 37 *McGill Law Journal* 681; Daenzer, *Regulating Class Privilege*.

25 Some of the most ardent supporters of the LCP in Canada have been the domestic placement agencies, which profit from the business of matching up potential employers with the workers who come in through the LCP. See Bakan and Stasiulis, 'Making the Match.'

26 Elize Delport, 'The Legal Position of Domestic Workers: A Comparative Perspective' (1992) 25, 2 *Comparative and International Law Journal of South Africa* 181–207. Delport compares the legal status of domestic workers in the United Kingdom, the United States of America, Zimbabwe, and Swaziland.

27 Ibid., 183.

28 Domestic service and prostitution/entertainment sectors are explicitly named as the two sectors where female migrant workers are most vulnerable to physical, sexual and psychological harm, and economic exploitation in the Report of the United Nations' Expert Group Meeting on Violence Against Women Migrant Workers, United Nations Division for the Advancement of Women, Manila, Philippines, 27–31 May 1996.

29 Frank Eelens, 'Migration of Sri Lankan Women to Western Asia,' in *International Migration Policies and the Status of Female Migrants* (Proceedings of the Expert Group Meeting on International Migration Policies and the Status of Female Migrants, Rome, 1995) 268.

30 Heyzer estimates that in Asian countries such as Hong Kong and Singapore, foreign domestic workers can earn five to six times the income in their own country. In the Gulf states, earnings can be fifteen times higher. These wage disparities are the major incentive for overseas migration, but regular payment of promised wages is often subject to abuse. Noeleen Heyzer, 'Introduction: Creating Responsive Policies for Migrant Women Domestic Workers,' in Noeleen Heyzer, G. Lyckalama a Nijeholt, and N. Weerakoon, *The Trade in Domestic Workers: Causes, Mechanisms and Consequences of International Migration* (Kuala Lumpur: Asian and Pacific Development Centre and Zed Books, 1994) xxviii.

31 Cynthia Enloe, *Bananas, Beaches and Bases: Making Feminist Sense of Interna-*

tional Politics (Berkeley: University of California Press, 1990) 177; Noeleen Heyzer and Vivienne Wee, 'Domestic Workers in Transient Overseas Employment: Who Benefits, Who Profits' (1995) 15, 2 and 3 *Canadian Woman Studies* 98.

32 Labour exporting countries not only rely on remittances from their nationals working abroad to help pay back IMF and other foreign loans; they also benefit from a reduction in unemployment and potential unrest assisted by labour export. Labour importing countries such as Canada use the migration of household workers to cheapen the costs of child, elderly, and home care, and to dampen political demands for a national child care strategy from upper and middle class Canadians who employ live-in caregivers.

33 Pura Velasco, '"We Can Still Fight Back": Organizing Domestic Workers in Toronto,' in Abigail B. Bakan and Daiva K. Stasiulis, eds., *Not One of the Family: Foreign Domestic Workers in Canada* (Toronto: University of Toronto Press, 1997) 163.

34 Joan Fitzpatrick, 'The Gender Dimension of U.S. Immigration Policy' (1997) 9, 23 *Yale Journal of Law and Feminism* 221.

35 For a historical overview of the migration of foreign domestic workers to Canada and the treatment accorded domestic workers from different racial/ethnic backgrounds and source countries, see Sedef Arat-Koc, 'From "Mothers of the Nation" to Migrant Workers,' in Bakan and Stasiulis, *Not One of the Family*.

36 Landed immigrants generally have access to the same citizenship rights as full citizens with exceptions such as voting in elections, running as political candidates, or taking up jobs involving national security. Landed immigrants are eligible to become citizens following three years of residence in Canada.

37 See Claire F.L. Young, 'Child Care – a Taxing Issue?' (1994) 39, 3 *McGill Law Journal* 539–567.

38 Canada lacks a comprehensive federal child care policy that ensures reasonable access to regulated child care. The national government has largely limited its involvement in child care to a number of funding mechanisms, such as the National Child Tax Credit and the Canada Assistance Plan (CAP). The fact that in 1990, the federal government placed limits on the annual increases to CAP has further exacerbated the regional differences in income level eligibility for child care subsidies, and the amounts of these subsidies. See Mab Oloman, 'Child Care Funding' (Strategy paper for National Child Care Conference and Lobby, Ottawa, October 1992), 4. See also The Task Force on Child Care, *Report of the Task*

Foreign Domestic Worker Policy and Jurisprudence 283

Force on Child Care (Ottawa: 1986); Ruth K. Abbott and R.A. Young, 'Cynical and Deliberate Manipulation? Child Care and the Reserve Army of Female Labour in Canada' (1989) 2, 24 *Journal of Canadian Studies* 22–38; Dawn Currie, 'Re-thinking What We Do and How We Do it: A Study of Reproductive Decisions' (1988) 25, 2 *Canadian Review of Sociology and Anthropology* 231–53.

39 With the aging of the baby boomer population, the care-giving field is shifting from an emphasis on child care to elderly care. As one journalist researching a story on Filipino nannies in Toronto wrote, 'It appears that Toronto's old people will be looked after by the same women who looked after our children.' Geraldine Sherman, 'Nanny's Dream,' *Toronto Life*, vol. 30, no. 13 (September 1996) 78.

40 In allowing for the substitution of practical job experience for the six-month training criterion announced as part of the policy changes in April 1992, the federal government had come part way in responding to 'concerns expressed by employers, domestic workers and their representatives' as well as a recommendation to a report on the Live-in Caregiver Program by the Standing Committee on Labour, Employment and Immigration. Government of Canada, 'News Release,' 9 June 1993, 2. Domestic advocacy groups were most vocal in attacking the six month full-time training requirement, arguing that it would cut off access to the LCP of most women from developing countries, which lacked such training programs.

41 Other conditions of acceptance for landing include the absence of misrepresentation of an applicant's education or training qualifications; absence of statutory grounds for inadmissibility of applicant and her dependents, e.g., criminal, security, health, and self-support concerns; and application for landing to an immigration officer. See Jackman, 'Admission,' 4. In Quebec, because of the Quebec government's emphasis on maintaining the status of the French language in that province, linguistic competence in French (and not in French or English as in the other provinces) is an additional requirement for landed status. This causes difficulties in the landing of domestics from the Philippines, the largest source of foreign domestics. Interview with Miriam Elvir, past board member, Montreal Household Workers Association, 11 August 1993.

42 The employer of a departing employee is, however, obligated to provide a 'Record of Employment' (ROE), indicating the number of weeks worked by the employee, as well as a statement of earnings.

43 Laura Chapman, Director General, Policy and Program Development (Immigration), Department of Employment and Immigration, House of Commons, *Minutes of Proceedings and Evidence of the Standing Committee on*

Labour, Employment and Immigration, Issue No. 8, 26 February 1992, 8. While Ms Chapman argued that 'raising the education requirement to grade 12 equivalency would not adversely affect any world areas,' this claim was disputed by domestic worker associations and by data produced by Employment and Immigration. The latter's statistics indicate that '44 per cent of Filipina domestic workers and 49 per cent of Caribbean domestic workers approved for permanent residence in 1989 did not have twelve years of schooling' let alone the equivalent of Canadian grade twelve. Macklin, 'Foreign Domestic Worker,' 759.

44 Group Interview, West Coast Domestic Workers Association, Vancouver, 26 April 1993. See also Carmencita Hernandez, Chair, Women's Committee, Canadian Ethnocultural Council, 'Nanny Rule Will Have Racist Outcome,' *Globe and Mail*, 15 February 1992, D7.

45 Laura Chapman, House of Commons debates, 8.

46 Ibid.

47 *Domestics' Cross-Cultural News*, INTERCEDE, Toronto, March 1993. It is, of course, possible that INTERCEDE's members are not representative of the educational levels of entrants into the FDM.

48 *Pinto v. Canada (Minister of Employment and Immigration)* (1990) 12 *Immigration Law Reporter* (2d) 194 (F.C.T.D.); (1991) 1 F.C. 619 (hereinafter *Pinto*).

49 Macklin, 'Foreign Domestic Worker,' 705–6.

50 Jackman, 'Admission,' 7–8. Barbara Jackman has argued that the imposition of domestic workers' qualifications in the admission requirements of the LCP make live-in domestics the only group of workers whose educational standards are imposed under immigration regulations, as opposed to provincial licensing requirements. In addition, these formal qualifications as applied to foreign domestics diverge from the educational and training levels of standardized occupations listed in the Canadian Classification and Dictionary of Occupations [CCDO], under 'Housekeepers, Servants and Related Occupations.' Here, specific vocational preparation time is given as less than three months training, and educational levels as less than twelve years. Ibid., 8. '[U]nlike other workers whose occupational skills are standardized by the CCDO, the domestic worker's qualifications are imposed by regulation without regard to actual occupational skill.' Ibid.

51 'Operations Memorandum' (Draft), Live-in Caregiver Program, Employment and Immigration Canada, 23 April 1992, 2.

52 In the Operations Memorandum for the Live-in Caregiver Program, one of the key points of change in the program is stated to be the 'legislative basis' of the new program 'to ensure that participants possess certain

qualifications pertaining to their education, training and language skills before their application for an employment authorization can be considered.' Ibid.
53 Patricia Daenzer, 'Ideology and the Formation of Migration Policy: The Case of Immigrant Domestic Workers, 1940–1990' (Doctoral dissertation, Department of Social Work, University of Toronto, 1991) 245; Macklin, 'Foreign Domestic Worker,' 740; Jackman, 'Admission,' 1, 4.
54 Jackman, 'Admission,' 3–4.
55 Unlike the *Immigration Act* and the *Immigration Regulations, 1978*, which are publicly promulgated, formal, legal instruments, the *Immigration Manual* consists of 'Informal instructions addressed to bureaucrats charged with administering immigration policy ... The Preface to the Manual makes [explicit] that: "Where conflict or inconsistency exists between these guidelines (including related Operations Memoranda) and the provisions of the *Immigration Act*, Regulations and related legislation, *the latter must take precedence*,"' Macklin, 'Foreign Domestic Worker,' 698–9, original emphasis.
56 Jackman, 'Admission,' 2.
57 Ibid., 4; Macklin, 'Foreign Domestic Worker,' 759–60.
58 Chantal Tie, 'Only Discriminating Visa Officers Need Apply: Visa Officer Decisions, the *Charter* and *Lee v. Canada (Minister of Citizenship and Immigration)*,' unpublished manuscript (on file with authors).
59 Macklin, 'Foreign Domestic Worker,' 760.
60 This was the consensus expressed by representatives of domestic worker groups from Vancouver, Toronto, and Montreal who met under the auspices of the Canadian Advisory Council on the Status of Women, 1 February 1992, at which Daiva Stasiulis was present.
61 Data collected from Citizenship and Immigration.
62 Specifically, our survey indicated that 14 of 25 West Indian domestic workers entered Canada as visitors and one claimed asylum as a refugee; only ten entered through either the FDM or LCP. In contrast, 23 of 25 Filipinas entered Canada through the FDM or LCP, while only two entered as visitors. These results are further discussed in Daiva Stasiulis and Abigail B. Bakan, 'Negotiating Citizenship: The Case of Foreign Domestic Workers in Canada' (1997) 57 *Feminist Review* 112–39. We gratefully acknowledge the assistance of Maria Leynes, Marcia Williams, and Claudine Charley who worked as interviewers in this survey.
63 The temporary status of the foreign domestic worker's visa is a feature of foreign domestic policies that preceded the FDM, first instituted in the 1973 'Temporary Employment Authorization' program. This program

brought in foreign domestics on temporary work permits that could be renewed annually to a maximum of three years. The 1976 *Immigration Act* revoked the privilege granted under previous legislation of applying for landed status from within Canada. The 1981 FDM continued to bring in foreign domestics with temporary employment authorizations renewable on a yearly basis, but with the added eligibility for application for permanent, landed status following two years of live-in domestic service.

64 Macklin, 'Foreign Domestic Worker,' 697.
65 Ibid., 698.
66 Ibid.
67 Immigration Canada, 'The Live-in Caregiver Program,' 1992.
68 EIC, *Immigration Manual*, Appendix C. The predecessor to this agreement was called an 'Employment Contract.' The change in title suggests a deliberate attempt to make the contract unenforceable. The Operations Memorandum for the LCP abolishes the requirement for any employment agreement, stating: 'It is the responsibility of the employer and employee to set out the terms and conditions of employment in the form of a contract.' CEIC 'Operations Memorandum (Draft): Live-In Caregiver Program,' 23 April 1992. The booklet on the Live-in Caregiver Program that is distributed by Immigration Canada to both potential employers and applicants provides a 'Sample Contract.' See Diana Breti and Christina Davidson, 'Background Paper: Foreign Domestic Workers in British Columbia,' West Coast Domestic Workers Association, Vancouver (undated) 3.
69 Ibid., 3.
70 *Domestic Workers Association Newsletter*, WCDWA, Vancouver, vol. 1, no. 2 (April 1987) 7. This article was written when Immigration was still issuing 'Employment Contracts' as opposed to Agreements.
71 Macklin, 'Foreign Domestic Worker,' 723, n192.
72 *Domestic Workers Association Newsletter*, vol. 1, no. 16 (September 1988) 4.
73 This statement appears at the bottom of the 'Sample Contract' provided by Immigration Canada in the booklet, 'The Live-in Caregiver Program: Information for Employers and Live-in Caregivers from Abroad,' Minister of Supply and Services Canada, 1992.
74 INTERCEDE, 'Improving The Ontario Employment Standards Act To Protect Domestic Workers' (undated).
75 Macklin reports a case, *Khan v. Canada (Minister of Employment and Immigration)* (1989) (1990)1 F.C. 30, 30 F.T.R., involving the detention by immigration officials of Ms Khan, a Trinidadian domestic worker who was suspected of transgressing the 'live-in' requirement of the FDM. The Court

Foreign Domestic Worker Policy and Jurisprudence 287

ruled that immigration authorities had resorted to 'callous and unnecessary' procedures in detaining Ms Khan, who was eight months pregnant at the time of her arrest. Macklin, 'Foreign Domestic Worker,' 723 n192.
76 Ibid.
77 Ibid., 685.
78 Alma Estable, 'Speaking with a Common Voice: Filipino Domestic Workers in Canada' (a background paper prepared for the United Council of Filipino Associations in Canada, Ottawa, March 1989), 6.
79 In one reported case in London, Ontario, a domestic worker was kept imprisoned for three years in her employer's home and forbidden to have any outside contact, including use of the telephone or access to newspapers or television. Another case in the same city involved an African woman who was made to work in the employer's home in the day, and on a turkey farm at night where her wages were pocketed by her employer. 'Domestic Worker Treated like Slave,' *Globe and Mail*, 6 August 1992, A6.
80 The Association pour la Défense des Droits du Personnel Domestique de Montréal submitted a dossier of 'concrete cases of abuse' as part of their brief to the Standing Committee on Labour, Employment, and Immigration during the federal government review of the Foreign Domestics Program in 1991–2. These cases reported employers engaging in a whole range of violent and abusive behaviour including: one who chased his employee with a knife and threatened to kill her if she left; one who dragged his employee by the hair to the balcony in the middle of winter; one who asked for a massage and suggested more intimate relations; a couple who proposed a threesome with their African employee whom they constantly questioned about polygamy in her country; a few cases of employers who paid well below standard monthly wages which were forwarded directly to the employees' families. Association pour la Défense des Droits du Personnel Domestique de Montréal, *Recommendations Presented to the Permanent Committee of Work, Employment and Immigration* (sic), 30 January 1992.
81 Shellee Colen, '"Just a Little Respect": West Indian Domestic Workers in New York City,' in Elsa M. Chaney and Mary Garcia Castro, eds., *Muchachas No More: Household Workers in Latin America and the Caribbean* (Philadelphia: Temple University Press, 1989) 180. For a discussion of the asymmetrical behaviours of domestic workers and their employers involving forms of address, space, physical appearance and gift-giving, see Judith Rollins, *Between Women: Domestics and Their Employers* (Philadelphia: Temple University Press, 1985); and Bakan and Stasiulis, eds. 'Introduction,' in *Not One of the Family*, 3–27.

288　Daiva Stasiulis and Abigail B. Bakan

82　These were some of the findings of a participatory action research study of the housing needs of 58 Filipina live-in domestic workers in the Lower Mainland of British Columbia, conducted by the Philippine Women Center. Philippine Women Centre, 'Housing Needs Assessment of Filipina Domestic Workers,' Vancouver, 1996.
83　Denise Caron of the Association des Aides Familiaux du Québec (formerly the Association pour la Défense des Droits du Personnel Domestique) spoke of two cases of employer abuse in Quebec referred to the association involving women who claimed to have received better treatment from employers in the Gulf region. Personal communication, 4 September 1998.
84　Sedef Arat-Koc and Fely Villasin, 'Report and Recommendations on the Foreign Domestic Movement' (Toronto: INTERCEDE, October 1990), 8–9.
85　See Makeda Silvera, *Silenced: Talks with Working Class Caribbean Women about Their Lives and Struggles as Domestic Workers in Canada*, 2nd ed. (Toronto: Sister Vision Press, 1989); Estable, 'Speaking with a Common Voice,' 36–7.
86　*Guzman v. Dr. & Mrs T.* [1997] B.C.C.H.R.D. No. 1.
87　Ibid., 44, 43.
88　*Singson v. Pasion and Moore* [1996] B.C.C.H.R.D. No. 12, 24.
89　Her female employer, Ms Pasion, although not involved in the alleged conduct, was nonetheless found liable for the conduct of her husband by virtue of s. 21(2) of the Act.
90　Miro Cernetig, 'Nannies' Poor Treatment Outlined,' *Globe and Mail*, 28 January 1998, A4.
91　West Coast Domestic Workers Association, 'Brief to the Review Committee on the Foreign Domestic Worker Program: Foreign Domestic Workers in British Columbia – Recommendations for Change,' November 1989, 4; Arat-Koc and Villasin, 'Report on Recommendations,' 7.
92　Violations of workers' privacy include the common practice of children walking into workers' bedrooms without knocking and during their off hours; employers monitoring their employees' mail and telephone conversations; limiting and even forbidding use of the telephone; refusing to provide employees with separate keys to the house. West Coast Domestic Workers Association, ibid., 8; Arat-Koc and Villasin, 'Report on Recommendations,' 7–8.
93　Judy Fudge, 'Little Victories and Big Defeats: The Rise and Fall of Collective Bargaining Rights for Domestic Workers in Ontario,' in Bakan and Stasiulis, *Not One of the Family*, 127.
94　Arat-Koc and Villasin, 'Report on Recommendations,' 7.
95　As Macklin points out, the New Brunswick statute denies that private

Foreign Domestic Worker Policy and Jurisprudence 289

domestic service constitutes real work by excluding from the definition of employer, 'a person having control or direction of or being responsible, directly or indirectly, for the employment of persons in or about his private home.' Macklin, 'Foreign Domestic Worker,' 702, n96.
96 Ibid.
97 Ibid.
98 Québec, Commission des normes du travail, Labour Standard, 1991, 2.
99 We thank Denise Caron of the Association des Aides Familiaux du Québec for this information.
100 Ontario, *Employment Standards – Fact Sheet: 'Domestic Workers*, http://www,gov.on.ca/lab.es.ese.htm, 1998.
101 *Employment Standards Act, B.C.*, S.B.C. 1995, c. 38.
102 British Columbia, 'A Guide to the Employment Standards.'
103 Ontario Labor Relations Act, S.O. 1995, C.1, Schedule A.
104 Fudge, 'Little Victories,' 137–40.
105 Audrey Macklin, 'On the Inside Looking In: Foreign Domestic Workers in Canada,' in Wenona Giles and Sedef Arat-Koc, eds., *Maid in the Market: Women's Paid Domestic Labour* (Halifax: Fernwood Publishing, 1994) 32.
106 Arat-Koc and Villasin, 'Report on Recommendations,' 5. In a 1990 survey of 576 live-in domestics in Toronto, only 35 per cent reported working a 44-hour week (defined as the 'normal' work week for live-in domestics by the Ontario Employment Standards Act), while 65 per cent regularly were required to work overtime. Only 33 per cent who routinely performed overtime work received the legal compensation of time-and-a-half pay or time off in lieu of pay; 43.7 per cent received no compensation whatsoever. Ibid., 6, Table II.
107 Jeanne Mikita, 'Summary of Results, Foreign Caregivers Migration and Employment Survey,' in *Supporting Documentation for West Coast Domestic Workers' Association*, Brief to Employment Standards Act Review Committee, March 1993.
108 The underpayment of the nannies who took part in the survey is reflected in the gap between their average wage of $1,264 per month before taxes and the approximately $300 in room and board deducted from their paycheque and the average wage of $1,793 which they should have earned if they had been paid according to provincial employment standards for their overtime. Miro Cernetig, 'Nannies' poor treatment outlined,' *Globe and Mail*, 28 June 1998, A4.
109 Ibid.
110 *Baker v. Canada (Minister of Citizenship and Immigration)*, [1999] 2 S.C.R. 817.

111 Andrea Timoll, 'Foreign Domestic Servants in Canada' (Honours research essay, Department of Political Science, Carleton University, September 1989) 57–8.
112 Macklin, 'Foreign Domestic Worker,' 734.
113 *Lodge v. M.M.I.* (1979), 1 F.C. 775.
114 Jackman, 'Admission,' 2. For various accounts of this struggle, see Anne Bayefsky, 'The Jamaican Women Case and the Canadian Human Rights Act: Is Government Subject to the Principle of Equal Opportunity?' (1980) 18 *U.W.O.L. Rev.* 461–7; Ronnie Leah and Gwen Morgan, 'Immigrant Women Fight Back; The Case of the Seven Jamaican Women' (1979) 7:3 *Resources for Feminist Research*, 23–4; Macklin, 'Foreign Domestic Worker,' 734–5.
115 *Fernandez* (14 March 1989), Vancouver 9530-01-5955 (Bd Inquiry), discussed in Macklin, 'Foreign Domestic Worker,' 707.
116 Ibid.
117 The WCDWA reports on the practice of agencies in the home countries of domestic applicants advising them to lie about their marital status and dependants on the grounds that 'they have a better chance of being admitted as domestics if they say they are single and have no dependants. Although Immigration denies that this is true, in 1988, of the 24,000 new work visas issued, fewer than 2,000 were issued to women who admitted they were married. In other words, Immigration discriminates against women who are married or have children.' *Domestic Workers Association Newsletter*, WCDWA, Vancouver, vol. 2, no. 10 (October 1989) 3.
118 Ibid.
119 Correspondence of R. Jankowski, Canadian Immigration Centre, Vancouver to West Coast Domestic Workers' Association, 17 January 1990; *Domestic Workers Association Newsletter*, vol. 3, no. 8 (August 1990) 5.
120 *Mitra v. Canada (Minister of Citizenship and Immigration)* (1996), 36 Imm. L.R. (2d) 213 F.T.R.
121 Ibid.
122 Deborah Cheney, 'Valued Judgments? A Reading of Immigration Cases,' in Anne Bottomley and Joanne Conaghan, eds., *Feminist Theory and Legal Strategy* (Oxford: Blackwell, 1993) 24.
123 *Eugenio v. Canada (Minister of Citizenship and Immmigration)* (1997), 38 Imm. L.R. (2d) 165 (Immigration and Refugee Board [Appeal Division]).
124 Ibid., 170
125 Ibid., 171.
126 Ibid., 172.
127 Cheney, 'Valued Judgments,' 23.

128 *Bernardez v. Canada (Minister of Citizenship & Immigration)* (1995), 31 Imm.L.R. (2d) 90.
129 Ibid., 4.
130 Ibid., 5.
131 *Turingan v. Canada (Minister of Employment & Immigration)* (1993), 24 Imm. L.R. (2d) 113.
132 *Bernardez v. Canada*, 6.
133 *Turingan v. Canada*, 115.
134 *Caletana v. Canada (Solicitor General)* (1994), (F.C.T.D.) 23 Imm.L.R. (2d) 177.
135 *Peje v. Canada (Minister of Citizenship & Immigration)* (1997), (F.C.T.D.) 37 Imm. L.R. (2d) 270. Elsa Peje, a citizen of the Philippines, had entered the FDM in 1990, was employed by various employers, but developed health problems in the form of an ulcerated stomach, sinus problems, and migraine headaches. Her illness prevented her from working and in September 1994, Ms Peje went on social assistance. After recovering her health, Ms Peje found several employers willing to provide her with work, but the Immigration Department refused to approve work permits for her.
136 Ibid., 273–4.
137 *Peje v. Canada (Minister of Citizenship and Immigration)* (1998), F.C.J. No. 1048 (F.C.T.D.).
138 *Baker v. Canada*, 827.
139 Ibid., 830.
140 Ibid., 860.
141 Ibid., 866.
142 Justice Claire L'Heureux-Dubé was quoting from R. Sullivan, *Driedger on the Construction of Statutes* (3rd ed. 1994), 330.
143 United Nations, General Assembly, 45th Session, Third Committee *Report of the Open-Ended Working Group on the Drafting of the International Convention on the Protection of the Rights of all Migrant Workers and Members of Their Families*, UN Doc.A/c.3/45/1 (21 June 1990).
144 *Sarmini Mustaji v. Khi Yoeng Tjin and Rosna Elly Tjin* (1996), (Court of Appeal for British Columbia), Court of Appeal Registry.
145 Kim Bolan, '"Virtual prisoner" awarded $250,000,' *Vancouver Sun*, 14 January, 1995, A4.
146 'These include statutory rights under employment standards, labour and workers' compensation legislation, and contractual rights under the employer/employee agreement.' Macklin, 'Foreign Domestic Worker,' 739–40.

147 Jackman, 'Admission,' 293–4; Tie, 'Only Discriminating,' 3. Tie similarly argues that a lack of familiarity with the Canadian Human Rights Act among immigration lawyers helps to account for the low numbers of immigration complaints brought before the Canadian Human Rights Commission. Chantal Tie, 'Immigrant Selection and the Canadian Human Rights Act,' (1994) 10 *Journal of Law and Social Policy* 105–6.
148 Macklin, 'Foreign Domestic Worker,' 739.
149 Ibid., 739, n276; Fudge, 'Little Victories,' 10, 143–4, n16.
150 Ibid., 741, 744; Jackman, 'Admission,' 292.
151 Philippine Women Centre, Filipino Nurses Support Group, Press Release, Vancouver, 9 January 2000.
152 Personal communication, Denise Caron, Association des Aides Familiaux du Québec.
153 INTERCEDE, 'Bill C-31 – The Immigration and Refugee Protection Act Viewed through Migrant Women's Eyes,' Presentation to the House Standing Committee on Citizenship and Immigration, July 2000, 13.
154 These organizations recommended that: caregivers who had worked under temporary employment authorization(s) for one year be eligible for landing under the In-Canada Landing Class; that the live-in requirement be eliminated; that caregivers be permitted to bring or sponsor their families to Canada; that the temporary employment authorization be employment rather than employer-specific; that a pro-active independent monitoring system be introduced to examine working conditions of foreign domestic workers; and finally that families employing foreign caregivers be provided with orientations regarding their responsibilities as employers. National Association of Women and the Law, the West Coast Domestic Workers Association, La Table féministe francophone de Concertation provinciale de l'Ontario, The National Organization of Immigrant and Visible Minority Women of Canada, *Brief on the Proposed Immigration and Refugee Act, Bill C-31*, Submitted to the Standing Committee on Citizenship and Immigration, August 2000.
155 Jackman, 'Admission,' 291.
156 Philip L. Bryden, 'Fundamental Justice and Family Class Immigration: The Example of Pangli v. Minister of Employment and Immigration' (1991) 41 *University of Toronto Law Journal* 484.
157 Cheney, 'Valued Judgments,' 24. Deborah Cheney is here describing British immigration law, but her characterization of immigration legislation is equally applicable to Canada.
158 'Historically, one may find the roots of the current statutory regime in laws developed in the early 1900s, at a time when an awareness of human

rights was minimal among the public and our legislators.' Jackman, 'Admission,' 292.
159 This argument is elaborated in Daiva K. Stasiulis, 'International Migration, Rights, and the Decline of "Actually Existing Liberal Democracy,"' (1997) 23, 2 *New Community* 197–214.
160 Philip L. Bryden, 'Fundamental Justice,' 516–17.
161 Thus, Bryden argues that refugee cases, including Madame Justice Wilson's decision in *Singh et al. v. Minister of Employment and Immigration*, [1985] 17 D.L.R. (4th) 422 have been treated differently than immigration cases. In extending Charter protections to non-citizen refugee applicants, the courts have viewed refugee protection to be a more urgent matter than the protection of the rights of immigrant visa applicants. Ibid., 514.
162 Tie, 'Only Discriminating,' 4.
163 Jackman, 'Admission,' 292.
164 Ryszard Cholewinski, *Migrant Workers in International Human Rights Law: Their Protection in Countries of Employment* (Oxford: Clarendon Press, 1997) 193. The principle of state sovereignty in the context of immigration is underlined in Article 79, Part viii of the ICMW on General Provisions: 'Nothing in the present Convention shall affect the right of each State Party to establish the criteria governing admission of migrant workers and members of their families.'
165 L.S. Bosniak, quoted in Cholewinski, *Migrant Workers*, 193.
166 Susan Davis, Roslyn Kunin, and Robert Trempe, *Not Just Numbers: A Canadian Framework for Future Immigration* (Ottawa: Immigration Legislative Review, 1997).
167 Immigration Minister Elinor Caplan quoted in Brian Laghi, 'Ottawa Proposes Immigration Overhaul,' *Globe and Mail*, 7 April 2000, A2; Canadian Council for Refugees, 'CCR Comments on New Immigration Bill,' 7 April 2000, http://www.web.net/~ccr/c31news.htm.
168 As this book was in production, the Canadian government introduced Bill C-11 to the House of Commons in February 2001. See Bill C-11, 'An Act respecting immigration to Canada and the granting of refugee protection to persons who are displaced, persecuted or in danger,' House of Commons of Canada, 21 February 2001. The newest package of immigration and refugee policy proposals is not markedly different from that contained in Bill C-31. As this proposed legislation fails to mention the Live-in Caregiver Program, it again leaves the policy on foreign domestic workers to Immigration Regulations and thus subject to wide bureaucratic discretion. See Canadian Council on Refugees, 'Brief – Bill C-11,' Ottawa, 25 March 2001.

169 Isabel Vincent, 'Canada Beckons Cream of Nannies,' *Globe and Mail*, 20 January 1996, A5.
170 According to the Greek myth, Hydra was finally killed by Heracles who had his friend Iolaus burn the stumps with torches as soon as the heads were removed.

CHAPTER SEVEN

Beyond the Confinement of Gender: Locating the Space of Legal Existence for Racialized Women

Joanne St Lewis

Racialized women are a heterogeneous group. Their unity is found in their shared experience of vulnerability to the racist attitudes and practices of whites – both women and men. Racialized women live diverse lives, as do white women, where class, culture, citizenship, religion, sexual identity, and different abilities should preclude presumptions of a racialized monolith. The law has played a pivotal role in determining the nature and scope of the rights of women who are not white: the law has racialized women of colour. During the colonial period they were regarded by whites as mere property, indigenous (sub)peoples to be exploited, or indentured servants. Legally subordinated, they could be sexually abused with utterly no recourse available because of the prevailing social class arrangements and the racist fantasies of the European imagination. Their economic status was that of producers of surplus wealth in the expansion of the capitalist dream. The subordinate status of racialized women in the law continues in our day, as can be seen, for example, in the legal status of domestic workers and the racist double standard relied on by some Euro-Canadian judges. Throughout this chapter the term 'racialized' is used for those women, men, and children who are variously identified as visible minorities, racial minorities, people of colour, and by specific racial/cultural designations such as black. It is intended to focus attention on the sociopolitical impact that the construction of 'race' and racism has had on specific peoples.

Racialized women have frequently been defined through the eyes of others. Beyond the plethora of terms used in legislation (visible minority, racial minority, ethno-cultural/racial), there are the terms coined in various political contexts. From 'people of colour' to 'racialized communities,' all terms have been intended to assert a collective identity that would facilitate action – both legal and political – to combat racism. However, the community of interests that informs the critique brought by racialized women to feminist legal theory is made up of many, and diverse, voices, all as contingent or as fluid as my own: No one racialized woman can speak for the multiplicity of voices within our communities. All debates about authenticity, the prioritizing of issues, and the divergence of scholarship involve the identities of the one speaking, the subject, the one spoken about, and the one spoken to. Let us bear in mind, therefore, that difference is not just a concept that renders equality theory more transparent; it is also an internal reality of the self. Furthermore, the shared experience of oppression through racism does not preclude vigilance about the points of privilege that arise through class, sexual identity, able-bodiedness, education, or access to decision-making fora. For all of these reasons our participation requires a critical mass of us within the policy-making institutions. The policy-making institution under discussion here is the law.

In recent decades, many different kinds of people in Canada have organized for the purposes of making themselves heard and seen and formally recognized as having an equal space in Canadian society and in Canadian law. 'Equality-seeking communities' is a term that incorporates but is not limited to the designated groups listed in various provincial and federal human rights instruments and policy documents dealing with equality. It also captures those individuals for whom location at the intersections of these categories creates unique opportunities and vulnerabilities, such as racialized women who are poor, refugees, and women with disabilities.

Racialized women are among the many equality-seeking communities whose perspectives have been absent from the conceptual frameworks relied on by Canadian courts when defining rights. This has occurred in part because of the failure of rights activists – including feminists – to fully incorporate their experiences and expertise. The demands issued by racialized women are neither simple nor easily attained. They are demands for inclusion in the academic settings where these theories are debated. They are demands for recognition that life at the intersection of power relations gives rise to unique forms of discrimination that require unique solutions. Most of all, these demands are for accountability from both institutions and allies for concrete steps to eradicate the racist practices and attitudes that hamper our mutual efforts to advance equality.

This chapter will focus on the question of why feminist legal theorists and activists must apply the expertise and perspectives of racialized women in the arguments they make before the courts. This will require a movement beyond appropriation or token representation within feminist legal policy-making institutions. Racialized women have multilayered expertise. Their experiences as members of communities that are subject to the ongoing impact of colonialism and the socioeconomic distortions of global capitalism can provide insight into a range of issues. Their participation in the formulation of concepts, methodologies, and legal strategies is one possible starting point for evaluating assumptions about the nature of identity, citizenship, culture, and rights.[1] For feminists, it is yet another opportunity to investigate the boundaries of gender and the shifting content of this category.[2] The participation of racialized women is an essential element of the full realization of women's equality.

The absence of racialized women's perspectives in the formulation of legal feminist concepts and strategies has been treated as unfortunate in many contemporary feminist discussions. Their 'best efforts' response has not met with the expected patience and modest congratulations from racialized communities. The virtual exclusion of racialized women is the marginalization of women who, though a minority within Canada, are in actuality the majority of women globally. This means that the analysis of gender equality shaped in their absence will inevitably contribute to their continued subordination. By discussing this issue, this chapter will hopefully contribute to the development of a more sustained approach to feminist legal strategies.

Since the 1970s, Canadian feminists have invested much political effort in attempting to change the law.[3] Their efforts have included reliance on selective activism in the courts, greater participation in the legal policy-making initiatives of government,[4] and increasingly, more public demands for legislative reform.[5] One of the most visible feminist organizations to have taken up the challenges of activism in the courts is the Women's Legal Education and Action Fund (LEAF), an organization of legal feminists formed in direct response to the proclamation of the *Canadian Charter of Rights and Freedoms* in 1985 and which uses a test case litigation strategy to advance women's equality rights. A highwater mark of this type of work is the cutting-edge analysis provided by LEAF in its intervenor's factum in *Andrews v. The Law Society of British Columbia*.[6] This intervention produced a remarkable result in that, for the first time, the Supreme Court of Canada accepted a substantive rather than a merely formal definition of equality. Such interventions have enabled women to grapple with the reality of an entrenched legal system that continues to resist the fundamental changes being sought by equality-seeking communities.

The first part of this chapter will briefly discuss the nature of legal culture and the 'race of the law' in order to assess how the Euro-Canadian legal system has shaped the feminist battle for equality. I argue that the embodiment of the legal system, including the judiciary, legal practitioners, and the legal academy, is of critical importance, because racialized women and men have been largely excluded from their ranks. Indeed, a discussion of the first case in Canadian jurisprudence alleging judicial bias regarding race (*R. v. R.D.S.*)[7] demonstrates some of the effects of this exclusion, as it represented an attempt to impugn the integrity of an African-Canadian woman judge who had acknowledged, in general terms, systemic racism in the justice system.

In addition to arguing for the increased presence of racialized peoples within legal institutions, I argue that racialized women provide an opportunity for a revisioning of feminist legal strategies. Racialized women's lived expertise would nourish feminist strategies for a number of reasons: first, racialized women are diverse and come together through consciousness of their oppression; second, their experiences are informed by life at the shifting intersections of class, religion, citizenship, culture, sexual identity, and history; and third, their oppression brings into sharp relief the role of the state and colonialism in the contemporary context. However, the questions of who racialized women are and the scope of their contribution have often been constrained by a feminist vision that would deny or circumscribe them.

The discussion of a more expansive identity for racialized women will be followed in the second part of the chapter by an analysis of how feminist legal theories have approached issues of 'race' and racism.[8] Using several cases to illustrate the themes, the chapter will trace developments from early denial of race and racism to the prioritizing and essentializing of gender, to the recent recognition and valorization of difference. Each of these developments has had a direct impact on the selection of issues to be raised in the courts about women's right to equality.

Finally, this chapter will draw on the insights of critical race theory (CRT) – the omnibus term used to describe the critique that has been brought to social, political, and legal theory by African-American and -Canadian scholars and by other members of racialized communities – to demonstrate how the established understandings of feminist legal issues may be transformed through the analyses advanced by racialized scholars.[9]

The Context: Legal Culture and the Role of Gender and Race in Equality Advocacy

What Race Is the Law?

Feminists have challenged the legal system as a key structure that needs transformation in a society that remains inhospitable to many.[10] The notions of individuality and rights that flow from a liberal framework have stripped equality-seekers of their identities and the necessary context for critique. Neutral language masks the failure of constitutional, statutory, and common law to address the needs of many vulnerable communities.

The inequitable history of the law, which facilitated the acquisition of power by an elite few, is not discussed by the courts and is rarely a part of legal argument. Instead, the law and the legal system have been used to reinforce oppression and social inequality. This inequality has sometimes been built on specific policies of discrimination or exclusion, such as those used to foster the expansion of the colonial empire. Inequity has also resulted from the operation of seemingly non-discriminatory concepts and practices such as precedent (in the common law system) and adherence to liberal notions of individual rights.[11] These practices have been assumed to be neutral, in spite of their disparate impact on vulnerable equality-seeking communities.

The law is designed to protect the interests of a privileged minority. This design is reflected in what conduct is regulated and whose behaviours are sanctioned, as well as in the operation of procedural rules and the substance of many legal concepts. Historically, power has been inextricably linked to property ownership. Therefore, it is not surprising that many legal rules relate to the preservation of property and that concepts of property continue to delimit the rights of those who are not part of the politically and economically powerful elite. The law has also defined human beings *into* property. Women, slaves, and indentured servants, among others, have been among the most vulnerable, having been legally defined in various periods as the property of men, slave-owners, and latterly, their domestic employers. Entire communities have also been denied the right to own property or circumscribed in the types of property they may own. This has arisen in the area of the legal rights of indigenous peoples – First Nations peoples, Inuit, Métis, status, and non-status Indians – who have at various points in Canadian history been deprived of their traditional lands and the right to alienate such lands as they do possess.[12] Contemporary socioeconomic relationships of many racialized communities (domestically and globally) are substantially rooted in the property relationships developed during the colonial period.

Common law, with its reliance on the doctrine of *stare decisis* (precedent), reinforces these inequalities, as each case serves as a conduit to past errors. This most often occurs when the past relied on by the courts conforms to myths of equality and progress. Litigants who challenge that perception often find that history and values are masked, thus making attempts to link current legal inequities to past historical discrimination difficult, if not impossible. The past is passed and is no longer accessible for redress in the present. This is most clearly evidenced by the reliance on neutrality or colour-blindness as the goal of equality by the courts. Litigants who assert racism and who demand redress for past inequities are suspect. This is built upon a number of pernicious distortions that racialized communities have struggled to erode. These include the following beliefs: (a) that discrimination has been eliminated in the (mythic) present; (b) that equality is realized by same treatment; (c) that civic culture can only be strong through a monoculture; (d) that discrimination is the act of individuals; (e) that good intentions are the hallmark of a fair society; (f) that it is unfair to judge the past through contemporary lenses; (g) that the descendants of those who perpetrated discrimination and those in their communities are not illegitimate beneficiaries of that discrimination; and (h) that historical redress is inherently unfair.

Precedent is one of the mechanisms that has evolved in common law to protect those seeking just decisions from the arbitrary whims and biases of individual judges. The structure was designed to reinforce consistency in the courts by setting out the circumstances under which they would be bound by prior decisions and to what extent, if any, discretion remained to differ or to forge a contrary direction. The degree of predictability for the litigant/accused was seen as increasing the likelihood of a just decision. The value of precedent in increasing the level of confidence in the judicial system is clear when one is concerned about arbitrariness.[13]

Precedent allows the law to retain a measure of continuity with the past. However, when that past has failed to uphold the dignity and interests of all, then those who have been historically excluded may well question how precedent can serve them rather than impede justice. The notion of precedent is rooted in a history of decision-making in which women were not legal persons, when chattel slavery was enforced by the courts, when rape within marriage was a legal impossibility, when indigenous peoples' cultural practices were outlawed and their lands confiscated, and when property ownership was a precondition to the right to vote and hold office.[14]

The contortions that legal advocates undertake to find precedents or threads of reasoning that would redefine the rights that support their claims is evidence both of the potency of liberalism and of its limitations.[15] In this context, liberalism is intended to capture the pervasive preoccupation with individual rights – same treatment under the rule of law in an atmosphere of legal scientific reasoning or logic. Reliance on the tools of the very legal system that has sustained the injustice is an inherent limitation of the liberal approach to rights because it is that same legal system that sets the parameters of the rights to be obtained.[16] Relying on 'the master's tools'[17] may restrict a more expansive vision that would result in social justice.

Canadian jurisprudence is eloquent in its silence about the nature of racism in society. Courts have often avoided the context in which racism arises, only to grapple with abstractions of rights that leave racialized plaintiffs, accused, and communities dissatisfied. Often the issue of race is screened out by the time the judgment is rendered, particularly as the case is filtered through several levels of court.[18] Failure of the courts to find police officers guilty of manslaughter in the numerous shooting incidents involving the African-Canadian community has resulted in charges of collusion between police, Crown, and the courts.[19] The results of these judicial decisions exacerbate the feelings of mistrust and erode the confidence of racialized communities in the capacity of the system to render justice. These communities often interpret a decontextualized decision as an unjust decision. The justice system is then renamed the injustice system. The erasure of race has thus resulted in the perception of a two-tiered system of justice.

The perception and experience of racialized people that the system tolerates racism lives alongside the liberal and mainstream assertion that the system is race-neutral. The latter assertion is simply not true. The legal system has never been race-neutral. It has always borne the race and culture of its progenitors. In other words, the system reflects the perspectives and values of the community it was designed to serve. It is this denial of race that has been recast as race-neutrality. The law has been constructed within a European, Judeo-Christian framework and is essentially a reflection of European cultures.[20] British and French colonialism in Canada meant the imposition of the common and civil law systems over pre-existing indigenous legal systems. The racial and cultural divide reinforced within the colonizing framework is a key aspect of the European consciousness that undergirds the law. As put by Amina Mama: 'White supremacy can ... be conceptualized as a set of discourses and practices that subjugated non-European people and cast them in the position of subjected Others, while it advanced the interests of European nations.'[21] The extent to which feminist legal strategies have been affected by this reality will be the focus of discussion later in this chapter.

Acknowledging that the justice system does not serve racialized communities does not explain why it does not. Racialized peoples are among the marginalized in Canadian society; it is not surprising that a system that fails the poor, the homeless, children, persons with disabilities, and women would also fail them. Even the rhetoric of equality has yet to entrench many of the necessary conceptual tools. Feminist, class, and critical race theories are still at the fringes of the legal academy and advocacy in the courts.

Embodying the Legal System

Theoretical frameworks are, of course, only one part of the strategy to demarginalize racialized communities. Members of those communities, however, must have increased presence in the fora where these concepts are created and critically evaluated, at the decision-making points in the justice system, and as academics, law students, legal counsel, legal policy-makers, tribunal members, and judges.[22] Jennifer Nedelsky, for example, has offered an outline of the qualities necessary for effective judging: 'What ... makes it possible for us to genuinely judge, to move beyond our private idiosyncrasies and preferences, is our capacity to achieve an "enlargement of mind" ... the more angles of vision we are able to take into account, the less likely we are to be locked into one perspective.'[23] I would argue that one of the best ways to ensure that 'more angles of vision' are available to us is to increase the participation of racialized peoples in the judiciary. This is not to advance a form of standpoint theory suggesting that only racialized people can achieve the requisite 'enlargement of mind.' It *is*, however, to argue that the angles of vision offered by racialized people do not simply arise in the minds of enlightened Euro-Canadian feminist lawyers and judges; they need to be articulated by those whose experiences of marginalization challenge the habitual assumptions of universality, fairness, and impartiality that permeate the judicial system.

The justice system is not an inanimate abstraction; it is made flesh through the people who work within it. Legal culture is sustained by the micro-behaviours of the judges, lawyers, and legal academics who articulate its values. Racialized peoples are poorly represented in these areas. The scarcity of people from racialized communities in the judicial hierarchy is a manifestation of that hierarchy's cultural homogeneity. With the exception Mr Justice Julius Isaacs, Chief Justice of the Federal Court of Appeal, racialized people, insofar as there are judges among them, are overwhelmingly located at the provincial court level. It will take a concerted effort before their representation amounts to more than token appointments and there is in place the cricical mass that would allow the development of effective critical race jurisprudence. Members of racialized communities have attempted to address this scarcity by demanding education and employment equity within law schools, the legal profession, and a change to the judicial appointments process.[24]

The above discussion would suggest that I believe only racialized peoples can render effective judgments of racial issues. However, our legal system has already deemed the Euro-Canadian perspective to be the race-neutral one. For example, Her Honour Judge Corinne Sparks – the first African Canadian appointed to the bench in Nova Scotia, indeed the first African-Canadian woman judge anywhere in Canada – made reference, when making a credibility finding in *R. v. R.D.S.*, to the social context of racial tension between police officers and black youth in Nova Scotia. Judge Sparks's finding in favour of the black youth rather than the white police officer was appealed on the ground of a reasonable apprehension of bias. Indeed, the Nova Scotia Court of Appeal agreed with the Crown that Judge Sparks's comments in *R. v. R.D.S.* gave rise to such a reasonable apprehension of bias.[25] This was the first and is the only judicial bias case on the issue of racism to come before the Canadian courts. Ironically, other cases involving overt racist statements made by Canadian judges have not become the subject of appeals on the basis of judicial bias. The bias that was being complained of in this case was the acknowledgment by a judge that racism exists in Canadian legal institutions.[26] Thus, in the Province of Nova Scotia, home of the Donald Marshall Jr Inquiry,[27] which resulted in significant policy changes within the provincial attorney-general's department, and where Dalhousie University's Faculty of Law had instituted its Indigenous, Black, and Mi'kmaq program so that the almost total exclusion of these communities from the legal profession could be addressed, Judge Sparks made waves – was legally accused of judicial bias – for stating that there is racism in the Canadian legal system. Judge Sparks was not new to these issues. She had been a member of the Canadian Bar Association Task Force on Gender Equality in the Legal Profession, the group that produced *Touchstones for Change*, which included an appendix specifically reporting on 'Women of Colour in the Legal Profession.'[28] Far from being the idiosyncratic murmurings of one 'biased' individual, Judge Sparks's remarks in *R. v. R.D.S.*, were supported by numerous reports at both the provincial and federal levels, as well as by her professional expertise regarding the issue of systemic racism in the Canadian administration of justice.[29]

The Nova Scotia Court of Appeal's finding of reasonable apprehension of bias against Her Honour Judge Sparks demonstrates that the contributions of racialized peoples to the judiciary that directly challenge the previously unacknowledged Eurocentric norms within the system can be seriously devalued. The case and its appeal offer a fundamental challenge to the assumption that judges are supposed to be 'race-neutral.'[30] What this neutrality means is that judges are not supposed to see race even when it is there. Neutrality in law means that the fiction of obscuring institutional racism is to be maintained by judges unless that is the matter specifically at issue. Values such as 'impartiality,' 'neutrality' and adherence to liberal notions of the individual are all acceptable: an explicit commitment to equality and anti-racism is not.

The questions of how judges should take judicial notice of the social context and whether judges from racialized groups must meet a higher standard than their non-racialized colleagues were raised by LEAF in their intervenor submission to the final appeal before the Supreme Court of Canada.[31] The African-Canadian Legal Clinic also intervened, its submission placing the allegations in the context of the historical experience of African-Canadians, which flowed from slavery, and pointing out that Eurocentrism continued to inform the courts' decision-making processes. In the event, though much of this analysis was ignored by the Court, six of the nine justices found that Judge Sparks's remarks did *not* give rise to a reasonable apprehension of bias. Indeed, four of them found that Judge Sparks's comments 'were entirely supported by the evidence' and 'reflected an entirely appropriate recognition of the facts in evidence and of the context within which this case arose – a context known to the judge and to any well-informed member of the community.'[32] Although the decision ultimately supported Judge Sparks, it is nevertheless significant that the first time the Supreme Court of Canada was asked to consider the issue of racial bias in the judiciary was in the case of a black woman judge acknowledging systemic racism, instead of in any of the numerous cases in Canadian jurisprudential history in which white judges have exhibited racial bias against indigenous people and members of so-called visible minorities.

Crystallizing a Feminist Pathway in the Courts: LEAF

What has been termed 'feminist advocacy' has been the result of efforts by feminist lawyers, scholars, and activists working together to put women's demands for equality before the courts. Striving for sex equality is not a neutral objective, however. It is a commitment to an express goal and set of values. Sex equality is about a way of being. Reliance on the legal system as the primary tool for the attainment of equality is a commitment to incremental change. Litigation, all rhetoric to the contrary, is not the path of the revolutionary. Litigation is incompatible with true radicalism, if radical means to go to the root, to the heart of things.[33] The law is still basically a tool for the maintenance of existing power hierarchies, and it remains inextricably tied to the status quo. Nevertheless, feminist legal theorists have had a unique role to play in the development of strategies for greater access and participation in existing structures.[34]

The role of feminist legal academics has not been incidental to the quest for equality in the law. Without the extensive contributions of legal scholars to the theorizing of what was meant by women's equality, seemingly irreconcilable differences could not have been bridged, and creative solutions for the practical attainment of women's equality could not have been conceived. The participation of women in the legal academy should not be taken for granted, however. Despite significant gains in feminist participation in some legal institutions,[35] the number of tenured women law faculty members continues to lag seriously behind in most schools. Feminist legal scholarship continues to be marginalized within many institutions, and commitment to this work is often denigrated and is sometimes even a barrier to the attainment of tenure or advancement.

Since its founding in 1985, LEAF has played an important role in the development of constitutional equality strategies and jurisprudence, and it has been instrumental in getting the Supreme Court of Canada (and by extension, lower courts) to accept a substantive definition of equality (though not always consistently), in contradistinction to the formalist one that prevailed before the *Canadian Charter of Rights and Freedoms*. Although LEAF is neither the sole nor even the best representative of feminist use of the legal system or involvement with law, it has styled itself as the leading legal feminist organization.

LEAF has relied on the contributions of feminist academics for theoretical support of their advocacy efforts in the courts. LEAF's legal committee, which is responsible for case selection, has consisted of legal academics and practitioners who share a solid commitment to feminist principles. Committee members have been identified for their individual strengths and have not necessarily had any connection to the board or to LEAF branches. In fact, the decision-making influence of the legal committee has been such that some members of the board complained of 'a tail wagging the dog' syndrome, which resulted in the non-elected body determining the priorities for a more diverse and democratically structured board. Regardless of this contentious structure, however, the quality of the work of the legal committee has never been in question.

The passage of time since the formation of LEAF has seen an evolution in the selection of legal committee members (and its subcommittees). LEAF first appointed members from racialized communities to its legal committee in 1989.[36] The heavy reliance on academic credentials and/or expertise in women's equality was both necessary and understandable.[37] The impact on diversified participation on the legal committee was also predictable. There are fewer than ten women academics from racialized communities with tenure in the legal academy. The number of practitioners from racialized communities who have not only the expertise but also the luxury of time and economic support to pursue the pro bono work for LEAF is also small. These realities are a product of systemic racism, which was replicated in LEAF's appointment processes prior to the vigilance they undertook in the early 1990s.

To a great extent, feminist legal theorists work within the framework of the common or civil law system. They are educated within these systems and are unwilling to discard them in their entirety. Given the scarcity of racialized women academics in law schools, it is fair to say that feminist legal theory will continue to suffer grave weaknesses in its capacity to apply a critical race analysis, as evidenced by the analysis in the second part of this chapter. It is not only a question of who controls knowledge production, but also a matter of how racialized women can effectively participate in the shaping of feminist litigation. Just as white feminists would find it abhorrent for their jurisprudence to be shaped, taught, and applied by 'progressive' men, racialized women challenge white feminists in academia to move beyond words to ensuring that racialized women are members of their faculties. At present, few institutions can claim to have permanently hired even one woman of colour. The burden of challenging the system critically to assess the impact of its racist legacy is not made any easier by allies who caution patience in the face of the continued exclusion of racialized women from critical points of decision-making. The development of a substantive body of critical race jurisprudence in Canadian law is just as dependent on the presence of racialized scholars in the academy as feminist legal theory is dependent on women.[38]

Reconciling Differences in Feminist Theory or 'Black Feminism Is not White Feminism in Blackface'[39]

Feminism, with its call for social justice, has transformed the political and theoretical landscape in fundamental ways. Feminism has taken on the shibboleths of liberalism and global capitalism and has put issues that concern the marginalized in society on the public agenda. It continues to challenge the assumptions that underlie society's power relations. Feminism is predicated on unity through gender and coalitions with other equality-seeking communities. This is both its grand vision and its Achilles heel.

Women from many equality-seeking communities who would challenge the assumptions that undergird the dominant discourse have assailed the effectiveness of feminist strategies and the legitimacy of those who would pursue them. The conflict between conceptual frameworks and desired results has given rise to many debates. At times, these debates have been seen as an opportunity for the flowering of new possibilities, a source of pride and a badge of courage for those feminists who have attempted to take responsibility and open themselves to other knowledge. At the same time, the debates have been seen by some as heightening the vulnerability of the movement at a point when the resistance to equality has been emboldened by a neoconservative agenda that is gaining ascendancy.

Feminism has often been placed in an oppositional stance to other theories that appear to have a totalizing world view. A similar position has been assigned to those theories that speak to issues of racism. Some of the critiques that arise from a postcolonial perspective, critical race theory, and the more rigid applications of identity politics have been seen as incompatible with feminism. Like other areas of scholarship, these bodies of theory have a significant number of male voices, many of which deny the validity of feminist perspectives. Nevertheless, these areas have also seen the increasing recognition of scholars who bring a highly nuanced feminist critique to their work.

The litigation of women's equality cases has reflected broader social patterns regarding racial issues in society. Mary Joe Frug has identified several discrete phases, from the movement from equality doctrine (denial of 'racism') to feminist theory (gender essentialism) and feminist doctrine (applications of difference theory).[40] These phases are reflected in the way early cases were silent about race, a silence that fed the presumption of a universal experience. Later, this silence gave way to an acknowledgment of how the differences between women required the selection of cases that would specifically address their varying concerns. Frug's delineation of the phases of feminist legal approaches undergirds the discussion in the three subsections that follow.

Denial of Racism

Feminist litigation in Canada and the United States has attempted to make the issues that directly affect women's lives visible to the courts. The first advocates saw this as a key factor in the effectiveness of their work. Policies and legal strategies were formed that would ostensibly address the needs of all women. One way of addressing these concerns was to look at the range of privileges and rights that had been denied women and to make arguments that would ensure them access and opportunity.

In the early stage of race denial, the focus on women as a universal category was justified since their exclusion (like that of racialized peoples) from many spheres of public life was total.[41] Arguments directed towards 'writing' women into legislation and policies would theoretically benefit *all* women. This struggle to transform definitions of legal personhood was seen as a precursor to grounding any rights argument. Efforts focused on ensuring that women had access to economic and educational opportunities that would ensure their full participation in the workforce.

Unfortunately, this approach failed to acknowledge the way in which underlying differences in women's inequalities meant that some categories of women would not benefit. The argument focused on the idea that if women were similarly situated to men, then they should – and would – be treated equally. Racialized women, however, were not similarly situated, to either Euro-Canadian men *or* Euro-Canadian women: a range of federal and provincial laws explicitly or implicitly excluded, on the basis of race, indigenous peoples and Asians from the franchise and certain occupations, among other things.[42] Racialized women thus fell between the cracks of this advocacy.

A recent example of this approach in litigation is the *Symes* case.[43] A Euro-Canadian feminist lawyer, Beth Symes, advanced in that case the argument that the costs of child care should be considered as part of the cost of doing business for professional women.[44] This case resonated with the interests of many professional middle-class women (and the rare men who had child-rearing responsibilities) who, if they pursued their career goals, were weighing their potentially increased earnings against the costs of child care to be paid with after-tax dollars. Ironically, the severe discrimination faced by their child care workers – from the Philippines, the Caribbean and other poor regions – who are penalized through a double taxation scheme, has made barely a ripple in the legal literature.[45]

The image that made a most forceful impression appeared not in the factum of the court case, but in a television interview with the plaintiff. The shot of the woman with her child and her live-in caregiver spoke volumes about the effacement of race and class. The *Symes* case truly was about increased access for women beyond the glass ceiling of male privilege. *Symes* was also about the brick wall of socioeconomic policies that increasingly found racialized women not just in the position of domestics but in the position of workers with neither labour nor civil rights, in short, in the position of indentured servants. Thus, in *Symes* there were two women, both seeking the opportunity for meaningful work, but coming from very different economic circumstances. One was the plaintiff; the other did not exist. Some Euro-Canadian feminists have discussed the socioeconomic inequities inherent in the case.[46] However, the fundamental commodification of racialized women as tax write-offs is not raised in their discussions. The links between their commodification and the earlier relationships between slave women and European women in the colonial household is obvious, and yet not commented on.

Work related to woman as mother/nurturer is undervalued. Foreign domestic workers in Canada, who are disproportionately from Third World countries, perform women's work as traditionally defined – the care of children, elderly relatives, and the household. They are among the most vulnerable of workers.[47] Employers, who are disproportionately Euro-Canadian, are complicit in the subordination of Canada's domestic workers. The undervalued work of these domestic workers facilitates Euro-Canadian women's fuller participation in the labour market.

Isolation, lack of job mobility, restrictive immigration policies, and the threat of deportation are part and parcel of the lives of domestic workers. Live-in domestic workers are typically denied private space, and they are often subject to exploitation through long work hours and in many cases, sexual abuse.[48] Euro-Canadian employers – and a few class-privileged racialized women – are supporting systemic conditions that heighten the vulnerability of other women.[49] This is compounded by the fact that the majority of domestic placement agencies are owned by women. The commitment of these women to supporting the economic independence of racialized women in other contexts may be encrusted with a racist mindset when they engage in their placement work.[50] This situation remains fundamentally unchallenged by the women's movement.

One of the ways in which respect for women can be measured is in the value placed on the work they perform.[51] Demands for pay equity are based on the demonstrated structural biases that have resulted in women receiving lower wages for work of equal value. This has occurred where women are in the same occupational category and fulfil the same role as men and in circumstances where a different role has similar value to another role performed by men in the organization. Pay equity has been less successful in challenging systemic biases where the job is basically occupied by women performing a task that is viewed as 'women's work.'

Pay equity legislation is another example, then, of how the structural inequalities that have differential impacts on racialized communities are ignored. This is the policy initiative that is most linked to the similarly situated approach. Female occupational categories are compared to predominantly or exclusively male occupational categories. The differences in the wages and benefits are viewed as a prima facie indicator of discrimination. Racialized women can benefit if they find themselves within a job category that has been found to be structurally subordinated vis-à-vis the criteria. However, women in job categories that are disproportionately or exclusively racialized, and where no or very few distinctions have been made on a gender basis, will not benefit. Racialized women who are domestics or garment workers do not have ready male comparators. Even if comparators are available, equalizing the wages of male and female workers will not serve to address the overall poor wages and working conditions experienced by members of an entire occupational category that is subject to systemic racism.

It can be argued that Euro-feminist litigators, as illustrated by their intervention in cases such as *Taylor and the Western Guard Party v. Canadian Human Rights Commission and the Attorney General of Canada*, have occasionally squarely addressed the issue of racism.[52] In that intervention, it was argued that hate messages were not a form of protected speech and functioned to promote inequality, in direct contravention of the *Charter*. The Supreme Court of Canada adopted this position. What is interesting in the intervenor's factum filed by LEAF is the complete absence of the word racism in the discussion of hate speech and its impact on vulnerable communities.

The relationship between the extreme position of hate speech as one example of racism and the invidious nature of racism in society as a whole is unclear in the factum. This is evidenced in the statement at paragraph 13 of the factum: 'Negative stereotyping and the denial of a group's humanity *can* adversely affect individual members of the group ...' (my emphasis).[53] The distinction between stereotyping and hate is not clear, obscuring the more commonplace reality of racism in the lives of many racialized peoples. It also implies that the more virulent form of stereotyping contained in hate speech has a more significant impact on the individuals and communities concerned than do other forms of racism. This is not necessarily the case. The heightened visibility of hate speech also means that it is less pervasive and more socially deplored, whereas the systemic forms of racism that ensure the socioeconomic and political subordination of racialized men, women, and children go unchallenged.

A further blurring of the distinction between hate speech and issues of systemic discrimination occurred in the arguments put forward by LEAF as intervenors in *R. v. Keegstra*:[54] 'the willful public promotion of group hatred is a violent form of expression because it is an integral link in systemic discrimination that keeps target groups in subordinated positions through the promotion of fear, intolerance, segregation, exclusion, disparagement, vilification, degradation, violence, and genocide.'[55] While this paragraph is clearly meant to outline the devastating impact of hate speech on its subject groups, the failure explicitly to define systemic discrimination blurs the issue. This represents a missed opportunity to establish a working definition of racism which could have become a working definition for courts faced with systemic racism involving other communities. Is this meant to be a definition of systemic discrimination, in whole or in part, or is it an articulation of the impact of hate speech? Given the scarcity of theorizing on racism put before the Supreme Court of Canada, it becomes more important than ever to ensure that definitions are provided, experiences named, and subtleties articulated. This critique is directed to the obverse side of the coin of responsibility towards others, which comes with the authority of voice that LEAF has successfully established over the years. The valuable role LEAF has played in advancing equality arguments before the courts for women comes with the price tag of ensuring that the interests of the entire diversity of women are fully explored and protected.

Gender Essentialism

In the second phase of feminist litigation, prevalent in feminist academic work of the 1970s, the term 'woman' became a homogenization of women's experience. This approach was defined by its search for those qualities deemed unique to women and their social realities. It was not necessarily characterized by a denial of women's differences. All differences between women were subordinated to that which was held in common.

From the 1970s onward, feminist legal theory began explicitly to reject the implicitly male standards used earlier. What women wanted and how their desires could be achieved required adjustments to previous indicators of success. The role that institutional structures and values played in shaping women's understandings of themselves moved to the forefront of the debate.

The theoretical foundation of what later came to be termed 'feminist essentialism' rested on the way in which the identified 'female' qualities would be protected or responded to in the development of feminist legal theory. (By this time the reader has noticed my attempts to put in cultural identifiers whenever they might assist in understanding the context for a theoretical position. I have not done so with gender essentialism. Gender essentialism has been associated in large part with Euro-American feminists, of whom Catharine McKinnon is most often used as an example. However, the ideological position regarding notions of a female essence is not limited to women of European descent.)

Essentialism took on a naturalizing interpretation of 'woman' as a set of inborn biological attributes and focused on the ways in which social practices were informed by that biology.[56] Basic attributes (such as childbearing) and the rigid social roles that have developed from social understandings of women's sexuality have led to the prioritizing of a number of legal issues. Demands for universal child care, reproductive freedom, antiviolence campaigns, and amendments to legislation such as that governing pregnancy benefits were intended to reflect women's reality.

The result of the search for essential traits assisted theorists in establishing the boundaries of issues that were feminist. While debates about the scope and relevance of 'nature versus nurture' abound within feminism,[57] it was assumed in the mainstream feminist literature that shared vulnerabilities and experiences of sex discrimination did link women together across the divides of class, geography, and culture.

The uniqueness of women's experiences as women became the yardstick by which to define what social policies were needed. Yet accommodation of women's needs through maternity benefits and changing the environment of the workplace to accommodate child care are not sufficient. Issues such as the 'nature' of women's decision-making, the way in which our values may shape organizational structures, and the question of whether there is a transcendent 'woman's view' of the world remain unresolved.

The problem of acknowledging diversity and working towards solutions for the inclusion of difference has become increasingly complex. The omnipresent male 'enemy,' the strength of the forces of resistance, and the pressing need for action have often made criticism of gender essentialism appear ill-timed at best, an act of betrayal at worst. Euro-feminism sought to reconcile its theoretical gaps by an ever-widening ideology that consumes and subsumes other frameworks.[58]

The definition of 'woman' as seen from Euro-Canadian feminist perspectives is often incompatible with the actual experiences of racialized women. Feminist essentialism contributes to the maintenance of unconscious and explicit systemic racism.[59] Euro-feminism is part of the psychic dissonance that pervades much of Euro-western thought.[60] Euro-patriarchy has been constructed on the subjugation of others and the totalizing of other identities in furtherance of specific economic and cultural aims. When Euro-feminists seek equality within male structures, they often cease critically to inquire into how their location, education, and theoretical frameworks may make that position incompatible with the values, rights, and needs of racialized women.

Many racialized women have taken the view that 'white women's equality with white men is dependent upon race hierarchy.'[61] The balancing of an effective political strategy by racialized women that would address the relationship between Euro-patriarchy and patriarchy as a universal concept is a challenge that racialized women have been grappling with, while many Euro-feminists are alternately ignorant, appalled, or confused. Racialized women have acknowledged the impacts that Euro-patriarchy has had on their entire communities – men, women, and children and the lands to which they are inextricably connected.

Systemic racism, while gendered, affects all racialized women, men, and children at the social and institutional levels, though to varying degrees. From that perspective, Euro-patriarchy is embodied in both men and women who have power and influence over the lives of racialized peoples. There is no exemption simply because Euro-feminists may also be political allies. Thus, the tendency of Euro-feminists to totalize all male oppression without acknowledging their own participation in the exploitation and reinforcement of racist practices against racialized men and women is a source of divisiveness.[62] While Euro-feminists have a solid base of knowledge and experience from which to critique Euro-patriarchy, their largely unsuccessful attempts to address issues of racism within feminist organizations are symptomatic of the theoretical vacuum on which they base incorporation of racialized men into that world view.[63]

The way in which the gender category operates for racialized women has often been denied by Euro-feminists in their quest to advance sex equality. Two cases serve as illustrations of this point. First, in *Conway v. The Queen*[64] LEAF intervened, together with the Minority Advocacy Rights Council (MARC), against a challenge by a male prisoner who claimed that his privacy rights were being violated by the presence of female prison guards. LEAF argued for the rights of female prison guards to work in correctional institutions in circumstances that involved observing male prisoners at all times, including those when they might be unclothed and during the performance of intimate searches. In the second case, *R. v. Butler*,[65] LEAF argued that pornography is not a form of protected speech but rather it is discrimination against women as individuals and as a collectivity, and thus a violation of *Charter* equality rights. At first glance, these cases appear unrelated, one dealing with women's right to work and the other with the sexual objectification of women through pornography. However, the following discussion will focus on how the disparate ways of viewing male and female bodies seen through the valence of a critical race analysis affects the interpretations offered by LEAF in both instances.

In the first issue area, it must be noted that women's struggle to gain access to predominantly male fields of work has been a long and difficult one. The resistance to including women in correctional institutions has been a conflation of sexism (it is a man's job), machismo (it is a tough, violent job), and paternalism (women should not have to experience the harshness of prison life). Female correctional officers have struggled to gain respect for their competence in this area. The position taken by the individual prisoner in this case was one that would deny many women jobs. It is a simple fact that there are far more correctional institutions for men than there are for women.

The prisoner's privacy rights claim was viewed as suspect by many women's rights advocates. As a member of LEAF's legal committee at the time, I suggested in the initial legal committee meeting that as between the rights of a female correctional officer and a prisoner, the prisoner was the most vulnerable given his social location and lack of rights. Furthermore, I noted that the impact of systemic racism meant that a disproportionate number of the prisoners being spoken about were men from racialized communities and that the women being spoken of were largely of Euro-Canadian descent. At this point, I was informed that this was (a) not a proper gender analysis and (b) not a proper critical race analysis, either![66] After raising the issues of marginalization and exclusion that I experienced, I was informed that my comments were taken into consideration and addressed within the factum on further discussion. The group ignored that I explicitly defined my analysis as an integrated whole, and they selectively edited it to meet their own interest and comfort zones. I felt strongly that this was not an appropriate case for presuming that gender 'trumped' race without a more substantial analysis.

From my perspective, the legal committee's decision to fragment my analysis effectively invalidated my contribution and stripped me of expertise, and I therefore left the committee. Ironically, my absence somehow enabled the committee to discuss my ideas more openly. I was later informed that my feelings of anger were misplaced since some of my comments had indeed been considered and accepted. The power dynamic that enabled two Euro-Canadian feminists to define me out of the feminist fold and that of critical race scholarship remained unexamined by all participants. This was compounded by their willingness to presume consent in my absence for the very issue on which I based my objections – the piecemeal appropriation of my analysis.

The piecemeal approach to the analysis of how social inequality occurs was at issue between the different intervenors in the case. Prisoners are by definition among the least privileged in society, their transgressions being punished by the restriction of their freedom. The right to control what happens to one's body is one of our most elementary rights. In citing the ways in which men react to privacy issues, it is not sufficient to note the differences between male and female prisoners, since their privacy interests have been protected in different ways throughout history. Unlike the approach taken by LEAF in *Andrews*, which acknowledged rights in conflict, no suggestions were made which could serve as guidelines to negotiate these potentially conflicting bases for rights.

The factum failed to acknowledge the ways in which males from different cultures and social contexts might view privacy in the racist context of the Canadian penal system. Instead, a glib reference to difference actually served to trivialize it. Historically, the ways in which male bodies have been racialized have furthered racist stereotypes. In addition, notions of female privacy and pristine European womanhood have furthered the criminalization of racialized males for transgressions that have been transposed to the level of attacks on the body politic. Acknowledgment of this reality would ask whether a liberal approach of increasing the number of women correctional officers from racialized communities is really a solution.

In the second case, *Butler*, despite its obvious merit in advancing women's equality, the decision does raise the issue of how Euro-feminism has ignored the ways in which racialized men and women have been eroticized in the pornographic imagination.[67] LEAF's factum omitted analysis of how racialized men are used in pornography. There is also an assumption that the harm to men is individual, but as a group they are advantaged. This is evidenced in statements such as: 'this harm does not define the social status and treatment of men as a group. Indeed, there is *no systematic data* to support the view that men are harmed by pornography' (my emphasis). This only holds true if the experiences of racialized men are erased. The pornographic imagination is treated as unique, when it is merely an extension of how racialized peoples are perceived. The colonizing relationship sexualized the power relationship between racialized women and men and Europeans. The non-European Other was a distorted amalgam of the exotic, the forbidden, the feared, and the commodified.

The role of colonialism in the Americas in objectifying black African men and women gives insight to another face of pornography, its non-sensual, non-erotic face – the face of power unmasked. That the deepest race fantasies made flesh were sometimes sexual does not make them the only or the most significant aspect of colonial slave relations.[68] While it attributed dangerous sexuality to hyper-masculinized black men, slavery simultaneously masculinized black femaleness. The asexual worker and the nurturing mammy were part of the defining of enslaved women. The same woman could also be sexually rapacious. However, rape of black women by white men did not take place because consent could always be presumed.[69] The same period also solidified the construction of the black male rapist with his desire for white flesh, heightened sexual performance, and bestial aggression. It should be noted that while pedophilia is now and was then aberrant, no moral or legal sanctions protected African children. This process of sexualization was not only gendered – its targets and victims were the men, women, and children of Africa.

Various criticisms were levelled at the arguments in *Butler*, in part for its characterization of gay male sexuality and for its failure to distinguish gay and lesbian erotica from the heterosexist pornography at issue.[70] Some felt that the failure to consider that lesbian and gay erotica would be an immediate target of police and Customs officials revealed the pervasiveness of the heterosexist bias in the argument, although it should be noted that antipornography lesbian scholars were prominent strategists in the case. However, it was a costly oversight. There was a failure to recognize that the discretion to exercise judgments about what was pornographic or obscene would reinforce dominant societal views of what constituted sexual perversity.[71] Customs officials startled many by seizing a book of cultural criticism by a prominent African-American feminist, bell hooks, in one of the first applications of the *Butler* test. Government officials misread her text. Non-erotic, nonpornographic – it is blackness itself, and outspoken female blackness, in particular, that is aberrant.[72]

The *Butler* decision also raised questions beyond the heterosexist/non-heterosexist dynamic. Racialized peoples are eroticized within the European sexual imagination. Lesbian and gay erotica, like heterosexist erotica, is also rooted in the perversity of the colonial mind with its racist conceptualizations of the non-European. The commodification of the sexuality of black African people and other racialized peoples is similar whether directed towards heterosexuals or the gay and lesbian community. The non-heterosexual world is not necessarily less prone to fetishize and eroticize racial difference.

Pornography identifies a cultural battle zone where women and politics are sexualized.[73] It has always dealt with issues beyond the sexual, including a variety of practices that involve the exploitation of women. For example, Kathleen Mahoney analyses the link between pornography and a range of abusive practices against women – wife battery, prostitution, incest, genital mutilation, bride-selling, rape, sexual harassment, and child abuse.[74] All of these practices are sex discrimination and are a manifestation of patriarchal domination in the societies in which they occur. However, pornography does not necessarily play the same pivotal role in these practices everywhere and at all times. Pornography as referred to in this context is largely a western phenomenon of the nineteenth and twentieth centuries.[75]

Some practices discussed by Mahoney predate the phenomenon of western pornography or are present in cultures where the consumption of pornography is not the principal source of the subordination of women. This is particularly true in cultures where the practices find their justification in religious interpretation. Detached from history, a decontextualized and deracialized analysis may result in ineffective solutions with little chance of addressing the problem of the exploitation of black women and men in pornography.[76]

Critical sexual politics has challenged the ways in which sexualized identities have shaped contemporary social roles and affected sociopolitical relationships. To identify as lesbian, gay, bisexual, or transgendered is to stand in opposition to heterosexist hegemony. To be a member of a racialized community whether heterosexually identified or not, is also to participate in an interrogation of Euro-patriarchy. One of the intriguing aspects of this perspective is how the examination of the role of racialized images on the erotic/pornographic imagination provides insight into Euro-consciousness.

Beyond the Confinement of Gender 319

Race Consciousness and the Fracturing of Feminist Universality

In the 1980s, postmodern theory, with its shifting categories, provided a basis for feminist legal theorists to respond to the criticisms of gender essentialism.[77] What came to be known as anti-essentialism involved placing women in their specific contexts. Women's multiple identities were now taken into consideration.[78] The nature of difference and how it was articulated was validated as feminists moved to concern with the diversity within.[79] But as Razack points out, 'when it became impossible to ignore the whiteness of theory or practice, the omission was viewed as accidental and therefore easily remedied by adding on these new and troublesome subjects of research.'[80] This was a poor substitute for a critical understanding of difference, however.

Racialized women do not subscribe to the totality of Euro-feminist values. Notions of femininity and the nature of both the oppression and identification of the oppressor do not have agreed-upon definitions, nor are they understood in the same ways. For example, slavery and modern society have created different understandings of agency and autonomy. Racialized women existed in a realm outside middle-class norms of femininity. Differences in the experience of the family and the way in which consensual adult relationships were restricted provided racialized communities with opportunities to examine and shape male–female relationships that were not provided on such a systematic basis to European women, particularly those of the middle classes.

While racialized women's challenges to Euro-feminist gender equality discourses appear to have fractured the imagined solidarity of the 'women's movement,' Euro-feminists must acknowledge that while they challenge, they also participate in the replication of some master narratives – such as the state and the citizen. Liberal feminist quests for equality with men can mask racial inequalities. The argument about collective versus individual rights can mask that the state is about a particular interpretation of collective rights or group existence. Multiculturalism in service to the state becomes part of the master narrative. Uncritical support for multiculturalism with its liberal support for 'difference' means accepting a cynical government concept whose policies are often disjointed because of the absence of an equality-based analysis. What is most destructive, however, is the manipulation of diversity in a manner that meets the needs and interests of the dominant society.[81] A distorted multi-'culture' emerges that is actually one of 'managing diversity.' Euro-feminists continue to struggle to forge a notion of cultural difference that is truly transformative.

As Homi Bhabha has argued, 'The whole nature of the public sphere is changing so that we really do need the notion of a politics which is based on unequal, uneven, multiple and potentially antagonistic political identities.'[82] The incorporation of the politics of 'differences' within feminist legal theory has had a decidedly liberal cast, however. While 'difference' is not synthesized, it is presumed that an accommodation can be reached that would enable all feminists to coexist within the same political theoretical framework. The dangers of this approach have been discussed with regard to superficial correspondence between discrimination based on sexuality and that of race. That which is not reconcilable is deemed secondary, as the anticensorship feminists discovered in *Butler* when their points of view were defined out of the feminist theory being put before the courts.[83]

For racialized women, the incorporation of an analysis based on difference has meant that the impact of racism in their lives could become a legitimate part of feminist legal strategizing. It has also meant that the positive aspects of cultural differences could be acknowledged. In this approach, the acknowledgment of difference provides a small though limited opportunity for the participation of racialized women in the shaping of the discourse within Euro-feminist theory.

Racialized women have an 'epistemic advantage' that flows from their experiences.[84] It is this reality that flows through the work of black feminist critics who speak of voices of authenticity and the need for acknowledgment of the expertise that flows from historical and contemporary experience.[85] However, 'multiplicity of experience does not necessarily mean that one decided to inhabit two contexts critically.'[86] A critique based on consciousness permits the creation of a racialized identity unbounded by Euro-consciousness.

A very hopeful sign in the movement towards a more explicit acceptance of this approach can be found in LEAF's factum for *O'Connor v. The Queen*,[87] a co-intervention with the Aboriginal Women's Council, the Canadian Association of Sexual Assault Centres, and the DisAbled Women's Network. The immediate issue in the case involved the disclosure of therapeutic records to third parties, to wit, to the accused, Bishop O'Connor, who was tried for raping and/or sexually assaulting four Aboriginal girls at a residential school in the 1960s in breach of his fiduciary responsibilities. A number of records were at issue in this particular case, including the residential school records, although the issue of disclosure involves all manner of records, from abortion, to child welfare, to prison records. The records at issue in *O'Connor* were not neutral, neither did they carry the same privacy aspects as records generated by consent in a therapeutic context. These records were created in a context where: (a) institutional interests and personal biases would have shaped their creation and made them highly suspect as racist documents; (b) historically, confidentiality and privacy would not have been accorded to Aboriginal children or their parents in this context; and (c) the records would not have been made with their consent. It is ironic that the victims were in the position of having records, possibly created by their abuser, but certainly created in the racist context of the residential schools, form part of the case against them. In the event, the complainant's right to privacy lost ground in the Supreme Court of Canada's attempts to safeguard the interests of the accused, in the course of which the specific historical context and nature of the records at issue were lost on the court.

Throughout the discussion of the courts and legal policy-makers the role of colonialism and the significance of this case for Aboriginal peoples was a mere whisper in the background. Yet, while colonialism was not identified by the Court as the source of the residential schools, it is clearly the cause of the heightened vulnerability of Aboriginal children and women to violence.[88] The engagement with colonialism as a framework for the analysis was hinted at in the LEAF factum. It may be that the tentative nature of the language reflects a view that the Court is not yet ready to grapple with this concept as an essential point of departure for its analysis.[89] It remains to be seen whether this tentative step towards a critique of the fundamental historical structures of privilege in Canadian society will be followed by increasingly bolder steps on the part of LEAF.

Conclusion

The distinctions between race, racism, culture, and multiculturalism and who 'owns' these issues confounds many theorists. Nevertheless, those who are most vulnerable to the ravages of racism are not in exclusive possession of the discussion nor of the work towards solutions. The breadth of systemic racism and its impact on global economics leaves none of us untouched. Racialized women have raised a challenge to the hegemony of Euro-feminist theory: Let us transcend the shallow external construction of self based on colour alone and seek to advance a politic that acknowledges the historic realities of oppression while asserting the liberating possibilities embedded within our distinct cultures. We must remember that no one discourse or historiography has the ethicopolitical legitimacy to represent the totality, and that the concept of 'totality' should be understood not as a pre-given horizon but as the necessary and inevitable 'effect' or function of the many relational dialogues, contestations, and asymmetries among the many positions (and their particular-universal ideologies) that constitute the total field.'[90]

The practical implication of the critique offered by racialized women has been to change feminist legal strategy in theory and practice. Although commendable work has been done throughout the feminist engagement with Canadian courts, much remains to be done. Determining a proper course of feminist legal action into the future necessitates looking at where we have been. The denial of racism has resulted in the reinforcement of class and race inequity in the labour market. Gender essentialism has obfuscated the role which Euro-Canadian women have played in the economic, sexual, and political exploitation of racialized women and men.

The intention of this chapter was not simply to criticize feminist legal interventions with the benefit of hindsight. It was to show how the inclusion of racialized women is both a vibrant possibility and a necessity for feminist legal theory. We need not fear that adherence to difference will reduce feminist solidarity to its constituent elements.[90] Our training and exposure to Euro-western values and institutions can be used effectively, and a critical perspective can be brought into the courts.[91]

Feminist legal practitioners would benefit us all by following these broad steps: First, feminist litigators should approach their analysis of a given case from a critical historical perspective so that they may recognize how colonialism could have contributed racist practice under examination in the current situation. Second, we should analyse whether and how race enters the equation by distinguishing direct discrimination and systemic racism from issues of culture, cultural assimilation/integration, multiculturalism, and diversity. Third, once the issue at law has been identified, a critical examination should be undertaken of the procedural rules, legal concepts, and area of the law for inherent bias, Eurocentrism, and disproportional impact on racialized communities. Fourth, the litigation should be strategic in the use of expert testimony, academic literature, and consultations, taking into consideration how power both constructs knowledge and defines the issues. Fifth, we need to consider how to communicate effectively or engage in an educational process with the court, fellow counsel, and the client to further their understanding of the complexity of the issues as they relate to race and intersecting inequalities. Sixth, we must be vigilant to ensure that legal arguments are not made by analogy to other grounds of discrimination which could limit the applicability of the solution, deny the existence of racism, or erode the potential for a truly transformative jurisprudence to address issues of racism. Seventh, we should assess carefully the context and applicability of strategic solutions developed in critical race theory for other sociopolitical contexts to ensure that they are relevant to the community in which the case has arisen. Finally, feminist litigators should consider whether a simultaneous or alternative strategy beyond the courtroom is necessary or more likely to further the discussion about racism.

We must be ever vigilant to ensure that the identities of racialized women remain fluid. We must guard against the commodification of our cultures and the making of our differences into a fetish for consumption within the Euro-feminist academy. Most particularly, we must keep in mind that we are our own best advocates and our own most critical analysts, if we claim responsibility for ourselves. There has been an evolution in the strategies used by feminists to work in coalition as evidenced by the number of co-interventions. However, co-interventions with racialized communities are reflective of a lack of resources within our communities. Ultimately, racialized women must speak for themselves and design their strategies without equivocation. Unfortunately, the accumulated impact of systemic exclusion from law schools, law firms, and the judiciary means that much more remains to be done before our voices are powerful enough to make the eradication of racism a priority and source of heightened consciousness in Canadian courts.[92]

Notes

1 See L. Tran, 'The Canadian Charter of Rights and Freedoms: Justification, Methods and Limits of a Multicultural Interpretation' (1996) 26 *Columbia Human Rights Law Review* 33; and William Conklin, 'Human Rights, Language and Law: A Survey of Semiotics and Phenomenology' (1995) 27 *Ottawa Law Review* (OLR) 129.

2 For a discussion of how the search for categories has hampered the Supreme Court of Canada's capacity fully to realize equality, see Douglas Kropp, '"Categorical" Failure: Canada's Equality Jurisprudence – Changing Notions of Identity and the Legal Subject' (1997) 23 *Queen's Law Journal* 201.

3 The 1970 *Report of the Royal Commission on the Status of Women* is credited by many as the catalyst for feminist legal scholarship in Canada, but see Toni Williams, 'Re-Forming "Women's" Truth: A Critique of the Report of the Royal Commission on the Status of Women in Canada,' (1990) 22 *OLR* 725.

4 The federal government and some of its provincial counterparts have consulted with women's organizations in response to and prior to the promulgation of legislation they perceive will have a direct impact on women's lives. A clear example of an effective consultation process was the amendments to the *Criminal Code* on sexual assault after the Supreme Court of Canada struck down the 'rape shield' law in *R. v. Seaboyer* (1991) 83 D.L.R. (4th) 193. See also the discussion of this issue by Sheila McIntyre in this volume. These consultations have not been unproblematic, as shown in the extensive analysis of the process leading to the 'stalking' amendment by Rosemary Cairns-Way, 'The Criminalization of Stalking: An Exercise in Media Manipulation and Political Opportunism' (1994) 39 *McGill Law Journal (MLJ)* 379.

5 The activities of the National Action Committee on the Status of Women (NAC) were subjected to harsh criticism from within and outside the feminist community during the tenure of Sunera Thobani, its first president from a racialized community. Judy Rebick, a former president of NAC, has noted that the layers of racism which permeate NAC (or any organization committed to the eradication of racism) have distorted the perceptions of their political activism. See Judy Rebick, 'Bridging Identity: A Creative Response to Identity Politics,' in J. Littleton, ed., *Clash of Identities: Essays on Media, Manipulation and Politics of the Self* (Toronto: Prentice-Hall, 1996) 38. In fact, equality advocacy is an ongoing process and expectations are often greatest because the potential response of equality-seeking organizations is so great. We often forget that many social and political institutions are totally unresponsive to many of the concerns expressed in this chapter.

6 See Women's Legal Education and Action Fund (LEAF), *Equality and the Charter: Ten Years of Feminist Advocacy before the Supreme Court of Canada* (Toronto: Emond Montgomery, 1996) 5. See also Joan Brockman and Dorothy Chunn, eds., *Gender Bias: Law, Courts and the Legal Profession* (Toronto: Thompson Educational Publishing, 1993) 5–6.

7 [1997] 3 S.C.R. 484.
8 I problematize the term 'race' here to signify my understanding of it as a socially constructed category rather than as a biological distinction. See Sherene Razack, 'Beyond Universal Women: Reflections on Theorizing Differences among Women' (1996) 45 *University of New Brunswick Law Journal (UNBLJ)* 217. Also see R. Austin, 'Black Women, Sisterhood and the Difference/Deviance Divide' (1992) 26 *New England Law Review (NELR)* 7; P. Caldwell, 'A Hair Piece: Perspectives on the Intersection of Race and Gender' (1991) *Duke Law Journal (DJL)* 365; Kimberle Crenshaw, 'Mapping the Margins: Intersectionality, Identity Politics and Violence against Women of Color' (1991) 43 *Stanford Law Review (SLR)* 1241; Trina Grillo and Stephanie Wildman, 'Obscuring the Importance of Race: The Implication of Making Comparisons between Racism and Sexism (or Other-Isms)' (1991) *DLJ* 397; Angela Harris, 'Race and Essentialism in Feminist Legal Theory' (1990) 42 *SLR* 581.
9 The universalizing of the term 'critical race theory' has masked, however, the different streams of analysis which racialized scholars have advanced more broadly in social, political, and literary theory. See Carol Aylward, *Canadian Critical Race Theory: Racism and the Law* (Halifax: Fernwood Publishing, 1999). See especially Aylward's discussion of critical race feminism (35–8) and chap. 3, 'Canadian Critical Race Litigation: Wedding Theory to Practice,' 76–133; and E. Brown, 'The Tower of Babel: Bridging the Divide between Critical Race Theory and "Mainstream" Civil Rights' (1995) 105 *Yale Law Journal (YLJ)* 513.
10 Feminist legal activists have made it their primary concern to contextualize the law in such a manner that sex discrimination is acknowledged and addressed. But see Sherene Razack, 'Exploring the Omissions and Silences in Law around Race,' in Brockman and Chunn, eds, *Gender Bias*, 38.
11 See Joanne St Lewis, 'Judicial Decision-Making at the Crossroads,' prepared for the National Judicial Institute, and Joanne St Lewis, 'Race, Racism and the Justice System,' in Carl James, ed., *Perspectives on Racism and the Human Services Sector: A Case for Change* (Toronto: University of Toronto Press, 1996) 104.
12 Alienation of property in this context refers to the right to use and dispose of one's property. See the *Report of the Royal Commission on Aboriginal Peoples*, vol. 1, chap. 9, 'The Indian Act: Oppressive Measures' (Ottawa: Minister of Supply and Services Canada, 1996) 283.
13 For an extensive discussion of the history of the doctrine of *stare decisis* and its evolution see Christian Bourbonnais Hyde, 'Le précédent: de force morale à méthode administrative' (1992) 24 *OLR* 463.

14 See discussion of the role of precedent in shaping the judicial decision-making process in St Lewis, 'Judicial Decision-Making.'
15 Liberalism is situated in its theoretical context in Richard Devlin, 'Mapping Legal Theory' (1994) 32 *Alberta Law Review* (*ALR*) 602. Liberalism itself is a fluid term which has been criticized from different perspectives, as seen in Mark Tushnet, 'The Possibilities of Interpretive Liberalism' (1991) 29 *ALR* 276; or H. Bielefeldt, 'Carl Schmitt's Critique of Reconstruction and Countercriticism' (1997) 10 *Canadian Journal of Law and Jurisprudence* (*CJLJ*) 65.
16 Catherine Bell explains how precedent, which relies on the Euro-Canadian jurisprudential construction of status Indians and Inuit, is used further to disadvantage Métis people, in her article 'Métis Constitutional Rights in Section 35(1)' (1997) 36 *ALR* 180.
17 The full quotation from Audre Lorde bears setting out: '*For the master's tools will never dismantle the master's house.* They may allow us temporarily to beat him at his own game, but they will never enable us to bring about genuine change. And this fact is only threatening to those women who still define the master's house as their only source of support.' See *Sister Outsider: Essays and Speeches* (Freedom, CA: Crossing Press, 1984) 112.
18 See discussion in J. St Lewis and S. Galloway, 'Reforming the Defence of Provocation.' Prepared for the Federal/Provincial/Territorial Ministers of Justice Working Group, 1994.
19 Harry Glasbeek, 'A Report on the Attorney-General's Files, Prosecutions and Coroners' Inquests Arising out of Police Shootings in the Ontario Criminal Justice System 1993.' Identified as a background paper entitled 'Police Shootings of Black People in Ontario' in the *Report of the Commission on Systemic Racism in the Ontario Criminal Justice System* (Toronto: Queen's Printer for Ontario, 1995).
20 See a more extensive discussion about the link between liberalism and the legal system in St Lewis, 'Race, Racism.'
21 See Amina Mama, *Beyond the Masks: Race, Gender and Subjectivity* (New York: Routledge, 1995) 17.
22 For a reflection of the absence/presence of women in the Australian courts, see Regina Graycar, 'The Gender of Judgements: Some Reflections on "Bias"' (1998) 32 *University of British Columbia Law Review* (*UBCLR*) 1.
23 Jennifer Nedelsky, 'Address' at the Inauguration of the F.R. Scott Chair on Constitutional Law, McGill University, 1996, 20.
24 In 1997 the Canadian Bar Association appointed a working group on racial equality in the legal profession as a follow-up to the *Touchstones* report on gender equality in the legal profession; it tabled a final report with recom-

mendations at its midwinter meeting of February 1999. The report and recommendations are available at www.cba.org. See also 'Ontario, Report of the Canadian Bar Association Task Force on Gender Equality in the Legal Profession: 'Appendix on Women of Colour in the Legal Profession,' by Her Hon. Judge Corinne Sparks, in *Touchstones for Change: Equality, Diversity and Accountability* (Ottawa: Canadian Bar Association, 1993); Shelina Neallani, 'Women of Colour in the Legal Profession: Facing the Familiar Barriers of Race and Sex' (1992) 5 *Canadian Journal of Women and Law (CJWL)* 148; and Sherene Razack, 'Speaking for Ourselves: Feminist Jurisprudence and Minority Women' (1990–1) 4 *CJWL* 440.
25 Note the strong dissent by Freeman J., however, in *R. v. R.D.S.* (1995), 145 N.S.R. (2d) 292–5 (C.A.).
26 See Richard Devlin's extensive review of the history of judicial bias in 'We Can't Go On Together with Suspicious Minds: Judicial Bias and Racialized Perspectives in *R. v. R.D.S.*' (1995) 18 *Dalhousie Law Journal (DLJ)* 408.
27 *Royal Commission on the Donald Marshall Jr Prosecution* (Halifax: Royal Commission, 1989).
28 See Sparks, 'Women of Colour.'
29 In her oral reasons in the case, Judge Sparks remarked: 'The Crown says, well, why would the officer say that events occurred the way in which he has relayed them to the Court this morning. I am not saying that the Constable has misled the Court, although police officers have been known to do that in the past. And I am not saying that the officer overreacted, but certainly police officers do overreact, particularly when they are dealing with non-white groups. That to me indicates a state of mind right there that is questionable. I believe that probably the situation in this particular case is the case of a young police officer who overreacted. And I do accept the evidence of [R.D.S.] that he was told to shut up or he would be under arrest. It seems to be in keeping with the prevalent attitude of the day.' See *R. v. S. (R.D.)* [1997], 10 C.R. (5th) 1 (S.C.C.) 26.
30 See also Carol Aylward, 'The Long Way Home: *R.D.S.* – The Journey' (1998) 47 *UNBLJ* 249; P. Hughes, '*R.D.S.*: A New Direction in Judicial Impartiality,' (1999) 9 *National Journal of Constitutional Law (NJCL)* 251; Sherene Razack, '*R.D.S. v. R.*: A Case about Home' (1998) 9 *Constitutional Forum* 59.
31 Factum of the Intervenors, Women's Legal Education and Action Fund and National Organization of Immigrant and Visible Minority Women of Canada for *R.D.S. v. Her Majesty the Queen*. Other intervenors included the National Organization of Immigrant and Visible Minority Women, the Afro-Canadian Caucus of Nova Scotia, the African Canadian Legal Clinic,

and the Congress of Black Women of Canada. *R. v. R.D.S.*, [1997] 3 S.C.R. 484.
32 See reasons per Justices La Forest, L'Heureux-Dubé, Gonthier, and McLachlin in *R. v. R.D.S.*, [1997] 3 S.C.R. 484. For analyses of the case and its ramifications, see the Editor's Forum on *R. v. R.D.S.* in (1998) 10, 1 *CJWL*: 159–212.
33 See Angela Davis, *Women, Race and Class* (New York: Vintage Books, 1983).
34 See Sherene Razack, *Canadian Feminism and the Law: The Women's Legal Education and Action Fund and the Pursuit of Equality* (Toronto: Second Story Press, 1991).
35 In 1996, the University of Windsor Faculty of Law appointed Juanita Westmoreland-Traore to its deanship. She was the first racialized woman to become dean of one of Canada's twenty-one law faculties. She was appointed to the Quebec bench in 1999, where she became the first racialized woman to join the Quebec judiciary. While data on the faculty (tenured and tenure-track) representation is not available, representation of women has improved moderately in many faculties. At the same time, racialized professors have token representation, and many faculties have yet to appoint their first professor from a racialized community. The demographics of law school classes have been steadily shifting better to reflect the representation of women in the broader population. However, the participation of racialized communities in law school student bodies still lags far behind.
36 The appointees were Penny Desjarlais, then constitutional adviser to the Native Council of Canada, and Joanne St Lewis, then Director of the Education Equity Program of the Faculty of Law of the University of Ottawa. Both were graduates of the University of British Columbia Law Faculty class of 1983.
37 Himani Bannerji, a sociology professor from York University, was the first non-legally trained member appointed to the legal committee.
38 See Esmeralda Thornhill, 'Ethics in the Legal Profession: The Issue of Access' (1995) 33 *ALR* 810.
39 Lorde, *Sister Outsider*.
40 See Mary Joe Frug, *Postmodern Legal Feminism* (New York: Routledge, 1992) 4. The parentheses correspond to the headings in my section and do not reflect headings relied on by Frug.
41 This much became evident in the so-called Persons case in which the 1867 *Constitution Act*'s exclusion of women from eligibility for the Senate was challenged. See *Reference re: British North America Act 1867 (U.K.) Section 24*, [1928] S.C.R. 276.

42 See James W. St G. Walker, *'Race,' Rights and the Law in the Supreme Court of Canada* (Waterloo, ON: Wilfrid Laurier University Press, 1997).
43 *Symes v. Canada* (1993), 110 D.L.R. (4th) 470 (S.C.C.).
44 For more detailed discussions of the relationship between child care, women's equality, and taxation, see Claire Young, '(In)visible Inequalities: Women, Tax and Poverty' (1995) 27 *OLR* 99; and Lorne Sossin, 'Redistributing Democracy: An Inquiry into Authority, Discretion and the Possibility of Engagement in the Welfare State' (1994) 26 *OLR* 1.
45 See Geneviève Hamada-Plank, 'Double Taxation: Riding on the Backs of Filipino Export Labour' (1997) 29 *OLR* 395. See also Bakan and Stasiulis in this volume.
46 See Judy Fudge, 'Reconceiving Employment Standards Legislation: Labour Law's Little Sister and the Feminization of Labour' (1991) 7 *Journal of Law and Social Policy* (*JLSP*) 73; and Fudge, 'Limiting Equity: The Definition of "Employment" under the Ontario Pay Equity Act' (1990) 4, 2 *CJWL* 556.
47 Abigail Bakan and Daiva Stasiulis, 'Making the Match: Domestic Placement Agencies and the Racialization of Women's Household Work' (1995) 20 *Signs: Journal of Women in Culture and Society* 306.
48 See Bakan and Stasiulis in this volume and Audrey Macklin, 'Foreign Domestic Worker: Surrogate Housewife or Mail Order Servant?' (1992) 37 *MLJ* 681.
49 Bakan and Stasiulis, 'Making the Match,' 308.
50 Ibid., 313.
51 For a more extensive discussion about the structured inequalities of the labour market, see Judy Fudge, 'Rungs on the Labour Law Ladder: Using Gender to Challenge Hierarchy' (1996) 60 *Saskatchewan Law Review* (*SLR*) 237.
52 *Canada (Human Rights Commission) v. Taylor*, [1990] 3 S.C.R. 892.
53 LEAF, *Equality and the Charter*, 122.
54 *R. v. Keegstra*, [1990] 3 S.C.R. 697.
55 LEAF, *Equality and the Charter*, 140.
56 See Drucilla Cornell, *Beyond Accommodation: Ethical Feminism Deconstruction, and the Law* (New York: Routledge, 1991) 15.
57 See Frug, *Postmodern Legal Feminism*, 9.
58 See Gayatri Spivak, 'The Intervention Interview,' in S. Harasym, ed., *The Post Colonial Critic: Interviews, Strategies, Dialogues* (New York: Routledge, 1990) 121.
59 See Rozena Maart, 'Consciousness, Knowledge and Morality: The Absence of the Knowledge of White Consciousness in Contemporary Feminist

Theory,' in Debra A. Shogan, ed., *A Reader in Feminist Ethics* (Toronto: Canadian Scholars' Press, 1993).
60 The term 'Euro-western thought' is being used to identify those philosophical streams that have been developed by Europeans, Euro-Canadians, and Euro-Americans (though they may be used by racialized peoples). The use of 'western' as synonymous with 'white' erases the fact that indigenous peoples have older epistemologies that predate those of Europeans.
61 Radha Jhappan, 'Post-Modern Race and Gender Essentialism or a Post-Mortem of Scholarship' 51 (1996) *Studies in Political Economy* 25.
62 Mama, *Beyond the Masks*, 11.
63 Irshad Manji, *Risking Utopia: On the Edge of a New Democracy* (Vancouver: Douglas and McIntyre, 1997).
64 Also known as *Weatherall v. Canada (Attorney General)*, [1993] 2 S.C.R. 872.
65 *R. v. Butler*, [1992] 1 S.C.R. 452.
66 I cite this particular example here to illustrate how quickly one can be stripped of expertise. It was at this point that I reflected on how decisions and power operated within the legal committee. As with all structures there were informal pools of power and those that were less powerful. Agreement or support could be obtained: if the issue was not at odds with the views of the majority, including those with the most influence; if the issue did not contradict those with the most influence; and if the issue was being challenged by someone with less influence. Agreement or support could only be obtained when those with influence agreed or were persuaded. Engaging in vigorous debate has never been my concern; however, it was shocking to have my expertise denied when it was ostensibly the very reason I was invited on the committee and later hired as the executive director.
67 LEAF, *Equality and the Charter*, 214.
68 I engage in a more extensive discussion of how colonialism has shaped contemporary understanding of black African-Canadian / American identities in 'Only Skin Deep: the Social Construction of Black Women,' unpublished paper on file with the author.
69 See Davis, *Women, Race and Class*.
70 But for an analysis that gay erotica is not beyond a harms-based critique, see Christopher Kendall, '"Real Dominant, Real Fun!": Gay Male Pornography and the Pursuit of Masculinity' (1993) 57 *SLR* 21.
71 A multifaceted examination of the censorship issue in a post-*Butler* state is contained in Brenda Cossman and Shannon Bell, eds., *Bad Attitude/s on Trial: Pornography, Feminism, and the Butler Decision* (Toronto: University of Toronto Press, 1997).

72 Discussion of the seizure of her book, *Black Looks: Race and Representation*, can be found in 'Censorship from Left and Right,' in bell hooks, *Outlaw Culture: Resisting Representations* (New York: Routledge, 1994) 63–72.
73 See Lynn A. Hunt, ed., *The Invention of Pornography: Obscenity and the Origins of Modernity, 1500–1800* (New York: Zone Books, 1993) 13; and Jewel Amoah, 'Back on the Auction Block: A Discussion of Black Women and Pornography' (1997) 14 *National Black Law Journal (NBLJ)* 204.
74 Kathleen E. Mahoney, 'Pornography and Violence towards Women: Comparisons between Europe, the United States and Canada,' in Irwin Cotler and F.P. Eliadis, eds., *International Human Rights Law: Theory and Practice* (Montreal: Canadian Human Rights Foundation, 1992) 333.
75 Hunt, *Invention of Pornography*, 10.
76 As Amoah puts it, 'the lumping together of all women in the battle against pornography lessen[s] the impact of the fact that Black women were once white men's property.' Amoah, 'Back on the Auction Block,' 19.
77 For a specific example of this analysis in the context of family law, see Emily Carasco, 'Race and Child Custody in Canada: Its Relevance and Role' (1999) 16 *Canadian Journal of Family Law (CJFL)* 11.
78 As Minow notes: 'Assertions of a difference as "the truth" may indeed obscure the power of the person attributing a difference while excluding important competing perspectives. Difference is a clue to the social arrangements that make some people less accepted and less integrated while expressing the needs and interests of others who constitute the presumed model.' Martha Minow, *Making All the Difference: Inclusion, Exclusion, and American Law* (Ithaca, NY: Cornell University Press, 1990) 53.
79 Ibid.
80 Razack, 'Exploring the Omissions,' 40.
81 It becomes what Homi Bhabha has referred to as 'a containment of cultural difference.' Bhabha, 'The Third Space,' in J. Rutherford, ed., *Identity: Community, Culture, Difference* (London: Lawrence and Wishart, 1990) 208.
82 Ibid., 208.
83 The fallout from the *Butler* decision in the women's community demonstrates this point. Anticensorship feminists, some lesbians, and sex-trade workers challenged LEAF. They pointed out that the targeting of lesbian and gay erotica – see *Little Sisters Book and Art Emporium v. Canada (Minister of Justice)* (1998), 160 D.L.R. (4th) 385 (B.C.C.A.) and *R. v. Scythes* (1993), O.J. No. 537 (Ont. Prov. Div.) – was an obvious consequence of the decision and should have been anticipated in LEAF's legal argument. It should be noted that the position of the lesbian community was not unified on this

point and that lesbian theorists had been consulted by LEAF. Despite this, strong criticisms were raised about LEAF's failure to consult widely enough within the women's community.

84 Mama, *Beyond the Masks*, 12.
85 bell hooks, *Yearning: Race, Gender and Culture Politics* (Toronto: Between the Lines, 1992) 29.
86 See discussion in Mama, *Beyond the Masks*, 12.
87 *R. v. O'Connor*, [1995] 4 S.C.R. 411.
88 For an extensive discussion of the impact of the residential school system on Aboriginal communities, see chap. 10 of the *Report of the Royal Commission on Aboriginal Peoples* (Ottawa: Minister of Supply and Services Canada, 1996) 333.
89 See Christine Boyle, 'The Role of Equality in Criminal Law' (1994) 58 *SLR* 203 for a discussion of how the failure explicitly to discuss equality contributed to the result. It should be noted that the federal government subsequently enacted legislation which shifts the balance towards a greater protection of the victim's rights. See McIntyre's chapter in this volume for a discussion of the federal government's response to *O'Connor*.
90 R. Radhakrishnan, 'Nationalism, Gender, and the Narrative of Identity,' in A. Parker, M. Russo, D. Sommer, and P. Yaeger, eds., *Nationalisms and Sensualities* (London: Routledge, 1992) 81.
91 Jennifer Nedelsky noted that 'the infinite regress of specificity threatens to disrupt the very idea of a category.' 'Address,' 6.
92 Sylvia Yanagisako and Carol Delaney, eds., *Naturalizing Power: Essays in Feminist Cultural Analysis* (New York: Routledge, 1995), 14. The author has provided a more detailed analysis of these issues in her report as co-chair to the Canadian Bar Association Working Group on Racial Equality entitled *Virtual Justice: Systemic Racism and the Canadian Legal Profession* (Ottawa: Canadian Bar Association, 1999).

PART FOUR
Family and Reproduction

CHAPTER EIGHT

Abortion Litigation

Sheilah L. Martin, QC

Over the years women have engaged with law across a wide range of issues in various contexts and – with mixed results. While the main purpose of this book is to provide an overview of salient areas, issues, and opinions, the focus of my chapter is litigation on abortion. Litigation is only one of the many legal strategies available and actually employed in relation to abortion. Nevertheless, the decided cases merit special attention.[1] Litigated cases have figured prominently in determining access to abortion and defining public debate on this subject in both Canada and the United States.[2] They are dramatic illustrations of controversy in an area of central concern to women. Government controls on abortion have been numerous, invasive, and persistent, and they have generally sought to substitute state-sanctioned standards for women's autonomy and equality.[3] Women's bodies have been a significant site of gender-based struggles, and part of women's larger subordination can be traced to show how some people redefined biology as destiny and tried to transform a capacity to bear children into a limit.[4]

Litigation on abortion is not new. There has, however, been a significant shift in the type, number, and result of abortion cases. Abortion litigation in the 1980s focused on whether abortions should remain criminal under the Criminal Code. Most cases were criminal law matters where the state pursued persons who performed or facilitated abortions (only rarely did the state target the women who had them).[5]

R. v. Morgentaler, Smoling et al.,[6] is the case that de-criminalized abortion and held that women have *Charter* rights in the abortion context. This instigated a significant shift in the focus of abortion litigation. Since *Morgentaler*, attempts to use the courts have included *Borowski v. Canada*,[7] which involved a claim by an antichoice activist that all abortions infringed the alleged *Charter* rights of fetuses, and cases where disgruntled ex-boyfriends tried to prevent women from having abortions by injunction, notably *Daigle v. Tremblay*.[8] In addition, much of the litigation in the 1990s focused on whether the provinces, which have the power to legislate in the area of health, can choose where an abortion can be performed or decide to uninsure abortions performed outside of hospitals. There have also been issues around safe access to abortion services and the requirements of third-party consents.[9]

My two main goals in this chapter are to introduce readers to different types of abortion-related litigation in Canada and to analyse part of the complex interrelationship between law and the pursuit of women's equality. I analyse the landmark 1988 *Morgentaler* decision and use it as a case study to make some general observations on the difficulties of assessing the transformative potential of law, and then I attempt to explain its contributions and limitations in relation to more recent abortion litigation.[10]

The 1988 Supreme Court Decision in the *Morgentaler* Case

In *Morgentaler*,[11] the Supreme Court of Canada struck down section 251 of the Criminal Code (C.C.),[12] the provision that had governed the availability of abortions since 1969. Section 251 made it a crime to perform or have an abortion at all stages of pregnancy but provided that 'therapeutic' abortions were lawful, as long as numerous legally prescribed conditions were met. Under these conditions, a pregnant woman was obliged to apply to the 'therapeutic abortion committee'[13] of an 'accredited or approved hospital,'[14] and to prove that the continuation of the pregnancy would, or would be likely to, endanger her 'life or health.' Section 251 authorized, but did not require, the establishment of therapeutic abortion committees across the country.[15] Studies showed that section 251 operated to severely curtail access to abortion:[16] many hospitals did not have functioning committees,[17] and for those that did, each committee imposed its own procedures[18] and interpreted the term 'life and health' in its own, often restrictive way.[19] This meant that there were variable standards and procedures, with the result that women would be unsure whether they could obtain an abortion either in a particular hospital or at all.

Dr Henry Morgentaler and his associates operated outside this statutory system for many years, in more and more places. In so-called Morgentaler clinics, women could obtain abortions without first securing a certificate from the therapeutic abortion committee. For this reason, Dr Morgentaler was criminally prosecuted numerous times for acting outside section 251.[20] Despite the fact that no jury in Canada has ever convicted him, he spent time in prison in Quebec for performing abortions. In 1975, Morgentaler first challenged the legality of section 251 on the basis that it infringed women's rights under the *Canadian Bill of Rights*, but the Supreme Court upheld section 251 because of the limited nature of that legal document and the restricted rights it conferred.[21]

Times had changed by 1984, when Dr Morgentaler was again charged criminally for performing abortions, this time in his Toronto clinic. From a legal perspective, the most significant change was that in 1982 the *Canadian Charter of Rights and Freedoms* had become the supreme law of Canada, and it was a powerful legal tool with expansively phrased protections for individual and group rights. Under its terms women were entitled, among others, to equality rights and the section 7 right to 'life, liberty and security of the person and the right not to be deprived therefore except in accordance with the principles of fundamental justice.' In 1988, a majority of the Supreme Court struck down section 251 C.C. because it offended a pregnant woman's section 7 *Charter* rights, and in so doing the Court accepted many of the claims and arguments it had previously rejected in 1975. There were three different sets of judicial reasons supporting the majority's conclusion, and there was also a dissenting judgment.

In the majority, two judges found that the purpose and operation of section 251 violated women's physical integrity and psychological well-being protected under the section 7 'security of the person' interest.[22] Two other judges concluded that section 251 C.C. improperly infringed a pregnant woman's 'security of the person' because the criminal law restricted access to a medically necessary service.[23] Both of these judgments held that the therapeutic abortion committee system operated outside the procedural aspects of the principles of fundamental justice, and therefore breached section 7 of the *Charter*.[24] The only woman on the panel, Madam Justice Wilson, asked 'whether a pregnant woman can, as a constitutional matter, be compelled by law to carry the fetus to term'[25] and believed that, at a minimum, section 251 C.C. violated a pregnant woman's physical and psychological security of the person. She went on to state that section 251 violated a pregnant woman's right to 'liberty' because it took a personal decision away from a woman and gave it to the therapeutic abortion committee at all stages of the pregnancy. It also infringed her 'security of the person' because it treated her as a 'passive recipient of a decision by others as to whether her body is to be used to nurture new life.'[26] She held that section 251 C.C. infringed women's freedom of conscience and that the breach of section 2(a) of the *Charter* meant that there was non-compliance with the principles of fundamental justice. Section 251 C.C. breached section 2(a) because the state, in enacting this criminal law prohibition against abortion, was endorsing and enforcing 'one conscientiously held view at the expense of another.'[27] It improperly treated a woman as a means to an end – the reproduction of successive generations – and not as an individual with the right to make essential private decisions in a free and democratic society.[28] In her judgment, the decision to have an abortion was thus protected as a matter of personal morality and individual conscience.

All five judges in the majority concluded that the criminal prohibition against abortion could not be upheld under section 1 of the *Charter* as 'demonstrably justifiable in a free and democratic society,' but found that the federal government has a legitimate interest in protecting the fetus which may, under different legislation, justify the use of its criminal law power.[29] As a result, section 251 C.C. was declared of no force or effect, and the criminal charges against Dr Morgentaler and associates no longer had any basis in law and were quashed.

General Observations on the Transformative Potential of Law

An examination of what is accomplished by litigation involves difficult questions of theoretical importance, practical significance, and personal angst, and there are many reasons why persons inquiring into the transformative potential of law should expect to be confronted by complex questions without ready answers.[30] First, there are so many relevant matters at play: fundamental issues such as the nature of law, the role of the state, the dynamics of power, and the roots and manifestations of the subordination of women. Second, for each such matter there are bodies of literature which outline competing theoretical and political perspectives.[31] For example, some claim that law is an inherently conservative force ill-adapted, resistant, or even inimical to progressive social change. Proponents of this theory of the nature of law would see little transformative potential in any legal struggle, including abortion litigation. However, this theory reflects only one view of what the law is, and what it can do. Others believe the law can accommodate new concepts, embrace altered social realities, and respond to our increasingly deeper understanding of what discrimination looks like and what equality requires. Under this alternative view, the law can be used as something other than the 'master's tool,'[32] but such a jurisprudential position recognizes the real need for new thinking and works to create a gender-inclusive notion of justice, informed by a compassionate understanding of multiple inequalities, and supported by an alternative vision of individual potential.

Similar theoretical divisions exist over other relevant matters, such as the role of the state. There is considerable division of opinion over who or what the state is, and there is no uniform or shared position on what role the state has played in the subordination of women, even among feminists. Looking at the regulation of abortion,[33] it is clear that state action in relation to women has not been monolithic, static over time, or directed towards a single end.[34] Thus, the possible mix of relevant issues and various perspectives results in a complex, even daunting matrix under which complicated interrelationships may further confound any attempt at a linear, neat, or all-encompassing response.

Third, not only are there different theoretical and political perspectives on the transformative potential of law, there is also some evidence that we are in a state of transition. As women continue to enter all parts of the public sphere and make various types of claims, there has been some response. In part, constitutionally entrenched equality rights have shifted the institutional framework within which Canadian feminists struggle against women's oppression. In the past, the mainstream women's movement tended to focus its attention on pressuring politicians and bureaucrats, but the *Charter* signalled an increased role for the judiciary. The judicialization of politics and the politicization of the judiciary have profound consequences for Canadian women's movements. Not everyone agrees that the courts and judges will be up to the challenge, and there is also disagreement over the effects of shifting the struggle from politics to law.[35] While some express concern over the potential demobilizing effects of a legalistic feminist struggle,[36] others claim it may now be easier to get to the courts than to the legislature and that cases have the potential to mobilize women.[37] So while some would argue that the law has been a powerful weapon in the control of women, there may now be areas in which law-based strategies, including litigation, contribute to progressive social change.

Fourth, even with this increased experience, the task of assessing the impact of a legal strategy also suffers from the inherent dilemma of all questions that involve determinations of cause and effect. How can one ever fairly say that this consequence was caused by that action, especially when, as here, we have no way of measuring the extent to which law changes public opinion or is shaped by it. The complex interplay between law and other social forces, therefore, severely limits our ability to be certain, and leaves us only to speculate as to likely influences. In relation to litigation, while it is relatively simple to state whether the court granted or withheld the requested remedy, it becomes more difficult to say that a particular case was a 'success' because it may be difficult to construct a principled definition of success. The limited inquiry into whether litigation served its purpose assumes that the purpose is singular and knowable, but it fails to provide adequate guidance on what the effect of the change is, and whether it took the place of something else, and whether that something else would have been better or worse.[38] For example, Dr Morgentaler 'won' to the extent that the criminal prohibition against abortion was struck down, and women 'won' because they would no longer be subject to criminal prosecution or the fear of it. But the Supreme Court did not clearly articulate a woman's right to obtain an abortion, failed to address women's equality rights, and left the door open for new criminal abortion legislation when it found that the state has a legitimate interest in protecting the fetus.[39]

Fifth, the many different types of laws and various forms of litigation will have a bearing on the transformative potential of litigation. Great attention must be paid to the specifics of the case: the particular issue involved; its subject matter, its moment in time, its social context; the people involved and implicated; and the type of legal action. This involves asking questions like is the law a prohibition or a form of regulation, is a party seeking an injunction, is there a constitutional claim, what remedy is being sought, what evidence is available and admissible, who started the proceedings, and who controls the litigation. What may have 'worked' in one set of complex and intertwined circumstances may be inappropriate for another.[40] It is also best to remember that the impact of certain features of the case may only be gauged by reference to the context in which they are subsequently raised. Whether some aspects of a decision are seen as a good thing or a bad thing some time in the future depends on many variables. There may, however, be some advantage to highlighting certain features of the *Morgentaler* case to suggest some of its contributions and limitations, even though such a process assumes that individual features can be adequately segregated, fairly assessed, and properly classified.

Important Features of the *Morgentaler* Case

The transformative effects of *Morgentaler* are tied to certain features of the case. It is important to note the reactive nature of the litigation, that the case involved an attack on intrusive state action, and that it was a *Charter* case.

The *Morgentaler* case happened because, as recently as 1984, the Province of Ontario was prepared to invoke its considerable powers and criminally charge physicians performing abortions. (Any enthusiasm for the Supreme Court's ultimate statement of the rights of women must be contained by the fact that they were not so respected at the time by the Ontario government and were not so recognized in the lower courts.) While in other contexts, it has been the slow pace and narrow scope of positive legislative action which brings women to the courts,[41] the *Morgentaler* case grew out of the state's desire to enforce restrictive prohibitions. That Dr Morgentaler et al. stood accused means that the litigation was reactive and defensive and that, like some other Canadian cases on abortion, the people arguing for choice were not there by choice.[42] There was no luxury of deciding whether this was the most strategic case to best advance women's rights to life, liberty, security of the person, and equality,[43] and regardless of its relatively positive outcome, this case stands as a further reminder that women, and other disadvantaged groups, do not always control the circumstances in which they plan, participate, or perhaps even, progress.

The nature of this case as an attack on intrusive state action is also important. Those seeking comparisons should remember that Morgentaler challenged a criminal prohibition, the most stringent and invasive form of law there is: he was in court as an individual engaged in a classic example of civil disobedience, and the subject matter of abortion has often generated the acrimonious divisions and ideological cleavages to which an adversarial process like litigation is often said to respond best. This configuration of circumstances raised the less problematic scenario of women acting against government-imposed limitations and exemplified the more traditional terrain of a contest between women and the state.[44]

That *Morgentaler* was a *Charter* case is of key significance – although it began as a criminal case, it developed into a constitutional one when the defence challenged the very legality of the prohibition under which the physicians were charged. The main arguments against section 251 C.C. were based on women's rights under the *Charter*, and there are many implications to *Morgentaler* being a *Charter* case rather than any other type of litigation. The nature of the inquiry in a *Charter* case is quite wide,[45] judges have very powerful remedies available to them,[46] and there are special rules expanding who can be a party to[47] or otherwise participate in the proceedings.[48] Less positive features of *Charter* litigation will be explored in a later section, but they include that since the *Charter* only applies to state action, only government-imposed restrictions can be challenged under it,[49] and, given the large role for judges, the *Morgentaler* case was somewhat of a gamble because there was the potential to entrench the gender-biased approach to women's reproductive rights taken under the *Canadian Bill of Rights*.[50]

Contributions of the *Morgentaler* Case

In my view, the 1988 *Morgentaler* decision made positive contributions to women both in relation to direct benefits and symbolic gains. The most direct and obvious benefits as a result of this case are that performing or having an abortion is no longer a criminal act,[51] the cumbersome therapeutic abortion committee structure is no longer needed, and abortions performed in Dr Morgentaler's clinics are no longer criminalized.[52] The striking down of section 251 C.C. was dramatic, effective immediately, and changed the life circumstances of all women in Canada,[53] regardless of their politics or personal preferences. If the main criterion for determining the contribution of legal reforms is the impact the changes make on the lives of women, *Morgentaler* represented a step towards meeting women's material needs in relation to reproduction and abortion.[54] For women to enjoy the full plenitude of *Charter* rights in the reproductive context, there must be changes across the interrelated issues of control over sexuality, access to contraceptives and health care, an acceptance that abortion is a necessary and normal medical service, and the ability to manage pregnancy and deliver children according to the woman's choice. For abortion to escape its gender-biased treatment, criminal prohibitions and special rules and obstacles constructed to restrict access must be removed,[55] as must barriers such as augmented requirements for a second opinion from another physician about the propriety of the procedure, additional consents from spouses or parents,[56] limited rules, and harsh sanctions mandating where abortions can be performed. In addition to removing barriers, attention must be paid to the equitable, timely, safe, publicly funded provision of abortion services to women who need them because it is at the operational level that there is disparate treatment of the rich and poor, the young and old, the rural and urban.[57] In addition, international studies indicate that the toll on the life and health of women caused by illegal abortion does not significantly decline unless abortion services made lawful in theory are also made available in practice.[58]

The *Morgentaler* case was the crucial first step in this process. The invalidation of the criminal law prohibition not only removed a significant barrier to its availability, it generated other indirect or less obvious benefits. Even if women who sought and obtained abortions were not prosecuted often under section 251 C.C., criminal abortion laws impacted directly on women's lives. Criminalization restricted safe and timely access to abortion. The fear of criminal liability skewed the market and restricted supply and sent a clear message that abortion, as a medical procedure, was in a special category. The illegality of certain abortions therefore had a chilling effect on the acceptability and availability of lawful ones. Making abortion a crime also influenced, as well as dictated, individual conduct. Criminal sanction may have deterred women from seeking abortions or inhibited them from obtaining them. The prohibition against abortion likely exerted moral suasion and resulted in women reinterpreting their pregnancies according to the imposed 'public' perception. Defining abortion as a crime also stigmatized women as criminals, even if they were not 'caught,' charged, or punished. It asserted that society had something to fear if women were left to control their reproductive cycles in the post-pregnancy period. By imposing a criminal prohibition against abortion, the state also dictated to pregnant women and reinforced the stereotype that women cannot be trusted to act as morally responsible decision-makers. Such a position failed to acknowledge that traditionally women have been, and overwhelmingly continue to be, the caretakers and nurturers of children and instead attempted to cast them in the derogatory role of irresponsible destroyers of life.

Litigation may also have a symbolic effect. Even if you do not believe, like some writers suggest, that legal entitlements have greater symbolic significance than real benefit,[59] the importance of symbolic victories should not be underestimated.[60] While most people who engage in litigation want to 'win,' many court cases are more than adversarial means to a desired end. The interpretation and application of law, especially *Charter* rights, involves competing characterizations of reality and selection from among contested claims with the result that litigation on abortion has an immense symbolic, ideological, and discursive content, as well as a direct impact.

The symbolic gains in *Morgentaler* are significant. Women are acknowledged as full rights bearers under the *Charter*. The high profile of constitutional cases, augmented by the attention of the media also serves an educative function, teaching, at a minimum, that women have constitutional rights,[61] even while pregnant, and that law is a socially situated process.[62]

Second, women are recognized as full rights bearers in the abortion context. This is of great importance because where women's reproductive potential is in issue, some people have failed to see that sex equality was possible, or indeed even relevant. The supremacy of the *Charter* also means that constitutional cases such as *Morgentaler* may have large and lasting implications because the constitutional dimension will now become a critical aspect of any inquiry into abortion. Just as the enunciation of a woman's right to an abortion in *Roe v. Wade*[63] recast the abortion debate in the United States, the terms of the *Morgentaler* judgment will redefine the Canadian legal lexicon in such a way that women can insist that state action conform to constitutional standards. Women's rights will therefore be used as a filter through which any state action which seeks to limit women's control over their reproduction must now pass.

In addition, the distinctive women-sensitive approach taken by Madam Justice Bertha Wilson has not only added to our analysis and understanding of women and abortion, it has signalled a more general acceptance of gender-inclusive legal norms.

Limitations on the *Morgentaler* Case

Even with these direct benefits and symbolic gains, there are noteworthy limits to this decision that derive from the nature of litigation, the constraints of judicial reasoning, and the limited narratives of law.

The traditional criticisms levelled at courts and litigation are acutely felt in relation to women and abortion, and many of what may be perceived as the limitations of *Morgentaler* derive more from general things like the court structure, the nature of judicial reasoning, the limits to *Charter* remedies, the litigation process, and the composition of the judiciary than from particular features of that case. For example, it is sometimes said that courts are unresponsive, decisions come slowly, and determinations are ambiguous, inconsistent, and technical. While litigation may allow individuals and groups to force the political and legal agenda, it is a notoriously expensive[64] and slow process.[65] Like other means of political influence, litigation requires management and organization and protracted and repeated presentations of one's position.

Certain distinguishing features about judicial reasoning may operate to inhibit the effectiveness of litigation. How judges arrive at their decisions and what they say is important because it will affect how future and related cases are approached and decided. Even when a judge reaches a good conclusion, sometimes the end result is supported by reasoning which is ambiguous, incomplete, unacceptable, or even harmful.

Sometimes it is hard to say what the judges actually agreed on. In *Morgentaler* there was not only a division of opinion between the majority who struck down the criminal prohibition and the minority seeking to uphold it, there were three separate set of reasons given by the majority judges. As the various judgments indicate, there was a significant divergence of opinion on important matters. In reaching the same conclusion by different means, there was little clear direction given to subsequent courts hearing abortion arguments.

In addition, judges often go to great lengths to go no further in their reasons than they are required to decide a particular case. This has important implications, as the following two examples show. First, in *Morgentaler*, the defence put forward a comprehensive claim based on numerous *Charter* rights. Although the Court accepted the section 7 arguments, even these were not fully explored or delineated.[66] It was also contended that section 251 C.C. infringed a pregnant woman's section 2(a) right to freedom of conscience, section 12 right not to be subjected to cruel and unusual treatment or punishment, and sex equality rights under sections 15 and 28 of the *Charter*.[67] An equality analysis would have been especially welcome, and likely less abstract than the analysis of section 7 rights.[68] The failure to comment on all of the issues and arguments raised in the case may create a very narrow scope through which to view the issue of abortion unless people clearly understand that the Court's decision(s) in *Morgentaler* represents the first *Charter* case on the constitutionality of a criminal abortion law and does not establish a complete code on women's rights in the abortion context.[69] It would be a grave error to view their comments as precluding or implicitly rejecting a constitutional challenge based on other *Charter* interests. In this respect, one must remember the *Morgentaler* decision did not answer all the questions about women, the law, and abortion, and it would be a grave mistake to approach it as if it did. The

Morgentaler case should be approached as the Court's introductory remarks and not its definitive statement.

Another consequence of the limited nature of judicial reasoning was that the Court did not comprehensively address the legal status of the fetus. The fact that section 251 C.C. no longer existed, meant that by the time the Supreme Court heard Borowski's claim that a fetus was an 'everyone' with a right to life under section 7 of the *Charter*, there was no legal or factual context for Borowski's arguments.[70] The Court quite properly determined that the issue was moot and too abstract to be pursued by a private citizen,[71] but because it never turned its attention to whether fetal rights even exist under the *Charter* there is some uncertainty, even though courts in Saskatchewan consistently rejected the subject of Borowski's claims.[72] That the Court did not address the legal status of the fetus nor when life begins will continue to have meaning in the areas of new reproductive technologies, such as frozen embryo ownership, medical research, and attempts by the state to control the behaviour of pregnant women.

Ambiguity and a lack of clarity and incompleteness may be harmful to future cases. For example, all judges in the majority concluded that the federal government has a legitimate interest in protecting the fetus that would justify the use of its criminal law powers but there was no agreement concerning the extent of that jurisdiction.[73] When Brian Mulroney's Progressive Conservative federal government tried to reintroduce what it considered to be a clear *Criminal Code* prohibition on abortion in *Bill C-43* in 1989[74] it apparently hoped constitutionally valid and politically acceptable legislation would result if it could invoke this jurisdiction and try to tailor new law to cure some of the procedural defects of section 251 C.C. specifically outlined by some of the justices in *Morgentaler*.[75] Bill C-43, however, was built on the faulty premise that constitutional abortion legislation could be achieved simply by responding to the Court's decision in *Morgentaler*, and was so remarkably similar to section 251 C.C. it was unlikely to pass constitutional muster. The government's legislative response was a highly selective picking and choosing of various elements of the different concurring majority judgments to define the evils to be remedied. There is always some risk when attempting to infer what will work from what did not, and that risk is increased when the judicial comments were cautious and intended to go no further than strictly necessary to invalidate the legislation.[76]

Even a well-reasoned and complete judgment will not often provide an answer on other, even closely related, matters. For example, two of the three judges in the majority emphasized that they were thinking about women's *Charter* rights in the context of a criminal law prohibition. If the legal context changes, say to the non-criminal one of arguing that the government cannot selectively withdraw public funding for abortions performed in clinics, the application of the *Morgentaler* reasoning and its persuasive force become matters for argument and speculation. So while cases may provide a more rational and principled basis for prediction, they do not contain prescriptions. Thus, often even a good case needs other good cases to really clarify and crystallize the extent of the protection.

Another example that even a comprehensive treatment of the constitutional issues would still not resolve all legal issues around abortion is the case of *Daigle v. Tremblay*. It was one of a series of attempts by men to obtain court-ordered injunctions to stop women from having abortions after section 251 C.C. had been struck down. While certain claims were made during the currency of the criminal prohibition, these men argued that they had rights as the legal representative of the fetus, as a biological 'father,' or under an alleged agreement that the parties had agreed to have a family.[77] The injunction obtained by Jean Guy Tremblay against Chantal Daigle from the Quebec Superior Court was upheld by the Quebec Court of Appeal but set aside by the Supreme Court of Canada,[78] which unanimously held that ex-boyfriends and potential fathers have no right to veto the pregnant woman's decision to terminate her pregnancy. The Supreme Court reiterated that rights vest at birth in Quebec law and common law,[79] and concluded that a fetus has no independent right to life.[80] The Court rejected the claim that the potential father's contribution to the act of conception gives him any legal right to any say in the management of the woman's pregnancy because to do so would allow one person to effectively expropriate the reproductive services of another. The Supreme Court squarely confronted whether the applicant had the legal rights he claimed, rather than dispose of the matter on some alternative ground. They adopted this approach because of its logical priority, its great importance, and because: 'If this question is not addressed ... it will remain unclear whether another woman in the position of Ms Daigle could be placed in a similar predicament through the use of a different legal procedure. In order to try to ensure that another woman is not put through an ordeal such as that experienced by Ms Daigle, it is important for this Court to give the guidance it can. This can only be accomplished if the question of substantive rights is addressed.'[81]

The Supreme Court's clear position in *Daigle v. Tremblay* should inhibit those who are disposed to attempt similar cases in the future. Clarity is especially important when the substance of the issue which divides the parties is, in essence, decided expeditiously and at the pretrial stage before the full strength of the applicant's evidence and argument can be evaluated.[82] In this respect, the strong terms of the Supreme Court's position provided much-needed guidance; the threat of legal action by a disgruntled ex-lover or husband no longer qualifies as a risk to be factored into the decision-making process of the many people and institutions that continue to control access to abortion.

Judgments can be restricted by subsequent courts and institutions who may fail to embrace and employ their principles. Jurisprudential victories may also be seen as somewhat precarious because, at least theoretically, progressive decisions can be reversed by members of a subsequent court. While the Canadian Supreme Court does not consider itself bound by its own decisions, good reasons are generally required before it will depart from established precedent, and this may occur where there is no social consensus around an issue or the legal principle has failed to garner widespread jurisprudential support. However, with a few important exceptions, which have tended to advance the interests of women and equality-seekers in Canada,[83] judicial reversals are rare and are not rapid. In addition, it is important to place this aspect of judge-made law in context and remember that there are very few types of decisions that cannot be changed. Legislation can be altered, regulations can be amended, policies can be revised, and practices can be rewritten.

Despite the rules of precedent and *stare decisis* and the hierarchical structure of the courts, not every judge or lower court will readily embrace the progressive principles in the approach taken by the Supreme Court.[84] This may explain why the Court chose to rule upon Ms Daigle's appeal notwithstanding that it was moot – the case clearly exhorts lower courts to disallow similar claims for injunctions. While lower courts must follow the strict terms of the Supreme Court's decisions, there are many ways in which such decisions can be restrictively interpreted, read down, or altered in practice.

On the more positive side, because courts generally follow precedent, one favourable decision is likely to lead to others. Litigation, to a greater extent than other policy-seeking means, may pick up momentum as one victory provides precedent for subsequent cases, such that the number of cases in any given area may not adequately convey its potential political impact.[85] Judges are also independent, decide according to principle, and may therefore be more free to lead public opinion because they need not answer to it directly. While the judiciary is independent, it must still respond to the social realities of the day, judgments should be informed by modern notions, and it should be acknowledged that the pressure on courts to advance a particular public policy does not occur in isolation from related activities in other political arenas.[86] That one judge, or a panel of judges in an appeal, has the power to rule on issues presented in litigation means that far fewer persons need to be persuaded to achieve social change or to prevent it. While this practice may be rationalized on a number of grounds,[87] it can give rise to both positive and negative consequences for women using litigation for progressive purposes. For instance, many point to the homogeneous composition of the judiciary as a reason to be distrustful.

The litigation context permits rather limited narratives because it is rights based; the language of law does not always permit conversations about women, even when they are directly affected, because of its tendency to focus on what is winnable; and there are rules about evidence which outline how and who can say what. As a general matter, the fact that *Charter*-based litigation is essentially a discourse about 'rights' places limits on the usefulness of a litigation strategy.[88] The abstractness of rights often obscures the immediate reality of needs. While this dichotomy exists in most cases, it is particularly acute in a litigation paradigm and in relation to abortion, where timely access to free and competent services for those who need them is the ultimate goal.[89] This may be particularly problematic considering that *Charter* remedies tend to operate in a piecemeal fashion and that only state action comes under review. For example, the federal government was the only level of state control over women's reproduction that was directly affected by *Morgentaler*. A review of responses to the issue of abortion after the *Morgentaler* decision shows how provinces have used their powers in different ways and to serve different ends. While some provinces have used the range of regulatory options created by the absence of a criminal law to promote women's reproductive health, other provinces have employed a variety of mechanisms to continue to restrict access to abortion. To the extent that new provincial regulations and policies operate as substitutes for legally defunct therapeutic abortion committees, they run the serious risk of duplicating their inadequacies, stigmatizing this medical procedure, impeding access to it, and creating administrative delays.

When the decision-making framework is the legal system there may be a tendency to present the 'problem' in a legalistic manner, such that it could be more easily remedied by a law-based response, without addressing underlying social tensions or causes.[90] Litigation involves an articulation of the policy being sought as a series of narrow issues that are then packaged into what appear as private and individual cases, presented in the proper sequence.[91] While this has the advantage of allowing the debate to become focused, such neat, simple, and compartmentalized definitions may not take into account a complex social context and its multiple lines of causality and consequence, and its disparate impact on differentially situated groups such as women of colour, Aboriginal women, poor women, or women with disabilities.[92] In addition, in the litigation process, each new restriction must be challenged as it arises, resulting in an expensive, time-consuming process.

Litigation often involves strategic decisions which may not always best advance women's larger interests. Rarely will the choice be the stark one of winning the point at the expense of women as there are generally many ways of shaping the argument and presenting a position. It is more likely that tension could arise between legal arguments which have a good chance of winning the case and those which would best advance feminist jurisprudence. In a contest between the direct benefit of increased access to abortion services and the symbolic gains through sound judicial reasoning, the desire for a specific remedy often prevails. The otherwise sage advice not to make jurisprudence with your client's money does not always cover cases where public interest advocates pursue policy change through litigation. In this context, it is important to mention how certain restrictions on abortion imposed by various provinces have been successfully challenged under the *Morgentaler* decision. The judges' reasoning has not always focused on women's rights but on more narrow grounds which made the case 'winnable,' illustrating the interplay between desirable ends and pragmatic means.

For example, in 1988, the British Columbia government attempted to revoke public funding for abortions immediately after the *Morgentaler* decision. The decision to withhold funding was struck down by a B.C. court on administrative law principles because the enabling statute did not allow the government to act as it did.[93] The judge did not comment on whether, if a province de-insured abortion in the proper form, such state action may still violate the principles of universality, accessibility, and comprehensiveness in the *Canada Health Act* and infringe women's

Charter rights.[94] To deny public funding for abortion is completely inconsistent with the goal of a national health care system that provides medically necessary services to all Canadians, regardless of their financial resources and ability to pay. It also qualifies as sex discrimination and the double disadvantaging of poor women because access to abortion would be seriously curtailed if individual women were forced personally to pay for medically necessary services or if doctors were expected to provide this sex-specific procedure free of charge.[95]

In a series of cases, action has been taken against restrictive provincial funding practices for abortion. In a 1989 court action, Dr Morgentaler challenged the New Brunswick government's policy of not reimbursing physicians who performed out-of-province abortions unless two physicians stated that the abortion was medically required and the procedure was rendered in an approved hospital.[96] Although Dr Morgentaler was successful, the usefulness of the decision for further court challenges in different circumstances may be limited because this case concerned the particular problems of a provincial 'policy' for out-of-province abortions.[97] This case does not address whether these same criteria would be valid if applied to abortions performed in New Brunswick, or whether similar restrictions would be valid if they were imposed by changing the legislated definition of 'entitled services,' and thereby transforming the impugned policy into law. But the case does illustrate a certain judicial willingness to question the funding decisions of provincial health regulators.

The *Morgentaler*-style abortion clinic was the target of legislation in Nova Scotia. In *An Act to Restrict the Privatization of Medical Services*,[98] the provincial government prescribed that certain procedures, including abortion, could not be lawfully provided in private clinics and attempted to justify its 'hospital only' limitation on the grounds it promoted medical safety, prevented direct patient billing, and reduced the costly duplication of medical services. A person who performed abortions outside a hospital was guilty of a summary conviction offence with a penalty range between ten to fifty thousand dollars in fines.[99] In addition, such a person would not be reimbursed according to the provincial tariff for the medical service performed and could have been enjoined from committing further breaches.[100] This Act was successfully challenged on constitutional grounds.[101] Although Dr Morgentaler alleged that the Act was a thinly veiled attempt to restrict access to abortion in a manner inconsistent with women's *Charter* rights,[102] and that private clinics provide a medically safe, economically efficient, and humane environment for abortion operations, the court focused on the issue of whether the Act was within provincial legislative competence. After reviewing the provisions of the Act, exploring its legislative history and noting the punitive character of the imposed fines, the court concluded that the Act was in pith and substance a matter of criminal law and therefore within an exclusively federal field. This decision was affirmed by the Nova Scotia Court of Appeal and ultimately by the Supreme Court of Canada.[103]

A more recent case concerning the provinces and abortion funding involved the same actor, Henry Morgentaler. In *Morgentaler v. P.E.I.*,[104] the court considered a regulation (similar to that in *B.C. Civil Liberties*) de-insuring abortions unless they were performed in a hospital, and they were deemed necessary by a provincial agency or its medical advisory committee. The regulation was made by the agency and approved by the provincial cabinet. The court was asked to determine whether a therapeutic abortion is a basic health service. Rather than address this metaphysical (and political) question, however, the court merely noted that the Act considers basic health services to be 'services rendered by physicians that are medically required.' Therefore, it held, a basic health service that is medically required is one which is performed by a physician. The court held that the regulation did not further any of the purposes of the parent legislation, and struck down the regulation.

Such cases may appear disappointing: the arguments look technical and do not clearly capture and convey the rich and varied life experiences of the women they are intended to benefit. Some fear that the focus on women may be lost and that covert legal tools may have hidden, unacceptable, and unforeseen consequences. In my view, although the disappointment is real, it should be the disappointment of missing an opportunity to make a gain rather than feeling defeat or suffering a loss in any overall sense. In many of these cases the more expansive claims based on women's rights were argued and heard, and when the judges decided on more narrow grounds, it is more a function of the conservative nature of judicial reasoning than an implicit rejection of women's claims. The rights-based arguments can have an influence even if they are not cited in the reasons for decision, and they should be made whenever possible because they set the overall stage for the argument. After so many years in the assigned role of understudy, many may feel that women's rights, interests, and realities ought rightly to occupy centre-stage and enjoy the spotlight, but there is still something to be said for a good result, a proper resolution, with women waiting in the wings, ready to emerge like a Greek chorus if necessary.

When the language is 'rights talk' in a litigation forum, who is allowed to say what remains restricted even in constitutional cases. The narratives of laws are limited because certain evidence may simply not be put before or be admissible to the decision-makers. Sometimes this is because the appropriate person is not before the court, either as a party or intervenor, and sometimes because a person makes a strategic decision not to tender certain evidence or pursue a particular line or argument, and sometimes it is because some rule excludes what may otherwise be part of the legally relevant story. A related point to who is before the courts is who has conduct of the case. Given that judges decide cases on the basis of the arguments[105] and evidence[106] presented to them, this question can have profound implications for the success of litigation as a vehicle for social action. Generally speaking, it is the parties to litigation who control what evidence is led and what arguments are made.[107] Intervenors normally do not have full status in the litigation, and are limited to arguing on the basis of the issues and evidence put forward by the parties.[108]

In *Morgentaler*, the evidence led by the defence formed the basis for the Supreme Court's finding of a violation of section 7. The Supreme Court drew frequently on the evidentiary record established at trial. It canvassed the disparate access to abortion, the standards and procedures applied by therapeutic abortion committees, the mortality rate associated with abortion versus full-term pregnancies, and the myriad positions of various religious groups on the issue of abortion[109] in reaching its conclusion that the machinery set up under this section violated section 7 of the *Charter*.[110] The state chose not to call evidence to justify section 251 C.C. in *Morgentaler*; recent constitutional cases, however, illustrate that governments must back up their claims that the legislation in question is a reasonable limit on the *Charter* right(s) at issue.[111]

Conclusion

My comments can be read as a small contribution to the larger controversy over whether the law has a role to play in the empowerment of women. In my view, the law does have a role: an important, multifaceted, but ultimately limited one. As the study of the *Morgentaler* case on abortion illustrates, in large measure and for many years, legal controls on abortion have operated as gender-biased instruments of oppression in the lives of Canadian women. In recent years, however, litigation has been used to redress historic discrimination and systemic deprivations in an attempt to empower women. The use of *Charter* litigation as a means of invalidating abortion-related crimes as in *Morgentaler* may be seen as part of a process, long overdue, by which women are included as full rights bearers within basic legal protections. An understanding of how gender bias may infuse the law and legal analysis means, however, that women have good reason to distrust a purely law-based strategy to combat their inequality. While legal strategies in general, and litigation in particular, can achieve some positive results on different fronts, they are not sufficient. If the goal is to combat the many forms of inequality women experience, it is most unlikely that one case, a line of cases, or even all legal strategies taken together could adequately address ubiquitous, multifaceted, and pervasive power imbalance. Despite the reach of 'law's empire,' laws are not the only, or perhaps even primary way of shaping human behaviour, and some significant sites of gender-based struggle may not be amenable to legally framed action. Even when laws or other forms of state action are involved, rights and remedies do not always satisfy material needs. Women's current states of social, political, and economic disadvantage may mean, however, that they are in no position to 'opt out' of *Charter* discourse. For all of its limitations, the opportunity *Charter* litigation gives women to redefine rights that credit their biological capacity and acknowledge their position of social inequality is, pragmatically, simply too necessary to reject.[112] There is also a certain satisfaction in claiming rights that have been denied for so long and the prospect of being a litigant after being a supplicant for so long may well prove irresistible.

Many varied approaches are therefore needed effectively to challenge inequality. Legal strategies must be used with flexibility, creativity, and in tandem with others. 'Everything all the time' captures the level of commitment required to effect the transformative changes needed if the goal is gender-inclusive justice within a non-sexist society. Equality-seekers understand they are trying to create what has not existed before and that there are no templates, precedents, or road maps on how to get there from here. Strategies must fit the circumstances and be as extensive as the problems they address. So even though many authors point to the emerging importance of legal discourse,[113] litigation should not be embraced as a cure-all, seen as a quick fix, or adopted as an appropriate strategy in all cases.[114] Court-based fights are subject to many limitations, contain considerable downside risks, and should be viewed as only one among a range of possible alternatives.[115] Even 'successful' litigation is partial: maximum effectiveness is best secured when multiple routes are pursued aggressively and simultaneously.

Notes

1 The legal landscape on abortion includes calls for legislative reform, whether sponsored by the government or put forward in a private members' bill; wrangling over licences or zoning requirements for abortion clinics; injunctions against picketing at clinics; actions on funding for abortion and challenges to restrictive regulatory rules and practices. Other related matters deal with controls on pregnant women and the regulation of reproductive technologies.

2 There has also been significant litigation on abortion in the United States. See Naomi R. Cahn, 'Defining Feminist Litigation' (1991) 14 *Harvard Women's Law Journal (HWLJ)* 1, and Valorie Vojdik, 'Afterword: A Thought about Feminist Litigation Strategies' (1998) 20 *Western New England Law Review (WNELR)* 139. For an interesting debate on the possibility of truly feminist litigation on abortion in the United States, see R. Colker, 'Feminist Litigation: An Oxymoron? A Study of the Briefs filed in *Webster v. Reproductive Health Services*' (1990) 13 *HWLJ* 137; Sarah Burns, 'Notes from the Field: A Reply to Prof. Colker' (1990) 13 *HWLJ* 189; R. Colker, 'Reply to Sarah Burns' (1990) 13 *HWLJ* 207. See also Pamela S. Karlan and Daniel R. Ortiz, 'In a Different Voice: Relational Feminism, Abortion Rights, and the Feminist Legal Agency' (1993) 83 *Northwestern University Law Review* 858 *(NULR)*. See R.B. Cowan, 'Women's Rights through Litigation: An Examination of the American Civil Liberties Union Women's Rights Project, 1971–1976' (1976) 8 *Columbia Human Rights Law Review (CHRLR)* 373 for an article that examines the general litigation activity of the Women's Rights Project *(WRP)* in the United States, established by the ACLU to work towards establishing basic sex equality through litigation. In Canada, the Women's Legal Education and Action Fund (LEAF) was set up in 1985 to assist with important test cases and to ensure that equality rights litigation was undertaken in a planned, responsible, and expert manner. Women turned to the courts because of the governments' failure to use proactive means to remedy legislation that contributed to systemic discrimination

against women. For a contemplation on feminism and abortion see Erin Soros, 'The Law of Generation: The Ethics of Abortion' (1998) 10 *Canadian Journal of Women and the Law (CJWL)* 149.

3 Abortion allows women to separate pregnancy from motherhood and reject what some believe is their natural role. Abortion gives back to women part of the reproductive control which nature and social circumstances often deny them. Because women do not always control the circumstances in which they are impregnated, or are pregnant, abortion has become one response to women's more generalized disadvantage. Abortion is a procedure that permits those women who experience pregnancy as a violation to reverse the biological betrayal. It is the price some women pay to reassert control when pregnancy is seen as the palpable proof of their powerlessness. Without intending to make a reductionist or universal claim, there is still some limited sense in which, to borrow the title of a foreign film on the execution of a female abortionist in France, abortion is 'the story of women.'

4 The broad area of women's reproductive rights has raised other important issues in areas related to, but different from, abortion litigation. The issue of women's right *to* reproduce, most notably debated in the area of new reproductive technologies, parallels and intersects with the abortion debate. This chapter does not focus on these issues, but instead gives a brief nod to them in anticipation of their continued importance in feminist debate and future litigation.

5 A review of the journals discloses no reported case involving criminal charges against the pregnant woman for her part in an unlawful abortion. Most of the reported decisions concerned the conduct of physicians, abortionists, and druggists, or other persons, usually boyfriends, who helped the woman obtain the unlawful abortion. Many illegal abortions were only discovered because the woman either died or became so ill she sought medical attention. Rather than operating as a moral condemnation of the woman's conduct, prosecutions in these cases may have reflected a concern for the physical safety of women and an attempt to deter unskilled abortionists from injuring other women. There was implicit understanding of the callousness and injustice of formally penalizing women who were seeking abortions. Non-enforcement against pregnant women illustrates how the legislation's symbolic statement of protecting fetal life was actually weighed against the reality of women's lives and how the reasons given for the existence of the offence did not always infuse or influence its enforcement. In my view, this non-enforcement constitutes a tacit acceptance that the reasons why women choose abortion are numer-

ous, personal, and profound, and properly outside the legitimate realm of state intervention.

6 [1988] 2 S.C.R. 30.
7 *Borowski v. A.G. Canada*, [1989] 1 S.C.R. 342.
8 *Daigle v. Tremblay*, [1989] 2 S.C.R. 530.
9 For a review of Canadian cases centred around safe access to abortion, see *Elizabeth Bagshaw Society v. Breton* (1997), B.C.J. No. 2414 (B.C.S.C.); *R. v. Lewis* (1996), B.C.J. No. 3001 (B.C. S.C.); *Ontario (Attorney General) v. Dieleman* (1994), 20 O.R. (3d) 229.
10 It is also difficult to know where to start the analysis: where the story begins is a significant editorial choice and in one sense, this analysis of abortion litigation could start with *R v. Palmer* (1937), 68 C.C.C. 31 (Ont. C.A.), aff'ing (1937) 68 C.C.C. 20 (Ont. H.C.). From 1892 until 1969, the Criminal Code made it an offence to knowingly, without lawful justification or excuse, sell, advertise, or have for sale or disposal any medicine, drug, or article intended or represented as a means of preventing conception. If the accused could prove that the public good was served by the acts alleged, this was a defence. The prohibition came under increasing criticisms from many quarters. In the late 1930s, birth control reformers believed the time had come for a test case, and *Palmer* became the vehicle to both advocate for and reflect social change. In that case, the accused was acquitted on the basis that her actions in disseminating birth control information to poor mothers already overburdened by large families were saved by the public good defence. The *Palmer* trial has been compared by some writers as being to the birth controllers what the Scopes monkey trial had been to the evolutionists. See Angus McLaren and Arlene Tigar McLaren, *The Bedroom and the State: The Changing Practices and Politics of Contraception and Abortion in Canada, 1880–1980* (Toronto: McClelland and Stewart, 1986) 124.
11 The three appellants were qualified medical practitioners charged under s. 423(1)(a) and s. 251(1) C.C. with criminal conspiracy to perform unlawful abortions.
12 Criminal Code, R.S.C. 1970, c. C-34. Under s. 251(1) C.C., a person who performed an unauthorized abortion could be found guilty, whether or not the woman on whom the operation was performed was in fact pregnant at the time, and was liable for life imprisonment. In contrast, s. 251(2) C.C. provided that a woman who procured her own miscarriage could only be found guilty if she was actually pregnant at the time of the operation, and she was only liable to imprisonment for two years.
13 A 'therapeutic abortion' committee was composed of three or more quali-

fied medical practitioners. Committee members were appointed by a hospital's administrative board and could not, by law, be physicians who performed any abortions.

14 Only hospitals accredited by the Canadian Council on Hospital Accreditation qualified as 'accredited hospitals.' An 'approved hospital' was a hospital 'approved for the purposes of this section by the Minister of Health of a province.' Many hospitals in Canada were neither 'accredited' nor 'approved.'

15 An important factor in understanding this arrangement is the constitutional division of legislative power between the federal and provincial governments. Under s. 251 C.C., Parliament invoked its exclusive jurisdiction to regulate matters of criminal law, but it also sought to respect provincial powers over health by allowing provinces to regulate access to abortion in the same manner in which they controlled the availability of other medical services. Access to abortion as a medical matter was therefore under provincial jurisdiction, and the provinces allowed individual hospital boards to determine such matters as whether their hospital would have a committee, its procedures, and decision-making standards, and how many abortions would be performed there.

16 Two major reports studied how this therapeutic abortion committee system actually worked: the *Badgley Report*, a national survey completed in 1976; and the *Powell Report*, an Ontario based study completed in 1986. These reports outlined how unfairly and inequitably the system operated: significant delay, restricted availability of abortion services, arbitrary administrative procedures, variable decision-making criteria, and unequal access to abortion were commonplace.

17 For example, during 1983, only 257 Canadian hospitals had therapeutic abortion committees, and even if a hospital had a committee, it did not necessarily perform abortions. In 1983, 19 per cent of all hospitals that had committees performed no abortions at all. A further 43 per cent of hospitals that had committees performed fewer than 100 therapeutic abortions in that year.

18 Some committees required a waiting period, the signature of special informed consent forms, or the approval of the woman's husband, if she was married, or the parents if she was a minor. Some committees required psychiatric assessments. Almost all abortions were performed within the first twenty weeks of pregnancy (99.6 per cent). Statistics Canada, *Therapeutic Abortions, 1986* (Ottawa: Supply and Services Canada, December, 1988).

19 Some committees required an immediate physical threat, whereas others

adopted the World Health Organization's definition of health as a state of well-being. This allowed a wider range of inquiry. See R. Badgley, *Report of the Committee on the Operation of the Abortion Law* (Ottawa: Minister of Supply and Services, 1977) 32.

20 Dr Morgentaler successfully invoked the defence of necessity in response to criminal charges under s. 251 C.C. in both Quebec and Ontario. In each case he was acquitted by a jury who believed that the abortion operation was performed to preserve the health or life of the woman. That juries accepted Dr Morgentaler's defence of necessity highlighted how public sentiment and community standards varied from the strict terms of the criminal prohibition. The juries' decisions raised numerous questions about the fairness, efficacy, and continued relevance of s. 251 C.C. A subsequent Ontario Court of Appeal decision in *R. v. Morgentaler* (1985), 52 O.R. (2d) 353 (Ont. C.A.) restricted the defence of necessity.

21 *Morgentaler v. The Queen* (1975), 53 D.L.R. (3d) 202 (S.C.C.), where Mr Justice Dickson, as he then was, stated that the Court was not called on to enter into the 'loud and continuous debate on abortion.'

22 Ibid., 56–7 per Dickson CJ (as he then was). The two dissenting judges found that s. 251 did not violate a pregnant woman's s. 7 rights because there was no express language in s. 7 which specifically granted women the right to have an abortion. Ibid., 146 per McIntyre, J.

23 Ibid., 89–106 per Beetz, J.

24 The procedural problems were said to include the unfair and arbitrary manner in which therapeutic abortion committees restricted access to abortions and created delays (per Dickson, CJ 63 et seq.). Moreover, the requirement that abortions take place in 'an approved or accredited hospital,' as well as the make-up and procedures of the committees were found to violate the principles of fundamental justice (per Beetz, J 111 et seq.).

25 Ibid., 162.

26 Ibid., 173.

27 [1988] 1 S.C.R. 179.

28 Section 2 states that everyone has the following fundamental freedoms: freedom of conscience and religion.

29 Ibid., 76 (per Dickson, CJ) and 112 (per Beetz, J). Madam Justice Wilson suggested at 182 that Parliament may wish to devise any new abortion law from a stage of pregnancy approach similar to that adopted in the United States.

30 It has always nagged at me that perhaps part of my belief in the ability of the legal system to help women stems from a personal and professional

conceit: as a lawyer I may feel more comfortable with this strategy, and because I want my work to be meaningful, I may exaggerate its usefulness.

31 While most recognize that law seeks to control behaviour, punish law-breakers, resolve conflict, formally express the dominant values or collective aspirations of society, educate the public, and promote a broad range of social objectives, there are numerous theories that explain the function of law very differently.

32 For a general discussion of the role of law in relation to women, see Shelley Gavigan, 'Law, Gender and Ideology,' in Anne Bayefsky, ed., *Legal Theory Meets Legal Practice* (Edmonton: Academic Printing and Publishing, 1988); K. O'Donovan, *Sexual Divisions in Law* (London: Weidenfeld and Nicolson, 1985); K. O'Donovan, 'Engendering Justice: Women's Perspectives and the Rule of Law' (1989) 29 *University of Toronto Law Journal* (*UTLJ*) 127; Sheila McLean and Noreen Burrows, eds., *The Legal Relevance of Gender* (New Jersey: Humanities Press, 1988); F. Olsen, 'Law as Patriarchy (unpublished manuscript); F. Olsen, 'The Family and the Market: A Study of Ideology and Legal Reform' (1983) 96 *HLR* 1497; Catherine McKinnon, 'Feminism, Marxism, Method and the State: Towards a Feminist Jurisprudence' (1984) 8 *Signs* 635; J. Rifkin, 'Toward a Theory of Law and Patriarchy' (1980) 3 *HWLJ* 83; D. Polan, 'Towards a Theory of Law and Patriarchy,' in David Kairys, ed., *The Politics of Law – A Progressive Critique*, 294; Ann Scales, 'Towards a Feminist Jurisprudence' (1981) 56 *Indiana Law Journal* (*ILJ*) 375; C. Littleton, 'Reconstructing Sexual Equality' (1987) 75 *California Law Review* (*CLR*) 1279.

33 The criminal law regulation of abortion in Canada has undergone numerous revisions and has passed through many phases. The nature of the prohibited conduct has been redefined numerous times, the evidentiary requirements have changed over time, and the allocation of the burden of proof has migrated between the Crown and the accused. For years the criminal prohibition was restricted to performing an abortion, but it later became a crime for a woman to have one. Criminality has turned on when the abortion was sought, why the abortion was sought, or under a combined scheme that permitted abortions only at designated times and on certain terms and conditions. The penalties for the different offences have varied over the decades and have ranged from a maximum sentence of death to a maximum of two years imprisonment. Some statutes contained express exculpatory provisions that made certain abortions lawful, but even when the statute was silent, the common law defence of necessity could be relied on in appropriate cases.

34 There is some dissatisfaction with the vision of the state as a monolithic,

omnipotent, one-dimensional representation of patriarchy: 'This concept of an overly deterministic state which can co-opt all social movements is simply not a concept verified by history. It is also a concept which begs the question of what should feminists do while waiting for the revolution.' See Jane Ursel, 'Considering the Impact of the Battered Women's Movement on the State: The Example in Manitoba,' in Elizabeth Comack and Stephen L. Brickey, eds., *The Social Basis of Law: Critical Readings in the Sociology of Law*, 2nd ed. (Halifax: Garamond, 1991) 265.

35 Lise Gotell, *The Canadian Women's Movement, Equality Rights and the Charter* (Ottawa: Canadian Research Institute for the Advancement of Women [CRIAW], 1990) 22, explains that in pre-*Charter* times, the path for change for women had been, of necessity, largely political, but in the post-*Charter* era, there is a 'legislative mandate for governments to bring laws into compliance with enumerated rights. When governments fail to take legislative initiative, the *Charter* allows the women's movement and other social groups to use the judicial arena as a way of placing issues on the political agenda. It is the legislative path, however, which is recognized by feminist *Charter* analysis to be the most effective and flexible means of achieving change.' In the judicial arena, 'women's equality is subject to the non-negotiable decisions of bodies which are isolated from direct political pressure' (at 39). Moreover, early legal victories may encourage feminists to focus their energies on the judicial branch of state, possibly at the expense of other activities. This results in the legalization of the feminist struggle, sometimes in cases with no direct bearing on women's social condition. Thus, pursuing a litigation strategy requires not only a substantial commitment of resources to fighting feminist issues in the courts, but also requires a commitment to fighting cases in which approaches to the interpretation of equality are at stake. See also Judy Fudge, 'The Public/Private Distinction: The Possibilities and the Limits to the Use of Charter Litigation to Further Feminist Struggles' (1987) 25 *Osgoode Hall Law Journal* 485, who explains how the *Charter* sparked debate regarding the limits to and possibilities of using law in the struggle for social transformation. In her view the extension of legal rights may help to transform women's sexual and economic subordination and is a necessary condition for social transformation. However, at 54, she cautions that structural and institutional limitations mean that courts are 'perhaps the least suitable of the existing fora for engaging in struggles for social transformation.'

36 Gotell, *Canadian Women's Movement*, 40. See also Deborah L. Rhode, 'The "No-Problem" Problem: Feminist Challenges and Cultural Change' (1991) 100 *Yale Law Journal (YLJ)* 1791, who states: 'Women's most fundamental

problem [in ensuring equality in social experience and not just equality in formal treatment] is how to politicize the problem – how to increase a sense of shared identity, purpose, and power through collective action.' In this respect she believes problems generally are better addressed in legislative or collective bargaining contexts, rather than courts, and that law can play only a limited role, but a larger role than many opponents have acknowledged.

37 Judy Fudge, 'The Effect of Entrenching a Bill of Rights upon Political Discourse: Feminist Demands and Sexual Violence in Canada' (1989) 17 *International Journal of Society and Law (IJSL)* 445, argues that while the struggle that led to equality guarantees in the *Charter* mobilized and radicalized women's groups, the actual results of *Charter* litigation may be much less positive. See also Fudge, 'The Public/Private Distinction,' where she argues that the assertion of legal rights is an important step towards transformation because such rights function as catalysts for political mobilization. See also S. Altschu and C. Carron, 'Chronology and Some Legal Landmarks in the History of Canadian Women' (1975) 21 *McGill Law Journal (MLJ)* 476; G. Brent, 'The Development of the Law Relating to the Participation of Canadian Women in Public Life' (1975) 25 *UTLJ* 358. It was the public nature of the *Daigle* litigation, and on a matter otherwise so private, that was the source of its greatest impact. Individual women saw themselves in the place of Ms Daigle, and if not outraged, they tended to be at least deeply disquieted.

38 Carol Smart, 'Feminism and Law: Some Problems of Analysis and Strategy' (1986) 14 *IJSL* 111, warns that because law has an autonomy from the state, and law itself is not a unified entity, legal changes cannot be regarded as 'causing' economic or social change, although legislation may, in some instances, provide the means to achieve change. See also Elizabeth Comack, *Feminist Engagement with the Law: The Legal Recognition of the Battered Woman Syndrome* (Ottawa: CRIAW, 1993) 4, where she states: 'One lesson has been that realizing meaningful reforms is no easy or straightforward matter. What, on the surface, may appear to be a benefit for women may, upon closer scrutiny, carry potentially disastrous consequences.'

39 *Bill C-43, An Act Respecting Abortion*, 2nd sess, 34th Parl., 38 Eliz II, 1989. This Bill was introduced in November 1989 and defeated by a tie vote in the Senate on 31 January 1991. Parliament responded fairly quickly with *Bill C-43*. The tendency to view litigation as a zero-sum game, with a winner and a loser, is thus too simplistic to describe how a complex judicial process interacts with variable social realities.

40 See Fudge, 'The Public/Private Distinction,' who explores what she

believes to be the Supreme Court's poor track record in regards to labour relations. She notes, however, that just because a particular tactic does not work for one group does not mean that others cannot use it, especially if their complaint is not tied to class relations.

41 Gotell, *Canadian Women's Movement* 25–6. It is interesting to note that despite active lobbying by both pro- and antichoice factions in relation to the criminal prohibition against abortion, proposed legislative amendments have all attempted to reduce the availability of legal abortions.

42 In *Borowski*, pro-choice women were compelled to intervene to counter the argument that the unborn fetus had somehow acquired constitutional rights. And Ms Daigle was anything but a willing or compliant participant – she was forced to defend herself and her rights in response to the spurious claims of her ex-boyfriend.

43 Another variation of women not controlling the commencement of litigation occurs when someone challenges state action that women worked hard to achieve. Early s. 15 litigation saw men arguing that benefits which accrued to women violated their equality rights, and should be extended to men, or alternatively struck down. This was the case, e.g., with maternity leave benefits. See Gwen Brodsky and Shelagh Day, *Canadian Equality Rights for Women: One Step Forward or Two Steps Back?* (Ottawa: Canadian Advisory Council on the Status of Women [CACSW], 1989) for a survey of the first three years of litigation under s. 15 of the *Charter*. According to this survey, men brought three times as many 'equality'-based challenges as women in this period.

44 Much of the recent writing on feminist engagement with law concerns the extent to which equality-seekers should align with the state. For example, this writing assesses the costs and benefits of women's groups joining forces with government to stop violence against women. There is a real fear that the power of the state will silence or overpower women's voices through a complex process of coordination, co-option, and editing. While no consensus emerges, valuable insights are to be gained from the diverse perspectives presented. Caution, careful calculation, and contained enthusiasm are suggested. This body of literature and the experiences of women's movements may be helpful in the abortion context in the future if women align with the state to provide timely access to publicly funded abortions.

45 The concern that private litigation between interested parties is too narrow a forum to properly address social issues can be heard, but less loudly, in relation to *Charter* litigation.

46 Section 52 of the *Charter* provides that the *Constitution* is the supreme law

of Canada. It is for this reason that state action that unjustifiably contravenes the provisions of the *Charter* must be declared of no force or effect. In addition to the remedy afforded by s. 52, the *Charter* also contemplates 'such remedies as the court considers appropriate and just in the circumstances in s. 24(1). These provisions provide a *Charter* litigant with a broad range of legal remedies.

47 In *Borowski* there was an issue of who can participate as a party to litigation: this is referred to as 'standing.' The rules on standing depend, in large measure, on the type of case involved. In private litigation, a party must have a direct, immediate, and personal interest before being allowed to pursue a legal action before the courts. As a constitutional case the rule of standing was somewhat relaxed such that it was on this basis that Mr Borowski, and Dr Morgentaler, as genuinely interested citizens, were permitted to challenge s. 251 of the *Criminal Code* notwithstanding that they were not, nor ever would be, pregnant women seeking abortions. Some, like Borowski, may use litigation in an attempt to restrict the rights of women by claiming a constitutional status for the fetus and attempting to construct maternal-fetal rights conflicts. Thus, the broad notion of standing may result in a proliferation of claims and counterclaims about competing rights, without necessarily promoting the interests of women. Recent decisions of public interest litigation take a more limited view. See *Canadian Council of Churches v. Canada (Minister of Employment and Immigration)*, [1992] 1 S.C.R. 236. For a further discussion of standing in the health care and abortion context, see Katherine Cherniawsky, 'Enforcement of Health Care Rights and Administrative Law' (1996) 4 *Health Law Journal* 48–51.

48 In addition to granting standing in constitutional cases, appellate courts often permit intervenors to address issues as friends of the court and to present arguments that may otherwise not be made by the parties to the litigation. The person or group seeking intervenor status must show their 'interest' in the case and that their submissions will be useful and different from those of the other parties. In cases where intervenors are permitted, litigation provides as close to a public forum as the law allows. Intervenors are self-selecting and must be approved by the Court. The rules of the Supreme Court of Canada give that Court wide discretion in deciding whether to allow persons to intervene. This means that whole groups can be left out of the process, and all sides of an issue may not be presented. Interest groups from both sides of the abortion debate had a say in *Borowski*. LEAF, REAL [Realistic, Equal, Active for Life] Women of Canada, and the Interfaith Coalition on Rights and Well-Being of Women and

Children were granted intervenor status. In *Daigle*, the Canadian Abortion Rights Action League, LEAF, Canadian Civil Liberties Association, Campaign Life Coalition, Canadian Physicians for Life, Association des medecins du Québec pour le respect de la vie, and REAL Women were granted intervenor status. In *Morgentaler* only the attorney-general of Canada intervened.

49 Section 32 of the *Charter* provides that it applies to the Parliament and government of Canada, and the legislature and government of each province so that only those controls on abortion imposed by the federal, provincial, and territorial governments can be challenged under the *Charter*. Limitations on abortion access created by hospitals or health care professionals, or by antichoice activists, cannot be cured directly by constitutional remedies. While private law remedies may provide some relief in these circumstances, their scope is usually much narrower than that of constitutional remedies. For a discussion of the limits the state action requirement imposes on feminist struggle, see Judy Fudge, 'The Public/Private Distinction' 485.

50 *R v. Morgentaler*, [1976] S.C.R. 616; *Bliss v. A.G. Canada*, [1979] 1 S.C.R. 183. See *A.G. Canada v. Lavell*, [1974] S.C.R. 1349. There, the overwhelmingly male composition of the judiciary and documented gender bias in some decisions suggests that the legal system and its processes continue to be male dominated, even though there may be some participation by women.

51 The Crown initially took the position that if found to contravene the *Charter*, only those parts of s. 251 C.C. dealing with therapeutic abortion committees should be struck down. This remedy would have cured the procedural difficulties inherent in the section, but the criminal prohibition would have remained. The Crown abandoned this position on the appeal, and the Court found that s. 251 was a 'complete code' which must be struck down in its entirety.

52 It is true that abortions performed in Dr Morgentaler's clinics are no longer illegal, but this too has been a battle. See Michael Mandel, *The Charter of Rights and the Legalization of Politics in Canada* (Toronto: Thompson Educational Publishing, 1989) 291, where the author notes that within a few months of the *Morgentaler* decision, every province except Quebec and Ontario, had announced measures to limit the funding or performance of abortions. In large part, this was a reaction to women seeking abortions at abortion clinics rather than in approved hospitals.

53 See Jane Ursel, 'Considering the Impact of the Battered Women's Movement on the State: The Example of Manitoba,' in E. Comack and S. Brickey, eds., *The Social Basis of Law: Critical Readings in the Sociology of Law*, 2nd ed.

(Halifax: Garamond, 1991) 265. See also Dawn H. Currie, 'Battered Women and the State: From the Failure of Theory to a Theory of Failure' (1990) 1, 2 *Journal of Human Justice (JHJ)* 77, who adopts a similar approach and (at 80) concludes that 'although objectively there have been gains for women through the reform of law, the domination of women by individual men is being replaced by their social or public domination.'

54 Access to abortion can also be restricted where a province requires that abortions must be performed in institutions with higher standards than similar health care procedures require. There has been a marked reluctance in some provinces to accept that abortion services could also be provided outside hospitals and in other facilities such as a 'woman's reproductive health care clinic.' The theory behind these clinics is to provide a range of services to accommodate women's unique reproductive health care needs: including family planning, fertility counseling, cancer screening, general maternal health, and abortion services. Some clinics, like Dr Morgentaler's 'free standing' clinics, specialize in providing abortion services. This patchwork of provincial provisions and policies must be scrutinized to determine if there has been an increase in women's access to necessary abortion services in the immediate aftermath of the *Morgentaler* decision. It is important to remember that the old Criminal Code prohibition carried with it no entitlement to a therapeutic abortion, and in fact, did much to restrict the availability of abortion operations. So even though there may be some unevenness and inequitable availability, women are, in my view, still further ahead. The site of struggle and litigation may now be the provincial governments, but those worried about national standards should focus their attention on the *Charter* rights of women and the provisions of the *Canada Health Act*.

55 Abortion is often placed in a separate category and made the subject of special rules. Some hospitals have retained bodies similar to their therapeutic abortion committees for administrative reasons, even though they serve no legal purpose, or the opinion of a second physician is required before an abortion can be performed, while other provinces require a doctor performing an abortion to file a written statement that the procedure is medically necessary. Additional consent requirements have sometimes been superimposed over and above general ones, a mandatory waiting period between the giving of the consent and the performance of the procedure is established, some provinces have used their general power to regulate medical institutions and medical qualifications to require that abortions be performed in hospitals and/or by a specialist in gynecology and obstetrics, and in some cases, hospitals and doctors have

required pregnant women to 'consent' to sterilization before a necessary abortion operation will be performed. Sometimes a province or hospital has a mandatory 'counseling' process before the abortion will be approved. The acceptability of such a program depends on its purpose and content. 'Counselling' is often nothing more than an attempt to dissuade the pregnant woman, force her to change her mind, or delay her. It often does not truly have her interests or medical needs in mind, and it can be used as a vehicle to impose the values of others. The attempt to manipulate a woman's choice through this form of counselling has been invalidated in the United States as an unlawful and unconstitutional infringement of a woman's right to have an abortion.

56 The Saskatchewan government tried to make spousal and parental consent to abortion a legal requirement in its *Freedom of Informed Choice (Abortions) Act*. The proposed legislation would have made it an offence to perform, cause, or approve an abortion without the written consent of a married woman's husband or the parents or guardians of an unmarried minor. In a reference case to determine the constitutionality of the proposed law, the Saskatchewan Court of Appeal held that the province could not create these offences without improperly invading Parliament's jurisdiction over criminal law. See *Reference Re Freedom of Informed Choice (Abortion) Act* (1986), 25 D.L.R. 94th, 751 (Sask. C.A.).

57 R. Cook, 'Reducing Maternal Mortality: A Priority for Human Rights Law,' in S. McLean, ed., *Legal Issues in Human Reproduction* (Aldershot: Gower, 1989) 185.

58 R. Cook and B. Dickens, *Abortion Laws in Commonwealth Countries* (Geneva: World Health Organization 1977) 63.

59 Fudge, 'Public/Private Distinction,' 504.

60 See David Kairys, 'Introduction,' in D. Kairys, ed., *Politics of Law*, 6, 7 where the author explains how law enforces, reflects, constitutes, and legitimizes dominant social and power relations. Kairys notes that 'the law is not simply an armed receptacle for values and priorities determined elsewhere; it is part of a complex social totality in which it constitutes as well as is constituted, shapes as well as is shaped.'

61 S. Kaye, 'Women in Law: The Law Can Change People' (1991) *New York University Law Review (NYULR)* 1934, claims that although stereotypes and inequities have not been eradicated yet, the law and the courts have had a substantial role in facilitating change in public attitudes about women. In the past, law legitimated, perpetuated, and institutionalized society's belief that women were unequal and subordinate. But by the mid-twentieth century, it was clear that law could be a force for change.

'The law as it relates to women is an example of a recent 'civilizing change' that has not merely followed but also shaped and advanced society's perceptions. To be sure, people have changed the law, but the more interesting and significant point is that the law also has succeeded in changing people, and particularly some – though by no means enough – of their invidious stereotypes about women's roles and capacities' (at 1937).

62 Law is a process because it is in a state of constant flux and adaptation. It is socially situated because law emerges from social relations and contributes to their preservation or transformation. There is a complex interrelationship between law and the society it purports to regulate. Law both shapes and is in turn shaped by its social environment. Law is implicated in and reflective of larger social problems. This might be called the 'reactive' dimension of law. For example, in circumstances of inequality not all groups will have had the same access to law to entrench their preferences into legal positions. This has immediate implications for any current law reform process and means that existing law should not be uncritically accepted as a given.

63 410 U.S. 113 (1973).

64 Although broad in theory, the notion of access clearly has its limits, ability to pay being a major factor. There are few sources of public funding for constitutional litigation. This situation led Brodsky and Day to conclude: 'Corporations, criminally accused persons and Attorneys General have good access to the courts; women and other disadvantaged groups do not ... Public funding is essential if women are to have any meaningful access to the exercise of their *Charter* rights.' Brodsky and Day, *Canadian Equality Rights*, 138. It has also been reported that the prohibitive cost of seeking injunctions against antichoice harassment has caused some medical practitioners to stop performing abortions. (Aug. 1993) 27, 2 *This Magazine* 9.

65 It took almost three years for a final ruling on the constitutional validity of the *Medical Services Act*, a Nova Scotia Act prohibiting private abortion clinics in that province. Even though the Supreme Court expedited its hearing of the case, Ms Daigle's pregnancy was advanced to the point where she ignored the lower courts' injunction and had an abortion before the Supreme Court could rule on her appeal.

66 *Morgentaler* was also the first *Charter* case on women's reproductive rights to reach the Supreme Court and only one of a limited number of pivotal decisions on s. 7.

67 Moreover, Morgentaler submitted that s. 251 C.C. was *ultra vires* Parlia-

ment, or that it amounted to an unlawful delegation of Parliament's criminal law jurisdiction to the provinces and/or therapeutic abortion committees. Lastly, the defence argued that certain provisions of the *Criminal Code* violated their rights as accused persons under the *Charter*. It is conceivable that the Supreme Court could have rested its decision on these latter issues, such that the matters of real concern to women were not addressed.

68 There are many advantages to a sex equality analysis. Equality is essentially a contextual and comparative concept, whereas infringement of individual rights can often be discussed and resolved at fairly high levels of abstraction. Equality involves and requires a comparison with real life conditions. This is especially significant in relation to women's reproductive health where equality requires not just notionally similar rights but the actual provision of services. An equality analysis requires that attention be paid to the actual life circumstances of women and collectively based interests as well as personal autonomy. See S.L. Martin, *The Canada Health Act, the Canadian Charter and Women's Reproductive Health* (Ottawa: CACSW, 1989) 34–5.

69 *Daigle*, 550. The Quebec Court of Appeal judgment in this case illustrates another facet of judicial reasoning – selective treatment of evidence to achieve a desired result.

70 Borowski argued that the exculpatory provisions of s. 251 C.C. infringed a fetus's right to life under s. 7 of the *Charter*, and that they discriminated against a fetus on the basis of its age, and physical and/or mental ability, contrary to s. 15 of the *Charter*. Because of the decision in *Morgentaler*, the Supreme Court first heard submissions on whether the case was moot, and whether Borowski had lost his standing. Although the Court ultimately resolved the case on the basis of these preliminary issues, it also heard submissions from the parties and intervenors on the merits of the case. Thus, in *Borowski*, pro-choice women did have some control over the arguments presented in the Court.

71 The first set of Borowski cases were dealt with on the basis of a private citizen's legal standing to challenge a criminal prohibition. In *Minister of Justice of Canada v. Borowski*, [1981] 2 S.C.R. 575, 64 C.C.C. (2d) 97, the Supreme Court of Canada granted him standing because there was a serious and justiciable issue concerning the legislation's validity, he was genuinely interested in the legislation, and there was no other reasonable and effective manner in which the issue could be brought before the Court. Joe Borowski then began to assert the substance of his claim. The evidence presented at trial is available in Alliance Against Abortion, *Trial for Life in*

the Court of Queen's Bench for Saskatchewan, Judicial Centre for Regina (Winnipeg: Alliance Against Abortion, 1984). In *Borowski v. A.G. Canada*, [1984] 1 W.W.R. 15, 4 D.L.R. (4th) 112 (Sask Q.B.) the Saskatchewan court rejected his claim for constitutional rights for the fetus. The Court of Appeal also rejected his 'novel' claim at [1987] 4 W.W.R. 385 (Sask. C.A.). When the substance of the argument was addressed by the Courts it was consistently rejected.

72 In 1981 Joseph Borowski, an antichoice advocate, was granted standing to argue that the therapeutic abortion committee exemption infringed a fetus's alleged right to life under the *Canadian Bill of Rights*; claims he repeated and repackaged under the *Charter* when the *Charter* came into force in 1982. See generally M.C.U. Shumiacher, 'I Set before You Life and Death' (1987) *University of Western Ontario Law Review* (*UWOLR*) 1; 'Chaff from the Charter's Threshing Floor' (1983) 13 *Manitoba Law Journal* 435.

73 Chief Justice Dickson, as he then was, gave no indication how far he believed that state interest extended. Mr Justice Beetz would allow limitations on *why* a woman could obtain an abortion and the minimum administrative structure necessary to ensure compliance. Unlike Madam Justice Wilson, neither of these judges addressed the stage in the pregnancy at which the government's interest became pressing, legitimate, or substantial. She suggested that the government's interest in the protection of fetal life depends on the gestational age of the fetus. Some of Mr Justice Beetz's comments also support this approach. Ibid., at 128, where he suggests that a prohibition based on fetal age may achieve the requisite proportionality under s. 1 of the *Charter*.

74 This provision would have made it an indictable offence to 'induce an abortion' unless 'induced by or under the direction of a medical practitioner who is of the opinion that if the abortion were not induced, the health or life of the female person would be likely to be threatened.' The Bill defined 'health' to include physical, mental, and psychological health; a 'medical practitioner' is left to the definition of provincial authorities; and 'opinion' means an opinion formed using generally accepted standards of the medical profession.

75 In 1989, the same year that the federal government attempted to recriminalize abortion by way of *Bill C-43*, the Royal Commission on New Reproductive Technologies was formed to examine the legal and ethical questions surrounding the swiftly expanding area of reproductive technologies. The commission reported its findings in *Proceed with Care*, a two-volume report alongside fifteen volumes of research carried out by and for

the commission. In brief, the commission's two main recommendations were to prohibit several aspects of new reproductive technology, such as the sale of gametes and embryos, and to establish a regulatory and licensing body. In 1996, the federal government responded to these recommendations, in part, by tabling *Bill C-47*, 'The Reproductive and Genetic Technologies Act' (*Bill C-47*, Human Reproductive and Genetic Technologies Act, 2d Sess., 35th Parl., 1996). There are significant parallels between the legislation governing abortion (both the *Criminal Code* provisions prior to Morgentaler and the defeated *Bill C-43*) and the proposed *Bill C-47*, which would regulate reproductive technologies. See Alison Harvison Young and Angela Wasunna in 'Wrestling with the Limits of Law: Regulating New Reproductive Technologies' (1998) 6 *Health Law Journal* 239–77, for a thorough review of the parallels. This area will undoubtedly be the subject of litigation in the future. On the surface, there appears to be a wide gap between the criminalization of abortion and various aspects of reproductive technologies, and interference in a wanted pregnancy. And the issues *are* different. The fundamental sameness, however, centres around a woman's right to autonomy over her body, and the rights of women over the rights of a fetus.

76 By contrast, the United States Supreme Court has been faced with over thirty abortion-related cases since its landmark decision in *Roe v. Wade*, and the contours of a woman's rights in the abortion context have yet to be stated with precision.

77 In *Mock v. Brandenburg* (1988), 61 *Alberta Law Report* (*ALR*) (2d) 235 (Q.B.), the consideration for the agreement was said to be the mutual exchange of promises to have and support a child. As is common in these cases, he averred at 237: he is willing to resume cohabitation with the respondent, to support her emotionally and financially through the pregnancy, and to support a child born of the pregnancy emotionally, intellectually, and financially.

78 Although Ms Daigle was an unwilling participant in the case, she did have some control over the issues and evidence presented to the court. However, the lower courts selectively ignored or discounted Ms Daigle's evidence as to her life circumstances, her reasons for seeking an abortion, and her view of the impact a forced pregnancy would have upon her. In terms of evidence, Ms Daigle, her physician, and Mr Tremblay all filed affidavits. Ms Daigle's evidence set out her reasons for seeking an abortion, as well as her life circumstances at the time of the case. Despite this, one of the judges of the Court of Appeal in *Daigle v. Tremblay* (1989), 59 D.L.R. (4th) 609, 612 (Que. C.A.) chose to rely on evidence that Ms Daigle's

health was 'excellent,' and that the fetus was 'normal' in its finding that carrying the fetus to term would not endanger Ms Daigle's security of the person.

79 Canadian courts have consistently maintained that in the absence of an express statutory conferral, legal rights vest at the time of birth and by doing so have curtailed the legal ambitions of those who attempt to control women in their role as the self-appointed guardians of the fetus.

80 [1989] 2 S.C.R. 530, 560, the Court concludes that the arguments submitted to support the assertion that a fetus is a 'human being' under the Quebec *Charter* because of the provisions in the Quebec *Civil Code* and *Code of Civil Procedure* 'do not support his claim: rather, they provide grounds for the opposite conclusion, that a fetus is not a juridical person under the Civil Code.' A fetus was not intended to be included in the term 'human being' in the *Quebec Charter of Human Rights and Freedoms*. R.S.Q. c. C-12, ss. 1–2. The Court emphasized (at 558) that such a determination was a normative and legal one which could not be resolved by resorting to the purported dictionary meaning of the term 'human being' or a textual comparison between different usages of terms like 'human being' or 'persons.' The limited legal protections which vest retroactively under the Quebec *Civil Code* and *Code of Civil Procedure*, if the fetus is born alive, cannot be used to support a claim that the fetus has a complete and independent legal personality.

81 Ibid., 550. For an interesting review and critique, see Donna Greschner, 'Abortion and Democracy for Women' (1990) 35 *MLJ* 633. She argues that the decision advances women's self-determination because it is empathetic towards Daigle's plight and accords her the dignity of not assessing her actions, either her reasons for having an abortion or the fact that she did not wait for the Court's ruling to take action. Second, it recognizes that the question of fetal personhood is a normative one, not to be settled by the genetic and biological factors that constitute the mainstay of antiabortion arguments. Third, in several comments about rights asserted by Tremblay as the father, the court suggests that women and men are not in identical positions regarding reproduction. However, at 658, Greschner notes that the judgment is somewhat problematic because of its overall generality and abstraction and because it analysed the question of fetal rights as a question of legislative intention rather than by questioning the effect their recognition would have on women's rights.

82 In these cases, the injunction application tends to be interlocutory in form only because in the time it would take to bring such a case to trial it is most likely that the pregnancy would be terminated by abortion or birth.

Abortion Litigation 373

When the interlocutory application effectively disposes of the litigation, and the injunction would provide, not merely preserve, the remedy, courts must be especially concerned with the nature and extent of the rights asserted. The emergent nature of interlocutory injunctive relief presents similar stresses on the justice system as court-ordered caesarian sections or in utero apprehension orders. There is little time for adequate research, a full canvassing of the relevant issues, and the exercise of sound and balanced judgment.

83 For example, see *Bliss v. A.G. Canada*, [1979] 1 S.C.R. 183, reversed by *Brooks v. Canada Safeway*, [1987] 1 S.C.R. 1219, on the issue of whether discrimination on the basis of pregnancy constitutes gender discrimination.

84 Fudge, 'The Public/Private Distinction,' 487: The combined efforts of academic exhortation and repeated litigation have had little effect in persuading lower courts to adopt a radical new stance to equality rights in order to alleviate women's subordinate position in society.

85 On the other hand, it was 'precedent' that had the potential to entrench gender inequality in the *Morgentaler* case, in light of the earlier approach to women's abortion-related rights taken by the Supreme Court under the *Canadian Bill of Rights*. Fortunately, the Supreme Court is taking the view that the *Charter* widens its powers to review the substantive content of legislation, such that *Bill of Rights*' jurisprudence has little, if any, precedential value.

86 Cowan, 'Women's Rights through Litigation,' 373: 'Courts are affected by, and in turn affect, these other activities.' Judges often limit their decisions to what is strictly required to resolve a particular dispute, leaving important matters unresolved.

87 These grounds include conservation of judicial resources, reluctance to tread on the powers of the executive, or, from the Supreme Court's perspective, an unwillingness to bind lower courts and other state institutions on extraneous matters. That the *Charter* is a relatively young document may also serve to create a judicial reticence to define its boundaries too early on. In the words of Chief Justice Dickson in *Morgentaler*, 151, 'It is neither necessary nor wise in this appeal to explore the broadest implication of s.7 as counsel wish us to do ... I do not think it would be appropriate to attempt an all encompassing explication of so important a provision as s. 7 so early in the history of the *Charter*.'

88 See Fudge, 'The Effect of Entrenching a Bill of Rights,' 458–9, where the author notes that feminist discourse about power has been translated into a discourse about rights: 'Instead of directly addressing the question of how best to promote women's sexual autonomy under social relations

which result in women's sexual subordination, feminists who invoke the *Charter* must couch their arguments in terms of the rhetoric of equality rights.' In the context of sexual violence, the focus is on the law as the source of the problem, such that the social construction of sexuality and social relations of power in which sexual relations take place fade into the background. See also F. Olsen, 'A Feminist Critique of Rights Analysis' (1984) 63 *Texas Law Review* (*TLR*) 387, who argues that women's gains in the legal arena should be attributed to their concrete struggles, rather than characterized as achieving rights.

89 Issues around who controls and contributes to the litigation process are critical: how the process is started, who can participate, and who has conduct of the case are all essential factors in evaluating the appropriateness and responsiveness of a litigation strategy. Any empowerment consequent to litigation could derive from the process as well as the result of the case.

90 Gotell, *Canadian Women's Movement*, 41 comments on how, since the *Charter* applies only to government action, attention becomes focused on legislation as both the cause and remedy of women's oppression. The *Charter* tends to reify the ideological separation between public and private spheres, 'obfuscating the extent to which the "public" constitutes the "private."' This encourages the women's movement to articulate its grievances in terms of the law's limited categories, instead of struggling for structural change in underlying social arrangements. Thus, the legalistic process required may co-opt some of the radical impulse behind women's struggles.

91 Cowan, 'Women's Rights through Litigation.'

92 For example, a holistic approach to women's reproductive health would include a consideration of the imposed use of dangerous birth control devices, sterilization abuse, inaccessibility of abortion, forced hysterectomy, the availability of prenatal care, and accurate information about sex, conception, and contraception, access to safe, affordable abortion, protection from environmental and occupational reproductive hazards, and pharmaceutical experimentation. In the *Daigle* case, the Supreme Court expressly ignored the broader context of its decision. In the words of the Court [1989] 2 S.C.R. 530, 553: 'Ascribing personhood to a fetus in law is a fundamentally normative task. It results in the recognition of rights and duties. In short, this Court's task is a legal one. Decisions based upon broad social, political, moral and economic choices are more appropriately left to the legislature.' The broad approach to the admissibility of evidence in *Charter* cases may combat this difficulty to some extent, as illustrated by *Morgentaler*. In that case, the Court had before it evidence of the disparate

access to abortion created by the therapeutic abortion committee system. Although this evidence provided some context for the decision, a more socially relevant picture of abortion would have included evidence of how the system affected on women of colour, Aboriginal women, and poor women, for example.

93 In *B.C. Civil Liberties Assn. v. A.G.B.C.* (1988), 24 B.C.L.R. (2d) 189 (S.C.), the legal argument focused on whether the way in which the provincial cabinet de-insured abortion was within the scope of its statutory powers. The Court carefully examined the source and extent of the cabinet's powers, questioned whether proper procedures were followed, and concluded that the cabinet had exceeded its statutory mandate. In this type of legal challenge, the court's decision often appears to be rather technical as the judicial inquiry is limited to the question of the decision-maker's jurisdiction. The content of the provincial withdrawal was not assessed and its potential impact on women was not evaluated. In this case striking down the illegal or ultra vires regulation was both an immediate benefit, because the offending limitation can no longer operate, and a lasting one, because the government did not attempt to reintroduce the funding withdrawal in its proper form. But the government of British Columbia could have reintroduced the same type of funding limitation if it acted within the terms of its statutory powers. If that occurred, a *Charter* challenge would have been most likely.

94 In 'The Enforcement of the *Canada Health Act*' (1996) 41 *MLJ* 505, Sujit Choudry argues that litigation on the *Canada Health Act*, including abortion funding litigation, can have far-reaching effects. The value of such litigation, she suggests, is in the broader political arena where '[w]idely publicized litigation against the government would serve to highlight the value that Canadians place on access to quality health care and would feed into the larger political discourse.' For further discussion on the topic, see Moira McConnell and Lorenne Clark, 'Abortion Law in Canada: A Matter of National Concern' (1991) *14 Dalhousie Law Journal (DLJ)* 81; Claire Farid, 'Access to Abortion in Ontario: From Morgentaler 1988 to the Savings and Restructuring Act' (1997) 5 *HLJ* 119; Katherine Cherniawsky, 'Enforcement of Health Care Rights and Administrative Law' (1996) 4 *HLJ* 35; Timothy Caulfield, 'Wishful Thinking: Defining "Medically Necessary" in Canada' (1996) 4 *HLJ* 63; and Moira L. McConnell, 'Abortion – Provincial Legislation – Control over Health Care: *R. v. Morgentaler*' (1994) 73 *Canadian Bar Review (CBR)* 417. In this way, litigation under a specific piece of legislation can work to achieve social justice. This optimism is offset by Allan Hutchinson, who insists that 'whether as a categoric system of

political practice or as a contingent strategy of radical intervention, law and lawyering can never be productive of real or lasting social improvement.' See Hutchinson, 'Calgary and Everything After: A Postmodern Re-Vision of Lawyering' (1995) 33 *ALR* 776.
95 For an explanation see Sheilah Martin, *Women's Reproductive Health, the Canadian Charter of Rights and Freedoms, and the Canada Health Act* (Ottawa: CACSW, 1988).
96 *Morgentaler v. A.G. New Brunswick* (1989), 98 N.B.R. (2d) 45 (1989) 38 Admin L.R. 280.
97 The importance of this problem should not be underestimated because it is so difficult to obtain abortions in certain provinces that residents are forced to go to another province.
98 *An Act to Restrict the Privatization of Medical Services (The Medical Services Act)* 1989 SN.S. 38 Eliz II.
99 Ibid., s. 6.
100 Ibid., ss. 5 and 7. But under s. 6(3), no prosecution could be commenced without the written leave of the attorney-general.
101 *R. v. Morgentaler* (1990), 99 N.S.R. (2d) 293 (N.S. Prov. Ct.).
102 *A.G. N.S. v. Morgentaler* (1989), 96 N.S.R. (2d) 54 (N.S. Court of Appeal) which upheld the propriety of the pre-trial injunction which enjoined Dr Morgentaler from performing any further abortions outside a hospital before his constitutional challenge was heard.
103 Affirmed by the N.S. S.C. (Appeal Division) (1991), 83 D.L.R. (4th) 8, (1991) 104 N.S.R. (2d) 361; later affirmed by the Supreme Court of Canada [1993] 107 D.L.R. (4th) 537.
104 (1995) 122 D.L.R. (4th) 728 (Supreme Court, Trial Division).
105 Courts and judges depend on lawyers to enlighten them with new insights into old principles. As the world changes and values evolve, lawyers must deepen their understanding of the context and ramifications of legal issues, to help keep the law attuned to the needs of modern society, and to lead in the progress of law. See Mary Eberts, 'New Facts for Old: Observations on the Judicial Process,' in Richard F. Devlin, ed., *Canadian Perspectives on Legal Theory* (Toronto: Edmond Montgomery, 1991) 467.
106 The question of what evidence is admissible is construed relatively broadly in constitutional cases. The Supreme court of Canada recognized in *Andrews v. Law Society of British Columbia*, [1989] 1 S.C.R. 143, 152 that *Charter* determination must not only be made in 'the context of the law which is subject to challenge but rather in the context of the place of the group in the entire social, political, and legal fabric of our society.' The

act of abortion cannot be separated from the social conditions in which impregnation occurs and pregnancy is experienced. Ideally, legal controls on abortion should only be analysed after considering matters such as sexual aggression, inadequate or unavailable contraception, special legal controls on the conduct of pregnant women, and the patchwork of provisions which deal with related matters such as maternity leave, pregnancy discrimination, and child care. See S.L. Martin,'Toward a Women-Centred View of Legal Controls on Human Reproduction,' in Kathleen E. Mahoney and Paul Mahoney, eds., *Human Rights in the Twenty-First Century: A Global Challenge* (Dordrecht, Netherlands: Martinus Nejhoff, 1993).

107 At trial, Borowski relied on new medical and biological technologies in his attempt to draw attention to the intrauterine characteristics of a fetus that qualified it for legal personhood. The evidence and arguments presented at trial have been published in a two-volume set, and together they illustrate the new evidentiary approach required by the *Charter*. Borowski also led evidence on the way therapeutic abortion committees worked. It is interesting to note that both Joseph Borowski and Dr Henry Morgentaler, speaking for the anti- and pro-choice forces respectively, used similar data to support competing contentions. See Alliance Against Abortion, *Trial for Life in the Court of Queen's Bench of Saskatchewan, Judicial Centre for Regina* (Winnipeg: Alliance Against Abortion, 1984).

108 Brodsky and Day, *Canadian Equality Rights*, 134. In some cases, however, intervenors may be granted standing with all the rights of a party. See *Schacter v. Canada*, [1992] 2 S.C.R. 679, where LEAF was granted intervenor status on this basis.

109 (1984), 12 D.L.R. 517–18, 525, 528, 534, 558.

110 See Mary Eberts, 'New Facts for Old, 478.

111 *R. v. Seaboyer; R. v. Gayme*, [1991] 2 S.C.R. 792; *R. v. Butler*, [1992] 1 S.C.R. 479, 493; *Schacter v. Canada*, [1992] 2 S.C.R. 695.

112 S.L. Martin, 'The Control of Women through Gender-Based Laws on Human Reproduction,' in Devlin, ed., *Canadian Perspectives*, 308.

113 See Smart, 'Feminism and Law,' 117–19.

114 See Cowan, 'Women's Rights through Litigation,' 401–4. For a Canadian perspective, see M. Elizabeth Atcheson, Mary Eberts, and Beth Symes, *Women and Legal Action* (Ottawa, CACSW, 1984), who state at 170–1: 'The long-term goal of equality for women will best be furthered by a strategy which combines public education, lobbying, use of the media, law reform, education and lawyers and the judiciary, as well as litigation.'

115 If we recognize the essentially political role that law plays, then its poten-

tial to oppress or empower becomes apparent. Understanding the social context of law suggests that not only should law yield to social purpose, but that law must be justified in relation to its responsiveness to social needs, claims, and interests. An understanding of the social context of law also counsels against a strict adherence to some of the characteristics of legal method; those of carving up connected issues, objectifying situations and people, and using abstraction to remove them from their social surroundings.

CHAPTER NINE

Legal as Political Strategies in the Canadian Women's Movement: Who's Speaking? Who's Listening?[1]

Susan D. Phillips

Legal strategies, as efforts to address injustices in individual cases, are also political strategies. Conceived of as political strategies, legal tactics potentially serve three purposes: to frame issues so as to establish particular sets of meanings or discourses; to mobilize support in the form of allies, public opinion, and financial resources; and to have an impact on legal, policy, and procedural outcomes. For a social movement, litigation can be used directly or indirectly as a vehicle for enhancing its political objectives. First, a social movement organization may use the law and legal methods proactively by taking a case to the courts or by intervening in a case. The attractiveness of litigating varies widely depending on the financial and organizational capacity of a group to support a case, ability to frame the issue within an appropriate rights discourse, suitability of procedural requirements, and rules of the courts, as well as the political risk entailed in losing the case. The second use of litigation is more indirect, but nevertheless has important implications for political mobilization. Court cases brought by other parties often provide an opportunity for the development of shared perspectives and coalition building among a diversity of groups. The resulting mobilization may serve as the basis for initiating or intensifying lobbying efforts to enact new legislation or to ensure that protections or advantages already gained are not lost. In both uses, the significance and success of legal claims made by a social movement need to be viewed in light of its broader political strategies.

The choice and pursuit of political strategies depends on both the nature and agency of the political actor(s) *and* on the 'political opportunity structure,'[2] in which the claims are made and collective action encouraged. In other words, the success of political strategies is contingent on both who is speaking and who is listening. This chapter offers some observations on how the political strategies and opportunities for influence by the Anglo-Canadian women's movement evolved during a critical decade in the movement's development from the mid-1980s to the mid-1990s.[3] This was the period in which the movement met neoliberalism and issues of inclusiveness head on. As a result of these encounters, there have been very significant changes in both the nature of the claimants – and thus of the claims being made – and in the political opportunity structure for the expression of women's concerns. In terms of who is speaking as and for women in Canada, there has been a considerable – and long overdue – trend towards greater inclusiveness that takes more seriously than ever before the perspectives of non-white, non–middle-class women. Indeed, the leadership of Canada's largest women's organization, the National Action Committee on the Status of Women (NAC), was put to the test in the early 1990s as to its real commitment to internal democracy and inclusiveness over its involvement with the Canadian Panel on Violence Against Women (CPVAW). It passed. But the question of *who* is seeking and being represented remains at the heart of the political strategies of the movement, and, in this sense, it has become more democratic and open to all Canadian women. In terms of who has been listening to the movement, however, political opportunities have been significantly reduced because of the overarching focus of both the former Conservative and the current Liberal government on deficit reduction. As we will see in the case of advocacy on child care policy, even a cleverly crafted and diligently pursued political strategy may fail utterly if the government is unwilling to pay attention because it has a conflicting agenda.

Making Claims: Legal as Political Strategies

Political strategies are calculated efforts to influence government policy and to shape public values, opinions, and behaviour. They may be pursued through the electoral process, legal channels, or advocacy of public officials. The choice of channels, specific tactics, and selection of issues made by a social movement organization depends on both its own 'agency' and on the 'political opportunity structure.' As Jenson argues, political actors are 'simultaneously subjects of structure and acting subjects.'[4] The focus on agency considers political actors as responsible agents who make choices about action in accordance with their intentions and capacities.[5] For a social movement organization, this hinges to a large degree on its organizational capabilities (including financial resources, nature and size of membership, expertise, and collective identity) and on the discourse surrounding these issues (e.g., whether a particular issue is or can be framed as a gender or a rights issue).

The potential for political mobilization also depends on the political opportunity structure which may be defined as the 'consistent – but not necessarily formal or permanent – dimensions of the political environment that provide incentives for people to undertake collective action by affecting their expectations for success or failure.'[6] Particularly salient aspects of this structure include macro-level economic conditions, state structures, alignments among political parties and elites, electoral stability, the availability of influential allies, and the degree of openness or centralization of power within the machinery of government. More micro-level factors might include the political (both small and capital 'p') concerns of a relevant Minister and the appeal or pressing nature of other issues on the agenda at the time that a particular group is advancing its own claims. Within this structure, groups make choices about strategies, but their choices are not unconstrained. Not all political strategies are possible: some interests and actors will be recognized as legitimate by the state and other actors, while others will be dismissed or actively opposed. Neither the agency of a political actor nor the conditions of the political opportunity structure are solely determinative of the success or failure of a legal/political strategy. Rather, what counts is the fit between an actor's capacities, the available choices, and the external conditions.[7]

When are legal methods and routes likely to be used as a form of political strategy? In an excellent review of the literature and empirical analysis of cases in the U.S. court system, Scheppele and Walker cite four sets of explanations as to why civil society groups choose to use legal strategies.[8] First, a popular American theory has been that legal remedies are used most often by politically disadvantaged groups as a *last* resort because they are unlikely to succeed in the electoral process or through lobbying channels. Empirical analysis in both the United States and Canada, however, only partially supports this thesis because politically advantaged interests, notably corporations and trade associations, have made much more extensive use of the courts than have 'outsider' citizen groups.[9] Second, it is asserted that groups that can frame their objectives and interests in terms of a rights discourse are more likely to avail themselves of the courts. The debate over whether the *Canadian Charter of Rights and Freedoms* has greatly expanded rights discourses and ultimately produced the 'legalization of politics'[10] is beyond the scope of this chapter. But, as Roach notes, that it is premature 'to conclude that the Charter has entrenched the dominance of interest advocacy based on the litigation of rights.'[11] Because litigation is very expensive, a third explanation for use of the courts focuses on the financial capacity of groups (including the size and source of their budgets and availability of expert legal staff) and on the ability to form coalitions with other groups. Not only are citizen groups much less endowed with financial resources, but many are restricted by their charitable status under income tax laws from extensive legal and political activity.[12] Finally, the match between an organization's legal concerns and the jurisdictional basis and procedural rules of the court are important. Scheppele and Walker note that groups are much more likely to use the courts if they are involved in a long-standing and intense conflict with clearly identifiable opponents and if the court has clear jurisdiction to rule.[13]

The main conclusions reached by Scheppele and Walker on the basis of their analysis of U.S. court cases are that the two most important factors in determining preference for legal strategies are the threshold rules (particularly rules of standing) that govern when groups can use the courts and the availability of organizational resources (particularly financial assistance from foundations and other groups).[14] In comparison with the United States, the literature on legal strategies by interest groups and social movements in Canada is less extensive. In Canada, public interest legal advocacy as a means of advancing public policy has gained attention in recent years, but has been more modest than in the United States. For instance, a study by the Canadian Advisory Council on the Status of Women (CACSW) on the first three years of *Charter* litigation under the equality provisions of section 15 revealed that of 600 cases, only forty-four involved sex equality and only seven were initiated by or on behalf of women.[15] In contrast to the plethora of groups, law firms, and foundations available to support public interest legal advocacy in the United states, the resources in Canada have been limited. The creation of LEAF as the lead organization in soliciting and representing *Charter* cases on behalf of women, especially in the interests of doubly disadvantaged women, has had the effect of making it *the* women's group responsible for legal strategies. While other women's groups may be consulted and supportive of litigation or intervention sponsored by LEAF, they generally are not taking their own cases and have not developed the legal expertise or financial resources to do so. Clearly, the pursuit of political goals through legal channels represents only a minor part of the political activity of the women's movement in Canada. The indirect role of litigation as an opportunity for political mobilization, however, affects the entire movement at various times. It is these legal-turned-political moments, rather than the use of litigation as a strategic approach to change law and policy, that figure in the cases discussed below.

This chapter examines two cases – the involvement of women's groups in the Canadian Panel on Violence Against Women in 1991 and the mobilization around a national child care policy in the late 1980s and early 1990s – neither of which represent particularly successful political strategies for the women's movement. The importance of the cases, however, does not reside in their ultimate success in obtaining public policy outcomes. Rather, they serve as illustrations of the importance of considering both the agency of political actors and the nature of the political opportunity structure in explaining the actions and successes of the women's movement. The CPVAW highlights what was perhaps the central issue of politics within the women's movement in Canada in the 1990s – the concern over inclusion, voice, and representation of less-privileged women or, in other words, the issue of who is speaking. It also raises questions about the extent to which legal strategies can effectively serve as vehicles for the politics of inclusion. In this example, a court case did create an opportunity for expanding the litigation practices of LEAF towards greater participation and inclusion by a wide range of women's groups. The case of child care demonstrates how an unreceptive political opportunity structure can frustrate a movement's political strategies, even if a representative, well-organized campaign was undertaken. In this instance, a legal case was divisive, potentially pitting wealthier, self-employed women against salaried women, rather than serving as an opportunity for alliance building.[16]

Who's Speaking? The Test of the Panel on Violence Against Women

The Canadian Panel on Violence Against Women, established by the federal government in August 1991, was initially supported by national women's organizations. They soon abandoned it, however, as an exercise in token representation.[17] This case demonstrates the expansion of voices of women of colour and Aboriginal and disabled women that has occurred within the movement and shows that there have been some serious attempts by national organizations, notably NAC, to pay attention to these communities. In many respects, the panel was a test of the commitment of NAC to democratization within the movement, and it was a test they passed, although they were soundly chastised by the mainstream media which misunderstood the significance of this struggle over representation for the movement as a whole. Indeed, *Globe and Mail* columnist Jeffrey Simpson referred to NAC as 'mosquito bites' and urged policy-makers to shrug them off, thereby dismissing their concerns about inclusiveness as political correctness.[18]

To fully appreciate the tensions that developed between women's groups and the CPVAW, it is important to understand the backdrop of the ongoing structural changes within NAC that were attempts to democratize the organization and to better represent its increasingly diverse constituencies. Beginning in 1988, NAC undertook a series of internal reorganizations aimed at making it more regionally representative, enhancing member participation, and creating better means of establishing priorities among issues.[19] In 1991, an affirmative action and outreach policy were implemented: five of its twenty-five executive board positions were reserved for women of colour, immigrant women, Aboriginal women, and women with disabilities, with the stipulation that these positions would remain empty if there were no suitable candidates from the designated constituencies. These structural and attitudinal changes produced significant results in a short period of time. By 1993, roughly one-third of the member groups from Ontario and British Columbia primarily represented women of colour and three of its presidents in that decade were women of colour. It also built strong coalitions with other national organizations representing minority women.[20] Other national women's groups that once had a predominantly white, middle-class orientation, such as LEAF and the YWCA, also responded to the same imperatives of democratization and inclusivity, if less dramatically than NAC.

While violence against women has long been an issue in which women in grass-roots organizations, crisis centres, and transition houses have been active service providers and advocates, it is an issue to which national women's organizations came relatively late.[21] Violence against women exploded into national prominence as a political issue with the massacre of fourteen women by Marc Lepine at Montreal's Ecole Polytechnique on 6 December 1989. Many women's groups, including NAC, called for a royal commission on violence against women, although within NAC the preference for a royal commission was an issue that was supported by professional organizations and career women, but generally opposed by grass-roots groups and minority women.[22]

In the throne speech of May 1991, the federal government, which did not wish to appear to be ignoring the legacy of Lepine, announced its intention to establish a panel, rather than a more formal Royal Commission. Although the benefits of such a panel were again a disputed point within NAC, they could not condemn the government's proposal given their earlier pressure for a Royal Commission. However, they made known their demands that such a panel not be elitist but broadly representative and comprised of women who had been involved actively in antiviolence work at the community level. The nine-member panel that was announced by the Minister Responsible for the Status of Women, Mary Collins, in August 1991, had a budget of $10 million and, in fact, consisted of women (and one man) with solid credentials as feminists and as participants on the front line of services for victims of violence.[23] There was, however, only one woman of colour (a lawyer from Vancouver) and one Aboriginal woman. In spite of persistent internal concerns, especially among women of colour who felt that minority women were unrepresented on the CPVAW and by those who were leery of becoming too close to a Tory initiative, NAC as an organization publicly supported the panel because its basic demand generally had been met.

A concurrent legal event on the issue of sexual violence had important implications for the movement and its relationships with the CPVAW. In August 1991, the Supreme Court of Canada in the *Seaboyer* case struck down the rape shield provision (s. 276) of the *Criminal Code*. This came as a blow to the women's organizations that had struggled since the late 1970s to ensure that a victim's past sexual history was not used as evidence for the defence at a trial for sexual assault.[24] Under pressure from women's groups, Minister of Justice Kim Campbell moved quite quickly to organize a series of consultations with a wide range of organizations, the product of which was *Bill C-49*.[25] It was one of the relatively rare cases during the Conservative regime that the consultations were open and constructive and, as the litigation director of LEAF stated, 'It is clear that Justice Minister Campbell listened to the input from women's organizations.'[26] In fact, Kim Campbell was reported to have quipped, 'I am in deep trouble with my caucus: NAC said something nice about me.' Then aside, she added, 'Don't worry, this won't last.'[27]

The consultation that resulted from the *Seaboyer* case not only had a positive, if short-lived, impact on the relationship between the government and the movement, it had a significant impact within the movement. The discussions around *Bill C-49* and sexual violence served to bring together the grass-roots and national groups, as well as minority and more privileged women. It put differences into perspective, allowed common positions to be constructed with relative ease, and generally built trust within the movement. A widely shared political discourse about the issue was developed that included the concerns and experiences of minority women as well as those of middle-class white women. Therefore, as the CPVAW was beginning its own consultation process at this same time, there were some positive expectations about what could be accomplished, and there was a much more unified movement around the issue of violence against women than had existed previously. NAC, as well as other groups, continued to do extensive work on the issue which had been identified as one of three priority campaigns for 1991–2 at its June annual general meeting (AGM).[28]

Almost as soon as the panel began, trouble was evident. First, there were unresolved issues of representation that continued to bother the panel. As a result of their very vocal concerns about inadequate representation, Aboriginal women succeeded in obtaining the establishment of an Aboriginal Circle composed of four women who were representatives of national Aboriginal organizations. They also secured the commitment that the circle would have sufficient power to integrate the unique needs and concerns of Aboriginal women fully with the work of the CPVAW.[29] In contrast, the nineteen-member advisory committee, which comprised professionals in the field and some representatives of women's groups, and which had been appointed at the same time, had little power and money, minimal information, and no real input into the deliberations of the panel.

As soon as the panel began its cross-country process of community consultations in January 1992, further complaints were heard. The process was badly organized. The focus was on hearing the experiences of individuals so that front-line workers and representatives of rape crisis centres and women's shelters were given only five minutes each to present their experiences and positions.[30] There were no interpreters for those who spoke neither French nor English, no accessibility for the disabled, and no child care. Little outreach had been done to encourage women of different cultures to come forward. In fact, at one of the

Toronto meetings – a locale in which cultural, racial, and class diversity should have been anticipated as reflective of the community – all of the women in attendance were white.[31]

The model for the consultative process was that of national catharsis which had been used in the Spicer Commission, and subsequently in the Royal Commission on New Reproductive Technologies, consisting of rounds of meetings with individuals in communities across the country.[32] While the CPVAW congratulated itself for travelling to 139 communities and hearing from 4,000 individuals, many activists in the movement saw this as hugely expensive and largely unproductive. The decision to focus on the explication of experiences to the effective exclusion of discussion of policy solutions was a poor one given how much awareness of the issue had increased in the span of a few years. While at the time of the Montreal massacre, lack of public awareness of violence against women was a serious problem, by the time the panel began its consultative process, much work had been done to heighten public consciousness. In part as a result of the consultations surrounding the rape shield legislation, different constituencies within the women's movement more clearly understood the concerns of each other. Thus, the CPVAW could have been more effective had it concentrated on policy responses from the beginning.

Shortly before its spring AGM of 1992, NAC sponsored its own round table on violence which drew participation by sixty representatives of a wide diversity of women's groups. Their displeasure with the CPVAW was so strong that they called for it to be disbanded. After consultations between executive members of NAC and Minister Collins, NAC issued an ultimatum: the government must appoint three new members (a black woman, an immigrant woman, and a woman with disablities), create a more effective role for the advisory committee, and provide greater accountability, specifically that the panel's findings be submitted to a subcommittee of NAC before being released. The chair of the CPVAW responded with a much more restrictive offer of three new special advisers. At this point, communication between chair of the CPVAW Pat Marshall and president of NAC Judy Rebick was strained, to say the least.

The panel's offer was so completely unacceptable to both the leadership and membership of NAC that the AGM voted unanimously to withdraw the organization's support for the panel.[33] Eventually six other national organizations – including the Congress of Black Women, the DisAbled Women's Network (DAWN), the National Organization of Visible Minority and Immigrant Women, and the Canadian Association of Sexual Assault Centres – joined NAC in condemning the CPVAW as tokenism and withdrew their support for it.[34] Vice-president of the Congress of Black Women Fleurette Osborne described their sense of marginalization: 'The Panel is sitting in the dining room and the rest of us are in the kitchen.'[35] The basic concern was that a committee that represents primarily white middle-class women could not fully represent racial minority women, women with disabilities, or working-class women and that the distinctive experiences of these women as victims of violence thereby were being ignored.[36] The Aboriginal women did not withdraw their support because their demands for representation had been met. That the withdrawal by the other national organizations did not alienate the Aboriginal women attests to the growing integration of the movement that had developed over this period, in part as a result of close ties between NAC and the Native Women's Association (NWAC) on the constitutional debate and regular communication between them on this one.

In contrast, the media seemed almost gleeful over this 'infighting.'[37] Some journalists claimed that the demands for representation of constituencies by members of those constituencies was itself a form of racial purification.[38] What the media reports missed for the most part was how much the face of feminism has changed and the degree to which the women's movement has progressed in taking the politics of inclusiveness seriously. In this case, that meant direct representation by women of different races, cultures, and class, not merely a sensitivity to these concerns by elite women.[39] If the leadership of NAC had ignored the concerns of women of colour, disabled women, and grass-roots activists among its own membership and remained with the CPVAW, a serious and long-lasting hiatus in the movement would have been the likely result.

Almost two years after it had begun, the panel released its report, *Changing the Landscape: Ending Violence, Achieving Equality*, on 29 July 1993.[40] The report, which took an explicitly feminist approach linking violence against women to systemic inequality, made 494 recommendations. These ranged from specific measures, such as boycotting violent movies and challenging sexist jokes, to universal appeals, for example, that men pledge not to be violent. At best, the report was reviewed with mild hope; at worst, it was censured as a boondoggle. There were three main criticisms: (1) it contains little information or recommendations that are new and thus the $10 million might have been better spent on funding shelters and crisis centres;[41] (2) it did not address the special concerns of minority women;[42] and (3) the process of hearing individuals relating experiences rather than groups (and individuals) discussing solutions was misplaced. As O'Reilly (a former writer for the CPVAW) lamented, the result of this process was '[A] lot of well-meaning people in small communities and in the North were sucked into the vortex of Ottawa-think, the taxpayer-funded world where process becomes more important than production, and not much gets done but people spend a lot of time doing it.'[43] Joan Meister, a representative of DAWN and member of the advisory committee, summed up the feeling of many women in national organizations when she said that while the government claimed that it had zero tolerance for violence against women, 'zero tolerance seems to mean no tolerance for women's groups.'[44]

What are the lessons from the Canadian Panel on Violence Against Women? First, the *who* of representation is increasingly critical. There has been a considerable, albeit unfinished, process of democratization within the women's movement in Canada such that the politics of difference are being taken seriously by many women's groups.[45] It is no longer legitimate to provide representation by white middle-class elites sensitive to racial, disability, and cultural differences; instead, direct participation by members of these constituencies and real opportunities to have input has come to be seen as a requirement of legitimate inclusiveness. While less-privileged women had participated in NAC for years, what was new at this time was the way in which the concerns of these women affected the organization's politics. As Judy Rebick, past president of NAC, put it: 'The women's movement, not just NAC, is way ahead of everybody else in society in dealing with issues of inclusion. We're breaking new ground for an organization like NAC. Nobody else is doing it to the same degree and most institutions aren't doing it at all. Or if they're doing it, they're doing it through tokenism. It's the same way they do it with women: you get the tame, safe women, or you get the tame, safe people of Colour who aren't going to challenge anything and you include them. We're not doing it that way. I think what we're doing is real.'[46]

Another NAC past president Sunera Thobani noted, 'We have learned that, if the women's movement is to have relevance for the lives of women who seek equality, then NAC has to remain committed to opening the doors to women who have had all other doors in society shut in their faces. And, it is these women who understand our society better than those who live in the four walls of their relative privilege.'[47]

Second, the *how* of representation is also important. In recent years, the federal government has demonstrated a preference for using third parties (such as task forces and royal commissions) to handle a variety of hot issues and provide national prominence and visibility for these issues by taking them to communities across the country. This practice has the advantage of connecting government with citizens as *individuals*. This is often undertaken as a cathartic experience and, in part, reflected a mistrust of interest groups by both the Conservative and Liberal governments. There is little doubt that in some instances this approach can be very effective in raising awareness and providing extensive, fair, and constructive participation on public policy issues. The issue of violence against women, however, was a case in which considerable expertise was already resident in groups. This expertise could have been tapped and the CPVAW could have started drawing up its recommendations much sooner – at a greatly reduced cost. Many of the activists in these groups who had worked for years on antiviolence felt a considerable degree of ownership over the issue and, naturally, they were reluctant to concede quietly their stake to a government-sponsored body that appeared to be reinventing the issue anew. The panel's process and its alienation of these groups, therefore, had sewn its own seeds of conflict from the start. In addition, the media poorly portrayed the nature of the struggle over the meaning of inclusiveness to the Canadian public. Indeed, they fostered the image of women's groups, especially NAC, as hostile, critical but never constructive, and as operating on the margins of politics. The media's love of a fight meant that, in general, journalists and, therefore, the Canadian public missed the significance of the conflict over representation.

Third, the example shows how a legal event – here, the *Seaboyer* case – has the potential to reverse in a flash hard-won gains and protections for women. But such legal events can also be turned into constructive moments of political mobilization that serve to draw communities together. Razack notes that when LEAF first intervened in the *Seaboyer* and *Gayme* cases at the trial level in 1985, they developed the factum without consultation with other women's organizations and later were severely criticized for its lack of equality arguments.[48] LEAF responded positively, however, with a process of 'workshopping' that has become standard practice in most cases. This democratization of its own internal legal practices involves formation of a working group consisting of members of the LEAF national committee and local chapters that consults with women's groups and communities, thus usually producing a much deeper appreciation of these communities. When the Supreme Court rendered its decision on *Seaboyer* in 1991 and struck down the protection of the rape shield law, the potentially disastrous moment was transformed into a constructive political strategy. As Bourne notes, 'In a rare show of feminist solidarity, white women joined with black, visible minority, Aboriginal, lesbian, and disabled women in calling for a clause in the preamble [to *Bill C-49*] recognizing the special vulnerability of "doubly oppressed" women to sexual assault and their lack of accessibility to the justice system.'[49] Although *Bill C-49* passed to the general satisfaction of the women's groups involved, the government would not concede to such a clause.

Future big budget consultations would be well advised to heed the basic lesson of this example. Consultations designed to bring political advantage to a government that do not draw on the expertise of communities and groups are open to challenges to their legitimacy and probably doomed to expensive and unnecessarily failure. The case also highlights that while the legal system tends to be inherently exclusionary rather than inclusive, litigation can serve as a moment for alliance building. Its final lesson lies in how quickly an issue can fall off the government agenda. In spite of initial attempts to develop a coordinated response to the CPVAW recommendations across the many departments involved in policy-making related to ending violence against women, a change in government meant that momentum stalled. Not only did the federal government apparently lose interest, but so too did the media. By the end of the 1990s, it was much more difficult to get the mainstream media in Canada to pay attention to issues related to gender and the women's movement, whether given positive or negative coverage, than at the beginning of the decade.

Who's Listening? The Disappearance of a National Child Care Policy

The demise of a proposed national child care policy in the late 1980s and early 1990s demonstrates the inherent difficulties of influence by groups advocating government spending in an era of fiscal restraint and a shrinking state. The outcomes on the child care issue had little to do with how hard and well women's groups lobbied. The most significant factor was that the political opportunity structure shifted ground under the advocates from a government willing to fund a national program – although based on neoconservative assumptions about traditional families, a limited role of the state, and preferences for the use of market-based delivery mechanisms – to a totally uninterested and, indeed, resistant state.

The issue of child care first emerged on the political agenda in 1970 when the *Report of the Royal Commission on the Status of Women* argued that the state has a shared responsibility with parents for caring for children and that without a comprehensive, affordable, and accessible child care system, women would never achieve equality. In spite of the growing participation of women in the paid labour force and a serious shortage of spaces in day care centres, very little was done on the issue until 1984 when the Liberal government in its dying days established a task force (the Cooke Task Force) to investigate the issue. In the election campaign and Throne Speech of that year, newly elected Prime Minister Mulroney committed his Conservative government to the creation of a national child care policy. Three years later, the National Strategy on Childcare was finally introduced, although it bore little resemblance to the 1986 report of the Cooke Task Force which had recommended an integrated system, including measures of parental leave, that would be completely publicly funded and non-profit.[50]

In contrast, the National Strategy had the stamp of a neoconservative and neoliberal ideology. A third of the proposed $6.4 billion allocation was dedicated to transfers to individuals under the income tax system (in most cases, irrespective of whether the money was spent on child care services).[51] The other major part of the National Strategy was the *Canada Child Care Act (Bill C-144)* that would have authorized $4 billion over seven years as operating and capital grants to centres, including for-profit centres. Because the regulation of child care lies under provincial jurisdiction, and the Conservatives did not want to contest this authority or antagonize the provinces, and because they saw monitoring of the system as a responsibility of parents, the proposed Act did not attempt to impose national standards or objectives on the quality of care that the provinces would have to ensure as a condition of federal funding.

The amount of money to be allocated to tax expenditures versus subsidizing the creation of day care spaces was a contested one within the government. There reportedly was a head-to-head contest in cabinet between Minister of Health and Welfare Jake Epp, who could not be described as a wildly enthusiastic supporter of child care at all, but who publicly was committed to expanding the supply of spaces, and Minister of Finance Michael Wilson, who favoured use of the tax system and restrictive financial ceilings. Ultimately, it was the minister of finance who prevailed.

The leading advocacy organization on the issue which spoke for both the women's movement and the child care advocacy community was the Child Care Advocacy Association of Canada (CCAAC).[52] The organization, founded in 1983, is not explicitly a feminist organization, but a federation of local and provincial child care advocacy groups, child care workers, social policy groups, unions and day care parents. The CCAAC's position was based on a clearly articulated model centred on universal accessibility, comprehensiveness, high quality, and non-profit administration.[53] Given this approach, it is not surprising that the CCAAC was vehemently opposed to the Conservatives' National Strategy: it contained no national objectives; provided insufficient new money (only one-half of the total allocation actually would have been an infusion of new dollars); supported for-profit centres; and relied too heavily on the tax system.

Although child care was also an important issue for the women's movement, most national and local women's groups did not develop their own information and positions, but adopted those of the CCAAC. This was primarily a conservation of scarce resources that is common in social movements. Given that most women's groups face a multitude of issues, all critically important to their constituencies, and have grossly inadequate resources with which to pursue these issues, the opportunity to borrow solid research and a well-thought-out position from an ally that specializes in the issue is a welcome one. Not only is the CCAAC a member of NAC, but at the time it shared adjoining offices with NAC's Ottawa office, and several people, notably Martha Friendly of the Childcare Resource and Research Unit at the University of Toronto, were central in developing policy positions in both organizations. Thus, there was considerable communication and accessibility between the two groups.

The CCAAC led a multipronged and intensive campaign on the issue: they conducted a successful petition campaign that gathered thousands of signatures, sponsored numerous information and protest events at the local level, and put together a very broadly based coalition of national groups including organizations as diverse as the Canadian Labour Congress, Federation of Nurses, National Anti-Poverty Organization, Canadian Jewish Congress, and Federation of Students, as well as many women's groups. During the brief legislative committee hearings in September 1987, they presented and coordinated the presentation of briefs by numerous other groups, and over an extended period had several meetings with the minister.[54]

Although the tax measures had become effective immediately upon their announcement and the child care bill quickly passed the House of Commons, in spite of the broad coalition of groups that uniformly spoke against it, it was not simply rubber-stamped by the Senate. There were two female sympathizers in the upper chamber – Conservative Senator Spivak and Liberal Senator Marsden whose support the women's movement had cultivated. Long before *Bill C-144* came to the upper chamber, these women ensured that Senate committees took a close look at the complete package of child benefits. The Senate standing committee that reviewed the Bill chose to provide the opportunity for extensive testimony from the advocates, many of whom had been declined a hearing in the legislation's swift passage through the House of Commons. Indeed, the Senate dragged out this process as long as possible and, not by chance, was still meeting when Parliament was dissolved for the 1988 federal election. Consequently, the Bill died on the order paper.

Given that the government had been unwilling to modify the strategy, the advocates considered the loss of the *Child Care Act* to be an unmitigated victory. Their leaders believed that they would be able to persuade a different federal government to pass more appropriate legislation or that they could concentrate their lobbying efforts on provincial governments. However, the political environment changed dramatically in a very short period of time. Not only were the Conservatives returned to power in the 1988 election, more focused than ever on fiscal restraint, but provincial governments, too, soon lost interest in spending programs of any kind. In spite of this retrenchment, however, few advocates on the CCAAC's campaign felt that the loss of the Conservatives' bill was a mistake.[55]

In its second term, the Mulroney government announced a new initiative – a focus on 'children on risk' – that proved to be strong on rhetoric, but unmatched with policy commitments. This allowed the prime minister and his government in February 1992 to walk away completely from their earlier commitment on child care on the grounds that, because of tough economic conditions, the federal government could not afford a national child care strategy. Indeed, throughout the Conservatives' second term both the women's movement and child care advocates were at complete odds with the Mulroney government, so that any lobbying by them was ignored and even discredited.[56] The federal government went so far as to help create and fund an alternative, less radical voice to the CCAAC as the lead representative of the child care community and, by the mid-1990s, the Child Care Federation had in many respects ascended to that role. At the same time, the Conservative and later Liberal government began to de-fund women's advocacy organizations, with NAC taking the most dramatic and largest single cuts to its operational support. Not surprisingly, this had a profound effect on the number of issues in which it could be involved.[57]

In this example, a legal challenge also played an important role that helped to shift the discourse to some degree and that would have profoundly changed the course of policy had the Supreme Court made a different decision on it. In 1989, Beth Symes, a self-employed lawyer and founding member of LEAF (although the case was not officially supported by LEAF) took a case to the Federal Court.[58] Symes claimed that she should be entitled to deduct the full salary of her nanny (an actual cost of almost $50,000 between 1982 and 1985, compared with the allowable annual deduction under the *Income Tax Act* of between $1,000 and $4,000) because the full cost of care should be regarded as an expense necessary to earn income from her business. It was also argued that to disallow such as expense would be an abrogation of the plaintiff's equality rights under the *Charter*: that is, to fail to consider the real costs of care as a business expense would have a disproportionate impact on women who remain primarily responsible for caregiving and, therefore, would constitute discrimination on the basis of sex.

Justice Cullen of the Federal Court concluded that the appellant had suffered discrimination based on her personal characteristics as a parent and a woman and he agreed that the full cost of nanny care should be allowed on the premise that the high cost of day care 'constitutes a barrier to women's access to the economy.'[59] In rendering its decision on the appeal in December 1993, however, the Supreme Court split seven to two along gender lines. The male majority rejected the claim that the inadmissability of the tax deduction is a form of gender discrimination because paying for child care is a responsibility of both parents: 'Unfortunately, proof that women pay social costs is not sufficient proof that women pay child care expenses. Those social costs, although very real, exist outside of the *Income Tax Act*.'[60] In a scathing dissent, the two female justices argued that the cost of a nanny is as legitimate a business expense as male-dominated activities such as lunches, cars, or golf club memberships. The logic of the majority argument – that the responsibility of paying for care is shared by both parents – may leave open the possibility of future *Charter* challenges of the child care expense deduction by self-employed single mothers.

Had the Supreme Court found in favour of Symes, the federal government would have been forced to respond with new policy because it would have been politically intolerable to allow full deductions of the cost of child care for self-employed parents, but not for salaried ones. As it was, the case received a mere blip of media attention. Unlike *Seaboyer*, this case did not serve as a rallying point for the women's movement and child care advocates because they did not see the tax system as the appropriate vehicle for implementing a national strategy at all. But in subtle ways, the case altered the political discourse by directly equating the subsidies to business for the 'perks' (e.g., meals with clients, club memberships) with lack of support for child care.

Under the first two terms of the Chrétien government, favourable possibilities for federally sponsored child care initially re-emerged, but were then shut down by the imperatives of fiscal restraint. During this period, the nature of the discourse over child care shifted significantly – from concerns over equality of women, to economic productivity, to a focus on child development. The first positive sign was that the Liberal's 1993 election agenda, laid out in their *Red Book*, tied the creation of new spaces to economic growth: it promised to expand the number of child care spaces by 50,000 in each year following a year of 3 per cent growth (up to a total of 150,000 spaces). In its first year in office, child care advocates helped the Chrétien government reposition the political discourse on child care in ways compatible with its dominant focus on jobs and the economy by forging closer conceptual links between social and economic policy. This was evidenced by the fact that in the discussion paper on social security reform presented in October 1994 by Human Resources Development Minister Lloyd Axworthy, child care is discussed under the chapter heading of 'working: jobs in a new economy' and is seen as a critical support for employment.[61] Child care was viewed as having a double benefit: first, it turns unproductive workers (especially women who are receiving social assistance benefits) into productive ones and, second, by linking quality care with child development, it is seen as a preventative approach to avoiding social costs later in life that result from a lack of support for children in their early years. It appeared for a brief period that a national child care policy might succeed if it could be reconfigured as an issue about jobs and the economy.

This window of opportunity was slammed shut by Finance Minister Martin's 1995 budget that made deficit reduction the all-consuming priority, put social policy reform on hold, and initiated a sharp reduction in the role of the federal government in both society and the economy.[62] It appeared, momentarily, to be nailed shut by the 1996 Throne Speech which, in the interests of national unity, placed self-imposed quasi-constitutional restrictions on the federal government's use of the spending power, thereby limiting future federal leadership in establishing cost-shared programs in areas of provincial jurisdiction.

Over this period, child care organizations continued to work with other child welfare organizations and social policy groups to advance the agenda of reducing child poverty. This collaborative work culminated with the creation of Campaign 2000, a diverse coalition of more than seventy groups. It is interesting to note that while two quite traditional women's organizations – the National Council of Women and the National Council of Jewish Women – are part of this coalition, NAC has not participated, illustrating how far removed from gender equity the issue of child care has become situated. In 1999, the Liberal government again began hinting that it would introduce a national child care program, linked to the National Children's Agenda. The latter is a federal–provincial initiative, signed in May 1999, that involves a number of ministries at each level (e.g., health, social services, justice, and human resources) and is intended to be 'a comprehensive long-term strategy to improve the well-being of children.'[63] Although the federal and provincial/territorial governments have agreed to support an early childhood development initiative as part of this agenda, a national child care strategy is not an explicit aspect of it. Nor is it likely to be in the foreseeable future, as neither level of government has any interest in reopening this discussion.

The case of child care provides three observations on political strategies of the women's movement. First, success depends, in part, on who is listening. If the political opportunity structure closes, as it did in this case when the Conservative and Liberal governments became consumed with deficit reduction and were no longer willing to support any new spending on child care, no rational arguments by the advocates – no matter how compelling – and no protest tactics will make a major difference.

The second observation is that the CCAAC, like most social movement organizations, has been firmly attached to its first principles and relatively uncompromising in its demands. Consequently, the organization's leaders were not about to agree that some new government-subsidized spaces are better than none, if this required sacrificing the other principles of quality and non-profit administration. While there is real value in and a vital role for such principled behaviour, it often comes at a cost of some loss of accessibility to ministers and bureaucrats.[64] In this case, the federal government actively attempted and succeeded in displacing the organization in favour of an organization that it viewed as more flexible.

Finally, this case shows that the way in which an issue is framed and how a political discourse is constructed is critical. Child care has been pursued primarily in terms of a child-centred discourse initially developed by the CCAAC and later carried forward by Campaign 2000. This discourse has had the advantage that it did not alienate men as parents and facilitated support by a broad coalition. But it has not been a discourse situated around gender, and this has circumvented to some extent the discussion of women's work and the gendered nature of caregiving.[65]

Conclusions

These two cases are only a glimpse into the myriad of issues on which Anglo-Canadian women's groups have been active advocates over the past thirty years. In addition, we have focused on legal strategies as a dimension of political strategies, rather than as an end unto themselves. Thus, we should be cautious about generalizing to movement-wide trends and to all legal strategies. Nevertheless, the cases do offer some insights into the three questions posed in the introductory chapter.

Should women persevere with the legal project despite its manifest dangers? My response is a definitive yes, though I recognize that legal tactics are only one form of political strategies. The risk is that litigation will always entail the possibility of losing, sometimes in a big way, in terms of legal or policy outcomes. This risk has to be assessed as accurately as possible in deciding whether to persist with litigation, and it cannot be ameliorated completely. In many cases, as with *Symes*, the clear alternative is to gain nothing. Perhaps the greatest benefit of litigation lies in its capacity to frame or reframe issues in ways that convey new meaning and carry political momentum that will help to effect change through other channels such as legislatures, international conventions, or alterations in individual and institutional behaviour. Success in subsequent mobilization depends on organizational capacities, financial and human resources, alliances within and beyond the movement, and the willingness of government to recognize political advocacy as legitimate and to react constructively to it. In this respect, the determinants of the ultimate success of legal strategies are little different from those of other political tactics: they need to be connected to and are dependent on the broader political strategies of an organization or movement.

Has litigation in the cases discussed in this chapter been successful, and by what measures? As political strategies, litigation can be evaluated according to three general criteria: Did litigation help frame or reframe the issue in ways that can be used politically by the movement? Did the case facilitate political mobilization within the movement and among allies? Did the judicial decision lead to changes in the law, policy, or process? The two cases discussed in this chapter, *Seaboyer* and *Symes*, reflect the enormous variability in the success of cases in which the women's movement was involved in the late twentieth century. While the decision in *Seaboyer* was neither a victory for framing nor outcomes, it became an important opportunity for mobilization that had significant implications for the movement. It was a case to which women had to react through other political means or give up on some important basic principles. In contrast, the contribution of *Symes* was largely in framing child care as an employment issue, and it had virtually no impact on outcomes or mobilization.

What can we learn from the strategies pursued? One advantage of legal strategies is that it is possible that women's organizations – whether as appellants, intervenors, or bystanders – can lose but still win. They may lose on the specifics of the case, but they can effectively use the judicial outcomes as a starting-point for a political strategy aimed at changing legislation or practice. The likelihood of turning a legal defeat into a successful political strategy is linked to both the political and organizational capacity *and* to contemporary political opportunity structures. In this regard, the basic lesson of this chapter is that for legal strategies to be generally effective, a social movement needs to build and maintain as much capacity as possible. There is little that a movement can do to ensure a compliant political opportunity structure, however. And here, we can offer few reasons to be optimistic because, at the end of the twentieth century, the women's movement in Canada faced a more closed political opportunity structure than it had just a decade earlier. Even in a post-deficit era, governments in general are less permeable to advocacy by civil society organizations. They have become much more constrained by several factors: decisions of neoliberal policies that restructured many social and other programs, often offloading or subjecting them to market discipline; intergovernmental relations; and consultative processes targeted to hearing primarily from individuals. The result of this closure has been to radicalize NAC and other groups and force them to work more through the media and public opinion than through the traditional channels of political lobbying. However, as was evident in the conflict over the Canadian Panel on Violence against Women, the media often demonstrate a very limited understanding of the nature of the movement and its issues.

Finally, one of the most significant and long-lasting developments in the Canadian women's movements has been the shift away from an emphasis on *what* is being represented and *how* it is being claimed to *who* is being represented. While the recognition and discussion of differences within the movement has been talked about for many years, some significant steps towards internal democratization were taken and not only changed policy discourses on a variety of issues, but affected political strategies in important ways. Legal movements, whether the issue at hand is won or lost, can be very important opportunities for political mobilization and consensus mobilization in the less than favourable contemporary climate.

Notes

1 The constructive comments of Radha Jhappan, Miriam Smith, Martha Friendly, and Elizabeth Casuga are greatly appreciated. Research for this work was supported by a grant from the Social Sciences and Humanities Research Council. An earlier version of this work was first presented at a conference at Carleton University in October 1993.
2 Analysis of the concept of political opportunity structure perhaps has been developed most extensively by Sidney Tarrow, *Power in Movement: Social Movements, Collective Action and Politics* (Cambridge: Cambridge University Press, 1994); see also Herbert Kitschelt, 'Political Opportunity Structures and Political Protest: Anti-Nuclear Movements in Four Democracies'

(1986) 16 *British Journal of Political Science* 57–85. The concept originates with Peter K. Eisinger, 'The Conditions of Protest Behavior in American Cities' (1973) 67 *American Political Science Review* 11–28.

3 This chapter focuses on the political strategies of the national women's organizations in English Canada. It is important to note that, because of its ties to Quebec nationalism, a political focus on the Quebec rather than the federal government, and a more progressive history of social policy in Quebec, the story of women's groups in Quebec is quite different from that of English Canada. For discussions of the political strategies of women in Quebec see: Micheline Dumont, 'Women of Quebec and the Contemporary Constitutional Issue'; Roberta Hamilton, 'Pronatalism, Feminism and Nationalism'; and Manon Tremblay, 'Gender and Support for Feminism: A Case Study of the 1989 Quebec General Election,' in François-Pierre Gingras, ed., *Gender and Politics* (Toronto: Oxford University Press, 1997).

4 Jane Jenson, 'Paradigms and Political Discourse: Protective Legislation in France and the United States before 1914' (1989) 22 *Canadian Journal of Political Science* 236.

5 Amartya Sen, *On Ethics and Economics* (Oxford: Blackwell, 1987) 40–4.

6 Tarrow, *Power in Movement*, 85.

7 On the issue of 'fit' between political actors and external conditions, see Theda Skocpol, *Protecting Soldiers and Mothers: The Political Origins of Social Policy in the United States* (Cambridge, MA: Harvard University Press, 1992) 1–62.

8 Kim Lane Scheppele and Jack L. Walker, 'The Litigation Strategies of Interest Groups,' in Jack L. Walker, *Mobilizing Interest Groups in America* (Ann Arbor: University of Michigan Press, 1991) 157–83, and Susan Olson, 'Interest Group Litigation in Federal District Court: Beyond the Political Disadvantage Theory' (1990) 52 *Journal of Politics* 854–82.

9 Scheppele and Walker, 'The Litigation Strategies of Interest Groups,' 182.

10 The legalization of politics is discussed in Michael Mandel, *The Charter of Rights and Freedoms and the Legalization of Politics in Canada*, 2nd ed. (Toronto: Wall and Thompson, 1994). On the expansion of rights discourses with particular reference to a number of feminist issues, see Janet Hiebert, 'Debating Policy: The Effect of Rights Talk,' in F. Leslie Seidle, ed., *Equity and Community: The Charter, Interest Advocacy and Representation* (Montreal: Institute for Research on Public Policy, 1993) 31–60.

11 Kent Roach, 'The Role of Litigation and the Charter in Interest Advocacy,' in Seidle, *Equity and Community*, 182

12 For a discussion of the restrictions on charitable status in Canada, see A. Paul Pross and Iain S. Stewart,' Lobbying, the Voluntary Sector and the

Public Purse,' in Susan D. Phillips, ed., *How Ottawa Spends 1993–94: A More Democratic Canada ...?* (Ottawa: Carleton University Press, 1993) 121–32 and Panel on Accountability and Governance in the Voluntary Sector, *Building on Strength: Improving Governance and Accountability in Canada's Voluntary Sector* (Ottawa: Voluntary Sector Roundtable, 1999) 67–70; in the United States, see Scheppele and Walker, 'The Litigation Strategies of Interest Groups,' 162–4.

13 Roach notes that there are a number of differences between the Canadian and American courts in procedural rules that affect citizen group litigation. While in the United States a losing party is responsible only for its own costs, under Anglo-Canadian procedure, the loser may also be assessed a substantial portion of the costs of the winning side. Groups must also be able to attain standing, i.e., to show that they are directly affected in the case, and finally, class actions, with the exception of Quebec and Ontario, are much more restricted in Canada. See Roach, 'The Role of Litigation and the Charter in Interest Advocacy,' 173–4; see also Christopher P. Manfredi, '"Appropriate and Just in the Circumstances": Public Policy and the Enforcement of Rights under the Canadian Charter of Rights and Freedoms' (1994) 27 *Canadian Journal of Political Science* 435–63.

14 Jeffrey M. Berry reaches a similar conclusion in *The Interest Group Society*, 3rd ed. (New York: Longman, 1997) 176–7.

15 Canadian Advisory Council on the Status of Women, *Canadian Charter Equality Rights for Women: One Step Forward or Two Steps Back?* prepared by Gwen Brodsky and Shelagh Day (Ottawa: Ministry of Supply and Services, 1989).

16 In both cases, the methodology involved a series of semistructured interviews conducted with key informants as well as analysis of media coverage, legal cases, and other primary documents.

17 For a discussion of the role and implications of the panel, see Andrea Levan, 'Violence Against Women,' in Janine Brodie, ed., *Women and Canadian Public Policy* (Toronto: Harcourt Brace, 1996) 319–54.

18 Jeffrey Simpson, 'Shrug off the Mosquito Bites and Get On with the Good Work,' *Globe and Mail*, 20 August 1992, A20.

19 Ann Molgat, *An Action that Will Not Be Allowed to Subside: NAC's First Twenty Years* (Toronto: National Action Committee on the Status of Women, 1993) 10–11; Jill Vickers, Pauline Rankin, and Christine Appelle, *Politics as if Women Mattered* (Toronto: University of Toronto Press, 1993) 205–46. Marjorie Griffin Cohen, 'The Canadian Women's Movement,' in Ruth Roach Pierson, Marjorie Griffin Cohen, Paula Bourne, and Philinda Masters, *Canadian Women's Issues*, vol. 1, *Strong Voices* (Toronto: Lorimer

1993) 1–31; Judy Rebick, 'Interview with Judy Rebick' (1994) 44 *Studies in Political Economy* 39–71.
20 Michele Landsberg, 'Canada's Largest Women's Group Is Making Waves' (1993) 4, 2 *Ms Magazine*, 18–19. Sunera Thobani was not parachuted into the presidency, but had worked hard in member groups of NAC. Yet her uncontested nomination was attacked as illegitimate by a Tory member of Parliament (and by a number of 'old guard' women) because she is an immigrant woman of colour. On this point, see Ruth Roach Piersen, 'The Mainstream Women's Movement and the Politics of Difference,' in Pierson et al., *Canadian Women's Issues*, 207. Thobani was succeeded by Joan Grant-Cummings, a Jamaican Canadian, who, in turn, was succeeded by Terri Brown, a First Nations woman.
21 For a discussion of the relationships between the women's movement and the state on family violence, see Gillian A. Walker, *Family Violence and the Women's Movement: The Conceptual Politics of Struggle* (Toronto: University of Toronto Press, 1990). On the background and process of the panel, see Elizabeth Casuga, 'Women's Issues and the State: The Canadian Panel on Violence Against Women,' unpublished honours thesis, School of Public Administration, Carleton University, 1994.
22 Personal communication with member of the NAC executive, September 1993.
23 For biographical notes on the nine members of the panel, see Status of Women Canada, 'Minister Collins Announces National Panel to Address Violence Against Women' (Ottawa: Status of Women Canada, 15 August 1991).
24 *R. v. Seaboyer* (1991) 83 D.L.R. (4th) 193. See Roz Currie, 'Supreme Court Strikes Down "Rape Shield" Law,' 12, 1 (1991) *Jurisfemme: News from the National Association of Women and the Law* 1, 3; Sherene Razack, *Canadian Feminism and the Law* (Toronto: Second Story Press, 1991) 56–8.
25 For a discussion of this Act, as well as subsequent court cases and legislation, see Janet Hiebert, 'Transforming Policy Conflict into Debates about Fundamental Rights: How Has the Canadian Charter of Rights and Freedoms Affected Political Will?' Paper presented to the Fifth World Congress of the International Association of Constitutional Law, Rotterdam, NL, July 1999. Available at www.eur.nl/frg/iacl/papers/hiebert.html. See also McIntyre's discussion in this volume.
26 'New Sexual Assault Legislation a Step Forward,' 4, 4 (January 1992) *LEAFLines* (Newsletter of the Women's Legal Education and Action Fund) 1. The one issue on which the Minister would not make concessions was the demand for inclusion in the preamble to *Bill C-49* of a statement that

because of racism, certain women are at greater risk for sexual assault and have more limited access to the justice system.
27 Personal communication with member of the NAC executive.
28 The other two priority campaigns were the Future of Women's Work and the 52 per cent Solution. National Action Committee on the Status of Women, *Annual Report 1991/92* (Toronto: NAC, 1992): 6. For details, see National Action Committee on the Status of Women, *The Women's Agenda: Declaration of Principles and a Call to Action* (Toronto: NAC, 1991).
29 Status of Women Canada, 'Canadian Panel on Violence Against Women: Minister Appoints Members of Advisory Committee and Aboriginal Circle' (Ottawa: Status of Women Canada, 8 November 1991).
30 Kim Bolan, '4 Groups Quit Federal Panel on Violence,' *Vancouver Sun*, 1 August 1992, A3.
31 Personal communication with Judy Rebick, September 1993.
32 While it was the federal government that mandated that the panel would have rounds of meetings in hundreds of communities across the country, it is not clear whether it was the government or the panel itself that decided to focus on individuals to the effective exclusion of organizations. The decision undoubtedly accorded with the government's preference for individuals rather than interest groups, but the panel may have felt that they already were well aware of the positions of groups working on antiviolence issues. The co-chair of the panel Pat Marshall apparently said that the decision had been the panel's which is part of the reason that NAC focused its criticisms on the panel rather than the government.
33 Lila Sarick, 'Violence Panel Loses Support of Four Groups,' *Globe and Mail*, 1 August 1992, A3.
34 The only national group that had been associated with the panel but which did not withdraw its support was the YWCA. The media reported only that five, not seven of eight groups withdrew.
35 Dennis Bueckert, 'NAC Leads Boycott of Federal Panel,' *Montreal Gazette*, 1 August 1992, A7.
36 Judy Rebick, quoted in 'Feuding in the Family,' *Toronto Star*, 8 August 1992, C2.
37 Ibid.; and Carol Goar, 'Infighting Mars Task Force on Violence,' *Toronto Star*, 4 August 1992, A17; Dahlia Reich, 'Stop the Bickering, Experts Say,' *London Free Press*, 13 August 1992, B1; 'NAC Attack not Fair to Panelists,' *Saskatoon Star Phoenix*, 6 August 1992, A5.
38 'Feuding in the Family,' *Toronto Star*, 8 August 1992, C2.
39 An exception to the norms of reporting on this issue was Geoffrey York

who demonstrated an understanding of the broader issues and concerns: '$10-Million Inquiry Fuelled Bitter Fight,' *Globe and Mail*, 30 July 1993, A4.
40 This was just before the long weekend in early August which meant that few reporters were around to cover the story in depth.
41 Marina Jimenez, 'Violence-against-Women Report Same Old Talk, No Action, Critics Complain,' *Ottawa Citizen*, 31 July 1993, B1; Sherri Davis-Barron, 'Report Leaves Aid Workers Skeptical,' *Ottawa Citizen*, 31 July 1993, C2; Karen O'Reilly, 'Where's the "Plan" from Blue-Ribbon Violence Panel,' *Financial Post*, 27 July 1993, 11.
42 Glenda Simms, quoted in 'Violence: 'There Is a Knowledge That 120 Women a Year Don't Have to Die,' *Montreal Gazette*, 30 July 1993; even the only visible minority woman on the panel, Mobina Jaffer, was quoted as saying, 'The women of color have got 5 pages in the report. I believe being the lone member was a mistake.' '$10 Million Study a "Cheap" Play Critics Charge,' *Toronto Star*, 30 July 1993, A23.
43 O'Reilly, 'Where's the "Plan,"' *Financial Post*, 27 July 1993, 11.
44 Quoted in Kim Bolan, '4 Groups Quit Federal Panel,' *Vancouver Sun*, 1 August 1992, A3.
45 The term 'politics of difference' is taken from Iris Young, *Justice and the Politics of Difference* (Princeton, NJ: Princeton University Press, 1990). For a discussion of the development of difference politics in the women's movement in Canada see Pierson, 'The Mainstream Women's Movement and the Politics of Difference,' 186–214.
46 Amy Gottlieb, 'What about Us? Organizing Inclusively in the National Action Committee on the Status of Women,' in Linda Carty, ed., *And Still We Rise* (Toronto: Women's Press, 1993) 384.
47 Sunera Thobani, 'Making a Commitment to Inclusion,' reprinted in Pierson et al., *Canadian Women's Issues*, 262.
48 Razack, *Canadian Feminism and the Law*, 55–6.
49 Paula Bourne, 'Women, Law and the Justice System,' in Pierson et al., *Canadian Women's Issues*, 332.
50 Status of Women Canada, *Report of the Task Force on Child Care* (Ottawa: Status of Women Canada 1986).
51 For a discussion and critique of the specifics of the National Strategy, see: Martha Friendly, *Child Care Policy in Canada: Putting the Pieces Together* (Toronto: Addison-Wesley, 1994); National Council of Welfare, *Child Care: A Better Alternative* (Ottawa: Ministry of Supply and Services, 1988); Susan D. Phillips, 'Rock-a-Bye, Brian: The National Strategy on Child Care,' in Katherine A. Graham, ed., *How Ottawa Spends, 1989–90: The Buck Stops*

Where? (Ottawa: Carleton University Press, 1989) 165–208; Katherine Teghtsoonian, 'Neo-Conservative Ideology and Opposition to Federal Regulation of Child Care Services in the United States and Canada' (1993) 26 *Canadian Journal of Political Science* 97–122.
52 The Child Care Advocacy Association of Canada (CCAAC) was initially called the Canadian Day Care Advocacy Association (CDCAA).
53 One of the very strong member organizations of the CCAAC, the Ontario Coalition, was particularly uncompromising (more so than the CCAAC itself), that child care has to be non-commercial. The coalition's slogan, 'Kids Are Not for Profit,' was widely distributed on political buttons.
54 Personal communication with several key informants.
55 Personal communication with Martha Friendly.
56 In fact, the outspoken Conservative Minister John Crosbie publicly equated NAC with famine, pestilence, and war as a pox on contemporary Canadian politics. Crosbie's remarks are perhaps best portrayed as a political cartoon that appeared in the *Globe and Mail* in 1993; this cartoon is reprinted in the National Action Committee on the Status of Women, *Annual Report 1992–93* (Toronto: NAC, 1993) 5. For a more general discussion of the closed political opportunity structure faced by the women's movement under the Conservative government see Sylvia Bashevkin, 'Losing Common Ground: Feminists, Conservatives and Public Policy in Canada during the Mulroney Years,' *Canadian Journal of Political Science* 26, 2 (1996) 211–42.
57 For a discussion of the context of this de-funding, see Jane Jenson and Susan D. Phillips, 'Regime Shift: New Citizenship Practices in Canada,' *International Journal of Canadian Studies*, 14 (Fall 1996) 111–35.
58 *Symes v. Canada*, [1989] 3 F.C. 59 (F.C.T.D.). LEAF was not officially in the case, but it served to reinforce LEAF's elitist image among many women. Razack, *Canadian Feminism and the Law*, 58.
59 *Symes v. Canada*, [1989] 3 F.C. 24 (F.C.T.D.).
60 Stephen Bindman, 'Child-Care Ruling Divides Judges on Gender Lines,' *Ottawa Citizen*, 17 December 1993, A1. *Symes v. Canada*, [1993] 4 S.C.R. 695.
61 Government of Canada, *Improving Social Security in Canada: A Discussion Paper* (Ottawa: Human Resources Development Canada, 1994) 29–55.
62 The demise of the child care strategy under the Chrétien government is discussed in Sandra Bach and Susan D. Phillips, 'Constructing a New Social Union: Child Care Beyond Infancy?' In Gene Swimmer, ed., *How Ottawa Spends, 1997–98: Seeing Red* (Ottawa: Carleton University Press, 1997) 235–58.
63 Federal-Provincial-Territorial Council of Ministers on Social Policy Re-

newal, 'News Release: Federal, Provincial and Territorial Governments Launch Dialogue Process for National Children's Agenda,' 7 May 1999.
64 In contrast to authors such as Gelb and Palley, who argue that the route to success for women's groups is to be more conventional, take incremental steps, and accept 'small wins,' many social movement organizations will prefer temporary loss rather than severely compromising basic values. Joyce Gelb and Marion L. Palley, *Women and Public Policies* (Princeton, NJ: Princeton University Press, 1982). The notion of 'small wins' was developed by Karl E. Weick, 'Small Wins: Redefining the Scale of Social Problems,' *American Psychologist*, January 1984, 40–9.
65 For an analysis of the discourse and political strategies by child care advocates in Ontario, see Lois Harder, 'The Trouble with Democracy: Child Care Reform in Ontario and the Politics of Participation,' in Linda Carty, ed., *And Still We Rise*, 243–57.